Effectiveness of Anti-Corruption Agencies in Southern Africa

Angola, Botswana, DRC, Lesotho, Malawi, Mozambique, Namibia, South Africa, Swaziland, Zambia, Zimbabwe

A review by
Open Society Initiative for Southern Africa
(OSISA)

2017

Published by the Open Society Initiative for Southern Africa and African Minds
OSISA
President Place
1 Hood Avenue
Rosebank
Johannesburg, 2196
South Africa
www.osisa.org

African Minds
4 Eccleston Place, Somerset West, 7130, Cape Town, South Africa
info@africanminds.org.za
www.africanminds.org.za

 2017
All contents of this document, unless specified otherwise, are licensed under
a Creative Commons Attribution Non-Commercial 4.0 International Licence

ISBNs
Print: 978-1-928332-21-3
EBook: 978-1-928332-22-0
e-Pub: 978-1-928332-23-7

Copies of this book are available for free download at www.africanminds.org.za and www.osisa.org

ORDERS
To order printed copies within Africa, please contact:
African Minds
Email: info@africanminds.org.za
To order printed copies from outside Africa, please contact:
African Books Collective
PO Box 721, Oxford OX1 9EN, UK
Email: orders@africanbookscollective.com

CONTENTS

Preface — iv

Acknowledgements — vii

1. General overview — 1

2. Angola
   Dr Helena Prata — 21

3. Botswana
   Dr Gape I Kaboyakgosi — 42

4. Democratic Republic of Congo
   Prof. Andre Mbata Mangu — 72

5. Lesotho
   Dr Motlamelle Anthony Kapa — 104

6. Malawi
   Dr Henry Chingaipe — 132

7. Mozambique — 167

8. Namibia
   Prof. Lesley Blaauw — 191

9. South Africa
   Dr Ralph Mathekga — 221

10. Swaziland
    Ms Maxine Langwenya — 262

11. Zambia
    Mr Goodwell Lungu — 284

12. Zimbabwe
    Ms Teresa Mugadza — 330

PREFACE

This study complements previous studies that the African Regional Office (AfRO) has supported in East Africa in partnership with the Open Society Initiative for East Africa (OSIEA), as well as in West Africa in partnership with the Open Society Initiative for West Africa (OSIWA), respectively. Overall, the Open Society Foundations' focus on corruption trends and impact lies in lending support to the fight against corruption by supporting advocacy work and the development of laws, policies and institutions to effectively deter, detect and punish corruption. At OSISA, this work falls under the Democracy and Governance Cluster's Private and Public Sector Accountability Programme.

On 31 October 2003, in his capacity as United Nations secretary general, Kofi Annan argued that:

> Corruption is an insidious plague that has a wide range of corrosive effects on societies. It undermines democracy and the rule of law, leads to violations of human rights, distorts markets, erodes the quality of life, and allows organized crime, terrorism and other threats to human security to flourish ... Corruption hurts the poor disproportionately by diverting funds intended for development, undermining a government's ability to provide basic services, feeding inequality and injustice, and discouraging foreign investment and aid.[1]

While it is true that no nation – rich or poor, big or small – is immune from corruption, and that in fact, corruption, small or grand – in all its various forms and manifestations – is as old as time, the poor in the developing world bear the brunt of corruption far more than any other population group. While the poor get poorer, go to bed hungry and are unable to fend for their families, the rich and powerful get richer and pursue lavish lifestyles, funded through corrupt means.

Africa is not short of oftentimes instructive conventions that set out the broad parameters of confronting major democratic development challenges such as corruption. At the regional level, in July 2013, the African Union adopted the AU Convention on Preventing and Combating Corruption (AUCPCC), which seeks to, inter alia, '[P]romote and strengthen the development in Africa by each State Party, of mechanisms required to prevent, detect, punish and eradicate corruption and related offences in the public and private sector'.[2] The AUCPCC entered into force on 5 August 2006. The AU Advisory Board on Corruption (AUBC) has been established to advise on the implementation of

---

1 United Nations secretary general's statement on the adoption by the General Assembly of the United Nations Convention against Corruption, New York, 31 October 2003.
2 Article 2(1), AU Convention on Preventing and Combating Corruption, July 2003.

the AUPCC. In 2007, the AU adopted the African Charter on Democracy, Elections and Governance (ACDEG), which highlights the negative impact of corruption on elections, democracy and governance and enjoins AU member states to take the necessary measures to confront these challenges.

At the sub-regional level, the SADC Protocol against Corruption (2001) seeks to 'promote and strengthen the development, within each Member State, of mechanisms needed to prevent, detect, punish and eradicate corruption in the public and private sector'.[3] At national level, SADC member states have established various mechanisms – laws, policies and institutions – to 'prevent, detect, punish and eradicate corruption'. This notwithstanding, corruption has not abated.

Various studies indicate that corruption is on the rise and is getting sophisticated by the day. The most telling of these trends is the Transparency International's Perception Index. Data from the 2016 index ranks Southern African countries out of 176 countries in the following order Botswana (35 down from 28 in 2015), Mauritius (50 down from 45 in 2015), Namibia (53 down from 45 in 2015), South Africa (64 down from 61 on 2015), Zambia (82 down from 76 in 2015), Lesotho (83 down from 61 in 2015), Malawi (120 down from 112 in 2015), Mozambique (142 down from 112 in 2015), Madagascar (145 down from 123 in 2015), Zimbabwe (154 down from 150 in 2015), Democratic Republic of Congo (156 down from 147 in 2015), and Angola (164 down from 163 in 2015).

Granted this is a perception index, and only of perceptions of corruption in the public sector – however, perceptions do matter and are a reflection of how those most affected perceive the impact of public sector corruption in their lives. Given that the private sector is not immune from corruption and oftentimes fuels public sector corruption, one can surmise that if private sector corruption were included in the index, the rankings could only worsen, especially in the resource-rich countries where the private sector in general and multinational corporations in particular, are active.

In recent times, there has been a sharp focus on the trends and impact of illicit financial flows (IFFs), especially in relation to public service delivery. In 2015, for instance, the African Union's high-level panel on IFFs estimated that over the last 50 years, Africa lost in excess of USD1 trillion in IFFs and that annually, the continent loses USD50 billion through IFFs, which is roughly double the official development assistance (ODA) that Africa receives every year. Clearly, these are conservative estimates drawn from official annual import and export reports of countries. The AU's high-level panel on IFFs notes that if proceeds of bribery and trafficking in drugs, people and firearms were include the figure would rise significantly. A lot of work still needs to be done by legislatures, investigative, police and tax authorities, and justice systems to match the levels of sophistication in corruption and IFFs.

It is against this background that this study was commissioned. The study sought to investigate indepth, the nature and character of on anti-corruption agencies (ACAs) in

---

3   Article 2(1)(a), SADC Protocol against Corruption, 2001.

southern Africa as well as reasons for their successes and failures. In view of the growing nature and sophistication of corruption, the study also sought to understand the relevance of existing legal frameworks for ACAs, their roles and means and preconditions necessary for their improved performance as well as alternative and/or complementary measures/mechanisms in the SADC region. In short, the study sought to inform policy-makers, the donor community, civil society and others on what could to be done to accelerate the fight against corruption and reduce its impact on democratic development.

It is hoped that the findings from the study will improve and strengthen anti-corruption efforts in Angola, Botswana, DRC, Lesotho, Namibia, Malawi, Mozambique, Swaziland, South Africa, Zambia and Zimbabwe, and the region at large.

Siphosami Malunga
Executive Director, OSISA

ACKNOWLEDGEMENTS

We thank the following persons for their contributions to this publication: Siphosami Malunga, OSISA Executive Director; Ozias Tungwarara, Programme Support Division Director, Africa Regional Office (AfRO); Jeggan Grey-Johnson, Programme Officer, Research and Advocacy, AfRO; Takawira Musavengana, OSISA Democracy and Governance Cluster Team Leader; Lusako Munyenyembe, OSISA Democracy and Governance Programme Officer and Glen Mpani, OSISA Democracy and Governance Programme Manager; Brenda Madisha, OSISA Democracy and Governance Programme Associate, as well as Benedict Komeke, OSISA Democracy and Governance Programme Associate, who assisted in organising the review and related meetings.

We also extend our gratitude to all the chapter authors: Dr Helena Prata (Angola); Dr Gape I Kaboyakgosi (Botswana); Prof. Andre Mbata Mangu (DRC); Dr Motlamelle Anthony Kapa (Lesotho); Dr Henry Chingaipe (Malawi); Prof. Lesley Blaauw (Namibia); Dr Ralph Mathekga (South Africa); Ms Maxine Langwenya (Swaziland); Mr Goodwell Lungu (Zambia); Ms Teresa Mugadza (Zimbabwe); as well as the overall editor, Mr Job Agingu Ogonda. For professional reasons, the author of the Mozambique chapter requested not to be identified.

1
GENERAL OVERVIEW

A. State of corruption

The state of corruption in the Southern African Development Community (SADC) region varies widely as evidenced by Transparency International's Corruption Perception Index (CPI). Whilst most of the countries occupy the lower half of the global index ranking, Botswana has the distinction of consistently being in the top third of the rankings. The country was ranked 30th globally in 2013 and 31st in 2014.

It ranked Lesotho at 55 out of 174 countries and territories globally, and scores it at 49 for the years 2013 and 2014; an improvement from 45 in 2012. The Mo Ibrahim African Overall Governance Index scores Lesotho at 61.1 out of 100 in overall governance and ranks it 10th out of 54 countries in Africa.

Zimbabwe was in 2014 ranked 156th of 176 most corrupt countries. A 2014 local survey by Transparency International Zimbabwe (TIZ), 77.4 % of the respondents professed that they had been asked for a bribe.

B. Politics of corruption

The public finance, justice and administrative systems in all the countries in SADC can effectively manage corruption. Most countries have an understated but potentially powerful institution known as the financial intelligence unit whose purpose is to ensure that the executive has a finger on the pulse of all significant amounts of money moving within the country. It would therefore take deliberate effort to remain ignorant of, say two million dollars, moving from the proverbial Gupta's account to that of a relative of a senior government official. Another is the asset forfeiture institutions and the public performance management institutions whose administrative powers to clean up malfeasance are incontestable. For the asset forfeiture law will place suspicious assets under state custody and maintenance until the owner can satisfy a judicial officer as to how they got miraculously rich. And the public performance system will automatically fire the minister for water if citizens complain that they have to pay bribes for connections, or businesses complain that they have to pay bribes for piping contracts. The executive can also unleash the less encumbered institutions such as the revenue authorities and anti-money laundering institutions to respectively heavily punish those that didn't pay due taxes on 'miraculous' incomes, or those whose incomes are tainted by connection to racketeering or other conspiracies to commit financial crimes. As such, accountable democratic governance is straight forward.

Competitive democracy is, however, prohibitively expensive. In order to win, especially as an incumbent, one has to raise many times the size of the war chest of the opposition in order to bribe, scare and intimidate the constituency into staying faithful or jumping into your ship. More important than the party coffers are the party individuals who having been corruptly enriched through public procurement, faithfully contest or fund the party as a contractual obligation and economic self-interest. In real politik, upholding ideals such as integrity and accountability would be suicidally naïve in a competitive democracy. Statecraft in competitive democracies is also complex and vicious. Most people that wield power in African democracies have had to enter alliances of betrayals, murders, sabotages, robberies of public coffers, kidnappings, massacres and bigotry. Such alliances ensure that the partners are collectively and individually captive to the need to retain power, at whatever cost, in order to avoid the consequences of their crimes. Thus the corruption in SADC, as most corruption in Africa, is a deliberate executive machination.

Botswana

Politicians in Botswana are routinely accused of corruption by the public. A number of factors complicate the enforcement of electoral or campaign finance discipline in Botswana. For instance, whereas the electoral law requires candidates to declare their electoral expenses to the Independent Electoral Commission, this is hardly ever enforced thereby leaving open the risk of state capture.

Democratic Republic of Congo

A close relationship exists between politics and corruption in the DRC, leading some people to disengage from politics in the name of ethics. The 2011 elections like those of 2006 were fraught with allegations of vote-rigging in favour of President Kabila. Many of the electoral agents were overtly corrupt. So were many voters who were paid with public money to vote for the incumbent president, parliamentary, senator, governor and vice-governor candidates.

The political culture has created a governance environment of non-accountability, patronage and the use of public resources to enforce political ambitions.

Lesotho

All the positive reports notwithstanding, Lesotho has had cases of grand corruption. The sale in the early 1990s of Lesotho's international passports to Chinese nationals under a scheme devised by the Lesotho National Development Corporation (LNDC) is a case in point. The scheme was designed to award Lesotho passports to wealthy individuals under a newly established consulate in Hong Kong so that they could come and invest in the local economy. A certain Ms Lydia Wu was identified as Lesotho's honorary consul based in Hong Kong to facilitate the process of identifying and attracting potential investors. Corrupt high-ranking individuals within the military government working with Ms Wu sold these passports at an estimated USD 2 800.00 per individual and USD 3 300.00 per family to poor Chinese nationals and collected an estimated USD 8 million. A commission of inquiry was set up by the military government but no prosecutions were made.

Malawi

Since the onset of multiparty rule in 1993, new corrupt elites emerged that have undermined democratic accountability generally and the fight against corruption in particular. For the past ten years the elites of the different regimes in Malawi exploited this principle to their virtual advantage. Even the state presidents have been involved in corrupt practices and yet no one could hold the regimes accountable because these political elites have tended to mutate from one regime to another. It is only the political label that changes but the players are largely the same. As the ruling party assumes more power and the executive increases its dominance in the political system, there is a serious erosion of both vertical and horizontal accountability. It is because of this legitimating of undemocratic tendencies that institutions of state restraint such as the Anti-Corruption Bureau (ACB), police, public media and the judiciary have come under attack from the executive. Thus, any attempt to fight corruption is seen by some as a way of gaining political mileage and settling political scores. It may be undermined by perceptions that it is merely usurping legitimate functions of anti-corruption institutions for political gain.

The 'cashgate' scandal illustrates the incestuous nature of political power and corruption in Malawi. It involved payments to 16 companies valued at MK 6 096 490 705 where no evidence has been provided to support the provision of goods or services. In addition, payments were further made to two newly formed companies totalling MK 3 955 366 067.19. Further payments were made at inflated prices totalling MK 3 619 539 979. The companies and public officers involved have included politicians across party lines, senior public officers, the executive, the military and the private sector.

Even more concerning, Mutharika's government is allegedly meddling in the ACB's work against Bakili Muluzi, Malawi's former president, who is accused of stealing USD 11 million in donor funds during his tenure between 1994 and 2004. Reyneck Matemba, the ACB deputy director, who was also lead prosecutor on the Muluzi trial, recused himself from the case, a move that observers saw as bowing to undue pressure from the government.

Many people see the president's hand in shielding Muluzi, whose son, Atulepe Muluzi, is a key ally of Mutharika and is the leader of the United Democratic Front (UDF), an opposition party that is in coalition with the president's party. In other words, protecting Muluzi is in the president's political interest.

Mozambique

According to the corruption survey commissioned by USAID in 2009, over the last 20 years, corruption in Mozambique had spread rapidly, reaching every sector and level of government. TI's 'Corruption Perception Index' (2015) places Mozambique at number 119 out of 178 countries globally.

Mozambique has had a litany of mega scandals implicating those wielding political power. In 2015, a public debt contracted to off-set the new tuna fishing company, EMATUM, involved possible criminal acts during the negotiations and setting up of the tuna company (FMO, 2015). Mozambique's political opposition called EMATUM the greatest financial scandal since independence and has called on the attorney general's office to arrest the former president of the republic and minister of finance, who set up the offending company.

South Africa

Corruption has become part and parcel of politics in South Africa in two distinct ways. Firstly, corruption has an influence on the functioning of the body politic in the country where corruption is resorted to as a means to attain political influence.

Secondly, corruption has an impact on the effectiveness and legitimacy of state institutions including institutions of democracy. When political elites are facing allegations of corruption and impropriety; they tend to launch an attack on state institutions that are tasked to investigate corruption. This undermines genuine investigations into corruption. The political battle between former president Thabo Mbeki and the then ANC deputy president Jacob Zuma has brought to light the suspicion that at times state institutions can be used to wage a political battle against; and anti-corruption institutions are conveniently available for such a task. The emergence of the Economic Freedom Fighters (EFF), amidst allegations of tender irregularities against the founding leader of the party Julius Malema, is another example.

It is well understood that competition for political positions within the dominant African National Congress (ANC) is one of the key drivers of corruption in the country. As an incumbent political party responsible for the distribution of state resources, the ANC finds itself plagued by corruption resulting in the corrosion of internal processes within the party, on one hand, and also corrosion of the principle of fairness in the broader political spectrum in South Africa on the other. For example, the ANC's relationship with Hitachi Company has recently come under scrutiny, where the party is alleged to have improperly gained from procurement relating to the construction of Medupi power station. Through its investment arm Chancellor House, the ANC had secured a stake in Hitachi Africa which has been awarded USD 5.6 billion to build boilers in the Medupi power station in Limpopo province, South Africa (Wild, 2015).

Hitachi was subsequently investigated by the US Securities Exchange Commission (SEC) regarding allegations that the company's partner in the Medupi power station deal was merely a front for the ruling ANC. Hitachi Japan agreed to pay a 'settlement' fee amounting to USD 19 million the SEC. Although Hitachi did not agree that it has an improper relationship with the ANC-owned Chancellor House, its decision to pay a fine to the SEC is a demonstration that the company is aware that its relationship with the ANC investment arm is not beyond reproach.

When questions were asked relating to former police commissioner Jacky Selebi's relationship with a known drug dealer Glen Agliotti, the then commissioner Selebi responded that Agliotti 'is my friend finish and klaar'. Either the commissioner did not respect or fully understand what is required of him as a police commissioner, or he did not respect the legitimacy of the police services as an institution whose responsibility is also generally to fight against corruption. The questions of 'friendship' and integrity of leaders also came forth in the relationship between President Jacob Zuma and his then financial advisor Shabir Shaik. Shaik was convicted of two counts of corruption and one count of fraud. Shaik has made payments to Jacob Zuma, which implicates Zuma in corruption. The prosecution authority has since decided not to prosecute Zuma; a decision that is still under review. Perhaps the Nkandla issue, involving expenditure of public funds at President Jacob Zuma's private home shows how multiple probes by different institutions have resulted in contradictory findings on the same issue. It has been argued in relation to Nkandla that the institutions seems to be 'working against each other' (Madonsela, 2015).

Swaziland

Corruption is prevalent within the bureaucracy as companies and private entities pay public officials to avoid the reach of regulation. For a long time the police, the ministry of finance, the ministry of commerce, industry and trade as well as the department of customs and excise have often been implicated in corrupt practices. Corruption has also been prevalent in the government procurement and tendering processes. For instance, in 2011, Polycarp Dlamini, the former general transport manager of the Central Transport Administration (CTA), was convicted of defrauding the government after he admitted to authorising payments worth up to SZL 12 million to a private company for services that were never rendered. On another level the Public Accounts Committee (PAC) was informed that E 1.6 million was paid to service providers for the maintenance of a machine that was neither broken nor in use at the Swaziland Broadcasting and Information Service (SBIS). The PAC was informed that the officer who authorised the bogus job cards had since been promoted and transferred to another government department. This type of behaviour is common albeit covert and therefore difficult to monitor as goods and services are undersupplied or rerouted for personal use. The results of grand corruption are there for all to see in the ever increasing wealth of high-level civil servants and officers of state. It has been suggested that Swaziland has no less than 31 millionaires who are junior government officials.

In 2005, the then minister of finance Majozi Sithole stated that '[T]he twin evils of bribery and corruption have become the order of the day in the country ... the economy is dying gradually because of this practice, and the citizens are placed under a heavy yoke'. The then minister estimated that corruption was costing the Swazi economy approximately ZAR 40 million a month. Poor people who suffer as a result of corruption took the minister's statement as confirmation of the extent to which the country was being driven to bankruptcy through corrupt activities. The corrupt public officials thought the minister was exaggerating the extent of corruption while academics were sceptical of the statement as the minister did not provide a basis for his assertion. The minister's statement was significant in so far as it highlighted the fact that the economy of the country was being undermined by corrupt activities. The current minister of finance Martin Dlamini says government has put in place measures to fight corruption but has made little progress in prosecuting and punishing corrupt people.

In the past, ministers have been found by a parliamentary select committee to have acted in a manner that is tantamount to theft of state property. The ministers had allocated themselves and subsequently 'bought' land belonging to the state at ridiculously low prices without competing with other would-be buyers. The land was given to the ministers at below market value. The matter was never pursued by the ACC as it eventually died down.

In 2015 Judge Mpendulo Simelane stated that he had been approached by the former Minister of Justice-Sibusiso Shongwe and told that judges could and should make money from cases over which they presided. The then Minister of Justice is then said to have asked the Judge to preside in a case of wealthy business people who were suing the Swaziland Revenue Authority for goods they had imported. The then Minister is said to have told the Judge that the business people were willing to pay about R2million for help in winning the case. Shongwe suggested that Simelane should preside in the case and explained how the R2million would be shared between the parties. Simelane and Shongwe were subsequently arrested by the Anti-Corruption Commission and charged with corruption but charges were subsequently dropped against Simelane. Simelane remains on suspension while Shongwe is presently out on bail. This case illustrates how the Swazi justice system was abused to settle political scores and make it complicit with the actions of corrupt public officials.

Zambia

A Task Force on Corruption was set up in Zambia to investigate the alleged grand theft committed by the MMD administration between 1991 and 2001. The second president Frederick Chiluba was subsequently acquitted of all criminal charges despite significant evidence to the contrary. In 2007, the ex-president found guilty of stealing USD 46 million (£23m) of public money by a UK court.

The Levy Mwanawasa administration, though less kleptocratic, was plagued with accusations of nepotism. His successor, Rupia Banda, of the MMD, was accused of abuse of power in connection with a USD 2.5 million oil deal with a Nigerian company from which he allegedly benefited during his 2008–2011 presidency. In June 2015, Banda was acquitted, with a Lusaka court saying there was insufficient evidence to convict him.

The PF governments have taken some steps to fight graft; in 2012, the national assembly reinserted the key 'abuse of office' clause of the Anti-Corruption Act, which had been removed by the MMD-dominated legislature in 2010. The clause allows for the prosecution of public officials for violations such as abuse of authority or misuse of public funds. However, many prosecutions and court decisions in Zambia are thought to reflect political motivations. And corruption by politically connected people pervades public contracting to date.

Zimbabwe

Corruption in Zimbabwe can be traced back to the nascent years when, due to political and social developments at the time, the ruling party [and by extension, the state] started to consolidate power and limit space for scrutiny by citizens. It is important to state that in the aftermath of *Gukurahundi*,[1] the state clamped down on dissent and scrutiny of many of its actions for national security reasons. Thus began the consolidation of power by the state during the period 1980–1995 and Zimbabwe became a de facto one-party state. The perpetrators were thereby captive to the need to retain power by any means necessary.

Thereafter, patronage as a result of conflation between state and party has become an integral part of politics and the economy in Zimbabwe. It is commonly understood that you do not conduct business in Zimbabwe unless you are 'known' by those in the ruling party. Coupled with the economic decline that had started in 1997,[2] corruption has become the way through which one conducts successful business or rises through the political ranks.

C. Legislative framework

All the countries in the study have robust legal and policy frameworks that are more than sufficient in fighting corruption.

In Botswana, the Corruption and Economic Crimes Act, CECA, is the principal legislation for fighting corruption in the country. Others include the Public Procurement and Asset Disposal Act, Financial Intelligence Act, Proceeds of Serious Crimes Act, The Penal Code, Extradition Act and the Mutual Assistance in Criminal Matters Act.

All the countries in the study have one form or the other of the above laws. Some, such as Zimbabwe, have constitutional amendments that further strengthen the legal and policy frameworks. *All* the countries also have some kind of policy framework that guides the implementation of anti-corruption measures.

It is however worth noting that legislation, policy formulation and reforms tend to immediately follow public outrage about one corruption scandal or the other. The sincerity

---

1 See https://en.wikipedia.org/wiki/Gukurahundi and davidcoltart.com/wp-content/uploads/2006/10/breakingthesilence.pdf
2 Commonly referred to as Black Friday, when the Zimbabwean dollar lost over 70% of its value against the US dollar in one day in November 1997. See generally www.grips.ac.jp/r-center/wp-content/uploads/09-12.pdf

of the executive and parliament in enacting the laws and policies is thus questionable. Notwithstanding, in most countries the Penal Code is usually *technically* sufficient to prosecute abuse of public resources and power. It thus appears that the enactment of laws can be used as an excuse to avoid decisive and impacting action against corruption.

D. Effectiveness of anti-corruption institutions

In order to ensure the level of transparency and accountability, most constitutions create a number of independent commissions supporting democracy such as public service commissions, a public prosecutor, and ombudsman/public protector, an electoral commission, a human rights commission, a media commission and a cohesion commission. In addition to their respective specific mandates, one of the general objectives of these commissions is to promote transparency and accountability in public institutions.

The principal agents against corruption under most constitutions are however the anti-corruption agencies.

Botswana: Directorate on Corruption and Economic Crime

The DCEC was founded in 1994 with the promulgation of the Corruption and Economic Crimes Act (CECA). Modelled on the Independent Commission Against Corruption (ICAC) of Hong Kong, the DCEC also adopted the three pronged strategy used by the ICAC, and internationally accepted as best practice: corruption prevention, investigation and public education.

Stability of agency

The DCEC has enjoyed stability and support from the executive and parliament. It is however worrisome that the director general of the DCEC reports to the state president thereby raising the risk that the president interferes with the mandate of the agency.

Autonomy

The president appoints the director general of the DCEC, but CECA gives the director general the mandate of running the affairs of the directorate independently. This raises the risk of executive interference. It is however worth noting that the DCEC has pursued, in court, a number of high profile personalities, including ministers.

Capacity

The DCEC has approximately 300 members of staff. Its human resources programme maintains an annual vacancy target to maximum of 2% (DCEC, 2011). However, the DCEC operates in a specialised environment where competition for human resources is fierce, making this target difficult to maintain.

Performance

The performance of the DCEC has been dismal by most measures. For example, it received 1 400 cases in 2013 and completed only nine. Of these, it managed four convictions. Institutions of similar size and number of corruption complaints are doing a lot more with the level of resourcing.

Lesotho: DCEO

Stability

The government only established this agency in 2003 yet the constitutive law was passed in 1999. The appointments of director general and staff, though stable, have been slow and far-between leaving the institution in limbo.

Autonomy

There is a directorate appointment and promotion board, appointed by the minister for justice, which has responsibility for appointments, promotions, and conditions of service of all staff, except the director general. The director general is appointed by the prime minister, which raises the risk of executive interference in the affairs of the directorate. It is responsible for its budgetary planning process and its financial resources. The ministry of finance issues on annual basis a call circular instructing all government ministries and departments to submit their budget estimates and the DCEO also prepares and submits its own to the budget controller with all supporting documents or reasons in support of it. The ministry of finance then determines how much the directorate gets, depending on the availability of funds and justification provided.

Capacity

Since its establishment in 2003, the DCEO staff has grown extremely sluggishly from five to 62, thereby leading to serious overload, a backlog of cases and low conviction rates . Staff of the directorate undergo regular specialised training under the auspices of the Commonwealth Secretariat Unit in Botswana. This Unit serves all Commonwealth countries in Africa. The directorate has its own training plan, which is actually a requirement of the government. Besides, the 2015/2016 budget has provision for specialised training in forensic investigations. Its budget in the 2012/2013 financial year amounted to only 0.09% of the national budget against the 0.5% internationally recommended benchmark for institutions of its nature to operate at full capacity.

Performance

There is serious overload, a backlog of cases and low conviction rates. One investigator has to handle about 30 cases per year. Despite these capacity challenges, the directorate has done some work regarding investigation of cases of corruption. According to Transparency International, from 1999 to 2012, the directorate had submitted 37 cases for prosecution, out of which two received guilty verdicts, while in 2012, it brought 71 cases before the courts, resulting in 16 convictions and two acquittals.

The directorate has sometimes taken a very brave and unprecedented move in recent years by investigating cases involving very high profile individuals, some of whom while still in public office. The first case involved the former clerk of the national assembly (the third senior most officer from the speaker), who was involved in corrupt activity in procuring for the national assembly a heavy-duty photocopier worth M 1 475 259.29 (about USD 113 481.48) (about three times its actual price) from Konica Enterprises (Pty) Ltd, trading as Itec Lesotho, which was the second accused. It has also launched investigations against former minister of finance Dr Timothy Thahane, who faces two counts of corruption. In another case, Thahane and former principal secretary for finance Mosito Khethisa are accused of defrauding the government of Lesotho of M 19 066 667.35. Former minister of local government and deputy prime minister Mothetjoa Metsing is being investigated for undeservingly and illegally awarding a tender to construct roads.

Malawi: Anti-Corruption Bureau

Recent reforms, including ongoing changes to the state's public financial management system, indicate that some progress is being made to improve transparency. However, many observers contend that the government has been slow to push through the necessary reforms.

Additionally, advances have been made to fix loopholes in the government payment system that previously made it easy for officials to siphon off state funds. And by virtue of the graft-busting Anti-Corruption Bureau (ACB), over 70 people involved in the cashgate saga were arrested. These efforts persuaded the IMF to recently resume Malawi's USD 150 million extended facility programme, which had been suspended last year in the wake of the widespread corruption scheme.

Efforts to make the ACB an independent corruption-fighting body have proven futile. The government actively fought to prevent this from happening, but despite their efforts, Mutharika maintains the power to appoint the bureau's director, which exposes it to political influence. In March, the president's party, the Democratic Progressive Party (DPP), killed a parliament bill aimed at making the ACB more independent.

The Corruption Perception Index (CPI) published by Transparency International ranks Malawi as 112th out of 167 countries.

Stability
Given that they serve at the pleasure of the president, the director and the deputy must dance to the tune of the executive or else risk being fired. This has been evidenced by the fact that, except on rare occasions, every new government has fired the director and appointed another. During its 18-year life span, the ACB has had seven directors, and only two of the directors had a deputy. Hence, in its current state the ACB is destabilised, incapacitated and skewed towards serving the interests of the incumbent government

and not necessarily the desires of the public. There is hope nonetheless. According to the 2012–2017 Strategic Plan the ACB intends to enhance its independence by reviewing the Corrupt Practices Act to address issues of the appointment of the director and deputy director and lobby for the empowerment of an independent body to oversee its activities.

Autonomy
The ACB was not directly established by the constitution but rather by an act of parliament, the Corrupt Practices Act Cap.7:04, enacted into law in 1995. Consequently, the constitution does not guarantee and safeguard the existence of the ACB. Parliament can repeal the act and abolish the ACB without necessarily going through the rigorous process of changing the republican constitution. Section 4(3) of the act provides that the ACB 'shall exercise its functions and powers independent of the direction or interference of any other person or authority'. However, the ACB is not free from external influence. Administratively the ACB is under the ministry of justice and annually reports to parliament. The appointment and removal of the director and deputy director has always been contentious. Currently, in accordance with the act, the state president appoints and removes the director and the deputy director.

Capacity
The ACB annual funding ceiling is not enough for meeting the operational and administrative costs therefore, and sometimes the ACB requests special funding based on emerging needs. The cashgate investigations, for example, sometimes are funded outside the ceiling because of the enormous amount of funding required. The special funding notwithstanding, the ACB faces acute resource constraints compounded by erratic funding. Sometimes months pass without funding, and once the funding is supplied, a large chunk covers administrative costs such as rent, electricity, water and car servicing.

Performance
The ACB has not effectively prevented corruption in the public sector as evidenced by massive looting from the government treasury through dubious contracts. It is only in 2011 that a monitoring and evaluation unit was established, with limited staff. In 2010, it referred 152 cases for prosecution whist only 25 were persecuted with ten convictions. In 2011, 108 were referred and 34 prosecuted, with 18 convictions.

Mozambique: Central Office for Combating Corruption
Chapter II, article 8 of Decree 22/2005 provides that 'the Central Office for Combating Corruption [COCC] is an Organic Unit of the Attorney-General of the Republic, responsible for investigating crimes of corruption and illicit economic participation and acting on the instruction of the respective processes'.

Stability
The agency has been relatively stable. However, this stability can be attributed to its inadequate autonomy ensures that potentially impacting action and decisions are nipped in the bird by the office of the attorney general.

Autonomy
The COCC is not autonomous given that the director and deputies are appointed by the attorney general, who himself is appointed by the president of the republic. In addition Internal Regulation of the Central Office for Combating Corruption, the attorney general also has the power to direct meetings of the COCC.

Capacity
COCC currently has 100 employees, including the director, the magistrates and the investigators. Of these, only approximately 40% have the requisite skills for anti-corruption activities. Of the 62 vacancies available in 2014, only 34% were filled, leaving an acute shortage of investigators, law clerks, magistrates and professional technicians.

The agency is also seriously underfunded resulting in its strategies and plans not being implemented.

Performance
The combination of lack of autonomy, staff capacities and resource constraints has rendered its performance dismal. In 2012, the agency had 376 cases and processed 151. In 2013, it had 395 and processed 114. The prosecution and conviction rates were not available at the time of publishing.

South Africa

South Africa is experiencing a significant rise in corruption, particularly in the public sector. The 2014 Transparency International Corruption Perception Index ranks South Africa 67 out of 175 countries when it comes to corruption. It has been stated that in the last 20 years, South Africa has lot R 700 billion to corruption. That is equivalent to more than half of annual budget in the country.

It was reported in 2013 that 'almost half (47%) of South Africans who came into contact with government paid bribery' (SAPA, 2013). The 2013 Transparency International Survey indicates that South Africans believe public sector corruption is getting worse. It was also reported in 2013 that South Africa is losing R 25 billion a year in government procurement. The national treasury's 2015 Supply Chain Management (SCM) Review raises concerns with the 'negative effects of inefficient public sector SCM, particularly in the procurement phase of the chain'. Perennial violation of supply chain guidelines has become a norm in the public service. The treasury report also points to price distortions created by corruption. This refers to the practices of overcharging for goods and services.

South Africa's institutions have evolved into a complex, effective anti-corruption machine, in a decentralised manner. The evolution of these institutions owes to the notion of separation of powers and the general mechanism of constitutional democracy. However, these institutions would not be effective in their attempts to address corruption had South Africa not acceded to international and regional anti-corruption instruments.

Stability

Because of constitutional anchoring and multiple institutions of democracy, some of the democratic institutions have relative stability. Whilst those that are appointed through parliament such as the public protector tend to have a stable tenure, presidential appointments such as in the Special Investigations Unit (SUI), the Directorate for Priority Crime Investigation, the National Prosecuting Authority and the South African Police Service have consistently been influenced by the executive for ascending to, or retaining power, or to avoid or limit accountability. This has at times entailed the appointment or removal of key figures in the institutions thereby compromising their efficacy. In November 2011, President Jacob Zuma appointed retired judge Willem Heath to head the SUI. He subsequently resigned only days after his appointment amid scandal. Zuma then appointed Advocate Vas Soni in September 2013 and he too resigned after 16 months in the job, stating 'personal' reasons (Monama, 2015). In March 2015, President Zuma appointed Advocate Gerhard Visagie as the new head of the SUI.

Autonomy

The principle of constitutional democracy as provided for in South Africa envisages the intuitional framework whose proper functioning should eliminate corruption. This avenue for fighting against corruption needs to be outlined in the context of South Africa because it represents another institutional approach to anti-corruption. It is also necessary to outline how this institutional framework has thus far functioned in the case of South Africa.

The Constitution of South Africa does not explicitly provide for the separation of powers between the executive, legislature and the judiciary. The constitution however provides for the institutional framework that recognises the principle of separation of powers. In outlining the function of the judiciary, the constitution states in the founding provision (the preamble) that the constitution is the 'supreme law of the Republic'. This means that all laws should be compliant with the constitution. The constitution states also that the legislative authority is vested with parliament (the legislature). Section 85 of the constitution provides that the executive authority of the republic lies with the president, who is the head of the executive.

The relationship between the three branches of government is rather delineated in the constitutional provision for the role and authority of the courts. The constitution states that 'The judicial authority of the republic is vested in the courts', and the courts 'are independent and subject only to the constitution and the law'. This is where the principle of separation of powers is nearly explicitly expressed in the constitution. It is however explicitly stated that 'No person or organ of state may interfere with the functioning of the courts'. This provision provides for judicial review – one of the cornerstone of accountability in a constitutional democracy. Judicial review is a system whereby the courts have powers to review decisions or complaints relating to decisions made by government or individuals, thus the executive.

These institutions include the: National Prosecution Authority, South African Police Service, Office of the Public Protector, Directorate for Priority Crime Investigation (DPCI), Assets Forfeiture Unit, Auditor General, Independent Police Investigative Directorate and the Financial Intelligence Centre.

All these institutions either account to parliament or to the executive. Some of the institutions simultaneously account to the executive and also to parliament. The national treasury's 2015 Public Sector Supply Chain Management Review report refers to the above institutions as mandated to 'detect and combat corruption'. The core function of these institutions however is not to fight against corruption; their combined routine function however would bring about fighting corruption as an outcome.

Capacity

Most of the institutions here above have the capacity to meet their mandates. For example, in 2014 the Office of the Public Protector operated on a R 200 million budget, to handle 40 000 cases. Other constitutional bodies have the budgets, staff and equipment at sufficient levels for their responsibilities.

Performance

In 2014 the Office of the Public Protector operated on a R 200 million budget, which according to the public protector was not proportional to the workload of 40 000 cases handled that year (Mokone, 2014). The increasing work load of the office points to the increasing level of confidence the public seems to have in it. It can be argued that the Office of the Public Protector under the leadership of Advocate Thuli Madonsela carries a disproportionately high load of complaints on government conduct because of the perception that the office is effective in investigating the complaints.

Since her appointment in 2009, South Africa's third public protector Advocate Thuli Madonsela handled high profile investigations involving high ranking politicians in the country. Among some of the notable cases she has handled involve an investigation into the R 1.60 billion leasing of buildings to the South African Police Services, under former police commissioner Bheki Cele. The public protector also handled a high profile investigation into a Limpopo-based company, On-Point Engineering, on allegations that companies related to Julius Malema, the then ANC Youth League president, were involved is massive tender rigging activities in the province. She also undertook investigations into expenditure on the security upgrade by the president at his Nkandla private home and also the investigations of allegations of maladministration at the South African Broadcasting Cooperation (SABC).

GENERAL OVERVIEW

Other institutions have had varying measures of success but non comparable to the public protector's office.

Swaziland

Transparency International rated Swaziland 88th in the world in its 2012 corruption perception index, with a rating of 37 out of 100 where 0 is the most corrupt and 100 is the least corrupt. In 2013 Swaziland had a rating of 39 and in 2014 it was 43. Clearly, the country's ratings are changing for the worse even though there is improvement in the overall ranking – in 2014, it was rated at 69th in the world.

Although there is no recent empirical national data on corruption perceptions locally, Swaziland's international and continental corruption perceptions have improved favourably. The 2014 global perception index ranks Swaziland 69 out of 174 countries, a quantum leap from ranking 82nd in 2013. For the first time, Swaziland is also ranked among the least corrupt countries in Africa. According to a 2015 global perception study conducted by Transparency International and Afrobarometer, business executives, government officials and the police are the most corrupt. That the police are implicated in corrupt practices is telling as the police are held to the highest standards of probity as guardians of law and order.

Stability

Because of its not being a constitutional body, the Anti-Corruption Commission (ACC) has been very unstable. In 2002 the high court declared that the 1993 act that established the ACC unconstitutional and accordingly set it aside. The operations of the ACC came to a halt as a result of the invalidation of the law that created it. In 2005, the supreme court set aside the high court order and accordingly re-activated the ACC and its operations. In 2006, parliament passed the Prevention of Corruption Act (POCA) and established an Anti-Corruption Commission dedicated to fighting corruption through the prevention and investigation of corruption as well as educating the public and raising awareness about the need to fight corruption. The POCA re-established the ACC as an independent body and provided for matters incidental to the prevention of corruption. The Constitution of Swaziland was passed in 2005, before the POCA in 2006. Consequently, the ACC is not a constitutional body. This therefore means that the constitution does not guarantee and safeguard the existence of the ACC. By extension, parliament can repeal the POCA and abolish the ACC without necessarily going through the rigorous process of changing the constitution. The ACC needs to have a legal framework that ensures independence and helps maintain its autonomy and not depend on the whims of the government.

Autonomy

The POCA establishes the ACC with operational but not administrative independence because it is a government department under the ministry of justice and constitutional affairs. The ACC therefore reports to the ministry of justice.

Capacity

The ACC receives approximately E 13 million per annum. The staff complement of the investigation team stands at ten. It consists of two vacant posts of chief anti-corruption officers and three vacant positions for senior investigators and one vacant post for an investigator.

Currently, there are three senior investigators and three vacancies that need to be filled. There are four investigating officers' positions and three of these are vacant. There is thus need to prioritise the filling of vacant positions to enable this section to function at its optimum level.

Also, most personnel in this section come from a law enforcement background and there is need for greater specialisation in anti-corruption technical competencies. Such training will help in building investigative and support skills in the commission.

Performance

The performance of the ACC is poor by comparison. In 2012, only 78 cases were reported and a paltry 12 prosecuted with only two convictions obtained.

Zambia

The state of corruption in Zambia reveals that the overall aggregate bribery index for 2014 calculated from 22 public service institutions was 8.5%. However, when compared to the 16 public institutions covered in the 2012 ZBPI, the overall aggregate bribery index in 2014 was 11.9% and in 2012 it was 9.8%. In terms of progress, this is indicative of a decline in percent of 2.1% when compared to 2012. This means that an average public service seeker in 2014 had a 11.9% possibility of paying a bribe, to any of the 16 public service institutions. This also means that in 2014 the likelihood of paying a bribe to a public institution worsened from 9.8% in 2012 to 11.9% in 2014. On the other hand, the Transparency International corruption Perception Index (CPI) for the past five years from 2009 to 2014 has been showing slight improvements in the perceived levels of corruption in Zambia. In 2009 on the CPI, Zambia had an improved score of 3.0 out of 10 points. In 2014, Zambia's score remained the same at 38 compared to 2013. Overall, Zambia has been making steady but slow improvements on the TI CPI by an average of 10% to 20% points a year.

Stability

Because the Anti-Corruption Commission (ACC) is not a constitutional institution, its stability is not guaranteed. In May 2016, the director general, Rosewin Wandi, resigned under political pressure. She had replaced Godfrey Kayukwa, unceremoniously fired in 2011 by then President Sata for being perceived to be close to former president Rupiah Banda.

Autonomy

The ACC's autonomy is guaranteed under section 5 of the Anti-Corruption Act No. 3 of 2012 and provides that '5. Subject to the Constitution, the Commission shall not, in the performance of its functions, be subject to the direction or control of any person or authority'. The preceding 1996 Anti-Corruption Act No. 42 of 1996 also had the same section 5 provision. Despite having this section, the executive is on record as going against such a provision. For instance on 6 December 2012, the late Zambian president Michael Chilufya Sata castigated the ACC for not getting permission from him when investigating senior party officials. He explained that by law the commission was supposed to get permission from him to investigate any senior party official.

Capacity

The commission had 341 staff by the end of 2014. However, only 322 officers were in post by end of the year and this implied that there were 19 vacancies and these were as a result of staff reductions arising from resignations, redundancies and retirements. In its 2013and 2014 annual reports, the ACC confirms that it could not implement some of its planned training activities due to inadequate funding. The reports also confirmed that the ACC lacked presence at district level due to resource constraints.

Performance

With a budget of between ZD 5–7 million, the ACC's performance is poor by regional standards. It received 2 000 complaints per year in 2013 and 2014. It prosecuted a mere 32 and 17 respectively, with 26 and 11 convictions.

Zimbabwe: Anti-Corruption Commission

The ZACC was introduced in 2009 under Constitutional Amendment No. 19 and is therefore a constitutional body. However, the agency's stability is often affected by political interference.

Capacity

Section 254 of the constitution constitutes the Zimbabwe Anti-Corruption Commission, which should comprise a chairperson and eight other members.[3] The members of the commission are to hold office for a five-year term, which is renewable only once. The commission's employees do not form part of the civil service and are employed as provided for in section 234 of the constitution. Effectively, their terms and conditions are determined by the commission subject to the country's protective labour laws.

The commission relies on the police to effect arrests.

---

3 The basic requirement for eligibility for the commissioners remains the same under the old constitution from section 100K(2), 254(2) borrows verbatim the eligibility requirements.

The ZACC's lack of an independent budget poses challenges and has often incapacitated the execution of its mandate. It denies the commission the capacity to plan, organise and prioritise its work. On a number of instances, the ZACC has failed to receive adequate resources for operations from the line ministry, other than salaries and benefits for its commissioners and staff, thus effectively rendering it a white elephant. This has been interpreted in some quarters as further indication of the lack of political will by the state to support the commission's core mandate – the fight against corruption.

Autonomy

The constitution provides for ZACC to report directly to parliament, the same provision also requires that the reports be submitted through the 'responsible minister'. While it appears this was intended as a mere formality, in practice, the line ministry has somehow arrogated itself editorial or veto power with respect to these reports. Between 2010 and 2012, for instance, the ZACC produced its annual reports and forwarded them to the responsible ministry. The minister however never tabled the reports before parliament, thus denying the commission access to the legislature at the same time as denying the lawmakers their oversight powers envisaged by the constitution.

Performance

In spite of the available comprehensive constitutional and legal framework, the ZACC has struggled to effectively combat or contain corruption. A lack of resources (both financial and human) is clearly one of the reasons for this ineffectiveness. Its mandate and those of its collaborating partners like the police, the judiciary and the prosecuting authority further compromise its performance. Ultimately, these weaknesses can be traced back to a lack of political will by those in power, who –it has been argued – are themselves the major culprits in corruption.Yet, despite all the setbacks highlighted above, ZACC, including its predecessor the Anti-Corruption Commission (ACC), has done considerable work. The commission has achieved the following key successes:

- Notable cases by the Commission include the mission led by the ACC to ascertain activities in the Chiadzwa diamond fields, although the report was never made public. ZACC was also instrumental in unearthing the FIFA match-fixing scandals of 2010/2011,[4] in which the local football authority, the Zimbabwe Football Association (ZIFA) was implicated. The local investigation led to the arrest and prosecution of the former CEO of ZIFA.[5] The ZACC was also involved in the NIEEB investigations, already mentioned.
- Besides investigations, the commission has also played an important

---

4 See generally the Ebrahim Commission (2012) Asiagate Report'.
5 *State vs. Henrietta Rushwaya*, the accused was eventually acquitted but several players, coaches and journalists were implicated in the criminal trial, and a FIFA-mandated tribunal found several of the accused persons guilty of impropriety.

advisory role in line with the constitution. In 2009 the ACC undertook a study on the nature and prevalence of corruption in the country. The report is however yet to be made public.
- In collaboration with the ministry of state enterprises, the ACC was involved in the creation and launching of the National Corporate Governance Framework for State Enterprises and Parastatals.
- The ZACC was also a key participant in developing the National Corporate Governance Code,[6] recently launched.
- The ZACC has also been invited by several government ministries and departments to undertake forensic audits of their operations, with a view to reducing opportunities for corruption.

E. Commitment to international conventions on corruption

All the countries in this study have either signed or ratified the United Nations Convention Against Corruption [UNCAC]; the AU Convention on Preventing and Combatting Corruption, [AUCPCC]; and the SADC Protocol Against Corruption [SPAC].

F. Recommendations

The reports make several recommendations. The anti-corruption reform can be approached from three categories, namely the legal, the institutional framework and the demand-side by society. The legal and institutional frameworks are a technical regulatory regime, including the penal code and the accountability framework that sanctions corruption related activities.

The role of the demand-side of anti-corruption initiatives refers to the societal consciousness and action that creates a political imperative for accountability in governance. This is important in the sense that the demand-side mediates the political cost of corruption and ultimately empowering citizens to consider exercising their democratic rights to prevent corruption.

Policy reforms

Countries such as Malawi, South Africa, the DRC, Zambia and Swaziland need to undertake constitutional reforms that ensure autonomy and stability for their anti-corruption bodies. The reform needs to focus on anchoring, tenure, appointments and removal. It also ought to consider the political, administrative and financial independence of the said bodies.

---

6 There are indications that the NCGC will soon be made into a law to augment the anti-corruption regulatory framework.

Institutional reforms

There is urgent need to ensure that all public institutions, as well as the private sector, introduce user-friendly, efficient and transparent systems. Most instances of corruption, especially low-level corruption in the public sector, results from opaque or inefficient systems, which give rise to illicit backdoor practices. As highlighted in the discussion on the legal framework, already the constitution provides for an efficient and transparent public service. All that is required, therefore, is intensive lobbying to ensure implementation of these constitutional imperatives.

Regarding the autonomy and stability of the ACAs, there needs to be rethinking of the process regarding the appointment of key positions, including the director of commissions, public prosecutions and also police commissioners. These appointments need to be subjected to some form of effective confirmation by parliament, instead of only the executive. Therefore, dispersing responsibility regarding these appointments would ultimately alleviate political pressure from the executive.

Cooperation mechanisms: there is a need to create synergy among the institutions whose functions constitutes the broader anti-corruption initiative. Synergy will ensure a common approach towards anti-corruption instead of varied institutions with differentiated mandates. The approach across these institutions is too fragmented.

Demand-side activism

In the fight against corruption, it is therefore imperative to ask how members of the public could be motivated to take a stand and begin to bring about positive change. Citizens need to be made more aware regarding the impact of corruption on their daily lives. CSOs, including corruption watchdog Transparency International, could play a significant role in this process. The CSOs would need to come up with programmes of action that would include comprehensive audits of public service systems to identify the ones that do not work and thus breed corruption, and then come up with proposed recommendations, before engaging or lobbying the appropriate authorities. It is therefore necessary to activate the demand for anti-corruption initiatives among communities. For accountability to happen, it is important to re-emphasise the public participation of the general citizenry, particularly at local government level. There need to be popular will regarding the fight against corruption.

Political reform

Ultimately, especially in relation to high-level corruption, the people must, through the party, petition, ballot and other lawful means, reject a leadership that is either corrupt or shields corruption. This power solely lies in the hands of the people.

2
ANGOLA
Dr Helena Prata

A. Introduction

Once compared to an endemic disease, corruption is a phenomenon which dates back to the very beginnings of life in society and is today one of the biggest problems of the globalised world.

While not a phenomenon exclusive to the public sector, it is in this sector that the greatest incidence is seen. As a result, the introduction of specific ways of fighting corruption in the public administration is increasingly gaining fans and has become part of the order of the day in discussions within various segments.

The effects of this phenomenon are toxic for all of society, since it leads to the undermining of the rule of law, renders viable practices which heighten social tensions, reduces the number of services offered, facilitates organised crime and compromises development.

The fight against corruption is therefore a measure which falls to the state, given that it corrodes social structures, brings institutions into disrepute and acts as a limiting factor on development.

Although corruption is today one of the main concerns of governments, it is rare for the doer to be held accountable and punished.

At international level, there are a number of legal instruments which express the intention of the countries and international anti-corruption organisations, of which we will list but a few:
- Convention on the Fight against Corruption involving Officials of the European Communities or Officials of the Member States of the European Union (signed in Brussels on 26 May 1997).
- Convention on Combating Bribery of Foreign Public Officials in International Business Transactions, known as the Organisation for Economic Co-operation and Development (OECD) Anti-Bribery Convention (adopted in Paris on 17 December 1997).

- Council of Europe Criminal Law Convention on Corruption (signed in Strasbourg on 30 April 1999).
- Convention on the Protection of the European Communities' Financial Interests (signed in Brussels on 26 July 1995) and its two protocols.
- Inter-American Convention against Corruption (adopted in Caracas on 29 March 1996).
- African Union Convention on Preventing and Combating Corruption (AUCPCC – adopted in Maputo on 11 July 2003).
- United Nations Convention Against Corruption (UNCAC – adopted in Mérida on 31 October 2003).

This report will only discuss legislation relating to the corruption of public officials, which, according to article 2 of the UNCAC, also includes holders of political office.

The methodology used in preparing this report included: (i) a study of the anti-corruption legislation currently in force; and (ii) consulting the entities directly involved in preventing and combatting corruption. However, it should be stressed that it was only possible to gather and view information made available by the departments of the court of auditors and it was not possible to obtain data from the Anti-Corruption High Commission, since it is not instituted yet; nor from the attorney general's office.

B. Angola's political economy

Between 2002 and 2014, Angola experienced its best economic years, placing it among the global economies with the highest economic growth rates. This growth was mainly due to oil exploration and the increase of the oil price in the international market. It created a highly favourable macroeconomic background, which led to the government adopting an expansionist public budget policy in the last ten years (public expenditure in 2012 was twice as much as in 2004). Furthermore, between 2004 and 2012, the country was classified as the fastest growing economy in sub-Saharan Africa, with GDP growing at a rate of 11.5% per year and its per capita GDP reaching the USD6 600 mark. As a result, in 2012, Angola was classified by the United Nations as a low- to medium-income country.

This macroeconomic setting contributed significantly to the measurable improvement of the main social indicators. According to the most recent data from the Integrated Survey on the Well-Being of the Population (Inquérito Integrado sobre o Bem-Estar da População – IBEP) (2008–2009),[1] the proportion of the population with an income lower than USD1 per day was 68% in 2001. However, in 2009: the headcount poverty rate was estimated at 36.6%; the infant and child mortality rate went from 250 children per thousand live

---

1 Instituto Nacional de Estatística (2012) *Sumário do Inquérito Integrado sobre o Bem-estar da População (IBEP) 2009*. Luanda: INE.

births in 2001 to 164 per thousand live births in 2012; and life expectancy at birth was 45 years in 2000, 52 years in 2012 and subsequently 60 years in 2014, according to a general population census performed that year.[2]

However, despite these improvements, this progress does not correlate with the growth of GDP and public spending, nor is it part of a progressive strategy to promote sustainable socio-economic development. Angola is still among the five countries with the worst child mortality rates in the world. According to the Angolan national statistics institute, approximately half of childbirths take place at home (48%), with the situation in rural areas even worse, where 73% of childbirths take place at home and, in most cases, without the help of qualified healthcare professionals. In addition, 65% of the population does not have access to drinking water, 58% do not have access to basic sanitation[3] and 37% of the population is considered to be poor.[4]

Angola is rich in natural resources, having a wide variety of minerals, diamonds, copper and fossil fuels (oil and gas). In the last two decades, oil exploration overtook other resources, with many being 'neglected' to the advantage of oil. On its own, oil contributes 45% to GDP and more than 75% to the general state budget; it represents 95% of the country's exports, making the Angolan economy oil-dependent.[5] However, oil price volatility in the international market has exposed the country's fragility. Due to the decrease in the average price of a barrel of oil, the country is experiencing the worst macroeconomic times since the end of the civil war. This has resulted in: instability in the foreign exchange market; the reduction of public spending by almost half; the continuous devaluation of the kwanza against the US dollar; the dramatic fall of imports due to the currency deficit; the significant rise in the rate of inflation; and stagnant salaries with no budget flexibility for readjustments, with the consequent loss of purchasing power for families. The negative impact of the current crisis represents a significant step back from the progress made in the main socio-economic indicators over recent years, with severe negative consequences for the most vulnerable families.

Civil society and international organisations have emphasised for a long time the need for the government to diversify the Angolan economy, using all its natural resources to drive its economy and to promote sustained and equitable socio-economic development. However, very little has been done in this regard. Lately, the government seems to have 'woken up' to the necessity of diversifying the economy and ensuring the efficient use of revenue, and has been implementing a series of reforms. This have notably included: considerable cuts to public spending; an increase in the urban property tax; and the restructuring of Sonangol, which culminated in the controversial appointment of Isabel

---

2   Instituto Nacional de Estatística (2016) *Resultados Definitivos Recenseamento Geral da População e Habitação 2014*. Lunada: INE.
3   Instituto Nacional de Estatística (2011) *Inquérito de Indicadores Básicos de Bem-Estar(QUIBB)*. Luanda: INE.
4   Instituto Nacional de Estatística (2010) *Relatório do Inquérito Integrado sobre o Bem-estar da População – (IBEP) 2009*. Luanda: INE.
5   Ministério das Finanças (2015) *Relatório de Fundamentação do Orçamento Geral do Estado*. Luanda: Ministério das Finanças.

dos Santos, the daughter of the state president, as the president of the board of directors of what is the largest public company. However, these measures will take some time to generate measurable results that will benefit families.

This delay is of concern to the government, considering that elections are scheduled for August 2017. The electoral registration process is already underway. Opposition parties and civil society organisations have criticised this process heavily because registration is being run by the ministry of territorial administration, whereas, according to the terms provided in article 107(1) of the constitution, 'electoral processes are organised by independent electoral administration bodies, whose structure, operation, composition and competencies are defined by law'.

Municipal elections, initially planned for 2014, will only take place after the general elections. The government justifies the postponement by claiming that legislation still needs to be approved, staff trained and facilities built.

It should also be noted that, at the time of 11th ordinary session of the MPLA's central committee, held in July 2015, President José Eduardo dos Santos announced that he would be leaving the political scene in 2018.

C. State of corruption in Angola

Angola has been no stranger to this international movement for greater transparency, stringency and honesty in public affairs, namely in governance and acts of the administration. On 23 June 2006, by means of Resolution 20/06, Angola ratified the UNCAC. On 11 June 2003, Angola took part in the second Ordinary Session of the Assembly of the Union held in Maputo, which preceded the approval of the AUCPCC. On 8 August 2005, Resolution 38/05 approved the SADC Protocol against Corruption and, on 14 August 2006, by means of Resolution 27/06, it approved the ratification of the AUCPCC.

In 2013, Presidential Decree No. 81/13 of 5 September set up a working group for the purpose of studying and preparing a proposal for the implementation of the UNCAC, whose remit includes fostering and bolstering measures to prevent and combat the effects of corruption, as well as fostering and facilitating international cooperation in the prevention of and fight against corruption, including the recovery of assets and the promotion of integrity in the management of public accounts and assets.

Nevertheless, firmly entrenched in the social fabric is the idea that corruption is thriving in Angola, that it is increasingly affecting various levels of the administration, and that a large part of the economy is affected by it.

Yet, Angola has a range of legal instruments which envisage the auditing and oversight of public accounts, as well as rules of conduct on the prevention of and fight against corruption, in which some penalty procedures are established for acts of corruption.

In short, the legislation which is currently in force gradually added certain legislative innovations of meaning and reach to section VII of the 1886 Criminal Code:

- A broad concept of 'public servant' has been adopted (article 327 of the Criminal Code and Article 15 of Law 3/10 of 29 March);
- Some offences committed by holders of political office and high political office are established in a special law (Law 3/10 of 29 March);
- Active corruption offences are established (article 321 of the Criminal Code);
- A progressively more stringent definition of abuse of power has been adopted (article 39 of Law 3/10, previously established in general terms by section II of the Criminal Code as abuse of authority);
- Procedures have been introduced for derogating from the professional secrecy rules of credit institutions, financial companies and the tax authorities (Law 34/11 of 12 December on combatting money laundering and terrorism financing);
- Rules of criminal liability have been introduced for individuals/legal persons vested with public powers in certain circumstances (article 2 of Law 3/10);
- The court of auditors was set up to carry out the oversight of the state in accounting, financial, budgetary, operational and asset matters, and of direct and indirect administration bodies (Law 5/96 of 12 April, as amended by Law 21/03 of 29 August; Decree No. 23/01 of 12 April, approving the regulation on the organisation and procedure of the court of auditors; and Decree No. 24/01 of 12 April approving the provisions governing the court of auditors and its list of fees); and
- Law 3/14 of 10 February, which criminalises the acts that are forerunners to money laundering.

D. Administrative Probity Law

The Administrative Probity Law (Law 3/10 of 29 March) establishes the bases and the legal provisions governing public morality and respect for public assets by public servants (article 1), including elected public servants (article 15).

In addition, individuals or legal persons that are not public servants may also be considered as such for the purposes of Law 3/10 if they have been vested with public powers (article 2[2]). Its scope of material application also includes individuals or legal persons that have been vested with public powers.

The Administrative Probity Law is divided into six chapters: a general section containing definitions and principles; a chapter establishing a kind of code of conduct for public servants; a chapter on acts of improbity which lists situations where there is a conflict of interests; a chapter on probity guarantees and penalties which establishes the obligation for public servants to declare assets and income; a chapter establishing the rules of conduct to be followed by public officials in the pursuit of their duties; and a chapter of final provisions.

The general section contains basic definitions regarding the applicability of public ethics principles. Article 15(1) defines the public servant/official as being 'the person who holds a mandate, position, job or post in a public entity through election, appointment, engagement or any other form of investiture or assignment, even if transitory or unpaid'.

This definition is in harmony with the definitions of 'public official' in article 2(a) of the UNCAC and in article 1(1) of the AUCPCC.

The definition in question is clarified in article 15(2) of Law 3/10, to the effect that the term 'public servant' in article 2(3) must be considered a synonym for any other term used in other Angolan legislation, thereby guaranteeing its compatibility with international rules (particularly the UNCAC).

Article 15(2) of the law introduced a comprehensive list of specific positions which include public servants from all the powers and from all levels of government, including state-owned companies and companies vested with public functions.

It should be noted that the general definition of public servant in article 15 of Law 3/10 corresponds to the definition of public employee for criminal purposes in article 377 of the Criminal Code.

Codes and rules of conduct

Article 8(2) of the UNCAC requires the establishment of codes and rules of conduct for correct, honourable and proper performance of public duties. These codes clearly indicate how public servants must behave, emphasising certain fundamental values which may assist them in making decisions in specific situations. These fundamental values must include fairness, impartiality, transparency, accountability, responsible use of resources of the organisation and correct behaviour towards the public.

As to the implementation of the codes of conduct, article 8(6) of the UNCAC provides that the states parties must consider the possibility of introducing disciplinary and other measures for breaches of the code. These measures must be unified and should include the dismissal of the guilty party. Other possible penalties range from a warning, reprimand, admonition, censure, loss of seniority or suspension order to loss of position, suspension, expulsion, fine, and even imprisonment.

In any of these cases, the states parties must decide who or which agencies will guarantee the implementation of the code of conduct.

They must designate at least one authority to receive, verify and investigate allegations regarding goods, offers or accommodations. If the states choose to have more than one authority, they must ensure correct communication mechanisms between them as a means of guaranteeing efficacy. There must be some person or some agency responsible for sitting in judgment of the breaches.

Article 3 of Law 3/10 contains a series of principles and ethical duties with which public servants must abide. Articles 23 to 26 of Law 3/10 set down general prohibitions for public servants under the rules of conduct established therein.

The law further addresses public service and political activity issues, as well as defining rules for situations of conflicts of interests, with the objective of maintaining integrity in the political and administrative decisions emanating from public servants and public management.

The transparency requirements oblige public servants to declare their financial situation and their private interests (article 27).

Conflicts of interests are governed by articles 19(2), 25(1)(d), and 25(1)(h), which form a binding regulation of general scope to be applied across every level of the country's public service. Articles 28 and 29 lay down the general definitions of what should be understood as a conflict of interests for the purposes of the law but, generally speaking, this comes about when the public official finds himself in circumstances in which his personal interests interfere, or may interfere, with the performance of his duties of independence and impartiality in the pursuit of public duties.

These rules on conflicts of interests seek to identify the circumstances in which such conflicts may occur, and how to manage them, as well as the administrative, judicial and political guarantees applicable to public servants and to citizens, along with the penalties for any breach of the rules on conflicts of interests (articles 28(2) and 31).

It should be noted that the management of conflicts of interests contained in Law 3/10 is in harmony with that established in the OECD Recommendation on Managing Conflict of Interest in the Public Service.

Yet despite the relatively long reach of the law to cover typical situations of administrative improbity, there is still a vast range of matters which remain to be addressed, including active corruption offences with adverse effects on international trade, in harmony with the OECD Convention of 1997, which has not yet been ratified by Angola; and the criminalisation of the offences of influence peddling and money laundering. Unlike other countries, the offence of money laundering is not established either in the Criminal Code or in other criminal legislation and, accordingly, there is an urgent need for such conduct to be outlawed, as it can hardly be said that the scope of application of Law 34/11 (Money Laundering Law) is restricted to certain typical activities; nor is there any provision for a specific rule of procedure to be adopted, in order to neutralise pacts of silence, etc.

There are no guarantees for the integrity of the administrative probity system set up by Law 3/10, since no provision is made: for a control and oversight body responsible for managing the situations of conflict of interests defined by the law; for laying down rules, procedures and mechanisms capable of preventing possible conflicts of interests; for monitoring actual conflicts of interests; and for defining appropriate measures with a view to eliminating such conflicts.

In addition, no protection mechanism has been established for those who report conflicts of interest in conformity with the general rules for the protection of victims, complainants, witnesses and other parties to the proceedings.

It is important to highlight here the importance which anonymous complaints may have as a suitable mechanism for triggering investigative procedures, depending on whether or not they contain suitable and sufficient information to launch the relevant inquiry.

Declaration of assets

The obligation of public officials to declare assets is set down in article 27 of Law 3/10. Clause 1 of this article establishes that prior to taking up office, public officials are obliged to declare all their assets and income which constitute private property.

This declaration is, according to the provision in question, a necessary condition for holding public office and must be updated every two years. However, not all public officials are required to declare their assets – only those specified in article 27(1) are subject to this obligation.

In this particular aspect, we believe it is important for this provision to be harmonised with article 15(2) since it has the benefit of avoiding narrow interpretations which may give rise to inequality in the treatment of identical situations.

However, it must be stressed that the declaration of assets is a duty of the public official and the failure to fulfil this duty may lead to the official in question committing the offence of false declarations, as prescribed in article 27(3), and being held liable in disciplinary and criminal terms.

The law establishes what the content of the declaration of assets should be and there is a specific form for the declaration of assets from which it is possible to infer that the declaration of assets must be made prior to taking office and must be updated every two years, if there is no reason to update it beforehand (for example, transfer from one public office to another, re-election, etc.). If there has been no change in assets from one calendar year to another, the public official must make a declaration to this effect.

Law 3/10 also lays down disciplinary and criminal penalties. However, it is not possible to ascertain from the penalty framework established by Law 3/10 whether the evidence filed in a disciplinary procedure may or may not be transferred to criminal proceedings, since the threshold necessary for a finding against the defendant in a disciplinary procedure is lower than that required for a conviction in criminal proceedings.

Regarding access to the content of the declarations, article 27(6) of Law 3/10 provides that 'access by court order is only permitted whenever, within the scope of criminal and/or disciplinary and administrative proceedings, reasons of one nature or another so warrant'.

This provision, in our view, constitutes a major limitation on the right to information established in article 40 of the Constitution of the Republic of Angola and, within the scope of the principles of administrative procedure, is a logical corollary of the principles of openness and transparency.

According to these principles, any citizen should have the right to obtain certificates and documents in order to file an action for judicial review seeking to quash any act harmful to the public assets or administrative morality. As citizens, voters, taxpayers and holders of rights arising out of the democratic principle, they are entitled to be aware of the character of officials and to know whether they are honest people of integrity.

Moreover, without access to this information, it will be difficult to exercise the right to complain enshrined in article 32 of Law 3/10, which establishes that 'any individual or legal person may report to the public prosecution service or to an administrative body facts which reveal a lack of probity'. However, the exercise of this right will only be possible if there is a mechanism for access to information since the complaint must necessarily be, on most occasions, accompanied by evidence and even proof, which will enable, with no great effort, the subject-matter of the process to be specified and delimited, and to be able to support (using the facts described therein, and nothing more) an accusation (article 32[2] of Law 3/10).

In this way, access to the information contained in the asset declaration of public officials is an individual guarantee to the citizen of a transparent administration and it cannot be admitted (or permitted) that there should be secrets and mysteries in this regard.

The deprivation of access to information by the citizens about the development of the legal estates of these public servants is equivalent to the implementation of a 'silent complicity' model of administration.

E. Criminalising corruption, criminal proceedings and imposing penalties

In the catalogue of offences in the Angolan criminal law system, corruption is one of the most regulated; the lawmakers have criminalised, in the Criminal Code and other legislation (Law 17/90, Law 6/99, Decree 24/90 of 6 October), corruption and acting in conflict of interest on the part of public officials (public servants and/or holders of political office). They have criminalised corruption in respect of an unlawful act, corruption in respect of a lawful act, active and passive corruption, etc.

The UNCAC, the AUCPCC and the SADC Protocol do not specify the necessary penalties which the states parties should establish in their national legislation to punish corruption-related offences. However, article 30 of the UNCAC provides some guidelines which establish that the states parties must have penalties that are proportional to the gravity of the infringement and which must be sufficient to have a deterring effect.

The general rules regarding penalties for offences of corruption in Angola are laid down in the Criminal Code in articles 318 to 326, which establish terms of imprisonment and the forfeiture to the state of the assets received as a result of corruption or of the value of such assets. Article 318 provides that the sentence may range from a minimum of two years to a maximum of eight years.

The key features for punishing corruption-related offences are, on the one hand, the sentencing of the public official involved and the person who corrupted them to a term of imprisonment and/or the payment of a fine and, on the other, depriving the perpetrators of the unlawful gains made from the corruption. The investigations and accusations must, in accordance with article 31(2) of the UNCAC, not only discover the criminals, but also trace and identify the assets that have been unlawfully obtained by the perpetrators, so as to ensure that they cannot benefit from the proceeds of the crime.

Seizure and confiscation are therefore necessary measures for removing assets of criminal origins from the hands of criminals, while article 323 of the Criminal Code provides for the forfeiture of the items received to the state.

However, there are no proper regulations for the seizure and confiscation of assets. Article 13 of Law 22/92 defines the rules for seizing assets, establishing that the items which must be seized include those (i) which served as instruments for the commission of offences or were intended for this purpose, (ii) which were left at the scene of the crime by the perpetrator, or (iii) any other items which may need to be examined for the criminal proceedings.

These rules, however, appear to refer to the seizure of items which may be used as evidence in criminal proceedings and do not refer directly to the seizure of the proceeds and instruments of crimes where the main objective is financial gain.

It is important therefore to adopt a suitable regulation regarding the seizure and confiscation of the proceeds and instruments of crime, as well as assets which have been mixed up with others and transformed.

The adoption of a suitable regulation is also necessary to guarantee compliance with the international rules established in article 31(2) of the UNCAC and ensure the identification, trace and seizure of the proceeds and instruments of crime.

F. Anti-Corruption High Commission (ACHC)

Successful investigations and proceedings into offences related to corruption and money laundering depend on the gathering and presentation of suitable evidence and the existence of institutions that can conduct proceedings aimed at holding the perpetrators of the offence liable.

Articles 6 and 36 of the UNCAC contain provisions on the creation of anti-corruption bodies for the prevention and criminalisation of corruption. The wording of the UNCAC obliges the states parties to guarantee the existence of a body or bodies for the prevention of corruption. It stresses that the prevention of corruption may be a task for one or more institutions.

The single-agency approach embraced by some countries seeks to set up an institution with a broad mandate to prevent corruption, raise awareness about the issue, and investigate and file corruption charges. It is based on the fundamental pillars of prevention and investigation, such as policing, analysis and technical assistance for prevention, public information, monitoring and investigation.On 5 April 1996, Law 3/96 made provision for the Anti-Corruption High Commission as an independent body with the objective of preventing and investigating acts of corruption and fraud committed in the pursuit of administrative duties and reporting them to the appropriate body for disciplinary or criminal proceedings.

Article 2 of Law 3/96 established that the Anti-Corruption High Commission should operate from the national parliament, which would elect the anti-corruption high commissioner by a majority of two-thirds of the deputies in full exercise of office (article 6), upon a proposal from any parliamentary group, from among citizens in full enjoyment of their civil and political rights, of recognised merit, probity and independence. The applications must be duly accompanied by proof of the eligibility of the applicant and the relevant declarations of acceptance. The anti-corruption high commissioner is elected for a term of four years.

According to this law, the Anti-Corruption High Commission, in the pursuit of its powers, may investigate evidence or news of facts which justify grounded suspicions of an act of corruption or fraud, an offence against public assets, abuse of public office or any other acts detrimental to the public interest or to the morality of the administration. Also according to the law, the Anti-Corruption High Commission is responsible, firstly, for raising awareness about the fight against corruption and, secondly, for conducting the investigation which precedes the trial and for preparing the investigation into acts of corruption. This is subsequently sent to the public prosecution service, which will conduct the investigation and the criminal proceedings.

However, despite the 19 years that the law has been in existence, the Anti-Corruption High Commission has not yet been set up, a fact which renders the entire legal framework developed around it ineffective.

In other words, there is no practising institutional framework which: goes beyond procedural activity to develop social awareness against corruption; sponsors studies and the prevention of corruption; develops a multidisciplinary intervention methodology in anti-corruption matters; simulates organic adjustments to other inspection, oversight or judicial bodies, useful for bolstering the fight against corruption; provides support, within the scope of its own specific competence, for corruption and fraud investigations conducted as part of the inspections of the various government departments, the police and the courts; or arranges with the ombudsman, the attorney general of the republic and the court of auditors specifically responsible (and supplementary) for combatting the factors which facilitate unlawful or ethically reprehensible conduct.

The ACHC should be the centre for all the documentation and collection of information about cases linked to corruption, including the preparation of financial and criminal investigations.

This being so, and in accordance with the laws in force, the ACHC would have more interaction with the Financial Information Unit, the attorney general's office and the court of auditors, as well as interaction with the tax authorities, the criminal investigation police, etc.

It is notable that the ACHC will have to be conferred the necessary capacities and resources to be able to fully perform and implement all its duties, as set down in Law 3/10 (for example, training human resources for financial investigations, aiming to guarantee effective cross-referencing of information with a view to ensuring that more effective results are obtained).

Another problem which poses a major obstacle for the execution of Law 3/10 is the fact that no regulation has been drafted. While the intention of the law is commendable, if the various relevant practical aspects are not detailed in regulations, with the aim of making it real in order for it to achieve full effectiveness, the law is of no practical effect.

The constitution provides for the publication of regulations as a guarantee for proper execution of the law. The aim of regulations is to clarify legislative provisions, by way of complementary rules to the law, thereby guaranteeing proper execution of the same. This is because laws make no provision for detail and do not specify the form of application – a task which is left to regulations.

All laws involve two major variables: the text in itself and the capacity for implementation. In other words, the law is only truly useful if what it defends and/or recommends makes sense and if this can be in some way protected by whoever created it.

As there is no legal and institutional framework which empowers the action of the ACHC in the fight against corruption, we are forced to conclude that Law 3/96 has become a dead letter, either because of its inefficiency and uncontrollability or simply its lack of applicability.

G. Court of auditors

The court of auditors was set up by Law 5/96, of 12 April, later amended by Laws 21/03 of 29 August and 13/10 of 9 July, and came into actual effect in 2001, when the appeal court judge, who is the president of the court, took up office.

According to the preamble of this law, 'the creation of the court of auditors in Angola is not only a democratic imperative, in the area of oversight of public funds which it is urgent to implement, but also a fundamental instrument for assuring greater stringency and discipline in the public finances'.

The Constitution of the Republic of Angola enshrines the court of auditors as 'the supreme body for overseeing the legality of the public finances and appraising the accounts which the law subjects to its jurisdiction' (article 182). This concept shows the jurisdictional nature of the court, the hierarchical rank of this body as an upper court, and marks out its powers over the matters within its speciality.

The council of ministers, in the normal course of its activity and in order to equip the court of auditors with legal instruments that would complement the organic law so that it would be efficient and effective in the pursuit of its duties, approved the following legal instruments:
- Decree 23/01, of 12 April, approving the regulation on the organisation and procedure of the court of auditors; and

- Decree 24/01, of 12 April, approving the provisions governing the court of auditors and its list of fees.

Six years after the law was approved, a legal and institutional framework was created that would enable the court of auditors to begin its work.

The court of auditors is composed of nine appeal court judges, including the president and the vice-president, and has two chambers, the first of which deals with prior reviews and the second with subsequent reviews. It functions in plenary chamber sessions, daily approval sessions and regional and provincial section sessions. The court may only function in plenary sessions if at least five of the judges are present and the president or, by delegation, the vice-president is among these five.

The competences of the court lie in the degree or extent of powers which they have in determining the range of matters on which it is legitimate for the court to make a pronouncement. Generally speaking, the competences of the court are defined as follows:

To give its opinion on the general accounts of the state: within the scope of this competence, the court has a consultation or opinion function with the national parliament. Within this functional interdependence, the court of auditors provides an instrumental technical assistance service to the national parliament, as a specialised body in matters involving the control of public finances.

- To conduct prior reviews of the legality and regularity of the acts and contracts submitted for prior review: in order to prevent seriously irregular acts from having material or financial effect, the lawmakers made the efficacy of given acts and contracts conditional on prior review by the court of auditors.
- To conduct audits and inquiries into the agencies under its jurisdiction: in such audits, the court weighs up whether the accounts of a given agency gives a fair view of the true financial and asset status of the agency in question by analysing its financial statements; in such enquiries, the court conducts a brief study of how the body is managed in terms of the legality and regularity of how income and expenditure are made, as well as aspects relevant to the economics, efficiency and efficacy of the management of the resources at the disposal of the body or agency under review.
- To ensure that any wrongful incurrence of financial liability is penalised and any loss restored. Financial liability lies with any de jure or de facto manager who has engaged in acts which, in general, infringe the rules on budget execution or who has diverted financial resources.

Reviews may be prior or subsequent, depending on when they are conducted by the court.

A prior review is conducted before the acts and contracts being targeted give rise to any material and financial effect. In this respect, the approval of the court is a pre-condition for their effectiveness. The purpose of a prior review is to ascertain the legality and propriety of the expenses.

A subsequent review is conducted after the acts and contracts have brought about effects and have the purpose of weighing up the legality and regularity of how income and expenditure are made, as well as, where contracts are involved, verifying whether the conditions of such contracts are the most advantageous at the time of execution.

An examination of the activity of the court of auditors leads us to the understanding that both prior reviews and subsequent reviews have the objective of contributing to the enhancement of financial management and public assets. In pursuit of this end, the court has designed, alongside its review and oversight activities, educational projects to raise awareness of accountability and call for the adoption of good management practices by public managers.

The court also invested in empowering its human resources through training sessions and the adoption of methods and tools which guarantee greater oversight and control of the financial and asset management of the public purse.

Within the scope of its investigative powers, the court of auditors monitors, inspects and oversees the acts of the administration and the expenses arising therefrom, by way of accounting, financial, budgetary, operational, and asset inspections.

The creation and commencement of the court of auditors in 2001 has brought significant contributions to good public finance governance. Apart from contributing to legality and financial regularity, the court fosters improved financial management by making recommendations in the written opinions and the external and internal audits and checks of accounts which it has concluded over the 14 years it has been in existence.

We should highlight here the drafting and release of the written opinions on the general accounts of the state, including social security accounts, which constitute an important landmark in public life for the contribution they have made to transparency in the administration of the public finances.

The recommendations made by the court in these written opinions is clear and seeks not only to guarantee legality and financial correctness but also to contribute to perfecting legislation.

In the pursuit of its duty to carry out outside and independent control of the public finances through prior, concurrent and successive reviews and render financial liabilities effective, the court contributes to strengthening the bond of trust between the state and the citizen.

In relation to its activity of financial control, it is worth mentioning the way in which the audited entities have taken its recommendations on board, which has resulted in considerable savings for the public purse and corrections of thousands of kwanzas, as well as the decisions making financial liabilities effective.

Over the last fourteen years, the court of auditors, within the scope of prior control, has dealt with a vast number of cases; notable among which, insofar as it concerns subsequent reviews, are the processes for imposing fines and for restoring financial loss in cases of financial liability.

As for subsequent control, it is worth noting the analytic work done with a view to preparing the report and issuing the opinion on the general accounts of the state and the internal accounts verification process, which is aimed at examining the accounts subject to its jurisdiction.

Also in the field of subsequent control, the court has conducted audits which fall within its purview, as well as appraising the audit reports of the Inspectorate General of Finance (IGF). For example, out of all the cases in 2014, there was, with regard to the prior assessment of works contracts, a total of 349 cases, one of which spilled over from the preceding year. Also worthy of note with regard to preventive review are the 63 cases where visa applications were rejected for failure to comply with legal procedures; 50 cases of rejected admissions, appointments and promotions; and 23 visa suspension cases. With regard to subsequent review in restoration of financial liability actions, there were two completed cases in 2014; the decision on one of which has become final.

H. Public prosecution service

With regard to the public prosecution service, the powers conferred on it by the 2010 constitution turned it into a fundamental institution for controlling the actions of other state players and government bodies, as well as the defender of the interests and constitutional rights of the citizen and the society.

Article 187 of the constitution says that 'the public prosecution service is an essential institution for the jurisdictional function of the state, and has autonomy and its own status'. Article 186 of the constitution specifies its remit as being that of representing the state, defending collective and diffuse interests, defending inalienable social and individual interests, etc. The pursuit of criminal proceedings also falls within the scope of its powers. The organisation, powers and status of the public prosecution service are envisaged in Law 22/12 of 14 August.

With the prerogatives afforded by the constitution and by ordinary legislation, the public prosecution service has a prominent position in controlling the other public institutions and defending the citizens. Apart from public prosecution powers – it has a monopoly on criminal proceedings – it is also involved in investigating, denouncing and acting on issues involving constitutional rights.

Unlike the judiciary – a passive institution which is dependent on others to act – the public prosecution service can select its cases and has a greater margin of choice and discretion. As a result, the members of the public prosecution service can now act vis-à-vis several public institutions, investigating, denouncing and proposing terms for adjusting conduct.

However, notwithstanding the powers and competences conferred by the constitution, the Criminal Code and the Criminal Procedure Code, Law 3/10 of 29 March, and Law 22/12 of 14 August, little is known about how the public prosecution service operates with regard to criminal proceedings which involve the engagement in or suspicion of engagement in acts of corruption.

I. Legislature

The legislature, in accordance with article 141 of the constitution, comprises the national parliament, which is in turn made up of deputies (representatives of the people) elected in accordance with the constitution and the law.

The main functions of the legislature are to draft the laws, exercise political control, and analyse the accounts of the state and of all the institutions which deal with public funds. It also exercises outside institutional control over the administrative function of the state.

The legislature expresses the will of the people and the ideological diversity of society, since its members are holders of mandates given by the people in elections; in this way, they express the different existing political leanings. As a result, the legitimacy of the members of the legislature imposes on them the mandate to represent public interest, to legislate, to propose public policies, and to oversee the administrative activity of the state, within the parameters of a democratic state.[6]

There is currently a consensus in political science that parliaments tend to lose slices of their legislative power as they increase their power to oversee and monitor public management acts. With the increasing complexity of government, the growth of the administrative machine, and the modernisation of society, yet more activities are falling within the scope of the executive power.

It can be inferred therefore that regarding the three classic functions of the legislature (to represent, legislate and oversee), nowadays the importance of the function of control is clear.

In political science, the control exercised by the legislature goes beyond oversight, it involves monitoring everything which the government does. What is of interest here is the role of the legislature in overseeing the use of public funds.[7]

The relevant constitutional provisions are set down in article 162(b), which establishes that 'it is incumbent on the national parliament, within the field of control and oversight, to receive and scrutinise the general accounts of the state' and, in article 104(4), which establishes that 'the execution of the general state budget shall comply with the principles

---

6   Pedone L (2001) O controle pelo legislativo. In: B Speck (ed.) *Caminhos da Transparência*. São Paulo: Edição Electrónica pp. 89–101.
7   Ibid.

of transparency and good governance and shall be reviewed by the national parliament and by the court of auditors, on the conditions set down by law'.

Outside parliamentary control is carried out with the assistance of the court of auditors, which is responsible for reviewing the legality of the public finances and appraising the accounts which the law subjects to its jurisdiction and the accounts of those which bring about a loss, diversion, or other irregularity which has a detrimental result for the public purse.

The wording of the articles above implies the obligation for there to be an annual rendering of accounts to the national parliament as provided for by law. In addition to these articles, there are also the routine institutional mechanisms used by the legislature for exerting control over the executive, such as the National Planning System Base Law (Law 1/11 of 14 January), the General State Budget Framework Law (15/10 of 14 June), and the Public Assets Law (Law 18/10 of 6 August).

The national parliament has therefore expanded its responsibility in the control of the public accounts, since it is to this institution that internal control reports must be reported.

The laws referred to above also contain features which seek to evidence transparency of actions and to permit the assessment of the results and the costs, as well as to improve planning instruments.

It is clear from constitutional and ordinary law provisions that the national parliament has an important role in controlling the public accounts.

However, the constitutional court, in Ruling 319/2013 of 9 October 2013, in a case involving a subsequent review of the constitutionality of some of the provisions of Law 13/12 of 2 May (organic law approving the national parliament regimen), declared the following unconstitutional: article 261(1)(c) and (2) and articles 260, 269, 270 and 271. The ruling also declared article 268 to be partially unconstitutional. The provisions in question lay down certain kinds of oversight of state accounts by the national parliament, namely: asking questions, making formal demands, parliamentary hearings, and enquiries.

The constitutional court held that as they are not expressly provided for in article 162 of the constitution (which establishes the competences of the legislature in control and oversight matters) the prerogatives granted by the above-mentioned unconstitutional articles 'contradict the system of government established by the constitution and are in breach of articles 162 and 105 of the Constitution of the Republic of Angola', and are thus unconstitutional (Ruling 319/2013 of 9 October).

Without prejudice to our consideration that the ruling is based on a narrow interpretation of articles 105 and 162 of the constitution, we understand that it places serious limits on the actions of the legislature in its function of controlling and overseeing the accounts of the state, while the features created for the exercise of these powers of control have a rather limited range owing to the tight limits imposed by the ruling.

Thus, despite the various constitutional possibilities attributed to the legislature, the oversight process adopted needs to be much improved, since the control exercised has a corrective and not a preventive character.

Anti-money laundering legislation

Although the exact definition of money laundering ultimately depends on the legislation of each country, some considerations of a general character may be made on the basis of international rules. Money laundering is very often defined as the process whereby the perpetrators of criminal activities disguise the origin of the assets and income (benefits) obtained unlawfully, transforming the proceeds from these activities into legally reusable capital, by dissimulating the origin or the true owner of the funds. The money laundering process may have three distinct and successive stages, in order to conceal the ownership and origin of the unlawful benefits, to maintain control of these benefits and to give them an appearance of legality:

1. Placement: the assets and income are placed in the financial and non-financial circuits by way of, for example, deposits in financial institutions or investments in lucrative activities and high-value assets;
2. Circulation: the assets and income are subject to multiple repeated operations (for instance, transfers of funds) with the purpose of distancing them further from their criminal origin, eliminating any trace of their provenance and ownership; and
3. Integration: the already recycled goods and assets are reintroduced to legitimate economic circuits by using them, for example, in the acquisition of goods and services.

Money laundering and corruption are intrinsically linked. Corruption-related offences are normally committed with the objective of obtaining an unlawful benefit, irrespective of whether it is active or passive corruption, embezzlement or some other act of corruption. In turn, money laundering is the process of concealing and disguising these unlawful gains generated from the corruption. The advantage of money laundering, from the point of view of the corrupt person, is that it is only when the proceeds from a corruption offence have been laundered successfully that they can be enjoyed, without fear of detection or confiscation.[8]

The UNCAC draws a connection between money laundering and corruption-related offences in article 23(2)(a). However, money laundering involves not only the public servant who has accepted an unlawful benefit, but also all those who have assisted the public servant in the money laundering process; for example, accountants (who distort information), lawyers (who rely on the creation of complex legal structures to disguise

---

8 OECD (2010) Seminar proceedings: Effective Means of Investigation and Prosecution of Corruption. p. 104. Available at http://www.oecd.org/corruption/acn/47588859.pdf [accessed 10 November 2016].

the true nature, origin and ownership of the goods), bank managers (who help to open accounts in jurisdictions which offer more favourable terms for the protection of the proceeds of crime), etc.

In the Angolan legal order, there is no criminal definition of money laundering, however, under Law 34/11 of 12 December and Law 3/14 of 10 February, it appears to be clear, and indeed this is the understanding in other legal orders, that the offences of corruption, among others, are forerunners of money laundering.

Money laundering is not established as an offence in the Angolan criminal legislation currently in force, while Laws 34/11 and 3/14 seek only to establish a set of rules relating to the prevention of the use of the financial system and the specially designated activities and professions for the purposes of laundering money and financing terrorism, on one hand, and the type of crimes that are forerunners of money laundering, on the other.

This seems to suggest that the forerunning offences (corruption, drug-trafficking, terrorism financing, etc.) and the treatment of money laundering situations should function independently of each other; but the degree of autonomy is not clear, nor can it be inferred directly from the legislation in force.

J. Conclusions

In the light of the framework described above, we may conclude that the system for preventing and fighting corruption in Angola is quite weak, with many negative aspects and a low investigation success rate, notwithstanding the work done by the court of auditors, and, consequently, extremely unsatisfactory penalty statistics.

Angola today is living in a contradiction when it comes to combatting illegalities in public management. On the one hand, legislation (including the constitution) exists which seeks to punish administrative improbity, to establish positive mechanisms to achieve efficient public management and, at the same time, to impose penalties on those who divert public resources. On the other hand, the reality shows that, despite the legislation, the judiciary and the anti-corruption institutions are unable to provide a satisfactory response. It could be said that there is quite a fragile judicial culture in Angola in terms of the prevention, control and elimination of acts of corruption, while the penalties in themselves are insufficient to put a stop to the phenomenon of corruption.

It is evident that the fight against corruption is vital in democratic states and that this concern is felt at the legislative level. Not so obvious, however, are the 'checks and balances' which govern the action of the institutions that have the objective of combatting the phenomenon of corruption.

The mere production of laws is not sufficient for the fight against corruption, it is necessary to create a set of mechanisms so that the institutions that are formally entrusted with controlling and overseeing the use of public resources are able to effectively prevent and eliminate acts of corruption.

K. Recommendations

Generally speaking, the data given in this report enables us to argue that, essentially, the legislative package that is currently in force and the institutional anti-corruption system do not furnish adequate tools to prevent and combat acts of corruption and public improbity more effectively, even though some of their specific aspects may be fully in compliance with international rules.

We have seen that in order for there to be an effective fight against the phenomenon of corruption as a whole, there must be combined actions which enable the preparation and consolidation of risk prevention plans, oversight and elimination of acts of corruption.

Accordingly:

- It is vital that the ACHC be set up in order to take over the determining role in eliminating acts of corruption.
- It is particularly important to enhance the prospection capacity and reliability of the administrative oversight bodies charged with reporting to the formal control bodies (criminal investigation police and public prosecution service) the acts of corruption of which they become aware in the course of their duties (see article 8[4] of the UNCAC). These bodies should direct their actions towards overseeing transactions for the acquisition of goods and services and the licensing of activities, as well as procedures for the recruitment of officials and for the control of transparency, objectivity, efficacy, merit and aptitude requirements (articles 7 and 9 of the UNCAC).
- There must be a suitable system for collecting reports (complaints) from the citizens; this does not exclude anonymous complaints (article 13[2] of the UNCAC). The endemic character of corruption today, the involvement of holders of state power and the reasonable fear of retaliation mean that anonymous complaints should not be undervalued. Very often they are the only way in which citizens can be involved in controlling corruption.
- To this point, a guarantee system must be established for public employees/servants who report infringements of which they have become aware in the course of their duties.
- Fostering and protecting the freedom to procure, receive, publish and disseminate information about corruption, in harmony with article 13 of the UNCAC, is also of vital importance, without prejudice to the inherent interests of secrecy of the investigations (when required) and, proportionately, to the reputation of the targeted persons.

- The adoption of special measures for boosting the integrity of the judiciary and the public prosecution service is also required, given the core roles they play in the criminal law system (article 11 of the UNCAC).
- As regards elimination, the worrying lack of effectiveness of the legislation that is currently in force must be remedied, since some of it has become transformed into purely symbolic law, which is clearly mirrored in the risible number of convictions obtained and the negligible use of instruments produced years ago, specifically Law 3/39 (which provides for the Anti-Corruption High Commission) which has been slow in leaving the pages of the Official Gazette and taking its place in practice. This objective presupposes empowerment, experience, and specialisation, all of which require an adequate allocation of human and material resources, not only to the criminal investigation police but also to the public prosecution service and the courts.
- It is important also to stress the fundamental role that civil society can play in fighting corruption and, to this end, it is necessary to foster mechanisms for interacting with those responsible for controlling, overseeing and eliminating acts of corruption in the sense of (i) debating and filing for judicial review of public management by the civil society; (ii) promoting, incentivising and disseminating the debate and the development of concepts on social participation in the monitoring and control of public management; (iii) proposing mechanisms for the transparency of and access to public information and data to be implemented by public bodies and entities and fostering the use of such information and data by the society; (iv) debating and discussing mechanisms for raising awareness and mobilising society towards participating in the monitoring and control of public management; (v) discussing and filing actions to empower and qualify society for monitoring and controlling public management; and (vi) debating and proposing measures for the prevention of and fight against corruption which involve the work of the public administration, companies and civil society.

Only by these measures can the negative views (at national and international level) of Angola's capacity to prevent and eliminate corruption be reversed.

3
BOTSWANA

Dr Gape I Kaboyakgosi

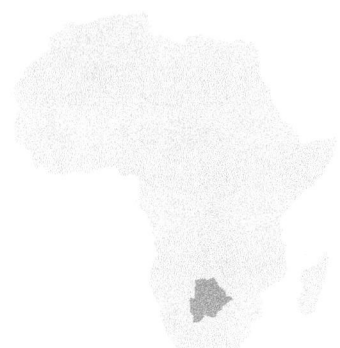

A. Introduction

This chapter profiles the opportunities and challenges faced by the Botswana Directorate on Corruption and Economic Crime (DCEC). The DCEC was set up in 1995, as a result of the adoption of the Corruption and Economic Crimes Act (CECA) to respond to what were then a number of lapses in ethical governance. Botswana is one of Africa's top performers in terms of governance indicators, and is also one of the continent's leading performers in anti-corruption. Since 1998 when Botswana was first assessed through Transparency International's Corruption Perception Index (CPI), the country consistently came out as Africa's leading anti-corruption nation in terms of the CPI. Globally, Botswana remains consistently in the 25% least corrupt countries of the world.[1]

The following section gives a brief overview of politics and the economy in Botswana, primarily showing that Botswana's track record in governance and economic growth sets it apart from its African peers. However, as a one-party dominant regime, Botswana still requires strong oversight mechanisms.

Politics and the economy

While the quality of its democracy can be questioned in some regards, Botswana is one of Africa's longest serving post-colonial democracies.[2] Since its inception as an independent republic in 1966, Botswana has practiced a multi-party electoral democracy; has consistently held five-yearly elections based on universal adult suffrage; and run a government based on a separation of powers – with the three branches of government, the judiciary, legislative and executive having clearly demarcated roles in governance. It is also a characteristic of Botswana's political landscape that the Botswana Democratic Party

---

1 Transparency International (2015) *Corruption Perception Index 2015*. Berlin: Transparency International.
2 Kaunda JM, Kaboyakgosi G, Kamaral B, Balule TB, Mpule K & Mapena KS (2008) *The Progress of Good Governance in Botswana*. Gaborone: BIDPA &UNECA; Taylor I (2005) The developmental state in Africa: The case of Botswana. In: P Mbabazi & I Taylor (eds) *The Potentiality of 'Developmental States' in Africa: Botswana and Uganda Compared*. Dakar: CODESIRA. pp. 44–56.

(BPD) has consistently won all 11 general elections, making the description of de facto one-party-dominant system apt for Botswana.³

Added to its democratic governance, Botswana is one of Africa's consistently high performers in terms of economic growth. Driven by minerals, particularly diamond revenue, the economy in Botswana has flourished in the last three decades. The country was Africa's only entrant into a list of 13 countries that had experienced growth of over 7% from the 1950s till the turn of the millennium, which is a very credible achievement.⁴

However, Botswana's growth rates have come with a number of undesirable characteristics including high unemployment, particularly amongst the educated youth, and high income inequality levels, particularly in view of the fact that Botswana is a middle income country.⁵

Botswana's performance in terms of many governance indicators is reasonably good, being rated consistently high by the World Bank Governance Indicators. Along with Namibia, South Africa, Mauritius, Cape Verde amongst others, Botswana is one of Africa's better governed states. Basic freedoms such as speech and association, are reasonably observed; the role of the media and its capacity to operate is well respected. However, parliament, the premier oversight institution, is dominated by the BDP. Such domination, coupled with the role of the BDP caucus and its capacity to control the agenda of parliamentary committees, means that the role of oversight played by parliament is often less than ideal, as the BDP is often accused of using its numbers to stifle debate. Similarly, the role played by the office of the auditor general (OAG), is compromised by the incapacity of the OAG to enforce its own decisions.⁶ Such incapacity is worsened by parliament's lack of capacity to function accordingly.

With the BDP majority reduced after the 2014 elections, a large proportion of BDP MPs have joined the executive, leading to a more rigorous parliament. However, this has resulted in a decidedly executive dominated parliament. In the context of this exercise, three major conclusions may thus be drawn about politics and the economy in Botswana:

- The government has a longstanding tradition of adhering to formal means of democratic governance, something for which it has received recognition. This includes multi-partyism, regular elections and the rule of law;

---

3   Sebudubudu D & Osei-Hwedie BZ (2006) 'Pitfalls of parliamentary democracy in Botswana'. *Afrika Spectrum* 41(1): 486; Maundeni Z, Sebudubudu D, Kebonang Z & Mokhawa G (2008) Dominant parties: What SADC can learn from the Botswana Democratic Party's compromises. *Studies on Political Parties and Democracy*. Maputo: Friedrich Ebert Stiftung. p. 3.
4   World Bank (2008) *The Growth Report: Strategies for Sustained Growth and Inclusive Development, Commission on Growth and Development*. Washington DC: World Bank.
5   World Bank & Botswana Institute for Development Policy Analysis (2013) Botswana Social Protection Assessment: Human Development Department Social Protection Unit, Africa Region. Washington DC: World Bank.
6   Marata K (2013) *Effective Budget Oversight in Botswana: Role of the Legislature and the Office of the Auditor General*. BIDPA: Gaborone.

- Government, on the strength of a high performing mining sector, has led an economic growth. This, however, occurred amidst inequality, and poverty levels that are arguably unbefitting of a middle income country; and
- Because of the dominance of the BDP in Botswana's democratic system, parliament's role of oversight is less robust than it could be.

B. State of corruption

That Botswana has earned a reputation for controlling corruption, this does not mean there are no challenges. The DCEC is fully aware of the challenges they face:

> Although Botswana continues to be the least corrupt country on the African continent according to Transparency International, we at the DCEC believe we should not sit on our laurels; as such we constantly look for new and improved ways of fighting corruption.[7]

The tone of realism in the DCEC is in line with frequent newspaper reports and allegations of corruption. There are concerns with suspected issues of conflict of interest and corruption. The crucial factor in these cases is that the ones involving senior government leaders lack any direct connections to electoral contest – they are made against individuals in government in their individual capacities. In 2010, then Minister of Defence, Justice and Security Ramadeluka Seretse was accused of not declaring his interests in a tender matter concerning procurement in his ministry. Similarly accused was current Minister of Trade and Industry Vincent Seretse whose charge was that he did not declare his interests in a tender matter during his tenure as chief executive officer of the state owned telecommunications corporation. Of interest to this exercise is that charging these ministers does not mean they were guilty of corruption. Of further interest is the idea that while Ramadeluka Seretse resigned his position, Vincent Seretse did not.[8] Perhaps the question that arises in terms of the wider management of corruption is the effectiveness of the links between the investigative aspects of anti-corruption and the prosecution aspect. In the corporate world, former managing director of Debswana Diamond Company, Louis Nchindo was accused of embezzling money from the company. However, he passed away before the conclusion of his trial. In all these matters, the concerned ministers duly won their cases in courts of law.

Other cases of suspected wrongdoing occur in the state-owned corporate sector. Among the recent reports of suspected corruption involves the state owned abattoir. the Botswana Meat Commission (BMC) came under scrutiny of the parliamentary commission in

---

7   Directorate on Corruption and Economic Crime (2012). Annual Report for 2011. Gaborone: DCEC. p. 4.
8   Bertelsmann Stiftung BTI (2014) *Botswana Country Report*. Gutersloh: Bertelsmann Stiftung.

2012/2013. A number of conclusions reached by the parliamentary commission include: that a number of members of the board of directors and the executive team were guilty of claiming monies for meetings held in Europe and in Botswana on similar days; and that the commission lacked efficient means of internal financial controls. The parliamentary commission described the corporate governance at BMC as 'shambolic'. Indeed, the parliamentary commission recommended that the DCEC must investigate the allowances to board members, for board meetings held for the six-year period of 2006–2012.[9]

Another major media story that became the subject of a parliamentary inquiry on corruption was that of the state owned investment company, the Botswana Development Corporation (BDC). The BDC embarked on the design and construction of what was to become Botswana's glass manufacturing plant in Palapye. However, there were soon suspicions of wrongdoing as the contractor was being paid at a rate faster than the work was being completed. The subsequent parliamentary inquiry revealed a number of challenges, including what was termed 'bad corporate governance practices', failure by management to execute due diligence and other conclusions that suggested suspicious undertakings. The project has since been abandoned officially by the BDC, which pointed out that it simply did not make economic sense to pursue.[10]

There are others, including the slow progress at Morupule B power station. The selection of the contractor to build the BDC's Morupule B power station was riddled with suspicion. In this instance it was pointed out that the contractor was picked despite manifest weaknesses and better qualified competitors. Other newspaper reports suggest that the state owned water utility, the Water Utilities Corporation (WUC) has somehow 'lost' P 327 million in the last financial year. Newspaper accounts revealed that the CEO had been dismissed, however, for non-performance.[11]

Politics and corruption

There is no public funding of political parties in Botswana. While the electoral campaign rules are not strict on party establishments, the BDP is usually funded by what are thought to be wealthy donors. These donors are unwilling to openly fund the opposition because the opposition parties are not credible, and thus not worth associating with. The BDP similarly gets funding from its own fund raising efforts.[12] A short-lived change towards private sector funding of political parties came about in 2004. Kgalagadi

---

9 Republic of Botswana Parliamentary Special Select Committee of Inquiry (2013) *The Report of the Republic of Botswana Special Committee into the Botswana Meat Commission and the Decline of the Beef Industry*. Gaborone: Government Printer.
10 Republic of Botswana (2012) *The Report of the Republic of Botswana's Parliamentary Special Committee of Inquiry into the Botswana Development Corporation's Fengyue Glass Manufacturing Botswana Palapye Glass Project*. Gaborone: Government Printer.
11 Gasennelwe U (2015, 5–11 December) WUC part ways with CEO. *Weekend Post*.
12 Gaotlhobogwe M (2011) Semenya, Mbulu to star at BDP fundraising dinner. *Mmegi online*. Available at http://www.mmegi.bw/index.php?sid=7&aid=1326&dir=2011/November/Wednesday9/ [accessed 30September 2016].

Breweries, the country's main brewery, donated P 1 million towards the parties for the campaign. However, this gesture was discontinued in the subsequent elections.

Besides politicians being accused of corruption, including conflict of interest, not too many are trying to link electoral politics to corruption in Botswana. A number of factors complicate the enforcement of electoral or campaign finance discipline in Botswana. For instance, whereas the electoral law enjoins candidates to declare their electoral expenses to the Independent Electoral Commission (IEC), this is hardly ever enforced.[13] Further complicating the electoral funding issue is that the law does not actually forbid party funding by external actors; political parties are thus allowed to approach any external donors for financing. The lack of a law requiring declaration of external funding means that the amounts will remain unknown as banks are not allowed to reveal these amounts.

To bring discipline to the electoral playing field, section 81 of the Electoral Act stipulates P 50 000 as the maximum for individual candidates to spend on their campaigns. However, the challenge with this law is that it is not effectively enforced. It is thus usually apparent, in terms of the external appearances, that candidates are likely to be spending beyond the P 50 000 limit. For example, the ruling BDP usually procures a campaign vehicle for each of the constituencies, of which there are currently 57. Similarly, even though the opposition parties often point out the unfair electoral playing field – particularly in that the BDP also benefits from the president and his deputy being shown on the state broadcaster during the campaigns, as well as being flown by official helicopters to all campaign events – the opposition has also, of late, shown itself to be capable fund raisers. In the last election, the opposition parties were able to rent two helicopters and a number of luxury bus liners. Further complicating the situation is that the law, by attempting to deter would-be wrongdoers, actually makes it worthwhile for politicians to overspend. In terms of section 87(5) of the act:

> Any candidate who makes material false statement of fact in his return knowing it to be false or not believing it to be true shall be guilty of an offence and liable to a fine not exceeding P 400 to imprisonment for a term not exceeding two years or both.

P 400 (about USD 40) is far too little to have any deterring effect. Thus overall, the following may be said of the law, and campaign finance:
- The law is too lenient on campaign finance cheats;
- The law is opaque, allowing external donations to go undetected, thus little is known about the amounts from external funders; and
- Enforcement of the law, particularly the P 50 000 limit, is too lax to deter would-be over-spenders, particularly given the stakes-control of the state and its machinery.

---

13 Molomo M & Sebudubudu D (2005) Funding of political parties: Levelling the political playing field. In: Z. Maundeni (ed.) *40 Years of Democracy in Botswana (1965–2005)*. Gaborone: Mmegi Publishing House. p. 150.

State of corruption

That Botswana is Africa's highest performer in anti-corruption indices must not be misconstrued to mean the country lacks challenges in managing corruption. From time to time, the national media reports on stories that show growing concerns regarding corruption within the country. This should not surprise, as corruption often tends to accompany economic growth.[14] However, the frequency of these reports is growing. Table 1 below shows the trends in the corruption perception indicators for Botswana over a five-year period.[15]

Table 1: Corruption perceptions indicators for Botswana (2009–2014)

Year	Score	Rank
2009	5.6	37
2010	5.8	33
2011	6.1	31
2012	6.5	30
2013	64	30
2014	63	31

Source: www.transparency.org.

From the table it can be seen that notwithstanding Botswana's ranking as Africa's least corrupt economy, the country's scores have fluctuated somewhat. For example, the 5.6 score in 2009 is Botswana's lowest in the last decade, as indeed the global ranking of 37 is the lowest. The scores of the latter two years, 2013 (rank number 30), and 2014 (rank number 31), show that Botswana's global rankings in anti-corruption, while improving from the lows of 2008/9, could be said to be improving. However, the consistent positioning of Botswana in the 30s means that its performance has stagnated, at least in terms of the CPI, particularly in comparison to the number 23 ranking the country obtained in 1997. Can Botswana therefore comfortably stay at a mid-thirties ranking? Decisions need to be made for higher targets, with strategies for ensuring the attainment of these targets.

Botswana's CPI ranking makes for uncomfortable reading in terms of the Africa-wide ranking. Whereas Botswana is consistently Africa's highest performer, globally the country fluctuates, including up to the 37th ranking realised in 2009, which is Botswana's historic lowest, and it remains Africa's top performer. Does this mean African nations' anti-corruption measures are so poor? By remaining in the 30s, does Botswana need to reconsider comparisons with the rest of its African counterparts, or need to revamp its strategies to improve on this?

---

14 Knuckles JA (2006) A study of corruption's causes in Botswana and Nigeria. Available at https://unpublishedworks.files.wordpress.com/2013/03/a-study-of-corruptions-causes-in-botswana-and-nigeria.pdf [accessed 5 September 2016].
15 TI CPI reports for 2009–2014.

C. History of anti-corruption measures

Botswana's primary anti-corruption agency (ACA), the Directorate on Corruption and Economic Crime (DCE) was set up in 1995 following the passing of the Corruption and Economic Crimes Act (CECA) in 1994. The CECA came about as a result of recognition by the Government of Botswana of the negative effects of corruption, and importantly, the urgency of fighting it.

The DCEC was government's response to a number of events that strongly pointed out a declining ethical governance in Botswana. Amongst these, following a parliamentary commission of inquiry, evidence was found of heavy borrowing from the National Development Bank (NDB), a finance development institution wholly owned by the government of Botswana by leading politicians. The over-borrowing brought the NDB to near collapse, yet rather than paying their loans, the politicians sought to write off their debts.

Soon after the NDB matter, another presidential commission of inquiry showed that affairs at the state-owned housing enterprises, the Botswana Housing Corporation (BHC) were not entirely satisfactory. The BHC carries the mandate of provision of housing for the country. Upon being charged with a wider mandate to provide more housing, the BHC soon became embroiled in allegations of irregular house allocations, irregular contracting and irregular land servicing. The subsequent death of the then CEO during the investigations of the BHC imbroglio increased suspicion that there was improper conduct involving important people. Prior to these occurrences, Botswana had been a quiet country, where democratic practice had been observed and trust in state institutions relatively assured. However, these occurrences changed that, and the DCEC was brought about.

Parliamentary records show that then minister of presidential affairs and public administration General Mompati Merafhe stated the following, in justifying the need for the DCEC:

> Government wishes it to become known both within and outside Botswana that ours is a country in which public and private business can be carried out honestly and fairly, and whose citizens do not tolerate the abuses of the law by those with the power and financial resources to usurp them. It is recognised that the current laws and the resources devoted to the fight against corruption and economic crime are inadequate to achieve that aim.

The minister's concerns were well founded; the episodes of corruption mentioned earlier were highly unusual in Botswana.

Legal instruments

Botswana has come a long way since the onset of the first major corruption scandals that prompted efforts to revamp anti-corruption legislation in the early 1990s. Beginning with the CECA, the government of Botswana has come up with a raft of other laws with the aim of controlling ethical behaviour in the public and private sectors. The CECA was first enacted in 1994, but later amended in 2013. A number of other laws have since been enacted to fight specific forms of unethical conduct, including money laundering. This section reviews the legal infrastructure of anti-corruption in Botswana.

Corruption and Economic Crimes (Amendment) Act, 2013
The CECA is the main anti-corruption legislation in Botswana. One of the purposes of the act is to provide for the establishment of a Directorate on Corruption and Economic Crime (DCEC) and to make comprehensive provision for the prevention of corruption. At section 3, the act both establishes the DCEC and confers upon it the authority to investigate suspected cases of corruption and economic crime.

The offences created by the act include the direct or indirect receipt of gifts by a public officer, to influence his or her behaviour in decision-making by bestowing benefits to either the public officer or a third party. Section 24(2) makes it an offence against the law for any persons to either directly or indirectly influence the behaviour of a public officer through inducement of either a gift or the promise of one, to obtain a desired outcome. Since the amendment of the act in 2013, the law has been extended to include 'abuse of offence' as an offence against the CECA.

The law extends to other aspects of public office. Section 25(1) makes it an offence for a public officer to accept bribes. Section 25(2) extends the burden of bribery to include those offering inducements to a public officer; the amendment to the CECA also extends the burden to 'any other person' who may directly or indirectly accept a bribe or valuable consideration. In particular, bribes constitute the crime of corruption at three levels: (i) if a public officer accepts valuable consideration after the performance of his public duty in relation to a specific act, then the public officer is deemed to have committed the offence of corruption; (ii) a promise to bribe the public officer after the doing of the act also constitutes corruption; and (iii) when a public officer accepts or agrees to accept for himself, or for any other person, any valuable consideration as an inducement or reward for, or otherwise on account of, his giving assistance or using influence in promoting, administering, executing or procuring any contract with a public body.

While the CECA is wide in its application, it does not exactly define corruption. Rather it describes the situation under which 'corruption' may be deemed to have occurred. Such a circumstance covers the action of a public officer who may act individually or with others to carry out the prescribed acts. Corruption is principally an offence that involves the participation of a public official; alone and or in concert with a private party to unfairly benefit a third party.

Section 23 of the CECA gives another key concept in the act that helps define corruption: the concept of valuable consideration. It ranges from a number of actions, which initially included liquidation of debt, loan and forbearing from exercise of any right or power. Under the amended CECA, valuable consideration has been expanded to encompass matters extending to abuse of office and influence peddling.

Section 45 of the CECA makes an attempt to rectify one of the major flaws in Botswana's anti-corruption fight (and by extension the capacity of the DCEC to be effective). The said section 45(1) states that:

> In any trial, in respect of an offence under part IV, a witness shall not be obliged to disclose the name or address of any informer, or state any matter which might lead to his discovery.

Public Procurement and Asset Disposal (PPAD) Act

The Public Procurement and Asset Disposal Act is the major legislation guiding the procurement of goods and services by government and its agencies. The law recognises the centrality of public finance into Botswana's economy. It promotes transparency and competition by regulating both the procurement and disposal of services and supplies for central government.

The act establishes the Public Procurement and Asset Disposal Board (PPADB) as well as its committees. Among the overall objectives of the PPAD Act is the attainment of a competitive economy; transparency, fairness and equity; as well as the maintenance of a level playing field in public procurement.

The act is, strictly speaking, not an anti-corruption law. A number of challenges are noted in the law, including that the law largely lacks a pre-emptive effect. For instance, by resorting to delisting offending contractors, the law leaves the door open for corrupt activities to occur. Added to that, the law does not make provisions for disciplining individual professionals such as artisans and other crafts, again being reactive, and thus susceptible to abuse. By not stipulating how the PPADB may engage with the DCEC the PPAD Act contributes to a fragmentary legal environment for anti-corruption.

Financial Intelligence Act

Amongst others, the Financial Intelligence Act sets up the Financial Intelligence Agency (FIA) at section 3 of the act. This is an important step in anti-corruption since the DCEC used to carry out this mandate (of enforcing anti-money laundering activities), stretching its resources. The act also provides for the establishment of the National Coordinating Committee on Financial Intelligence; sets up mechanisms for reporting of suspicious transactions and other cash transactions; and provides for mutual assistance with comparable bodies outside Botswana in relation to financial information

As set up by part II of the act, the agency's responsibilities are the requesting, receiving, analysing and disseminating to an investigatory authority, supervisory authority or comparable body, disclosures of financial information (with particular reference to suspicious transactions), or matters required by or under any enactment in order to counter financial offences, and matters concerning the financing of any activities or transactions related thereto.

Proceeds of Serious Crimes Act

The Proceeds of Serious Crimes Act, like the PPAD Act, the Mutual Assistance Act and a number of other legal instruments in this section is, strictly speaking, not an anti-corruption law. However, the act can be brought to bear in specific circumstances where corruption is concerned as corruption can be deemed as a serious crime. Specifically, section 3 of the act states that:

> Where a person has been convicted of a serious offence, the director of public prosecution may apply to the court before which the conviction was obtained, or to the high court, for a confiscation order in respect of that serious offence, or, if convictions were obtained for more than one serious offence, in respect of all or any of those offences.

Its importance to enforcement is that section 3(2) of the act makes it imperative that only by gaining conviction can a confiscation order be obtained. Thus, when a conviction is not obtained for any reason, the proceeds of any crime may continue to be enjoyed.

The major challenge with this act is that, by strictly relying on first gaining a conviction before the director of public prosecution (DPP) can apply for confiscating proceeds of crime, its stance weakens enforcement officials as offenders may, in the meantime, interfere with such proceeds of crime. It has been suggested, however, that even the constitution at section 8 (where it guarantees the right to privacy), may be offended by a stricter law on forfeiture of assets.[16]

Penal Code

The Penal Code is another piece of legislation that addresses aspects of managing corruption in Botswana. Matters of corruption under this law are mostly enforced by the Botswana Police Services, bringing this particular law enforcement organ into contact with the DCEC. In recognition of the constitutional status of the DPP as the primary prosecuting authority in Botswana, the police, like the DCEC must obtain permission from the DPP in order to proceed with prosecution. In terms of the Penal Code, those found guilty of corruption are liable to a prison term of three years or less. The offence of abuse of office, which is also found in the CECA, makes one liable to a jail term of three years or less. Most corrupt acts under the Penal Code fall under the rubric 'abuse of office' and they include the following transgressions:

- Section 99 – Official corruption;
- Section 100 – Extortion by public officers;
- Section 101 – Public officers receiving property to show favour;

---

16 De Speville B (2007) *Review of Botswana's National Anti-corruption Strategy and its Implementation*. Gaborone: Delegation of the European Commission to Botswana.

- Section 102 – Officers charged with administration of property of a special character or with special duties;
- Section 103 – False claims by officials;
- Section 104 – Abuse of office;
- Section 384 – Corrupt practices by and of agents; and
- Section 385 – Secret commission on government contracts.

The Penal Code also includes the following offences under the rubric of corruption:
- Section 276 – Stealing by persons employed in the public service;
- Section 277 – Stealing by clerks and servants;
- Section 278 – Stealing by directors or officers of companies; and
- Section 279 – Perjury and subordination of perjury.

The Penal Code has a number of challenges. Amongst these is the inconsistency between it and the CECA. For example, whereas the Penal Code defines a public officer as 'any person in the service of, or holding office under the state whether such service is permanent or temporary, or paid or unpaid', the CECA goes further, and defines it as any person working for an entity where, while government may not hold majority ownership, public finance is used to pay for the activities of such a corporate entity.

Other notable clashes between the two are in the application of penalties. In the Penal Code, conviction for any of the offences may earn the convict a maximum of three years, while under the CECA conviction may earn such a convict a maximum of ten years, and the possibility of over half a million pula in fines, or both. The inconsistencies between the two may lead to confusion in ensuring similar standards in application. Indeed, there are suspicions that since it is easier to convict under the Penal Code, the police prefer to use it than the more rigorous CECA. However, the CECA has stricter, harsher sentences.

Extradition Act No. 18 of 1990

Though strictly speaking the Extradition Act is not an anti-corruption law, it has an effect on management of corrupt activity. Section 3(1) of the act makes the following provision:

> Where an arrangement has been made with any country, with respect to the surrender to that country of any fugitive criminal, the minister may, having regard to reciprocal provisions under the law of that country, by order published in the Gazette, direct that this act shall apply in the case of that country subject to such conditions, exceptions and qualifications as may be specified in the order.

The said section facilitates the extradition of any criminal suspect to any country, which has a prior arrangement with Botswana in such matters. Thus the act assists in making it difficult for criminals who commit corrupt or other acts of illegality in Botswana to hide away from the application of the law in their home countries.

Mutual Assistance in Criminal Matters Act, 1990

The Mutual Assistance in Criminal Matters Act facilitates the provision of assistance to Botswana by foreign countries in the event that Botswana requires such. As in the Extradition Act, the Mutual Assistance Act anticipates a bilateral arrangement being in place between Botswana and a country from which assistance is sought. The act covers a number of issues including: the obtaining of evidence, documents or other articles; provision of documents and other records; location and identification of witnesses or suspects; the execution of requests for search and seizure; making of arrangements for persons to give evidence; confiscation of property in respect of offences; recovery of pecuniary penalties in respect of offences; restraining of dealings in property, or the freezing of assets that may be confiscated, or that may be needed to satisfy pecuniary penalties imposed, in respect of offences; location of property that may be confiscated, or that may be needed to satisfy pecuniary penalties imposed; and others. In the words of a former deputy director at the DPP, there are two challenges to the application of either of the two treaties:

- The absence of an extradition treaty with a requested state often makes it difficult to get the required assistance. Even where these instruments are in place, various legal requirements and restrictions, jurisdictional problems and differences in criminal law and procedure often pose serious barriers to co-operation and mutual legal assistance; and
- Resorting to informal requests which are less cumbersome and capable of yielding quick results may not always pass constitutional muster.[17]

Role of competition law and policy

In 2010, through the Competition Act of 2010, Botswana set up its competition authority. Botswana's anti-corruption laws also speak to the possibilities of addressing corruption in the private sector. The FIA assists in ensuring that money laundering matters are addressed. Added to this are the Competition Act and the competition policy. Speaking at an occasion to mark the beginning of an UNCAC review in Botswana, then director of public prosecutions, Leonard Sechele made this point:

> Our laws should therefore be stretched to cover the private sector as it has been evident that corrupt officials/individuals in government launder public assets to their privately owned companies.[18]

---

17 Khan R (n.d.) Effective Legal and Practical Measures for Combating Corruption. Training course on the criminal justice response to corruption: Participants' papers. p. 165.
18 Africa loses billions to corruption (2014, 26 February) *Botswana Daily News*. Available at http://www.dailynews.gov.bw/mobile/news-details.php?nid=9222&flag [accessed 30 September 2016].

Among others, the capacity for private sector corruption is addressed in the Competition Act. The competition authority is made to address some of the malpractices in the private sector that could pass as corruption. These include regulating mergers; advising government on anti-competitive practices; undertaking market inquiries on the effectiveness of competition; and evaluating contraventions on the act, including looking at such malpractices as bid rigging, resale price maintenance, and market allocation.[19]

While not an anti-corruption law, the act helps avert private sector related malpractices. Indeed, if the private sector, for instance, engages in bid rigging or dividing the market between them, this may be to the detriment of public procurement practices. Ultimately the effects of these malpractices are passed on to consumers.

D. Directorate on Corruption and Economic Crime (DCEC)

The DCEC is Botswana's focal point in matters of anti-corruption. It was founded in 1994, with the promulgation of the CECA.

Historical development of the institutional framework

Both the CECA as the primary anti-corruption law in Botswana, and the DCEC which it gave rise to, came about as a result of recognition by the government of Botswana of the negative effects of corruption, and importantly, the urgency of fighting it. Modelled on the Independent Commission Against Corruption (ICAC) of Hong Kong, the DCEC also adopted the three-pronged strategy used by the ICAC, and internationally accepted as best practice: corruption prevention, investigation and public education.

Stability of the agency

Since its formation in 1995, the DCEC has led the national fight against corruption in Botswana. It was initially under the ministry of defence, justice and security but moved to the ministry of presidential affairs and public administration. The agency has been stable, with its three leaders serving longer than five years each before allegedly being asked to retire against their wishes. Amongst these are the founding director, Graham Stockwell, who was also a former deputy director at Hong Kong's famed ICAC. Upon setting up the DCEC, Stockwell was deputised by Tymon Katlholo who came from the Botswana Police Services. Katlholo became director and retired in 2008. Rose Seretse, the current director general of DCEC took over from Katlholo in 2008.

The DCEC has support from the executive and parliament as evidenced through budgetary support. Though the director general of the DCEC reports to the state president, to date, no evidence has been brought to show that the president interferes with the mandate of the agency.

---

19 Competition Authority (n.d.) *Fair Competition and Prosperity.* Gaborone.

Responsibilities, and investigative and prosecutorial powers

The functions of the DCEC, as listed under section 6 of the CECA, are to:
- Receive and investigate any complaints alleging corruption in any public body;
- Investigate any alleged or suspected offences under this act, or any other offence discovered during such an investigation;
- Investigate any alleged or suspected contravention of any of the provisions of the fiscal and revenue laws of the country;
- Investigate any conduct of any person, which in the opinion of the director, may be connected with or conducive to corruption;
- Assist any law enforcement agency of the government in the investigation of offences involving dishonesty or cheating of the public revenue;
- Examine the practices and procedures of public bodies in order to facilitate the discovery of corrupt practices and to secure the revision of methods of work or procedures this, in the opinion of the director, may be conducive to corrupt practices;
- Instruct, advise and assist any person, on the latter's request, on ways in which corrupt practices may be eliminated by such person;
- Advise heads of public bodies of changes in practices or procedures compatible with the effective discharge of the duties of such public bodies that the director thinks necessary to reduce the likelihood of the occurrence of corrupt practices; and
- Educate the public against the evils of corruption; and enlist and foster public support in combating corruption.

With the exception of sections (d), (i), and (j), the sections of the CECA are actually reactive. They are either investigative (occurring after harm has occurred), or otherwise reactive to a request by some other actor who may wish to enlist DCEC guidance or support. Sections (d), (i), and (j), on the other hand, allow the DCEC the latitude to act entirely on its own volition, through mainly means of persuasion. Though onerous, the three sections hold great potential for preventing corruption.[20]

The DCEC is internally organised in a manner that both responds to the CECA, and to the need to support the sections that support the CECA. The investigation division; legal services; public education and corruption prevention divisions are all directly linked to the DCEC's three-pronged strategy of communication, education and investigation, while the corporate services division provides support services.

---

20 Khan R (n.d.) Effective Legal and Practical Measures for Combating Corruption. Training course on the criminal justice response to corruption: Participants' papers. p. 160.

Investigation division
The investigation division investigates all cases of corruption as reported to the DCEC. In response to signals of corruption prone areas, the division is divided into sector-specific areas, such as construction, land allocation, transport, immigration, and education. The division also has working relations with other law enforcement agencies of Botswana.

Legal services division
The primary role of the legal services division is the provision of legal advice to the DCEC. Since 2013 when the DCEC adopted the strategy of having legal expertise along all stages of the investigative process, this division has assisted with investigations along the various stages of pre-and post-investigation and with conferences with investigators. The division has working relationships with the DPP.

Public education division
The role of the public education division is to sensitise stakeholders of the downside of corruption and to enlist the cooperation of these stakeholders to fight corruption. It includes anti-corruption workshops, talk shows, fairs, and the development of brochures and exhibitions.

Corruption prevention division
The corruption prevention division works through the review of records of public bodies as well as advocating for positive changes for effective service delivery. In line with the DCEC's emphasis on prevention as the best approach to managing corruption, the division has developed internal structures to respond to its mandate. These divisions are the public sector integrity, partnerships research and policy; and quality assurance units.

Corporate services division
The corporate services division works as service provider to the other divisions within the DCEC. It provides information and technology support, as well as a library, financial management, records management and provides leadership in the reforms process required to make the DCEC respond to its environment better.

Autonomy

The DCEC, like any statutory organisation, exists in a political, legal and economic environment which provides both constraints and opportunities for action. The president of Botswana appoints the director general (DG) of the DCEC, as empowered by section 4(1) of the CECA. In order to safeguard the independence of the DCEC, the CECA gives the DG the role of running the affairs of the directorate. This provision is further enforced by the statement that the DG takes no direction from any authority in the running of the DCEC.

However, the DCEC does occasionally face suspicions of lack of independence. Over and above these issues, citizens and the media tend to find it unbelievable that the DCEC can be independent when the DG is appointed by the president of the republic.[21] Despite the new amendment of the CECA clarifying that the DCEC shall be subject to no other authority in carrying out its mandate, these suspicions persist. However, in the DCEC's defence, it can be pointed out that, not only do they pursue matters in court, involving important people, their conviction rate is actually high as shown earlier. In addition, the DCEC has pursued, in court, a number of high profile personalities, including ministers. Losses of these cases cannot be blamed entirely on the DCEC, which carries out investigations before handing over prosecution roles to the DPP.

Prosecution

Section 39 of the Corruption and Economic Crimes Act clarifies the question of who may prosecute matters. It essentially bestows the duty to prosecute upon the DPP (which is part of the attorney general's chambers), and thereby, separates investigative powers from prosecutorial powers. As per section 39:

(1) If, after an investigation of any person under this act, it appears to the director that an offence under part IV has been committed by that person, the director shall refer the matter to the attorney general for his decision.

(2) No prosecution for an offence under part IV shall be instituted except by or with written consent of the attorney general.

The problem with this arrangement is that challenges with the DPP, particularly in terms of manpower, are transferred to the DCEC. In other words, the capacity of the DCEC to prosecute its matters is a direct function of the DPP's capacity to do so. With the DPP facing the challenge of retaining its experienced prosecutors, the capacity of the DCEC to prosecute matters expeditiously is challenged.[22]

Other agencies

Apart from the DCEC, a number of other organisations contribute to the fight against corruption in Botswana, these are described below.

Directorate of Public Prosecutions

Section 51A of the Constitution of Botswana establishes the Directorate of Public Prosecutions as the primary body responsible for instituting criminal proceedings against any party (with

---

21 De Speville B (2007) *Review of Botswana's National Anti-corruption Strategy and its Implementation.* Gaborone: Delegation of the European Commission to Botswana.

22 Khan R (n.d.) Effective Legal and Practical Measures for Combating Corruption. Training course on the criminal justice response to corruption: Participants' papers. p.160; Directorate on Corruption and Economic Crime (DCEC) (2014) *Annual Report.* Gaborone: DCEC.

the exception of the court martial). This means that, amongst others, cases investigated by the DCEC are in turn referred to the DPP for prosecution. Whereas the DPP may delegate its functions to such bodies as the DCEC and the police, it is the primary prosecution authority in Botswana, and is subject to no other authority in the execution of its duties.

Botswana police

The Botswana Police Services has the mandate of prevention of crime and the protection life and properly nationwide, as well as the maintenance of Botswana's internal peace and stability. When it comes to corruption matters, the police rely on the Penal Code. This often causes challenges in that the Penal Code prescribes more lenient sentences.

Judiciary and the corruption court

Botswana's judiciary forms part of the anti-corruption landscape. The system consists of the magistrate's court, high court and high court of appeal. In 2013 a branch of the high court was formed to provide specialist handling of anti-corruption matters. The aptly named corruption court is essentially a part of the high court, but with specialist focus on corruption matters.

Financial Intelligence Agency

Section 3 of the Financial Intelligence Act sets up the Financial Intelligence Agency (FIA), as the primary agency carrying the mandate of enforcing matters related to financial intelligence in Botswana. Amongst others the Financial Intelligence Act empowers the FIA to receive, and analyse information on suspicious transactions and to send whatever information it discovers to relevant authorities. Amongst a list of organisations who may report suspicious transactions to the FIA are gambling interests, law firms, banks, accountants, accounting firms and audit firms.

Resources

The DCEC is funded from the Consolidated Funds of Botswana. The consolidated funds amalgamate funds from taxes, mineral revenue and other sources of public finance.

Funding for the DCEC is through allocations by the national assembly. Annually the budget as allocated is divided into recurrent budget and development budget. The development budget is expenditure on new, budgetary undertakings, including procurement of buildings and other capital items; whereas the recurrent budget covers ongoing items such the salaries of employees, rentals, training and others. Figure 1 below shows that the development expenditure has been steadily rising for the last three years. The only time this failed to be the case was after the onset of the global recession, where government made a policy decision to not increase expenditures to its organisations. Government funding to the DCEC is such that, periodically when there are exigencies, the state does pick up the shortfalls; as in the financial year 2010/11, when a 3% allowance was made.

Figure 1: Budget allocations to the DCEC (2010–2014)

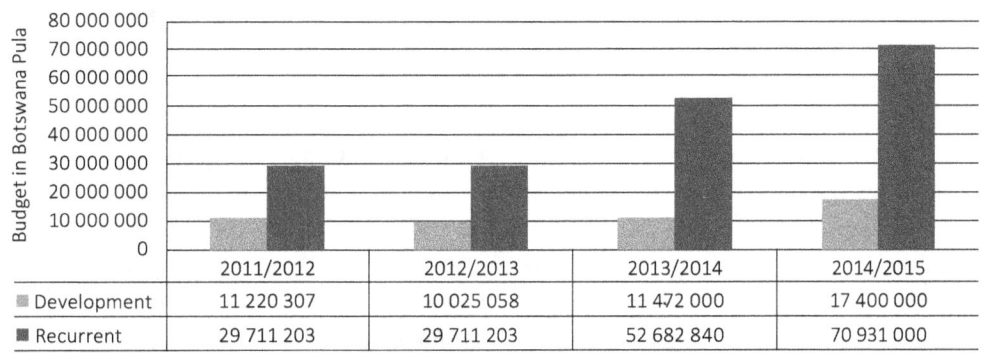

Source: DCEC Annual Reports

In terms of Figure 1 above, the development budgets show the amounts dedicated to creating new programmes. Essentially the recurrent budget, which shows the amounts allocated to upkeep of DCEC programmes, includes money spent on maintenance, salaries, and related effects. In any given year, the recurrent budgets outstrip the development budgets.

A review of the DCEC strategy made the finding that, though the DCEC faced financial constraints in some of their programmes, the seemingly low amounts of finance outlays are not due to refusal by government. As stated in the review of Botswana's national anti-corruption strategy and its implementation:

> The point should be made that the low level of resources invested up to now has not been caused by any refusal to accede to DCEC requests. Rather it has been the result of the DCEC not fully appreciating the need to extend its operations and its presence over the whole country.[23]

Agency staff and staff-related challenges

As with any organisation, the DCEC's mandate is carried out by its employees with varying competencies. In terms of the law, the accounting officer of the DCEC is the director general who is appointed by the president of Botswana in terms of section 4(1) of the CECA.

It is important to note that while the CECA stipulates that the president appoints the DG, it protects the independence of the DCEC in specifying at section 4(3), that 'any decision, including investigations by the director general shall not be subject to the direction and control of any person or authority'. Prior to the 2013 amendment of the CECA, the law stated only that the DG, who then was simply referred to as director, was 'responsible for the direction and administration of the directorate'. The rest of the DCEC staff, who are essentially public servants, are recruited on terms determined by the minister. Staff is allocated along the DCEC organisational structure, which includes a number of divisions,

---

23 De Speville B (2007) *Review of Botswana's National Anti-corruption Strategy and its Implementation*. Gaborone: Delegation of the European Commission to Botswana. p. 47.

including legal services, corporate services, investigation services, public education and corruption prevention services. An implication of this arrangement is that the DG does not have full control of staffing matters.

In terms of staffing, government continues to support the DCEC by providing resources for recruiting more staff. From the staff complement of 65 that began with the DCEC in 1995, the total employed members of staff stood at 297 in 2013/14. What is notable is that the DCEC increases its staff complement almost annually. In the last three years, the establishment has increased from 284 in 2012, to 291 in 2013, to 297 in 2014. Instructively, however, the corresponding years also had the DCEC experiencing vacancy rates beyond its target of 2% per annum. These are 4%, 3.5%, and 3.37%.[24]

Besides an annual training budget, the DCEC human resources programme has a number of other initiatives such as health and wellness, a rewards ceremony to recognise performance and an in-house library which covers subjects beyond just those of professional interest.

In order to operate optimally, the directorate has come up with the target of maintaining an annual vacancy rate at 2%.[25] However, the DCEC operates in a specialised environment where competition for human resources is fierce. Between the police, commercial banks, and the intelligence organisations, competition for human resources is intense. Skills such as investigations, legal services and prosecutions are in high demand between the DCEC, the FIA and other law enforcement agencies. As a result, the DCEC has consistently struggled to meet this target. As per the DCEC:

> The directorate experienced difficulties in maintaining the 2% vacancy rate mainly because it is not easy to find experienced investigators in the market... The other challenge is that all employees are vetted before they could be offered employment, thus increasing the turnaround time for recruitment process. The attrition rate stands at 2.5%.[26]

Performance and challenges
Reports made to the DCEC

Figure 3 below show the number of reports received by the directorate. In essence, the figure shows the number of cases to be in decline year on year. This could mean that the DCEC has been effective in carrying out its mandate. The various measures such as the public education, anti-corruption clubs and other interventions are bearing fruit, resulting in fewer cases reported.

However, it is also possible that the cases reported at newer courts such as the FIA are receiving the reports that would otherwise would have gone to the DCEC. Indeed, places such as the ombudsman could be receiving reports that could be forwarded to the DCEC.

---

24 Directorate on Corruption and Economic Crime (DCEC) (2012/13/14) *Annual Report*. Gaborone: DCEC.
25 Directorate on Corruption and Economic Crime (DCEC) (2011) *Annual Report*. Gaborone: DCEC.
26 Directorate on Corruption and Economic Crime (DCEC) (2010) *Annual Report*. Gaborone: DCEC. p.24.

BOTSWANA

Figure 2: Reports received by the DCEC (2009–2013)

2009	2010	2011	2012	2013
1926	1851	1800	1646	1471

Source: DCEC Annual Reports.

Number of cases in court

Other performance measures are the number of cases that the DCEC brings to court, and the number that it actually wins by gaining convictions. By these measures, the DCEC performance appears mixed. However, in 2013, with the establishment of the corruption court, the DCEC had to assist the court to understand some of the cases, hence a low completion rate. Nevertheless, the acquittals have been rising in proportion to the completed matters, strongly suggesting that the conviction rates were declining as a result.

Figure 3: Number of cases handled by the DCEC (2009–2013)

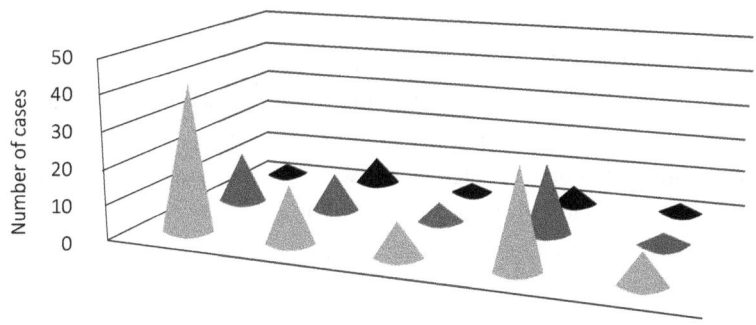

	2009	2010	2011	2012	2013
Completed	41	16	9	28	9
Convictions	16	11	6	20	4
Aquitals	3	8	3	5	3

Source: DCEC Annual Reports 2009–2013.

A number of challenges detract from the performance of the DCEC. These include the incapacity of the law to protect informers or would be informers of the DCEC; lack of laws to facilitate the revelation of information necessary to combat corruption; intractable media relations due to the CECA; and delays in the prosecution of anti-corruption cases. These issues are discussed in the following sections.

Complexity of corruption

One of the emerging issues confronting the DCEC is the complexity of corruption. The multiplicity of challenges leading to corruption, which in turn means a multiplicity of laws, have to be applied by different actors in order to enforce the law. As stated in the DCEC 2013 annual report for instance:

> Corruption cases are increasingly becoming complex and the magnitude of these cases requires that stakeholders consistently review their business processes and have monitoring measures in place to guard against any probable corrupt practices.[27]

While the details of this matter were not expounded at length, one of the related issues is the incapacity of the DCEC to use the full extent of the legal mechanisms at their disposal. As an example, the ability to impound the proceeds of corrupt practices is one way of curbing corruption. Yet, as the following lengthy citation from Khan demonstrates, the application of the law is seldom straightforward a matter. In attempting to confiscate goods the DCEC faces an issue:

> The Act empowers the director of public prosecutions to apply for constraining order whenever a person investigated for an act of corruption has been charged or is about to be charged for an offence. However, such an application has to be made under section 8 of the Proceeds of Serious Crimes Act. In this connection, identification of property representing the proceeds of crimes still remains a daunting task for investigators and prosecutors alike. Failure to establish a connection or link between the alleged unlawful activity and the property concerned results in criminals getting away with the proceeds of a crime that they eventually use to commit more crimes.[28]

Delays due to the corruption court

As shown in the foregoing figures, there is a low completion rate of cases, which, at the very least, suggests inefficiency. Cases take long to be disposed. The DCEC attributes this to the slow justice process; for instance, the DCEC notes in 2009 that some of the challenges that delay them from completing disposing of cases are external:

> Completion at court is very slow and it impacts on the disposal rate. For instance, the *State vs. Nchindo* case which was registered three years ago has not yet

---

27 Directorate on Corruption and Economic Crime (DCEC) (2013) *Annual Report*. Gaborone: DCEC. p. 10.
28 Khan R (n.d.) Effective Legal and Practical Measures for Combating Corruption. Training course on the criminal justice response to corruption: Participants' papers.

commenced. The wheels of justice turn slowly and therefore delay finality of cases.[29]

The establishment of the corruption court has however led to delays in the legal process. In terms of Botswana's jurisprudence, one can only have their case committed to the high court, after lower level courts have dealt with it. According to the DCEC, the cases have to first go to the magistrate's court, and for any defendant:

> After having charges read to him and a summary of evidence submitted to court, then the magistrate's court will, on application by the prosecutor transmit the record to the high court for trial, in what is known as committal proceedings.[30]

Such procedure thus leads to delays in the prosecution processes, reducing the effectiveness of the DCEC's mandate.

Inadequacy of laws to reveal corruption
Another matter affecting the performance of the DCEC is the lack of laws to reveal wrongdoing. Corruption is complex. It occurs between the parties who have an incentive to want it to remain hidden, which is why as many laws as possible are required to reveal corruption. In this regard, the DCEC has consistently decried the lack of laws to reveal corruption where it might exist. As an example, in its 2012 annual report, the DCEC clarifies the challenge with the lack of introduction of these pieces of legislation as thus:

> Inadequate legislative protection of whistleblowers and witnesses remains a challenge as it has direct effect on the number and quality of reports submitted to the directorate due to fear of victimisation. It is hoped that once the whistle blowing legislation is in place, quality of reports will be enhanced and more people will come forward to report corruption.[31]

Added to the lack of whistleblower and witness protection laws are other statutes that would ordinarily assist in revealing information. These include a law on the declaration of assets and liabilities of public leaders as well as a law on freedom of information. According to the government-owned newspaper, the *Daily News*, in 2009, then leader of the Botswana Congress Party, Dumelang Saleshando proposed both bills in parliament. While neither motion was successful, then minister of presidential affairs and public administration promised that the law on whistle blowing would be brought to parliament. However, in 2015, such a law still does not exist.

---

29 Directorate on Corruption and Economic Crime (DCEC) (2009) *Annual Report*. Gaborone: DCEC. p. 7.
30 Directorate on Corruption and Economic Crime (DCEC) (2013) *Annual Report*. Gaborone: DCEC. p.13.
31 Directorate on Corruption and Economic Crime (DCEC) (2013) *Annual Report*. Gaborone: DCEC. p. 17.

Whose role it is to fight corruption?
One of the challenges to the DCEC's mandate is a misguided view that regards anti-corruption issues as primarily a DCEC problem. The requisite support and commitment of all stakeholders is perhaps suboptimal at best, or non-existent at worst.

Another view, from academia, is that perhaps even media reporting is not necessarily intended to inform the nation or obtain their cooperation in fighting the corruption scourge. This is perhaps a by-product of a bigger agenda: to report on something juicy, something that will make the readers take note. No matter the motive, however, commitment seems to be lacking, particularly outside of the law enforcement fraternity.

Resources from donor sources
The DCEC's sources of finance are broader than just the government. Other sources include financial and technical assistance from development partners. A typical example occurs in the 2011/12 fiscal year when the directorate's training budget was constrained due to government's budgetary position which was unfavourable.

In response, a number of cooperating partners came to the DCEC's rescue. Whereas the DCEC training budget was only P 140 000, contribution by cooperating partners enabled the directorate to attain its objectives. As per the DCEC:

> The funds were augmented by funds sourced from donors, namely the United Nations Development Programme (UNDP) and the US government. The UNDP funded the DCEC training with USD 140 000, while the US government donated USD 25 000 and availed experts in investigations who conducted training to DCEC officers at the expense of the US government. The Australian government also paid for training of DCEC officers in South Africa.[32]

Relations with the public and other stakeholders

The DCEC has a number of mechanisms for reaching out to external stakeholders. The lead structure in this regard is the public education programme of the DCEC. Through this programme, the DCEC carries out a number of activities including radio shows, house-to-house campaigns, management workshops, youth sensitisation workshops and others.

The media
The DCEC has periodic interactions with the media in which it shares information on progress on various undertakings and investigations. These announcements often appear in the state owned *Daily News* newspaper. The summaries of these cases are then compiled in the annual report for public consumption.

---

32 Directorate on Corruption and Economic Crime (DCEC) (2012) *Annual Report.* Gaborone: DCEC. p. 35.

An important aspect of the CECA is at section 44, where the law attempts to protect the sanctity of investigative processes. The said section makes it an offence to:

> ...without authority or reasonable excuse disclose(s) to any person who is the subject of an investigation in respect of an offence alleged or suspected to have been committed by him under this act the fact that he is subject to such an investigation or publishes or discloses to any other person either the identity of the person who is subject to an investigation...

This section is particularly important given that the media in any democracy would be inclined to publish stories on corruption; this would tend to create tension between the media and the DCEC.

A recent illustration of this matter: DCEC raided the offices of *The Gazette* newspaper, a private weekly. According to *Mmegi* newspaper, the DCEC raided *The Gazette* because they had published a story that the DCEC was investigating. Yet, upon being asked if they were investigating the story, the DCEC are said to have offered only a 'neither confirm nor deny' response. Upon finding the story however, the DCEC are alleged to have pointed out that such reporting could alert the culprits they were after.[33]

What is problematic in this instance is that the DCEC's reluctance to take the media into its confidence is viewed with suspicion by the media. Similarly, the media's desire to report stories could, realistically, compromise investigations. It is a case of two competing public interests that need to be balanced.

While the DCEC has both proactive and reactive relations with the media, via its public relations unit, there are tensions between the two parties. On one side, there are fears by the DCEC that the media, by reporting on matters under investigation, may unwittingly alert a subject under investigation, thereby disturbing the sanctity of the investigation. On the other hand, the media questions the DCEC's reluctance to confirm, when asked, whether or not they are investigating matters that the media may wish to report on. The media argues that most of the matters they report on, and which bring them into conflict with the DCEC, are not sub judice, and thus, they are not breaking the law. Instead, the media finds fault with the DCEC for refusing to even confirm or deny they are investigating certain things, yet expects the media to self-censor by not reporting on these.

The media is thus unhappy with what they deem to be an unreasonable expectation by the law that puts the burden of knowing on the DCEC; it is for the media to discover whether the DCEC is investigating or not. According to media, expecting the media to come to the DCEC to ask if a subject of their intended stories is being investigated or not, is tantamount to saying the DCEC must take charge of their editorial policy.

---

33 Mathala S & Charles S (2015, 8 May) Why the DCEC raided *The Gazette*. *Mmegi online*. Available at http://www.mmegi.bw/index.php?aid=51026&fb_comment_id=765191076929888_765284730253856#f1b1d26fb3163a4 [accessed 30 September 2016].

Such a stance they see as 'very invasive' and 'trampling on their rights as the fourth estate'. Added to this is the fact the law gives the DCEC the right to come into their premises and demand computers and other journalistic tools of trade; this, they argue has rendered the DCEC dictatorial.

Communities
DCEC relations with the communities in Botswana include a number of approaches. Amongst these are the Community Anti-corruption Clubs (CAC) road shows, media briefings, house-to-house campaigns and outreach campaigns. The first instance involves dissemination of information on the evils of corruption to the concerned groups, including the youth and general communities. For example, in the 2013/14 financial year, Setlalekgosi Community Secondary School, Maun Secondary School and Mater Spei Senior Secondary School community clubs were resuscitated. At the same time, Mahalpye, Moshupa, Thamaga and Maun (all large villages) had formed community clubs.[34]

The DCEC assists the communities to register these clubs with the registrar of societies, a government department responsible for registering non-profit making entities. Such status enables the clubs to raise funds, open bank accounts and accept deposits so that they can operate normally. In house-to-house campaigns, typically the DCEC visits specific population sectors that may, for various reasons, be unable to attend the regular outreach activities. These sectors include the disabled, the sick, the elderly and those whose normal daily schedules do not allow for attendance of the outreach programmes.

Anti-corruption units and corruption prevention units
The DCEC also assists in managing corruption by setting up anti-corruption units (ACUs) in government ministries. The ACUs are made up of ministerial staff in ministries where incidents of corruption are considered to be high. Their duty is to diagnose possible areas of corruption and take corrective action. The corruption prevention committees (CPCs), on the other hand, emphasise prevention in their mandates. They devise approaches for lessening corruption, including information sharing, and education.

The challenge with either type of committee is that as they are voluntary, often regarded as extra work, and thus possibly receive less attention. Added to that, either structure faces resource constraints.

Relationship with the private sector

DCEC relationships with the private sector are primarily through its interactions with the umbrella body for private business in Botswana, the Botswana Chamber of Commerce, Industry and Manpower (BOCCIM).

---

34 Directorate on Corruption and Economic Crime (DCEC) (2014) *Annual Report*. Gaborone: DCEC.

BOCCIM is the predecessor to Business Botswana. In partnership with the DCEC, BOCCIM designed a code of conduct for the private sector. The code is, strictly speaking, not public law, but a voluntary set of principles guiding the private business sector on issues of corruption

The primary aim of the code of conduct is to work as a persuasive instrument that commits members to accede to self-regulatory behaviour against corruption. The code sets out a number of principles by which members ought to abide in their business affairs. Members are therefore exhorted to aspire to higher conduct through some of the following issues:

- Observation and compliance with business ethics;
- Strict avoidance of conflict of interest;
- Prohibition of solicitation, offering, acceptance and promising of bribes;
- Avoidance of political interference in the conduct of business; and
- Commitment to ethical and legal procurement and tendering procedures.

A major challenge with the BOCCIM code of conduct is that it is not binding on members, as it is, in essence, a voluntary undertaking. Though desirable to have all businesses sign up to the code as a sign of commitment to ethical behaviour, BOCCIM has reiterated that accession to the code is too limited. A number of reasons make accession difficult, including the fact that those businesses outside of the remits of the code can still conduct business in Botswana. There are no consequences for not acceding to the code; thus enforcement is problematic.

The public and other stakeholders
Due to the fragmentary nature of anti-corruption undertakings, the DCEC has a number of strategies through which it effects relationships with other stakeholders, including communities, government agencies, the media, and the private sector.

The DCEC's external relations strategy is also facilitated by a number of memorandums of understanding (MoU). Such MoUs work to improve coordination, information and other resources exchange, including capacity-building. One of the DCEC's notable MoUs is that with the Competition Authority of Botswana, as well as Public Procurement and Asset Disposal Board (PPADB). The MoU was signed in 2010, and seeks to improve relations between the three organisations. To that extent, information exchange and other mutual support is improved; for instance, the DCEC has been able to call on information technology support from the PPADB.

MoUs are also signed with external organisations. The African Development Bank's anti-corruption department signed an MoU with the DCEC in 2013. A number of areas were identified:

- Capacity-building initiatives, possibly including on the job training for DCEC personnel;
- National, regional and international forums and symposiums;
- Review and research activities;
- Development and peer-to-peer partnerships; and
- Additional activities.

DCEC in the international arena

Through the DCEC, Botswana is a member of the Southern African Development Community (SADC) Forum Against Corruption (SAFAC). Since attaining membership of the body, the DCEC has actively participated in SAFAC activities.

While Botswana has ratified the United Nations Convention Against Corruption (UNCAC), the country has yet to domesticate it. This means that the potential benefits and duties of the UNCAC are limited. However, Botswana has already undergone review processes by the UNCAC.

On behalf of Botswana as host government, the DCEC is also host to the Commonwealth Africa Anti-corruption Centre (CAACC). This centre was launched in 2013 through the signing of a MoU between the government of Botswana and the Commonwealth secretariat. Through this initiative, the Commonwealth aims to assist anti-corruption agencies in commonwealth nations on the African continent to improve their performance. Included in the strategies of the CAACC are: training and development; peer reviews; twinning and other exchanges; research; annual review meetings; communications such as newsletters, innovation awards; and providing mutual support.

While the CAACC initiative has begun its operations, including targeting the ACAs in 19 countries for training, it appears that the responses have been less than enthusiastic. The DCEC is a member of the SAFAC. The directorate has consistently attended SAFAC meetings since it became a member.

Reporting mechanisms and public perception

In terms of section 31 of the CECA, the DCEC is obligated to report annually to the president on 31 March. Section 22(1) of the CECA states that such submission shall 'on or before 31 March in each year, or by such later date as the president may allow, where the DCEC is to submit to the president a report on the activities of the Directorate in the previous year'.

Section 31 of the CECA also empowers the president to extend the reporting period for submission. What this means in practice, is that the DCEC may make requests for extensions to the deadline(s) of reporting to the president. The reports made to the president are usually in the form of an annual report, which is then made publicly available.

While on the one hand, the law is not explicit that upon receipt of the annual report that the president must publish it, in practice, the presidency in Botswana has always interpreted this to mean that the report must be published. No report has thus been withheld from public consumption to date.

Public perceptions of the performance of the DCEC vary with official versions. However, whereas most of the indicators (such as that by Transparency International, are mostly driven by academics, business people and civil servants), public perception studies suggest a growing cynicism with corruption in Botswana. Table 1 below shows the results of the Afrobarometer study on perceptions of corruption amongst public officials. When asked the question about perceived levels of corruption amongst public officials, respondents in Botswana showed the following results:

Table 1: Public perceptions of corruption by public servants in Botswana (2002/3, 2008/9 and 2011/13)

	2002/3	2008/9	2011/13
None	8.1	18.1	6.8
Some of them	42.1	43.8	55.2
Most of them	19.7	20.9	23.9
All of them	5.1	3.3	3.7
Don't know/haven't heard enough	25.1	13.9	10.2

Source: Afrobarometer (various years).

The general trend is towards more perceptions of corruption. For instance, whereas in 2002 42.1% of the respondents had perceived 'some' of the public servants as corrupt, this number grew to 43.8% in 2008/9, and ultimately to 55.2% in 2011/13. Similarly, the public's perception that most public servants in Botswana were corrupt grew from 19.7% in 2002/3 to 20.9% in 2008/9, and 23.9% in 2011/13. Thus, there is certainly a case to be made that the general publics' perceptions of corruption are at variance with those of international ranking agencies.

This should, perhaps, not be much of a surprise. One of the oft-made criticisms of the DCEC is that it lacks independence. The criticism, among others, is made that the directorate only goes after the 'small fish', unimportant people in society, ignoring those that are influential.[35]

E. Conclusions

A number of conclusions may be drawn in relation to the DCEC, its operations, and its resources. The DCEC was established due to a felt need. Corruption was certainly emerging as a new policy challenge that needed addressing. Whereas Botswana brought

---

35 Gbadamosi G (2005) Corruption perception and sustainable development: Sharing Botswana's anti-graft agency experiences. Available at https://eprints.worc.ac.uk/88/3/Corruption_Perception_and_Sustainable_Development_revised-_SAJEMS.pdf [accessed17 November 2016]. p. 17.

in Mr Stockwell to spearhead the development of the DCEC, the initiative to create the DCEC was taken locally. The following are some of the significant findings from this study:

- The DCEC has had a continual, stable existence since inception. For instance, its leaders have served out their terms with relative assurance of tenure.
- Whereas Botswana's anti-corruption efforts are notable, citizen surveys are less positive in corruption outlooks when compared to major global surveys like Transparency International's Corruption Perception Index. The differences ought to be investigated.
- Botswana's Electoral Act has a number of loopholes that make it difficult to enforce ethical conduct in campaign financing in Botswana.
- Botswana lacks a number of laws needed to assist the DCEC in fighting corruption. Such laws that are necessary, but currently absent, include the whistle-blower protection act, declaration of assets and liabilities law, and freedom of information law. Such absence of laws compromises the DCEC's capacity to enforce its mandate.
- Variations between laws central and incidental to anti-corruption have the potential to cloud the anti-corruption fight. In this regard, The Penal Code and CECA have a number of inconsistencies that need to be addressed.
- Perceptions persist that the DCEC is not independent. Whereas independence is subject to interpretation, the perceptions will compromise DCEC standing with the public.
- The DCEC has mechanisms for interacting with the public, the private sector, government and the media. However, weaknesses in the law tend to work against cordial relations with the media, leading to unnecessary friction.
- While the DCEC has mechanisms for interacting with the public, the weakness is the lack of involvement of the public on a more sustained, more regular basis.
- The setting up of the corruption court in Botswana ought to help the DCEC address its mandate more effectively.
- The misinformed perception by some that anti-corruption is solely the mandate of the DCEC, compromises the capacity for essential networking.
- The DCEC has not domesticated the UNCAC. The delay is costing Botswana the capacity to reform its anti-corruption approaches.

F. Recommendations

The following recommendations are made to improve anti-corruption efforts in Botswana:

Botswana must close the loopholes in the Electoral Act which make campaign finance reform difficult to enforce currently:

- In order to strengthen efforts at measuring citizen views on anti-corruption, academia must devise more surveys of citizen perception. The more regular these surveys, the more comprehensive the picture.
- In order to strengthen anti-corruption management in the country, government must come with laws that will assist in revealing information on possible corrupt practices. The laws include: a freedom of information law, a whistleblower protection act, and a law on declaration of assets and liabilities.
- Botswana must address inconsistencies between the CECA and other laws, such as the Penal Code.
- In order to bolster DCEC standing amongst the media and the public, government must consider changing the appointment processes of the head of the DCEC. The president thus being an appointing authority, ought to be enjoined in law to appoint the director general of the DCEC, but in consultation with the leader of opposition in parliament.
- In order to further strengthen anti-corruption measures in the country, Botswana must, as a matter of urgency, domesticate the UNCAC.

4

DEMOCRATIC REPUBLIC OF CONGO

Prof. Andre Mbata Mangu

A. Executive summary

As many African leaders acknowledged through the ratification or accession to instruments such as the United Nations Convention Against Corruption (UNCAC), the African Convention on Preventing and Combatting Corruption (AUCPCC) or the Southern African Development Community (SADC) Protocol against Corruption, corruption undermines socio-economic development and good governance. Specialised and independent institutions as recommended by the UNCAC and AUCPCC therefore have had to be established and fully equipped to wage an effective war against the scourge of corruption.

This chapter reflects on the fight against corruption in the Democratic Republic of Congo (DRC) with a focus on the strengths and weaknesses of the Office of the Presidential Special Advisor on Good Governance, Corruption, Money Laundering and the Financing of Terrorism (the office of the special advisor, hereafter), the Congolese specialised anti-corruption body.

The main finding of the study, which is based on independent and reliable reports and studies undertaken previously, is that corruption is rampant, endemic and systemic in the DRC. No sector is immune. The most corrupted sector appears to be the political sphere, which impacts on all the other sectors, given the importance of politics in society.

The DRC is a state party to the UNCAC and the SADC Protocol. It signed and recently ratified the AUCPCC, which is now binding on the DRC. However, it does not comply with these instruments. This contrasts with numerous statements from the Congolese authorities that they are strongly committed to promoting good governance and combatting corruption. Several pieces of legislation enacted by parliament could help combat corruption but generally remain empty rhetoric. The Ethics and Anti-Corruption Commission established by the 2003 constitution did not survive the transition. It does not feature in the 2006 constitution, which currently governs the country. Corruption continues unabated.

Established in July 2016 by an ordinance of the president of the republic, the office of the special advisor has been vested with important powers. The special advisor who presides over this office is appointed and reports directly to the president of the republic, who may also dismiss him at will. Located in the office of the president, its main function is more to 'advise' than act, putting the president himself at the heart of the fight against corruption. Its main weakness lies in the fact that it has been established by the president and thus lacks the necessary independence.

The special advisor has no power over the state president himself, the members of the government, the chief executive officers of public services or enterprises, political leaders and others persons close to the state president or associated with him/her. Without term limits or specific qualifications required, the position is also unlikely to survive change in the presidency. The fight against corruption in the political and public sector is emphasised while the economic and private sectors, where corruption is also rampant, remain relatively unscrutinised. The citizenry, civil society organisations, and even public institutions such as parliament are not closely connected to the special advisor. Since the appointment of the special advisor in 2015, there has been more talk than action. No single high-ranking official has been prosecuted, sentenced and imprisoned for mismanagement, corruption, money laundering or financing terrorism. The judiciary has failed to act against corruption. Due to political patronage and clientelism, parliament, which has also an important role to play in combatting corruption and is mandated to oversee the government and public services and enterprises, has not succeeded in dismissing any single manager in the civil service. All the no-confidence motions tabled by the members of the opposition and calling for the removal of the prime minister and various ministers for mismanagement have been defeated by the ruling coalition, showing solidarity with the government.

'Zero-tolerance for corruption' remains an empty slogan. The office of the special advisor remains largely ineffective, giving the impression that it was established to impress donor countries, with the aim of attracting investment into the country. A strong political will to combat corruption seems to be lacking, as evidenced by the non-ratification of the AUCPCC despite the DRC signing it in 2010.

The fight against corruption must be taken more seriously – not only by the president, the government, parliament and the judiciary – but also by every Congolese citizen, international institutions, multinationals, and all foreign companies and their governments. It should also embrace all sectors, public and private. International organisations and foreign governments should not tolerate acts and practices considered crimes in their own countries.

The DRC needs a specialised and independent anti-corruption body, well equipped with professional staff, endowed with the necessary resources and accountable to the people. The ratification of the AUCPCC and its implementation – which requires the establishment of such an independent entity – will be the first step and send a clear message that the DRC government is taking the 'zero-tolerance against corruption' mantra more seriously in order to foster socio-economic development and democratic governance of the country. At the SADC level, efforts should be made to strengthen the SADC Protocol and monitor member states' compliance to its edicts.

B. State of corruption in Africa, Southern Africa and the DRC

Corruption is neither native nor peculiar to Africa. It is inherent to human societies. It affects all countries, whether developed or underdeveloped, democratic or undemocratic, rich or poor. It is a worldwide phenomenon with negative consequences for development, governance, and even peace and security. This explains why the member states of the United Nations (UN) adopted the Convention Against Corruption[1] to combat it.

Corruption undermines democracy, justice, and the rule of law. It leads to violations of human rights, distorts markets, and erodes ethical values and justice. Corruption threatens human security and sustainable development.[2] Although it is found in all countries, it is in the developing world that its effects are the most destructive. Corruption hurts the poor disproportionately by diverting funds intended for development, undermining the government's ability to provide basic services, feeding inequality and injustice and discouraging foreign aid and investment. It is a key element in economic underperformance and a major obstacle to poverty alleviation and development.[3]

Over the past years, international institutions such as the World Bank, the International Monetary Fund (IMF), the UN Economic Commission for Africa (UNECA), civil society organisations (CSOs), including non-governmental organisations (NGOs), and initiatives such as Global Witness, Global Integrity, Transparency International, the Extractive Industries Transparency Initiative and Doing Business, have produced numerous reports and indexes on corruption in Africa. All these reports confirm that corruption has reached cancerous proportions on the continent. It is widespread, systemic, endemic and corrosive. However, corrupt people are not only African peoples and their leaders, but also non-Africans, including governments, businesses, companies, institutions and individual citizens.

According to UNECA, corruption is the single most important challenge for eradicating poverty, the creation of predicable and favourable investment environments and socio-economic development in general. It deepens poverty and stalls the realisation of the Millennium Development Goals (MDGs).[4] Corruption ranks first among the 14 leading

---

1 UN (2004) United Nations Convention Against Corruption. New York: UN. Available at https://www.unodc.org/documents/brussels/UN_Convention_Against_Corruption.pdf [accessed 30 July 2016].
2 Anan K (2004) Foreword to the UNCAC. p. iii. Available at https://www.unodc.org/documents/brussels/UN_Convention_Against_Corruption.pdf [accessed 30 July 2016].
3 Ibid.
4 See UN Economic Commission for Africa (UNECA) (2009) *Africa Governance Report II*. p. 12. Available at http://www.uneca.org/sites/default/files/PublicationFiles/agr2-english_0.pdf [accessed 12 December 2016]; UN Economic Commission for Africa (2000) *Assessing the Efficiency and Impact of National Anti-Corruption Institutions in Africa*. p. VII. Addis Ababa: UNECA; UN Economic Commission for Africa (UNECA)

obstacles to good governance and state delivery in Africa.[5] Many African countries are trapped in the vicious circle of corruption, poverty and underdevelopment. Corruption affects the executive, the legislature, the judiciary, public administration, political parties, public entities and companies, unions, NGOs and private companies.

Corruption is an indicator of weak and undemocratic governance. It has virtually become an acceptable way of life for many people on the continent.[6] This is not only an accusation from western countries and their organisations, but it has also been admitted by African leaders themselves since the inception of the African Union (AU), which superseded the Organisation of African Unity (OAU).[7] In terms of its Constitutive Act adopted in 2000,[8] the objectives of the AU are, inter alia, to 'promote democratic principles and institutions, popular participation and good governance'.[9] One of its principles is 'Respect for democratic principles, human rights, the rule of law and good governance'.[10] In as much as it opposes good governance and is 'literally the antithesis of development and progress',[11] corruption poses a challenge and a great risk to the objectives and principles of the AU and should therefore be combatted.

The New Partnership for Africa's Development (NEPAD)[12] was launched as an African initiative to promote socio-economic development and good governance. In the NEPAD Declaration[13] – adopted at the first meeting of the heads of state and government implementation committee of NEPAD in Abuja, Nigeria, in 2001 – African leaders implicitly identified corruption as an obstacle to development, and committed themselves to fighting it.

The African Peer review Mechanism (APRM) was established later as a voluntary mechanism to assess and make recommendations to improve governance among AU member states participating in NEPAD. The APRM is based on the Declaration on Democracy, Political, Economic and Corporate Governance adopted by the AU assembly

---

(2008) *Africa's Economic Report: Africa and the Monetary Consensus: Performances and Progress of the Continent*. Addis Ababa: UNECA; Le Pere G & Ikome F (2012) The future of Africa's development. In: E Lundsgaarde (ed.) *Africa towards 2030: Challenges for Development Policy*. London: Palgrave McMillan. pp. 233.

5   Mangu AMB (2007) Assessing the effectiveness of the African Peer-Review Mechanism and its impact on the promotion of democracy and good political governance. *African Human Rights Law Journal* 7: 361.
6   UN Economic Commission for Africa (UNECA) (2002) *Guidelines for Enhancing Good Economic and Corporate Governance in Africa*, Final Draft. Addis Ababa: UNECA. pp. 13–14.
7   OUA Charter. Available at http://www.au.int/en/treaties/oau-charter-addis-ababa-25-may-1963 [accessed 30 July 2016].
8   AU Constitutive Act. Available at http://www.au.int/en/sites/default/files/ConstitutiveAct_EN.pdf [accessed 30 July 2016].
9   AU Constitutive Act, article 3(g).
10 Ibid., article 4(m).
11 UN Economic Commission for Africa (2000) *Assessing the Efficiency and Impact of National Anti-Corruption Institutions in Africa*. p. 3. Addis Ababa: UNECA.
12 Heyns C & Killander M (eds)(2006) *Compendium of Key Human rights Instruments of the African Union*. Pretoria: Pretoria University Law Press. pp. 308–354.
13 Declaration on Democracy, Political, Economic and Corporate Governance, paragraph 8. In: C Heyns & M Killander (eds)(2006) *Compendium of Key Human Rights Instruments of the African Union*. Pretoria: Pretoria University Law Press. pp. 338–341.

of heads of state and government in Durban, South Africa, in July 2002. This instrument clearly identifies corruption as the major obstacle to democracy and political, economic and corporate governance. African leaders undertook to 'eradicate corruption, which both retards economic development and undermines the moral fabric of society'.[14] In support of good political governance, they agreed to ensure the effective functioning of parliaments and other accountability institutions, including parliamentary committees and anti-corruption bodies'.[15]

Different APRM reports have singled out corruption as the major obstacle to democracy, good political, economic, social and corporate governance, and Africa's development. Corruption was considered one of the cross-cutting obstacles to good governance in Benin,[16] Burkina Faso,[17] Ghana,[18] Kenya,[19] Rwanda[20] and South Africa.[21]

On 11 July 2003 – after several declarations in which they expressed their commitment to fighting corruption as one of the major challenges to Africa's development and renaissance, particularly within the framework of the NEPAD and its APRM – African leaders adopted the AU Convention on Preventing and Combatting Corruption (AUCPCC).[22] The AUCPCC came into force on 5 August 2006.

The first objective of the AUCPCC is to 'Promote and strengthen the development in Africa by each State Party, of mechanisms required to prevent, detect, punish and eradicate corruption and related offences in the public and private sectors'.[23] The AUCPCC established the advisory board on corruption (ABC) as the follow-up mechanism mandated to popularise it, help AU member states comply with its provisions, and to promote and encourage the adoption and application of anti-corruption measures. The questionnaire for the APRM country self-assessment, developed in 2004, selected the AUCPCC as one of the regional standards and codes to be considered when assessing good governance of any AU member state under the APRM and within NEPAD.[24]

---

14 Ibid.
15 Ibid., paragraph 14.
16 MAEP (2008) *Rapport d'évaluation No. 6 de la République du Bénin*, Janvier 2008. pp. 273–291, paragraphs 904–994.
17 MAEP (2009) *Rapport d'évaluation No. 9 de la République du Burkina Faso,* June 2009. Paragraphs 1051–1061.
18 Mangu AMB (2007) Assessing the effectiveness of the African Peer-Review Mechanism and its impact on the promotion of democracy and good political governance. *African Human Rights Law Journal* 7: 368, 376.
19 Ibid.: 376, 379.
20 Ibid.: 376.
21 State of the Union Africa (2010) State of the Union South Africa Report 2010. Available at http://www.southernafricatrust.org/docs/State_of_the_Union_South_Africa_Report_2010.pdf [accessed 19 December 2016]
22 African Union Convention on Preventing and Combatting Corruption (AUCPCC). Available at http://www.au.int/en/treaties/african-union-convention-preventing-and-combating-corruption [accessed 30 July 2016].
23 AUCPCC, article 2(1).
24 Country Self-assessment for the APRM (2004) In: C Heyns & M Killander (eds)(2006) *Compendium of Key Human Rights Instruments of the African Union.* Pretoria: Pretoria University Law Press. pp. 305, paragraph 2.2.

The AUCPCC defines several offences related to corruption[25] and obliges state parties to 'Establish, maintain and strengthen independent national anti-corruption authorities and agencies'.[26] It also provides for the strengthening of accountability in the public sector, the protection of witnesses and informants in corruption cases, regular reporting and public education on corruption. In 2007, AU member states adopted the African Charter on Democracy, Elections and Governance (ACDEG), which entered into force in 2012. The ACDEG underscores the negative effects of corruption in the areas of democratic governance, the rule of law, and in the conduct of free and fair elections.

Southern African countries adopted their own anti-corruption treaty in 2001.[27] The SADC Protocol does not require state parties to establish specialised anti-corruption agencies. However, Southern African countries are obliged to adopt national legislation establishing such specialised independent anti-corruption authorities or agencies as part of compliance with the AUCPCC. Unfortunately, despite these legal and political developments and the progress made in some countries, little change has actually occurred and the scourge of corruption continues unabated.

The purpose of this chapter is to report on corruption and on the strengths and weaknesses of the office of the special advisor,[28] as the main anti-corruption body in the DRC. In addition, the chapter will make recommendations for combatting corruption more successfully and to eradicate its consequences on the political, social, economic and cultural development of society, as a prerequisite for sustainable development, peace, and democracy.

C. Political economy of corruption in the DRC

Background

At about 2.4 million square kilometres and with a population of around 80 million, the DRC is the second largest (after Algeria) and the third most densely populated country (after Nigeria, Egypt and Ethiopia) on the African continent.

To better understand the developments that have occurred in the country, including those related to corruption, it is worth considering the strategic importance of the DRC, which is located right in the middle of the continent, and its immense natural resources. Anyone who exerts influence on politics and the economy in the DRC, either directly or indirectly, is likely to control a great part of Africa and even the entire continent.[29]

---

25 AUCPCC, article 4.
26 Ibid., article 5.
27 SADC Protocol against Corruption. Available at http://www.sadc.int/files/7913/5292/8361/Protocol_Against_Corruption2001.pdf [accessed 30 July 2016].
28 Ordonnance No. 16/065 pf 14 July 2016, *Journal Officiel de la République Démocratique du Congo*, 1er août 2016, Première Partie, No. 15.
29 Mangu AMB (2002) *The Road to Constitutionalism and Democracy in Postcolonial Africa: The Case of the Democratic Republic of Congo*. LLD Thesis. Pretoria: UNISA. pp. 309.

The DRC is surrounded by nine other countries, namely Angola, Zambia, Tanzania, Rwanda, Burundi, Uganda, South Sudan, Central African Republic and Congo. Its geographical position makes it belong to Central, Southern and Eastern Africa. This explains why it holds the membership of three regional economic communities, namely the Economic Community of Central African States (ECCAS), the SADC, and the Common Market for Eastern and Southern Africa (COMESA).

Thanks to its natural resources, the DRC is one of the richest countries on earth, with the paradox that the Congolese people are currently among the poorest. Around 450 ethnic groups inhabit the DRC, which is currently divided into 25 provinces and the city of Kinshasa, the capital of the republic.

During the 1885–1886 Berlin Conference, the territory now known as the DRC was allocated to Leopold II, the King of Belgium, as the Congo Free State. The DRC therefore entered modern history not as a Belgian colony, but as the personal possession of the King of Belgium. Despite the name, the Congo was no free state. It was not even a state understood in international law as a sovereign entity consisting of a people inhabiting a specific territory and subjected to a government. It was rather the private domain of the King, who owned everything, including the land and the people.

In 1908, the King transferred his domain to Belgium. The Congo Free State then became a Belgian colony known as the Belgian Congo. After a long liberation struggle led by Patrice-Emery Lumumba and other nationalist leaders, the colony became independent from Belgium on 30 June 1960 and became the DRC, with Joseph Kasavubu as the president of the republic, and Patrice Emery Lumumba as his prime minister. Shortly after independence, the DRC went through its first political crisis, involving mutiny in the army, secessions, rebellions and interference from Belgium under the pretext of protecting its nationals. This resulted in the establishment of the first UN operation in the Congo under the code name of the 'ONUC'.

For about five years, from 1960 to 1964, the DRC was governed by the Fundamental Law of 19 May 1960. The Fundamental Law of the first Constitution of Independent Congo was an interim Belgian law. It was drafted by the Belgian government, adopted by the Belgian parliament, assented to and promulgated by the Belgian King Baudouin and published in the Belgian Monitor like any other Belgian law.[30] The Fundamental Law was replaced with a constitution adopted by the Congolese people themselves by referendum and promulgated by President Joseph Kasavubu on 1 August 1964. The 1964 constitution paved the way for the organisation of general elections in 1965.

On 24 November 1965, General Mobutu led a military coup that overthrew President Joseph Kasavubu. He established an authoritarian regime based one-party rule. Mobutu's 32-year long authoritarian and corrupt rule lasted until 17 May 1997, when he was deposed by the rebellion of the *Alliance des Forces de Liberation du Congo* (AFDL), led by Laurent-Desire

---

30 Mangu AMB (2002) *The Road to Constitutionalism and Democracy in Postcolonial Africa: The Case of the Democratic Republic of Congo.* LLD Thesis. Pretoria: UNISA. pp. 331.

Kabila and backed by the governments of some neighbouring countries, notably Rwanda and Uganda, who invaded the DRC to control its natural resources. President Laurent-Desire Kabila quickly distanced himself from his comrades within the AFDL and from Rwanda and Uganda. In response, several rebellions broke out against his government. The DRC was divided into several administrations controlled respectively by the Kabila government and the most important rebel groups, namely the *Rassemblement congolais pour la démocratie* (RCD, Congolese Rally for Democracy) and the *Mouvememt de libération du Congo* (MLC, Movement for the Liberation of the Congo). Due to the number of foreign armies that intervened to support the Kabila government or the rebel movements, the armed conflict in the DRC was labelled the 'First Congolese World War' or the 'African War'.[31] On the basis of the Lusaka Agreement[32] signed in July/August 1999 with the assistance of the international community, a new UN operation mission, which later developed into MONUSCO, was sent to help the Congolese leaders reunite the country and bring the armed conflict to an end. On 16 January 2001, President Laurent-Desire Kabila was assassinated and replaced by his son, Joseph Kabila.

The Inter-Congolese Dialogue was held in Sun City, South Africa, between 2002 and 2003. It brought together the belligerents and ended up with the adoption of an interim constitution that led to the formation of a government of national unity led by President Joseph Kabila. A new constitution was adopted by referendum held from 18–19 December 2005. It was promulgated on 18 February 2006 by President Joseph Kabila, who still governs the DRC.

Joseph Kabila was elected in 2006 and re-elected in 2011. Both presidential elections were reportedly rigged. The DRC is confronting yet another political crisis due to the failure of the government to organise a presidential election despite President Kabila's second and final term of office ending on 19 December 2016. As Thandika Mkandawire rightly pointed out in his preface to *Zaire: What a destiny:*[33]

> Ever since the Congo crisis and Mobutu's accession to power, Zaïre (as the DRC was named under Mobutu) has represented the full range of African problems, from colonial domination and exploitation through corruption, authoritarian rule and ethnic conflicts, to military regimes and mismanagement. The country offers a caricatural case history of the outstanding waste of African potential.[34]

---

31 Mangu AMB (2002) *The Road to Constitutionalism and Democracy in Postcolonial Africa: The Case of the Democratic Republic of Congo.* LLD Thesis. Pretoria: UNISA. pp. 312.
32 United Nations Peacemaker Ceasefire Agreement (Lusaka Agreement). Available at http://peacemaker.un.org/drc-lusaka-agreement99 [accessed 31 July 2016].
33 Mbaya K (ed.) (1991) *Le Zaïre vers quelles destinées?* Dakar: CODESRIA.
34 Mkandawire T (1991) Introduction. In: K Mbaya (ed.) *Le Zaïre vers quelles destinées?* Dakar: CODESRIA. pp. IX–X.

Corruption was singled out as one of the main causes of the 'outstanding waste of African potential' in the DRC and of the 'paradox' of being one of the richest countries in the world at the same time as having one of its poorest populations.

Overview of corruption in the DRC

The AUCPCC and the SADC Protocol contain lengthy definitions of corruption. According to the AUCPCC, the following are constitutive of the crime of corruption and related offences:

(a) the solicitation or acceptance, directly or indirectly, by a public official or any other person, of any goods of monetary value, or other benefit, such as a gift, favour, promise or advantage for himself or herself or for another person or entity, in exchange for any act or omission in the performance of his or her public functions;

(b) the offering or granting, directly or indirectly, to a public official or any other person, of any goods of monetary value, or other benefit, such as a gift, favour, promise or advantage for himself or herself or for another person or entity, in exchange for any act or omission in the performance of his or her public functions;

(c) any act or omission in the discharge of his or her duties by a public official or any other person for the purpose of illicitly obtaining benefits for himself or herself or for a third party;

(d) the diversion by a public official or any other person, for purposes unrelated to those for which they were intended, for his or her own benefit or that of a third party, of any property belonging to the State or its agencies, to an independent agency, or to an individual, that such official has received by virtue of his or her position;

(e) the offering or giving, promising, solicitation or acceptance, directly or indirectly, of any undue advantage to or by any person who directs or works for, in any capacity, a private sector entity, for himself or herself or for anyone else, for him or her to act, or refrain from acting, in breach of his or her duties;

(f) the offering, giving, solicitation or acceptance directly or indirectly, or promising of any undue advantage to or by any person who asserts or confirms that he or she is able to exert any improper influence over the decision making of any person performing functions in the public or private sector in consideration thereof, whether the undue advantage is for himself or herself or for anyone else, as well as the request, receipt or the acceptance of the offer or the promise of such an advantage, in consideration of that influence, whether or not the influence is exerted or whether or not the supposed influence leads to the intended result;

(g) illicit enrichment;

(h) the use or concealment of proceeds derived from any of the acts referred to in this Article; and

(i) participation as a principal, co-principal, agent, instigator, accomplice or accessory after the fact, or on any other manner in the commission or attempted commission of, in any collaboration or conspiracy to commit, any of the acts referred to in this article.[35]

The SADC Protocol includes all of the above, except for 'illicit enrichment', as 'acts of corruption'.[36] The Congolese Penal Code also punishes acts of corruption.

According to Transparency International,[37] corruption entails 'the abuse of entrusted power for private gain'. It includes many acts such as 'bribery or any other behaviour in relation to persons entrusted with responsibilities in the public and private sectors which violates their duties as public officials, private employees, independent agents or other relationships of that kind and aimed at obtaining undue advantage of any kind for themselves and others'.[38]

Corruption can be classified as grand, petty and political, depending on the amounts of money lost and the sector where it occurs. Grand corruption consists of acts committed at a high level of government that distort policies or the central function of the state, enabling leaders to benefit at the expense of the public. Petty corruption refers to everyday abuse of power by mid-level public officials in their interactions with ordinary citizens as they try to access basic goods or services in places like hospitals, schools, police departments and other agencies. Political corruption is a manipulation of policies, institutions and rules of procedure in the allocation of resources and financing by political decision-makers, who abuse their position to sustain their power, status and wealth. Undoubtedly, grand, petty, political and socio-economic corruption have become endemic and permeate all sectors of life in the DRC.

Since 2011, the DRC has improved is ranking on Transparency International's Corruption Perceptions Index (CPI), but the score has not improved (between 20 and 22) and the DRC remains one of the most corrupt countries in Africa. The perceptions of the Congolese peoples themselves seem to confirm this situation – a hundred students from the University of Kinshasa interviewed in July 2016 even ranked their country among the most corrupt in the world.[39]

As under Mobutu, public resources continue to be siphoned off to sustain a web of patronal networks.

---

35 AUCPCC, article 4.
36 Ibid., article 3.
37 Transparency International (no date) What is corruption? Available at https://www.transparency.org/what-is-corruption/#define [accessed 30 July 2016].
38 SADC Protocol, article 1.
39 The interview was conducted in Kinshasa from 10–20 July 2016. Out of the 100 students, 60 were female students and both females and males equally consider corruption endemic and permeating all the sectors of life. Law enforcement officials (in the judiciary, the army, the police) and politicians were considered the most corrupt.

Table 1. DRC TP CPI ranking and score, 2011–2015

	2011	2012	2013	2014	2015
Ranking	168	160	154	154	147
Score	20	21	22	22	22

Source: Transparency International CPI 2010–2015[40]

Politics and corruption

Politics is the most corrupt sector in the DRC. Given the role of politics and leadership in any society, the corruption of politics has dramatic consequences for all the other societal sectors. A close relationship exists between politics and corruption in any society, leading some people to disengage from politics in the name of ethics. The situation is even worse in the DRC, where ethics seems to have been excluded from politics. This corruption of politics usually manifests during elections and in all the spheres of governments, whether national, provincial, municipal or local.

Political corruption and electoral politics

As in many other countries, electoral politics is marred by corruption. Under the current (2006) constitution, presidential and parliamentary elections have been held twice, in 2006 and 2011 respectively. They were won by the incumbent president, Joseph Kabila, and considered rigged by the independent electoral commission which organised them. Accused of vote-rigging in favour of President Kabila during the 2006 elections, Father Malu Malu, one of his former advisers who chaired the electoral commission, was replaced with Pastor Ngoy Mulunda, one of the founding members of President Kabila's Party of the People for Democracy and Reconstruction (PPRD). The 2011 elections highlighted major political and electoral corruption challenges in the country, especially with regards to voter and candidate registration, result manipulation and campaign financing.[41]

In some areas, security forces also interfered in the electoral processes while in others, voters burned down polling stations in protest against allegations of electoral fraud and ballot stuffing. In three constituencies of the Katanga Province, for instance, a 100% voter turnout was registered – with all the votes in favour of Kabila. This raised major suspicions among election observers, leading the European Union, the Carter Center and national observers' groups to question the credibility of the results. Parliamentary elections were

---

40 See http://www.transparency.org/cpi2010/resultshttp; http://www.transparency.org/cpi2011/result http://www.transparency.org/cpi2012/resultshttp; http:///www.transparency.org/cpi2013/results ; http://www.transparency.org/cpi2014/results; http://www.transparency.org/cpi2015#results-table [accessed 30 July 2016].

41 Freedom House (2012) Countries at the Crossroads – Democratic Republic of Congo. Available at www.freedomhouse.org/report/countriescrossroads/2012/democratic-republic-congo [accessed 12 December 2016]; http://www.transparency.org/files/content/corruptionqas/Country_Profile_DRC_2014.pdf [accessed 30 July 2016].

also rigged. It was the same for the elections of senators, governors and vice-governors of provinces.[42]

Ahead of the 2011 elections, the ruling coalition felt it could lose the presidency if the opposition was to rally behind a single candidate under article 69 of the constitution, which provided for a second round if no candidate obtained an outright majority during the first round.[43] PPRD strategists decided to amend this particular constitutional provision to remove the second round.[44] At the same time, the PPRD interior minister, acting under the instructions of the PPRD secretary general, registered more than two hundred parties which competed for election under the leadership of President Kabila as their 'Moral Authority'. This act has been referred to as 'extreme political engineering'.[45]

Like Mobutu, Joseph Kabila has become a 'master of [political] manipulation'.[46] The *divide et impera* rule once used by the foreign colonial masters and Mobutu was aimed at helping him retain power through electoral engineering. Mulambu reported that by the end of 1995, as Mobutu resisted the opposition against the three decades of his authoritarian and corrupt rule, there were around 460 parties in Zaire.[47] Almost two-thirds of these parties were created by Mobutu's cronies or sycophants and funded by Mobutu himself.[48] Liniger-Goumaz referred to multi-partyism under Mobutu as 'multi-mobutism'.[49] This led François Bayart[50] to hold that no one was more democratic than Mobutu because he had created more than a hundred parties himself.

The situation is perhaps even worse under Joseph Kabila. The number of political parties registered by his government has gone beyond five hundred, with the overwhelming majority belonging to the presidential majority and having him as their supreme leader. Multi-partyism under Joseph Kabila is nothing more than 'multi-kabilism'.

---

42 See Bertelsmann Foundation (2014) BTI 2014 Democratic Republic of Congo Country Report. Available at www.btiproject.de/uploads/tx_jpdownloads/BTI_2014_Congo_DR.pdf [accessed 30 July 2016]; http://www.transparency.org/files/content/corruptionqas/Country_Profile_DRC_2014.pdf [accessed 30 July 2016].
43 Article 71 of the 2006 constitution.
44 See http://www.droitcongolais.info/files/1.09.1.-Loi-constitutionnelle-du-20-janvier-2011_Revision-de-la-Constitution.pdf [accessed 30 July 2016].
45 Mangu AMB (2002) *The Road to Constitutionalism and Democracy in Postcolonial Africa: The Case of the Democratic Republic of Congo*. LLD Thesis. Pretoria: UNISA. pp. 422.
46 Ibid.
47 Mulambu M (1997) Les masses populaires et les préalables d'une transition démocratique au Zaïre (1990–1992). In: G Nzongola-Ntalaja & L Lee (eds) *The State and Democracy in Africa*. Harare: AAPS Books. p. 57; Mangu AMB (2002) *The Road to Constitutionalism and Democracy in Postcolonial Africa: The Case of the Democratic Republic of Congo*. LLD Thesis. Pretoria: UNISA. p. 428.
48 See Liniger-Goumaz M (1992) *La démocrature, dictarure camouflée, démocratie truquée*. Paris: L'Harmattan. p. 273; Mangu AMB (2002) *The Road to Constitutionalism and Democracy in Postcolonial Africa: The Case of the Democratic Republic of Congo*. LLD Thesis. Pretoria: UNISA. p. 428.
49 Liniger-Goumaz M (1992) *La démocrature, dictarure camouflée, démocratie truquée*. Paris: L'Harmattan. p. 16.
50 Ibid.: p. 310.

Corruption in the presidency

Despite promises to put an end to corruption and those involved behind bars,[51] President Kabila has done little to combat it. Corruption remains rampant in the DRC, especially among state officials and public servants. Opponents argue that one of the reasons why the fight against corruption remains an empty slogan under Kabila's presidency is that the state president himself, the first lady, members of the first family (his sister, brother and close friends and allies) are themselves involved in this 'business'.

The state president has reportedly secured a huge fortune that makes him one of the richest leaders on the continent. His precise remuneration and perks are unknown. He and the first lady allegedly make 'donations' to friends and supporters out of the national budget. Unconfirmed reports hold that Dan Gertler, a businessman close to Joseph Kabila, has invested billions offshore as a cover for the president.[52] Gertler has been involved in many corruption scandals within and outside the country.[53] It is also said that key decisions such as signing contracts with foreign multinationals are concluded via bribes, which make their way towards the president through his close associates. Multi-billion contracts with Chinese companies are said to have followed the same path.

The president's twin sister, Jaynet Kabila, and his young brother, Zoe Kabila, are also counted among the wealthiest people in the DRC. They are said to have accumulated immense wealth through huge commissions and through investing millions in business directly or indirectly.

President Kabila recently inaugurated a luxury five-star hotel in Tanzania,[54] shortly after inaugurating another hotel belonging to young brother Zoe Kabila in the Congolese province of Central Kongo.[55] In the Panama Papers, released in the course of 2016, Jaynet Kabila also had her name cited among politicians and business people accused of illicit enrichment and even money laundering, transferring billions of US dollars to tax havens.[56]

Other members of the presidency have also been accused of involvement in corruption. During the transition, Mr Evariste Boshab, President Kabila's chief of staff, was accused of enriching himself with USD 32 million meant for the national electricity company, SNEL,

---

51 Kabila sonne 'la fin de la recreation' (2006, 6 December) *La Libre*. Available at http://www.lalibre.be/actu/international/kabila-sonne-la-fin-de-la-recreation-51b8910fe4b0de6db9aee24b [accessed 25 November 2016].
52 'Panama papers': Dan Gertler, roi du Congo et de l'offshore (2016, 7 April) *Le Monde Afrique*. Available at http://www.lemonde.fr/afrique/article/2016/04/07/panama-papers-dan-gertler-roi-du-congo-et-de-l-offshore_4898097_3212.html [accessed 20 December 2016].
53 Ibid.
54 RDC: Joseph Kabila inaugure son immeuble à Dar es Salaam où la DGDA est locataire (2016, 5 October) *VAC*. Available at http://vacradio.com/rdc-joseph-kabila-inaugure-son-immeuble-a-dar-es-salaam-ou-la-dgda-est-locataire/ [accessed 20 December 2016].
55 RDC: Alias Joseph Kabila inaugure l'hôtel de Zoé Kabila à Muanda le 'Beviour Hôtel'! (2016, 24 July) *Mediapart*. Available at https://blogs.mediapart.fr/freddy-mulongo/blog/240716/rdc-alias-joseph-kabila-inaugure-lhotel-de-zoe-kabila-muanda-le-beviour-hotel [accessed 20 December 2016].
56 DRC president's sister named in Panama Papers (2016, 4 April) *Media24*. Available at http://www.news24.com/Africa/News/drc-presidents-sister-named-in-panama-papers-20160404 [accessed 20 December 2016].

from the government of neighbouring Republic of Congo.[57] The funds never reached their destination. Mr Boshab was dismissed, but never prosecuted. Instead, a few months later, President Kabila appointed him as the general secretary of the PPRD, before appointing him deputy minister in charge of the interior and security, the second highest position in the government. Many have assumed that if the man was never prosecuted and ended up being promoted, it is because he acted on behalf of the president. All the presidential chiefs of staff and other senior officials in the presidency have done similar things. There is the case of Mr Lumanu Nsefu, who succeeded Boshab as the presidential chief of staff, then Mr Beya Siku who replaced Mr Lumanu, and finally Mr Nehemie Mwilanya, the current chief of staff. Surprisingly, all of them teach at the University of Kinshasa. Like his predecessors, Boshab and Lumanu, Prof. Beya Siku was only dismissed before his appointment as the DRC ambassador to Angola. He was not prosecuted despite several accusations of corruption made against him.[58]

In July 2016, a well-known Congolese online journal reported that the current presidential chief of staff, Nehemie Wilanya, had bought a house worth USD 400 000 in the US and had yet been refused a visa for his family members.[59]

In November 2016, Mr Kimbembe Mazunga, who had served many years as President Kabila's senior advisor in charge of infrastructure before his deployment as the chief executive officer of ONATRA, was accused of the misappropriation of several million US dollars and the plundering of the enterprise's coffers. This corrupt advisor to the president was suspended, and not prosecuted.

Corruption in the national and provincial governments and parliaments

The 2006 constitution establishes a quasi-federal state with three spheres of government, namely the national, the provincial, and the municipal and local spheres of government. At the national level, the prime minister is the head of the government, consisting of deputy prime ministers, state ministers, ministers and deputy ministers. The members of this government are appointed and can also be dismissed by the state president on the recommendation of the prime minister.[60] Actually, the president is the de facto head of government and the prime minister is a figurehead with little or no power over the other members of government. Each member of government is assisted by a cabinet constituted on the basis of patronage and political clientelism. The members of these cabinets are essentially appointed among the militants of the political party and the relatives of the ministers. The same occurs in the provincial governments led by the provincial governors.

---

57 See http://unenouvelleafriquevoitjour.blogspot.co.za/2016/07/affaire-evariste-boshab-et-32-millions.html and http://www.iledelareunion.net/video-reunion/rdcpourquoi-toujours-evariste-boshab-dans-la-meme-case-de-detournement-du-denier-public--video-G3M6gf4A9nI.htm [accessed30 July 2016].
58 See http://www.jeuneafrique.com/239952/politique/rdc-un-conseiller-de-kabila-poursuit-katumbi-pour-fraude-douaniere/ [accessed 25 November 2016].
59 See Pas de visa US pour la famille du 'dircab' de 'Joseph Kabila'! (2016, 23 August) *Congo Indépendent*. Available at http://www.congoindependant.com/article.php?articleid=11067 [accessed 20 December 2016].
60 Articles 78 and 90 of the 2006 constitution.

This creates a political environment where political corruption can only prosper. On the other hand, members of parliament either at the national or the provincial level – who are mandated to control the executives and make their members accountable in cases of mismanagement or corruption – are themselves also involved in corruption.

The most interesting form of corruption has been that of the president or the ruling coalition corrupting its own members of parliament to have a law passed or defeated or to save the government from a motion of no-confidence.[61] The same tactic has been used by the ruling coalition, which corrupts the members of the provincial legislatures, including those from the coalition, to protect the governors and provincial governments.

When the provincial assemblies are to elect the governors, the tradition has been for the ruling coalition to deploy its leadership to persuade and give money to secure the votes of the members of the provincial legislatures for their candidate.

Since 2006, despite well established irregularities and misconduct in the exercise of their functions, no prime minister, minister or even a chief executive officer of a public enterprise has lost his position through a decision of the national assembly. What's more, regardless of accusations of embezzlement and corruption, no prime minister, minister, parliamentarian (either national or provincial) or governor has ever been prosecuted – let alone convicted.

Corruption in the judiciary

According to the constitution, the judiciary is independent from the other two branches of government, namely the executive and legislature. Justice is administered in the name of the people, and judgments are handed down in the name of the president of the republic.[62] Unfortunately, the reality is different. The judiciary is dependent on the executive and the ruling coalition under the leadership of the state president, who appoints and can also dismiss its members as the judicial independent commission plays a minor role. The judiciary, which should play a key role in combatting corruption, is itself corrupt from the lowest to the highest courts. Many courts' rulings are paid for if not politically motivated. This is particularly manifest in electoral disputes.

Corruption in the civil service

Corruption is also rampant in the government administration sector. Many public servants are poorly paid and rely on corruption to survive. Lack of oversight provides public officials with both opportunities and incentives for extorting money from the population.[63]

---

61 See International Crisis Group (2010) Congo: A Stalled Democratic Agenda. Available at www.crisisgroup.org/en/regions/africa/central-africa/drcongo/b073-congo-a-stalled-democratic-agenda.aspx; http://www.transparency.org/files/content/corruptionqas/Country_Profile_DRC_2014.pdf [accessed 30 July 2016].
62 Article 149 of the 2006 constitution.
63 Global Integrity (2006) Global Integrity Report: Democratic Republic of Congo. Available at https://www.globalintegrity.org/research/reports/global-integrity-report/global-integrity-report-2006/gir-scorecard-2006-democratic-republic-of-congo/ [accessed 12 December 2016]; Transparency International (2014) Overview of Corruption and Anti-Corruption in the Democratic Republic Of Congo (DRC). Available at http://www.

Bribes are paid in contacts with the police, judiciary, administration, the education and tax revenue services, as well as with registry and permit officials. Private companies are also routinely confronted by petty and bureaucratic corruption. For instance, more than 65% of the firms interviewed in the 2010 World Bank Enterprise Survey reported being expected to make informal payments to get things done, while 75% expected to make a gift of an estimated 9% of the contract value to secure a government contract. This is not just the case of small companies, but also multinationals.[64]

Corruption in the mining industry

Many reports have documented the long tradition of predatory management of the country's natural resources. The DRC's considerable natural wealth is generally exploited for the commercial benefit of a small number of business and political actors to the detriment of the population.[65] Global Witness reports have also denounced extensive corruption, a lack of transparency and life-threatening labour conditions in the natural resources sector.[66]

Tax and customs administration

Corruption in tax and customs offices undermines the government's capacity to generate revenue. Most generally, customs administration is poorly structured and suffers from a lack of resources, infrastructure and equipment, but also from extensive red tape, the overstaffing of posts and widespread corruption.

Customs officers tend to declare goods that are taxed at a lower rate than their import value, and take bribes to waive customs fees. Citizens are poorly informed of which fees are legal, and remain largely unaware of their rights in this regard. Taxes are mostly collected informally and illegally, undermining accountability between citizens and the state. At another level, mining companies take advantage of the tax administration's lack of resources and capacity to develop tax avoidance schemes.

State-run enterprises and corruption

The management of state-run companies remains an area of concern. Corruption, mismanagement, and massive looting by management and governing boards are regularly reported. Audits are never conducted. Management teams routinely decide on their own benefits or grant themselves 'loans' that are never paid back. None of the companies

---

transparency.org/files/content/corruptionqas/Country_Profile_DRC_2014.pdf [accessed 21 December 2016].
64 Enterprise Surveys (2013) Democratic Republic of Congo: Sampling Procedure. Available at http://www.enterprisesurveys.org/nada/index.php/catalog/646/sampling [accessed 21 December 2016].
65 Global Witness (2004) The Same Old Story: A Background Study on Natural Resources in the Republic Democratic Of Congo. Available at https://www.globalwitness.org/en/archive/same-old-story/ [accessed 21 December 2016]; Transparency International (2014) Overview of Corruption and Anti-Corruption in the Democratic Republic of Congo (DRC). Available at Transparency International (2014) Overview of Corruption and Anti-Corruption in the Democratic Republic Of Congo (DRC). Available at http://www.transparency.org/files/content/corruptionqas/Country_Profile_DRC_2014.pdf [accessed 21 December 2016].
66 Ibid.

reviewed had internal auditors.⁶⁷ There is little indication of any progress made in the management of state-owned enterprises since Kabila appointed his own people to lead many of them.

Corruption in the education system

The level of corruption in the DRC education system has contributed to its being discredited, along with graduates and their degrees. In many cases, success at school depends on corruption. Students have to pay their teachers or professors to pass an exam or obtain a degree. Those registered for a state diploma at the end of high school have to pay the inspectors to allow them to get their exams completed outside the exam hall and then reintroduced into the hall.

The situation is the same at university. Of female students interviewed at the University of Kinshasa, 80% are of the view that they need to pay or sleep with their lecturers to pass their exams. The phenomenon of 'sexually transmissible marks' is known in all institutions of higher education in the country. Another phenomenon tantamount to corruption is the system whereby lecturers request their colleagues to pass their girlfriends or relatives. It is also possible that political leaders interfere with the education system. The last scandal to date relates to the economics masters awarded to Prime Minister Augustin Matata Ponyo at the University of Kinshasa. With the rector of the university being a former advisor to the prime minister, instructions were given to the dean of the faculty to circumvent the rules and let the candidate defend his dissertation in camera and not in public. The examining panel was changed in violation of the rules and Prime Minister Matata was proclaimed as having passed the degree with distinction. When the deputy dean and some other faculty members wrote to the academic registrar to complain and the news reached the media, they were summarily suspended by the rector.⁶⁸

Corruption in the allocation of state contracts to multinational companies

It is well known that no one can do business successfully in the DRC without resorting to corruption. It takes a very long time to establish a business in the DRC, which is why Doing Business ranked the DRC among the countries where it is difficult to do business for several consecutive years.⁶⁹ Foreign investors are often faced with the dilemma of working with corrupt officials and being allowed to do business, or refusing and returning home.

---

67 Kodi M (2007) Anti-corruption Challenges in Post-election Democratic Republic of Congo, Chatham House Report. Available https://www.chathamhouse.org/publications/papers/view/108381 [accessed 21 December 2016]; Transparency International (2014) Overview of Corruption and Anti-Corruption in the Democratic Republic of Congo (DRC). Available at http://www.transparency.org/files/content/corruptionqas/Country_Profile_DRC_2014.pdf [accessed 21 December 2016].

68 Saga d'une maffia scientifique à l'UNIKIN (2016, 13 February) *Congo Synthese*. Available at http://www.congosynthese.com/news_reader.aspx?Id=15298 [accessed 21 December 2016].

69 Doing Business (2016) Ease of doing business in the DRC. Available at http://www.doingbusiness.org/data/exploreeconomies/congo,-dem~-rep~ [accessed 21 December 2016].

The corruption of state officials is commonly used to win government contracts.[70] The forestry sector, like the mining sector, is run by 'mafia-type networks with close connections to the political establishment' and industrial logging companies contribute only less than 1% of GDP. There are also indications that actual timber exports could be as much as seven times higher than official figures claim.[71]

Recruitment and bidding procedures are rarely competitive or made public. Auditing and expenditure tracking are rare, and the DRC performs very poorly – well below the region's average in the 2012 Open Budget Index, with a score of 18%. The government provides scant information to the public on the central government's budget and financial spending, making it impossible for citizens to hold the government accountable for its management of public-funded entities. As a result, state resources can easily be syphoned off for private or political purposes.

D. Legal and policy framework against corruption

Several efforts have been undertaken to combat corruption in the DRC. These efforts started during the transition period (2003–2006). An anti-corruption legal framework and institutional and non-institutional arrangements do exist, and could help to combat corruption.

Legal framework

The legal framework against corruption in the DRC consists of binding international and domestic instruments. With regard to the relationship between international and domestic law, it is worth stressing that like many other African Francophone countries, the DRC is 'monist', where international and domestic law are two sides of the same law. Accordingly, any international agreement duly ratified is automatically incorporated and enforceable in domestic law. Such international agreements even prevail over domestic legislation, but are inferior to the constitution. This is different from many Anglophone countries who have inherited the Anglo-American system, which is dualist. According to the dualist theory, international law and domestic law are different laws. For an international agreement to become law in a country, apart from its ratification or accession, it should be domesticated

---

70 See Africa Panel (2013) Africa Progress Report 2013: Lost Revenues in the Democratic Republic of Congo. Available at http://www.africaprogresspanel.org/publications/policy-papers/africa-progress-report-2013/ [accessed 21 December 2016]; Transparency International (2014) Overview of Corruption and Anti-Corruption in the Democratic Republic of Congo (DRC). Available at http://www.transparency.org/files/content/corruptionqas/Country_Profile_DRC_2014.pdf [accessed 21 December 2016].

71 See International Crisis Group (2006) Escaping the Conflict Trap: Promoting Good Governance in the Congo. *Africa Report* No. 114. Available at www.crisisgroup.org/en/regions/africa/central-africa/drcongo/114-escaping-the-conflict-trap-promoting-goodgovernance-in-the-congo.aspx [accessed 21 December 2016]; Transparency International (2014) Overview of Corruption and Anti-Corruption in the Democratic Republic of Congo (DRC). Available at http://www.transparency.org/files/content/corruptionqas/Country_Profile_DRC_2014.pdf [accessed 21 December 2016].

or transformed by an act of parliament that gives it effect in domestic law. Even when it has become law, it is subject to ordinary legislation.

In view of the above, the anti-corruption legal framework in the DRC consists of the following instruments:

- The previously mentioned UNCAC (the United Nation's Convention Against Corruption), which was ratified by the DRC in September 2010 and can therefore be invoked directly by the Congolese courts and other legal institutions in their fight against corruption;
- The SADC Protocol against Corruption, which was signed and ratified in 2007;
- The previously mentioned AU protocol on corruption, namely the AUCPCC, which was ratified on 8 November 2016;[72]
- The 2006 constitution, which contains a number of provisions aimed at promoting transparency and combatting corruption, including provisions that oblige the president of the republic and members of the government to declare their assets to the constitutional court before taking up and or shortly after leaving their position, as well as provisions preventing them from benefitting from any public procurement or tender;[73]
- The 2005 Anti-corruption Act is considered to provide an adequate legal framework to fight corruption in the DRC;[74]
- The 2004 Money Laundering Act, which criminalises money laundering and under which the DRC cooperates with African and European crime-fighting organisations;
- The Criminal Code, which criminalises corruption; and
- The ordinance appointing the Presidential Advisor on Good Governance, Corruption, Money Laundering and the Financing of Terrorism (the previously mentioned 'office of the special advisor') and the ordinances providing for the organising and functioning of this office.

---

72 Law No. 16/029 of 8 November 2016, authorising the ratification of the AUCPCC, Official Journal of 15 November 2016.
73 Articles 98 & 99 of the 2006 constitution.
74 See Freedom House (2010) Countries at the Crossroads – Democratic Republic of Congo. Available at https://freedomhouse.org/report/countries-crossroads/2010/congo-democratic-republic-kinshasa [accessed 12 December 2016]; Transparency International (2014) Overview of Corruption and Anti-Corruption in the Democratic Republic of Congo (DRC). Available at http://www.transparency.org/files/content/corruptionqas/Country_Profile_DRC_2014.pdf [accessed 21 December 2016].

Unfortunately, due to a lack of political will, this strong legal framework has not resulted in the effective prosecution of corruption, even in cases where there was solid evidence of abuse.[75]

As part of its efforts to combat corruption, the DRC joined the Extractive Industry Transparency Initiative (EITI) in 2005 and had to implement several steps to promote transparency before becoming an EITI-compliant country. In 2008, the DRC became a candidate country, but, after only publishing its first report after considerable delays, its candidacy status was suspended as the government did not show demonstrable commitment to financial and contractual transparency.[76] In July 2014, the suspension was lifted and the DRC was accepted as a compliant member of the EITI.[77]

Institutional arrangements and stakeholders in combatting corruption
Ethics and anti-corruption commission
Known as the *Commission éthique et lutte contre la corruption*, this commission was established as one of the five 'citizen' institutions supporting democracy by the interim constitution of 2003,[78] which was adopted during the Inter-Congolese Dialogue held in Sun City, South Africa. Like any other institution, the commission faced several major resource and logistical problems. Its board consisted of the representatives of the signatories to the Sun City Agreement, which resulted in bloated staffing, complicated decision-making processes and no common vision or coherent strategy.[79] Its work was further hampered by weak leadership, insufficient technical expertise and lack of independence. Little could be expected from this institution, which had few powers. After all, it was a 'commission', an advisory body, with its main mandate to 'advise'. It was not a judicial or a quasi-judicial institution that could investigate and prosecute or bring cases of corruption before the competent courts. It had no 'teeth' and could not 'bite'. Accordingly, this anti-corruption agency failed to investigate or prosecute any case of mismanagement and corruption during the transition, and the authors of these acts went unpunished. It did not go beyond the interim constitutional order and was not carried into the 2006 constitution. It would therefore be wrong to consider this commission as a specialised anti-corruption agency in the DRC.

---

75 Kodi M (2007) Anti-corruption Challenges in Post-election Democratic Republic of Congo, Chatham House Report. Available https://www.chathamhouse.org/publications/papers/view/108381 [accessed 21 December 2016].
76 International Crisis Group (2012) Black Gold in the Congo: Threat to Stability or Development Opportunity? Available at https://www.crisisgroup.org/africa/central-africa/democratic-republic-congo/black-gold-congo-threat-stability-or-development-opportunity [accessed 21 December 2016]; Transparency International (2014) Overview of Corruption and Anti-Corruption in the Democratic Republic of Congo (DRC). Available at http://www.transparency.org/files/content/corruptionqas/Country_Profile_DRC_2014.pdf [accessed 21 December 2016].
77 See ITIE (2016) 2016 DRC Report. Available at http://www.itierdc.net/wp-content/uploads/2016/03/rapport-ITIE-RDC-2014-Final-sign%C3%A9.pdf [accessed 21 December 2016].
78 Article 154 of the 2003 interim constitution.
79 Kodi M (2007) Anti-corruption Challenges in Post-election Democratic Republic of Congo, Chatham House Report. Available https://www.chathamhouse.org/publications/papers/view/108381 [accessed 21 December 2016].

Financial intelligence unit

CENAREF, the *Cellule nationale des renseignements financiers* (financial intelligence unit) was established in October 2009 as part of the 'zero-tolerance' campaign to combat money laundering and the misappropriation of public funds by civil servants and members of public institutions. It is responsible for collecting and analysing information as well as for conducting investigations into money laundering and terrorism financing. Limited human and financial resources hampering the government's ability to enforce regulations and lack of competent and qualified personnel have so far prevented CENAREF from fully carrying out its responsibilities. A weak judicial system also impedes the enforcement of anti-money laundering regulations.[80]

Auditing court

Established by an act of parliament, the *Cour des Comptes* (auditing court) is responsible for reviewing public expenditure and auditing state-run companies. It can be tasked by the national assembly to investigate the government's management of public resources. Despite its name, it is not a court, but an administrative body under the authority of the national assembly. Its mission is to assist the national assembly in the performance of its constitutional oversight duties of the executive, public services and enterprises. Unfortunately, it is as ineffective as the national assembly to which it reports. Its recommendations are largely ignored by public institutions as well as by the national assembly itself. No single state organ or official has been investigated, prosecuted and convicted on the basis of the documented reports of the *Cour des Comptes*, and the national assembly itself has so fair paid little attention to its recommendations.

The judiciary

In line with the powers vested in it by the constitution, the primary role in combatting corruption, money laundering and the financing of terrorism should be played by the judiciary, which is designed to be independent and impartial. However, as emphasised earlier, the judiciary lacks independence and suffers from widespread political interference and generalised corruption. It is largely dependent on the president of the republic and his government. The justice minister also tends to behave as the line manager of the members of the judiciary, especially the prosecutors. The minister has the power to instruct them and decide who should be investigated, prosecuted, sentenced or not.

In February 2008, President Kabila forced 89 judges into retirement, including the president of the supreme court of justice and the prosecutor general, and replaced them with 28 largely unqualified magistrates appointed on the basis of patronage and political

---

80 See US Department of State (2012) International Narcotics Control Strategy Report (INCSR) – Volume II: Money Laundering and Financial Crimes. Available at www.state.gov/j/inl/rls/nrcrpt/2012/database/191291.htm [accessed on 30 July 2016]; Transparency International (2014) Overview of Corruption and Anti-Corruption in the Democratic Republic of Congo (DRC). Available at http://www.transparency.org/files/content/corruptionqas/Country_Profile_DRC_2014.pdf [accessed 21 December 2016].

clientelism. The presidential ordinance could be declared unconstitutional and invalid by the supreme court of justice acting as a constitutional court, which was still to be established. While the supreme court decided to keep quiet, the African Commission of Human and Peoples' Rights recently ruled that the presidential ordinance violated the rights of the members of the judiciary who had been retired or dismissed and ordered the DRC government to reinstate them.[81]

Furthermore, the Congolese courts are reported to give favourable verdicts to the highest bidders or those close to the ruling political elite.[82] They are particularly harsh towards the elite's opponents. The case of Mr Moise Katumbi – a former governor of Katanga, who resigned from all his duties and announced his candidacy in the forthcoming presidential election – demonstrates how far the president, his government and the ruling coalition can go in manipulating the courts and using them to serve their political interests. Several charges of fraud were fomented against Mr Katumbi and the judiciary was obliged to sentence him *in abstentia* just to remove him from the political competition. Mrs Ramazani Wazuri, the judge-president of the Kamalondo tribunal in Lubumbashi, denounced this situation, acknowledging that her signature on the judgment sentencing Moise Katumbi to a three years' imprisonment had actually been forced by high-ranking officials in the presidency of the republic, the government, the security services and her own superiors in the judiciary.[83] However, Mr Katumbi was not prosecuted and convicted for corruption. Earlier, presidential special advisor Luzolo Bambi, who was justice minister at the time, had publicly announced that several governors of provinces would be investigated as part of the presidential campaign of 'zero-tolerance' towards corruption.[84] Unfortunately, the charges were dropped and no single governor was prosecuted, let alone convicted.

In spite of the strong anti-corruption legal framework, this study cannot report on any single case of a high-profile official or politician being prosecuted, judged, or convicted for corruption or corruption-related offences. This has contributed to fuelling a culture of impunity and cynicism in the DRC.[85]

As has recently happened in the case of Mr Kimbembe Mazunga, the chief executive officer of ONATRA (national office of transportation, a public enterprise) – or earlier with

---

81 See La requête des magistrats congolais reçue par la Commission Africaine des Droits de l'Homme et des Peuples (2013, 18 September) *Le Phare*. Available at http://www.lephareonline.net/la-requete-des-magistrats-congolais-recue-par-la-commission-africaine-des-droits-de-lhomme-et-des-peuples/ [accessed 21 December 2016].
82 See Bertelsmann Foundation (2014) BTI 2014 Democratic Republic of Congo Country Report. Available at www.btiproject.de/uploads/tx_jpdownloads/BTI_2014_Congo_DR.pdf [accessed 30 July 2016].
83 Condamnation de Katumbi: la juge Ramazani Wazuri dit avoir subi des menaces (2016, 29 July) *Radio Okapi*. Available at http://www.radiookapi.net/2016/07/29/actualite/justice/condamnation-de-katumbi-la-juge-ramazani-wazuri-dit-avoir-subi-des [accessed 23 December 2016].
84 RDC: Kabila porte plainte pour corruption contre quatre gouverneurs, dont Katumbi (2015, 25 June) *Le Vif*. Available at http://www.levif.be/actualite/international/rdc-kabila-porte-plainte-pour-corruption-contre-quatre-gouverneurs-dont-katumbi/article-normal-402393.html [accessed 23 December 2016].
85 Kodi M (2007) Anti-corruption Challenges in Post-election Democratic Republic of Congo, Chatham House Report. Available https://www.chathamhouse.org/publications/papers/view/108381 [accessed 21 December 2016].

professors Evariste Boshab, Lumanu Nsefu and Beya Siku, chiefs of staff in the presidency – the only sanction faced by corrupt high-ranking officials has consisted in their suspension … and redeployment. Not a single one has been prosecuted and the judiciary has not played any significant role in combatting corruption. This has also been denounced by the office of the special advisor, who himself wrote to the president and complained about the public prosecutor's lack of collaboration and commitment in the prosecution of high-ranking corrupt officials.[86]

Other stakeholders in the fight against corruption
From 16–19 December 2009, the DRC hosted a *Forum national sur la lutte contre la corruption* (national forum on the fight against corruption). The forum recommended the creation of a number of anti-corruption institutions such as a national council of ethics, an independent commission on ethics and the fight against corruption, a government anti-corruption agency, and an ombudsman.[87] All these institutions have yet to be established.

A number of parliamentarians have also joined in the fight by adhering to tenets of the Organisation of Parliamentarians against Corruption. A Congolese section of the Network of African Parliamentarians against Corruption was established under the leadership of the Hon. Jean Pierre Pasi Zapamba Buka.[88] In 2015, the Network organised a seminar on corruption and initiated a national campaign in partnership with the Open Society Initiative for Southern Africa (OSISA).[89] Unfortunately, its recommendations have been ignored. Other stakeholders in the fight against corruption include the media, CSOs, human rights activists and all DRC citizens. However, whistleblowers are not protected and many journalists, reporters and human rights activists have been silenced, intimidated or prosecuted for defamation.

---

86 See Obstruction aux enquêtes: Luzolo Bambi accuse le PGR (2016, 24 June) *Politico*. Available at http://www.politico.cd/actualite/la-une/2016/06/24/obstruction-aux-enquetes-luzolo-bambi-accuse-pgr.html [accessed 21 December 2016]; Luzolo Bambi: 'La corruption est devenue endémique, il faut l'arrêter' (2015, 5 August) *Radio Okapi*. Available at http://www.radiookapi.net/emissions-2/linvite-du-jour/2015/05/05/luzolo-bambi-la-corruption-est-devenue-endemique-il-faut-larreter [accessed 21 December 2016]. https://edrcrdf.wordpress.com/2015/05/08/je-denonce-jedenonce2015gmail-com-luzolo-bambi-a-la-chasse-de-ces-vieux-demons http://congonouveau.org/lutte-contre-corruption-mur-personnes-visees-menacent-luzolo-bambi/ [accessed on 30 July 2016].
87 See En RDC, la corruption assimilée à 'une pandémie qui détruit le tissu socioéconomique' (no date) *Le Potentiel Online*. Available at https://www.lepotentielonline.com/index.php?option=com_content&view=article&id=4867:en-rdc-la-corruption-assimilee-a-une-pandemie-qui-detruit-le-tissu-socio economique&catid=90&Itemid=514 [accessed 21 December 2016].
88 Le Parlement de RDC s'engage dans la lutte contre la corruption (2015, 17 January) *Kongo Times*. Available at http://afrique.kongotimes.info/mobile/mobile/rdc/parlement/8889-parlement-rdc-engage-dans-lutte-contre-corruption.html [accessed 21 December 2016].
89 See Pour lutter contre la corruption en RDC:L'Apnac exige le changement de mentalité (2015, 4 April) *7sur7*. Available at http://7sur7.cd/new/pour-lutter-contre-la-corruption-en-rdclapnac-exige-le-changement-de-mentalite/ [accessed 21 December 2016]; https://www.facebook.com/pages/Apnac-Rdc/1538701473010374 [accessed 30 July 2016].

E. Office of the Presidential Special Advisor on Good Governance, Corruption, Money Laundering and the Financing of Terrorism

This office (discussed here previously as the office of the special advisor) was created to fill the gap since there was no anti-corruption body established by the constitution or a parliamentary act. At this juncture, it is worth providing the background to the creation of this office and examining the mandate of the special advisor prior to assessing his autonomy, administrative and financial independence, and performance.

Background

On 31 March 2015, President Joseph Kabila appointed Professor Luzolo Bambi, a former minister of justice and a criminal law professor at the University of Kinshasa, to serve as his special advisor on good governance, corruption, money laundering, and the financing of terrorism.[90] The appointment of Luzolo, who had initiated the 'zero-tolerance' campaign against corruption when he was the minister of justice, sent the message that the DRC government had decided to take the fight for good governance and the war on corruption, money laundering and the financing of terrorism more seriously. Professor Luzolo's appointment was therefore welcomed and expectations were high that he would finally deliver on his earlier commitments. However, the special advisor was only one of the presidential advisors with no specific status or powers in the presidency. His mandate was to 'advise' the president and recommend measures aimed at fighting corruption, not to prosecute or bring to justice the presumed corrupt officials. He was therefore weak and the ordinance appointing him did not provide for the relationships with other state organs involved in the fight against crimes, especially the judiciary.

To overcome these challenges, President Joseph Kabila signed another ordinance detailing the competences of the presidential special advisor and providing for the organisation and the functioning of his office.[91]

Mandate, autonomy, administrative and financial independence

Presidential Ordinance No. 16/065 of 14 July 2016 provides for the mandate, organisation and functioning of the office of the special advisor.

Mandate

In terms of this ordinance, the special advisor is vested with the following powers:
- Initiate and recommend to the head of state any strategies and policies to be enforced by the institutions of the republic in order to promote

---

90 Ordinance No. 15/021 of 31 March 2015, *Journal Officiel de la République Démocratique du Congo.*
91 Ordinance No. 16/065 of 14 July 2016, 1 August 2016, *Journal Officiel de la République Démocratique du Congo.*, Première Partie, No.15. pp. 23–26.

good governance and fight against corruption, money laundering and the financing of terrorism;
- Initiate any investigations, inquiries, and proceedings to help identify, prosecute and punish any person or group of persons, organisations, entities, enterprises or other services involved in corruption, money laundering and the financing of terrorism;
- Cooperate with the general inspection of finances, financial intelligence unit and other relevant services in order to open preliminary investigations prior to bringing before the courts the cases of corruption, money laundering and the financing of terrorism, fraud, brought to his attention by the head of state or any whistleblowers;
- Monitor the acts of corruption, money laundering and the financing of terrorism;
- Recommend to the head of state the measures and possible sanctions, depending on each case or circumstance in line with the constitution and the laws of the republic, in order to facilitate the cooperation with the investigating or prosecuting authorities. To this end, some members of the office of the special advisor are vested with the authority of judicial police officers with jurisdiction across the country;
- The special advisor can resort to the services of the competent prosecuting authorities and the minister of justice for any act of his competence to initiate public action after informing the president of the republic;[92]
- The special advisor can also request any person or service to assist him in the determination of the cases under his examination after informing the chief of staff of the president. The requested person or service is obliged to respond.[93]

Autonomy

In carrying out his responsibilities, the special advisor is assisted by a cabinet that he appoints (and may also dismiss), consisting of a chief of staff, a deputy chief of staff, principal advisors, special envoys, a personal assistant, analysts, and a technical secretariat headed by a technical assistant. The size of the cabinet is determined by the chief of staff and can change depending on what is required. The special advisor can also request the cooperation of other services after securing authorisation of the chief of staff.[94]

---

92 Ordinance No. 16/065 of 14 July 2016, 1 August 2016, *Journal Officiel de la République Démocratique du Congo* Première Partie, No.15, p. 24, article 2.
93 Ibid., article 3.
94 Ibid., articles 5 & 6.

The special advisor and his office staff are members of the cabinet of the president, which is under the leadership of the chief of staff. The special advisor reports to the chief of staff before reporting to the president. The position and role of the chief of staff in the organisation and functioning of the office of the special advisor impact negatively on its autonomy. However, the special advisor enjoys some autonomy as compared to other presidential advisors. He or she is obliged to inform the chief of staff of the president before requesting the expertise of anyone or any public service outside his office[95] or be expressly authorised by the chief of staff when he or she needs their services.[96] However, the special advisor is entitled to appoint and even dismiss the members of his/her own office (cabinet) even though the chief of staff has to be informed before any decision is taken.[97]

Administrative and financial independence

As an integral part of the president's cabinet, the office of the special advisor has no administrative or financial independence. This is due to the role of the chief of staff in the determination of the size of the personnel of his office, in their appointment and dismissal. The budget and logistical means required for the functioning of the services of the special advisor are determined by the president of the republic.[98] The same goes for the remuneration and other perks due to the special advisor and the members of his office.[99]

Performance

As stressed earlier, the special advisor on good governance, corruption, and related crimes was only appointed on 31 March 2015. At the time, his mandate was similar to that of other advisors in the presidency: advise the president, initiate and recommend any strategies and policies to be enforced by the institutions of the republic in order to promote good governance and the fight against corruption and related crimes.

It was only on 14 July 2016 that the president signed an ordinance that established a cabinet for the special advisor, making it a quasi-judicial institution with powers to investigate and prosecute any case of mal governance, corruption, money laundering and financing of terrorism. This ordinance also gave some administrative autonomy to the special advisor, who could appoint and dismiss his staff. The first priority of the special advisor since the coming into force of the presidential ordinance was to find offices for his cabinet away from the presidency in order to make it easily accessible to the people and other stakeholders involved in the fight against corruption and related crimes. The second was to recruit competent personnel. A few months after its establishment, it is somewhat premature to assess the office's performance. However, some lessons can be learned from its initial activitiess.

---

95 Ibid., article 3.
96 Ibid., article 5.
97 Ibid., article 6.
98 Ibid., article 9.
99 Ibid., article 10.

The special advisor started his work on a high note by initiating investigations, inquiries, and proceedings which could help identify, prosecute and punish the managers of two public enterprises, namely Mr Constantin Mbengele, chief executive officer of the *Fonds de la Promotion de l'Industrie* (Funds for the Promotion of Industry – FPI), and his colleague of *Régie des Voies Aériennes* (Airports Company – RVA). After both failed to respond to his invitation to be heard on the charges against them, the special advisor dispatched his personnel to arrest them. In the meantime, he issued an order preventing them from leaving the country during the investigations and requested other public services, such as the security services and the judiciary, to cooperate with his office. These investigations hit the headlines in July–August 2016. The two managers belong to the ruling coalition and are close to the president and the prime minister. After a few weeks, during which time they went into hiding and even attempted to leave the DRC for fear of prosecution and arrest, they publicly returned to their offices. The relevant security services and the public prosecutor, who should have facilitated their arrest, did not cooperate with the special advisor as required by the presidential ordinance establishing his office.[100] The charges seem to have been dropped for political reasons, disappointing many people who had hoped the special advisor would play a major role in fighting the scourge of corruption by targeting the high-profile officials involved in grand corruption. Although it is premature to make conclusions, the special advisor has so far failed to deliver on his mandate of combatting corruption in the DRC. Unless there is some positive change in the political, legal and social environment, it is unlikely that the DRC will ever win the fight against corruption or even reduce its negative impact.

F. Findings

- Endemic and rampant corruption taking place on the African continent in general and in Southern Africa hampers development, peace, democracy and good governance.
- Despite legal and political developments and progress that has been made in some African countries, little change has actually occurred in terms of governance on the continent. The scourge of corruption remains unabated, resulting in the worsening of the state of governance and the living conditions of the overwhelming majority of African people to the benefit of a few corrupt leaders, their entourages and associates.
- Many high-ranking officials referred to as 'criminals with ties' are involved in corrupt acts.[101] The DRC is one of the worst cases of

---

100 See Obstruction aux enquêtes: Luzolo Bambi accuse le PGR (2016, 24 June) *Politico*. Available at http://www.politico.cd/actualite/la-une/2016/06/24/obstruction-aux-enquetes-luzolo-bambi-accuse-pgr.html [accessed 21 December 2016].
101 This emanated from a meeting with the presidential special advisor in July 2016 and from several

- governance and corruption in Southern Africa. Corruption has become a normal way of life, affecting all the sectors of society.
- The presidential special advisor has complained several times to the president that other law enforcement services – especially the general prosecutor, the police, the security services and even the government – are not cooperating in the fight against corruption because of their own involvement. Until the Ordinance of 14 July 2016, he had failed to get the required backing from the president of the republic, signalling the lack of strong political will to combat corruption despite numerous statements to the contrary from the presidency.
- There is no single court case involving a right ranking official (minister, governor, chief executive officer of a public enterprise or service) who has been prosecuted and sentenced for corruption. In March 2015, the president signed an ordinance dismissing 38 public service servants in the department of finance for corruption.[102] However, they were not prosecuted.
- The establishment of the office of the special advisor represents a positive development in the fight against corruption, which is multifaceted, rampant and systemic in the DRC. Located in the office of the president of the republic, the highest political institution in the country, the appointment of the special advisor invested with important powers and directly reporting to him raised hopes that President Kabila was committed to fighting corruption during his second and last term of office, constitutionally ending on 19 December 2016. There were renewed expectations that this time around, the President could deliver on his early promise of putting an end to the 'recreation' by opening the doors of prisons to all those who were involved in the 'business' of corruption and by adopting and

---

other public statements from his Office. See Luzolo Bambi: 'La corruption est devenue endémique, il faut l'arrêter' (2015, 5 August) *Radio Okapi*. Available at http://www.radiookapi.net/emissions-2/linvite-du-jour/2015/05/05/luzolo-bambi-la-corruption-est-devenue-endemique-il-faut-larreter [accessed 21 December 2016]; Spoliation des immeubles de l'Etat: Luzolo dénonce Egwake dans une note confidentielle à Kabila et Matata (2016, 14 March) *Africa News*. Available at http://www.africanewsrdc.com/politique/2016/03/14/luzolo-denonce-note-confidentielle-a-kabila-et-matata.html [accessed 21 December 2016]; Je dénonce 'jedenonce2015@gmail.com': Luzolo Bambi à la chasse de ces vieux démons? (2015, 8 May) *The Eastern Congo Tribune*. Available at https://edrcrdf.wordpress.com/2015/05/08/je-denonce-jedenonce2015gmail-com-luzolo-bambi-a-la-chasse-de-ces-vieux-demons/ [accessed 21 December 2016]; Dos Au Mur, Les Personnes Visées Menacent Luzolo Bambi (2016, 4 July) *Congonouveau*. Available at http://congonouveau.org/lutte-contre-corruption-mur-personnes-visees-menacent-luzolo-bambi/ [accessed 21 December 2016].

102 See Corruption: Le président Kabila révoque à la pelle (liste complète des révoqués ci-dessous) (2016, 5 May) *7sur7*. Available at http://7sur7.cd/new/corruptionle-president-kabila-revoque-a-la-pelle-liste-complete-des-revoques-ci-dessous/ [accessed 21 December 2016].

enforcing a 'zero-tolerance' policy against corruption. Unfortunately, expectations were too high.

- While being located in the presidency, which could constitute its strength, this actually impacts negatively on the fight against corruption. First, this is a political position. The special advisor is a politician appointed by the president, who can also dismiss him at will. His appointment is political and he would not survive a change of president. The special advisor has no fixed term limits, he is dependent on the president and lacks independence. As a member of the ruling party/coalition, he cannot act against the president and the first family, or against their political and business allies. It is unlikely that the special adviser would act in the same way as South Africa's now former public protector Tuli Mandonsela did against President Jacob Zuma. Lack of independence and autonomy are therefore the main weakness of the office. Second, as the designation implies, the main task of the special advisor is to 'advise' the president. There is no direct line of collaboration with other oversight institutions such as parliament and the judiciary. Third, the private sector is excluded from the jurisdiction of the special advisor despite the fact that corruption is rampant in all sectors, including the private sector. Four, foreign states and multinational companies are also involved in corruption. Unfortunately, the ordinance establishing the office of the special advisor does not refer to judicial cooperation or legal assistance. It also ignores corrupt acts committed by the officials of foreign states and the representatives of foreign or multinational companies.

- The office of the special advisor was established after the DRC ratified the UNCAC and the SADC Protocol, and after it signed the AUPCC, which was finally ratified on 9 November 2016. However, it does not comply with these instruments and is not the specialised body state parties are required to establish. With regard to the UNCAC, the ordinance governing the office of the special advisor does include corruption in the private sector,[103] and the participation of society.[104] It does not elaborate on money laundering,[105] the financing of terrorism, the criminalisation of law enforcement agents involved in corruption,[106] the bribery of foreign public officials and officials of public international organisations,[107] the embezzlement,

---

103 Article 12 of the UNCAC.
104 Ibid., article 13.
105 Ibid., article 14.
106 Ibid., article 15.
107 Ibid., article 16.

misappropriation or other diversion of property by a public official,[108] trading in influence,[109] abuse of functions,[110] illicit enrichment,[111] bribery and embezzlement of property in the private sector,[112] laundering of proceeds of crime,[113] concealment,[114] obstruction of justice,[115] freezing, seizure and confiscation,[116] protection of witnesses, experts and victims,[117] protection of reporting persons,[118] and international cooperation.[119] The UNAC provides that each state party should ensure the existence of a body or bodies or persons specialised in combatting corruption through law enforcement and such body or bodies or persons should be granted the necessary independence to carry out their functions effectively and without any undue influence. Such persons should have the appropriate training and resources to carry out their duties.[120] Unfortunately, the office of the special advisor does not comply with any of these stipulations. The ordinance does not even comply with the SADC Protocol, which is a weak instrument in the fight against corruption since the office of the special advisor is not the competent organ to report to the committee established for the implementation of the SADC Protocol.[121]

G. Recommendations

Corruption threatens the social fabric and undermines the accountability and transparency in the management of public affairs as well as socio-economic development in many African countries, including the DRC. Accordingly, the fight against corruption should be taken seriously and efforts should be made to ensure that that 'zero-tolerance' for corruption ceases to be an empty slogan to become a reality.

---

108 Ibid., article 17.
109 Ibid., article 18.
110 Ibid., article 19.
111 Ibid., article 20.
112 Ibid., articles 21 & 22.
113 Ibid., article 23.
114 Ibid., article 24.
115 Ibid., article 25.
116 Ibid., article 31.
117 Ibid., article 32.
118 Ibid., articles 10 & 33.
119 Ibid., article 43.
120 Ibid., article 6.2.
121 SADC Protocol, article 11.

Policy

- As a state party to the UNCAC, the AUCPCC and the SADC Protocol against Corruption, the DRC should adopt legislative and other measures to prevent and combat all forms of corruption and related offences in the public and private sectors, encourage the participation of the private sector and citizenry in the fight against corruption, prevent companies from paying bribes to win tenders, proscribe the use of funds acquired through illegal and corrupt practices to finance political parties, incorporate the principle of transparency into funding of political parties, give effect to the right of access to any information that is required to assist in the fight against corruption and related offences, proscribe any illicit enrichment, and hold corrupt persons in the public and private sectors accountable and take appropriate action against persons who commit acts of corruption in the performance of their functions and duties, in full compliance with its international obligations.
- The country should harmonise its policies and domestic legislation in order to prevent and punish corruption and establish enforceable standards of good conduct for public officials, leaders of political parties and managers of companies.
- Strong political will and leadership are essential ingredients for waging an effective war against the scourge of corruption.
- The DRC should establish an effective and independent anti-corruption body to fight against corruption. The Office of the Special Advisor on Good Governance, Corruption, Money Laundering and the Financing of Terrorism as a political position established by a presidential ordinance and not by the constitution or an act of parliament, and which is subjected to the president, does not qualify as the kind of independent anti-corruption body prescribed by the UNCAC and AUCPCC.
- Having signed the African Charter on Democracy, Elections and Governance, which is also aimed at combatting corruption, the DRC should also ratify, and comply with, it.

Institutional

- The independent anti-corruption body in the DRC should regularly report on the fight against corruption, collect and document information on corruption and related offences in the country, and collect information and analyse the conduct or behaviour of foreign officials and multinational companies.

- Other state organs, especially the judiciary, CSOs and the private sector should cooperate with such an anti-corruption body in order to prevent, detect, prosecute and eradicate the scourge of corruption in the country.
- People should be well trained and motivated to effectively fight against corruption.
- Public anti-corruption campaigns and training programmes should be organised regularly to raise public awareness about the pernicious effects of the scourge of corruption.
- The DRC anti-corruption body should also cooperate with similar bodies on the continent to effectively fight against corruption and related offences.

Citizen action

- Either individually or collectively through CSOs, citizens should play an important role in the fight against corruption in all its forms. They should participate as whistleblowers to denounce perpetrators of corruption, and also become active participants in the fight against this scourge.
- In as much as corruption permeates all the sectors of life, the fight against it should be made a people's affair including everybody in the country, and with the assistance of the international community.
- Civil society and the media should be at the forefront of this fight.
- At the regional and sub-regional levels, the AU and SADC should put pressure on member states such as the DRC to comply with the AUCPCC and the SADC fully, monitor states' compliance on the basis of a number of indicators of good governance, and promote regional cooperation in the fight against corruption, money laundering and the financing of terrorism among law enforcement agents.

5
LESOTHO

Dr Motlamelle Anthony Kapa

A. Executive summary

This report assesses the effectiveness of the Directorate on Corruption and Economic Offences (DCEO) since its establishment in 2003. It focuses on:
- The extent to which Lesotho aligns itself with international instruments against corruption;
- The legal framework for combating corruption;
- Staffing issues of the anti-corruption body;
- Responsibilities and prosecutorial powers of the DCEO;
- Relations between the DCEO and its key stakeholders in the fight against corruption;
- The DCEO's financial resources; and
- The overall performance of the DCEO in combating corruption.

Interviews were conducted with respondents from civil society organisations (CSOs) with a focus on good governance, as well as with the top leadership of the DCEO. Relevant international instruments against corruption, academic material, appropriate laws and reports on the DCEO, and newspaper reports were also used.

The study finds that the DCEO's performance has not been quantitatively impressive, particularly on the prosecution of corruption cases, due to the many challenges the agency faces. However, the agency has, in recent years, been bold to embark on investigating cases of grand corruption involving very powerful individuals, whose cases are still pending in the courts of law.

B. The state of corruption in Lesotho

Corruption pervades all societies to varying degrees, causing more harm in some than in others. The United Nations (UN) regards corruption as 'an insidious plague' that poses serious threat to stability and security of societies. It undermines the institutions and values of democracy, ethical values and justice; jeopardising sustainable development and the rule of law.[1] In similar a vein, the African Union (AU) notes that corruption 'undermines accountability and transparency in the management of public affairs as well as socio-economic development on the continent'.[2]

While there are many ways of defining corruption, Transparency International defines it aptly as 'the abuse of entrusted power for private gain' and classifies it into three categories,[3] depending on the amount of money involved, and where it occurs. The first category is grand corruption, which consists of:

> Acts committed at a high level of government that distort policies or the central government functioning of the state, enabling leaders to benefit at the expense of the public good.

The second is petty corruption, which refers to:

> Everyday abuse of entrusted power by low- and mid-level public officials in their interactions with ordinary citizens, who often are trying to access basic goods or services in places like hospitals, schools, police departments and other agencies.

The last is political corruption, which involves:

> A manipulation of policies, institutions and rules of procedure in the allocation of resources and financing by political decision makers, who abuse their position to sustain power, status and wealth.

This is how corruption is conceived in this report.

Since its return to multi-party politics in 1993 (after a hiatus of 23 years), Lesotho has consistently been receiving favourable reports in terms of its attempt to fight corruption. The general picture emerging from assessments of public perception about corruption in Lesotho, carried out by external organisations, is that the country is doing better than other African countries in combatting corruption. Recent results from two of these organisations, namely, Transparency International's Corruption Perception Index and the Mo Ibrahim Foundation are the most useful, for the purposes of this report. The 2015 report from Transparency International and the Afrobarometer[4] shows that only 5% of people surveyed in Lesotho say they paid a bribe in the previous year. This makes Lesotho the fourth least corrupt country in Africa after Mauritius, Botswana and Cape Verde,

---

1 UN (2004) *United Nations Convention against Corruption*. New York: UN. p. 5.
2 AU (2003) *African Union Convention on Prevention and Combating Corruption*. Adopted by the 2nd Ordinary Session of the Assembly of the Union, Maputo, 11 July 2003.
3 Transparency International. Available at www.transparency.org./what-is-corruption [accessed 28 September 2015].
4 Pring C (2015) *People and Corruption: Africa Survey 2015, Global Corruption Barometer*. Berlin: Transparency International.

respectively. In addition, 60% of people surveyed in Lesotho believe that ordinary people can make a difference in the fight against corruption. This is a very useful finding because it speaks to potential for a missing variable in corruption discourse – one of popular will (deliberate action by society to tackle corruption) to fight corruption. It shows that the majority of citizens are not indifferent about corruption, nor do they condone it; they believe they have a stake in combating it. The small percentage of those who paid a bribe in 2014 may suggest that, not only do Basotho regard corruption bad, but they actually act against it by not paying a bribe; thus reducing the incidence of corruption in the country as the reports have been indicating consistently. Similarly, in 2014, Transparency International rated Lesotho at 55 out of 174 countries and territories globally, an improvement from 45 in 2012.[5]

The Mo Ibrahim African overall governance index scores Lesotho at 61.1 out of 100 in overall governance, an overall improvement of 2.2 since 2011. It is also in the top ten out of 54 African countries in overall governance; a score which places it higher than both the African average and the regional average for Southern Africa; it ranks fifth in overall governance in the Southern African region.[6]

According to Mr Litelu Ramokhoro, director for training and public education, Lesotho is working towards conducting its own national survey on corruption. This exercise has been budgeted for already and tender documents are being prepared with the assistance of the commonwealth secretariat. The expectation is that it will have commenced before the end of 2015. This survey is intended to give a much clear picture than is presently available.[7]

This generally positive picture regarding the state of corruption notwithstanding, perceptions of corruptions in both grand and petty forms persist.

Politics of corruption

A former British colony from 1868 to 1966, Lesotho inherited state institutions established, not to promote democratic principles, good governance and accountability, but to serve as instruments of control, law and order maintenance, and extraction of economic resources.[8] Perhaps this explains why the anti-corruption agency was not even provided for in the national constitution, even after the 1993 transition to multi-party politics and constitutional rule.

With very limited natural resources and an export-oriented, low-wage textile industry,[9] Lesotho has a very weak economic base. Its traditional and main source of revenue,

---

5   Transparency International (2014) *Corruption Perspective Index 2014*. Berlin: Transparency International.
6   Mo Ibrahim Foundation (2015) *Ibrahim Index of African Governance 2015*.
7   Interview with Mr Litelu Ramokhoro, Director for Training and Public Education, Maseru, 7 September2015.
8   Clapham C (1985) *Third World Politics: An Introduction*. Wisconsin: The University of Wisconsin Press. Chapter 3.
9   Under the United States African Growth and Opportunity Act, which employs about 47 971 people as at the end of December 2014, a figure slightly higher than that of the public sector employment of 44 234 during the same period. Central Bank of Lesotho (2013) *Annual Report 2013*. Maseru: Central Bank of Lesotho. p. 15.

the Southern African Customs Union (SACU), which accounted for 50% of the total government revenue, faces challenges.[10] The South African mining industry, the main source of employment for the Basotho for about a century, has not been employing new workers in recent years; it has, in fact, been retrenching those who were already employed in large numbers. Their numbers declined by about 9.5% (from 37 051 to 33 513) between December 2012 and December 2013.[11] This compounds the already high level of unemployment, estimated at 25.3%.[12] Lesotho is ranked 162 out of 187 countries in terms of human development.[13] Lesotho's human development index is also low at 0.486 (in 2013); down to 0.313, when accounting for inequality. Life expectancy is similarly low at 49.4 years in 2013, down by 4.4 years from 53.8 in 1980. About 49.5% of the population is multi-dimensionally poor (i.e. suffers from multiple deprivations in education, health and living standards), while 18.2% live in severe poverty, and 43.4% live below the income poverty line of USD 1.25 a day.[14]

The above is, generally, the socio-economic context in which the discourse on corruption has to be understood in Lesotho. Corruption has always featured in Lesotho with government not taking a decisive action against it; this is potentially a demonstration of a lack of political will. While a nebulous concept, political will would, in this context, be defined as: deliberate action of government against those alleged to be corrupt; allocation of resources in anti-corruption endeavours and institutions and, more importantly, prosecuting those implicated in corrupt activities irrespective of their social or political positions. Several cases of grand corruption are instructive; government's political will to deal with them has varied, largely depending on who was the head of government. In other words, political will has not been institutionalised such that it is a defining feature of the political system. But, as indicated earlier, ordinary citizens of Lesotho believe that they can reduce corruption, implying the potential for popular will, though it is not clear how this can be achieved.

That Lesotho seems to be doing so well in corruption perception assessments is an enigma, given the cases of grand corruption. One of the main cases was the sale of Lesotho's international passports to Chinese nationals in the early 1990s, under a scheme devised by the Lesotho National Development Corporation (LNDC), a parastatal organisation created to attract foreign direct investment in Lesotho. The scheme was designed to award Lesotho passports to wealthy individuals under a newly established consulate in Hong Kong, so that they could come and invest in the local economy. A certain Ms Lydia Wu was identified as Lesotho's honorary consular based in Hong Kong to facilitate the process of identifying and attracting potential investors. Corrupt high-ranking individuals within

---

10 Parliament of the Kingdom of Lesotho, Budget Speech to Parliament for the 2015/16 Fiscal Year, by Dr 'Mamphono Khaketla, Minister of Finance, 22 May 2015.
11 Central Bank of Lesotho (2013) *Annual Report 2013*. Maseru: Central Bank of Lesotho. p. 16.
12 Bureau of Statistics. Available at http://www.bos.gov.ls [accessed 3 December 2015].
13 United Nations Development Programme (2014) *Human Development Report 2014*. Available from http://www.undp.org/content/lesotho/en [accessed 3 December 2015].
14 Ibid.

the military government working with Ms Wu sold these passports at an estimated USD 2 800 per individual and USD 3 300 per family, to poor Chinese nationals, collecting an estimated USD 8 million. A commission of inquiry was set up by the military government[15] but no prosecutions were made.

The most cited grand corruption case, which put Lesotho on the map in terms of fighting corruption involved bribery in the Lesotho Highlands Water Project (LHWP), the largest water transfer project in the world, between Lesotho and the Republic of South Africa. Under this project, Lesotho signed a treaty in October 1986 with the Republic of South Africa, in which the former sells water to the latter. Several multinational corporations were accused of having paid bribes to the chief executive of the Lesotho Highlands Development Authority (LHDA),[16] Mr Masopha Sole, for the award of the project-related contracts. After protracted court cases, Sole was found guilty of accepting bribes and sentenced to 15 years imprisonment, which he served. Several of these companies were fined tens of millions of US dollars.[17]

After the 2012 elections, Lesotho's first coalition government declared in its policy document that it would fight corruption and strengthen the relevant institutions, including the DCEO, and implement policy on declaration of assets by public servants.[18] This undertaking was forcefully implemented first when, for the first time in the history of Lesotho, a minister (Timothy Thahane) was charged with corruption and fired from his ministerial position. He always maintained that he was innocent and the charges were politically motivated. He later contested elections in his constituency as an independent candidate but lost to the All Basotho Convention (ABC) candidate. Another case concerned the deputy leader of the Democratic Congress (DC), Mr Monyane Moleleki, as to the irregularities regarding the granting of mining licences to some companies. The case was postponed several times due to his serious illness. The case is still pending at the time of writing.[19]

We are yet to see if this case will continue now that the DC is back in power. Similarly, Mr Mothetjoa Metsing, who was deputy prime minister in the Thabane-led coalition government, also has corruption cases to answer to after his bid to stop them failed in the court of appeal. Whether or not these will also proceed under the current government (in which he is still deputy prime minister) remains to be seen. However, the post-February 2015 elections seven-party coalition government has indicated in its agreement that it will 'make transparency and good governance a hallmark of the government' and 'eliminate corruption at all levels of society and government'.[20] The coalition government comprises

---

15 Machobane LBB (2001) *Kings Knights: Military Governance in the Kingdom of Lesotho, 1986–1993*. Roma: Department of History, National University of Lesotho. pp. 129–131.
16 An institution tasked with the implementation, supervision and maintenance of the LHWP in Lesotho.
17 Earle A (2007) The role of governance in countering corruption: An African case study. *Water Policy* 9(2): 18.
18 ABC, LCD & BNP (2012) Leano la `Muso oa Kopanelo, 2012–2017. Maseru, Unpublished.
19 Tefo T (2015, 13 August) Moleleki's 'Corruption case postponed once again'. *Lesotho Times*. Available at www.lestimes.com/moleleki-corruption-case-postponed-once-again/ [accessed 29 September 2015].
20 The Coalition Agreement for Stability and Reform: Lesotho's Second Coalition Government Agreement, April 2015.

the following parties: the DC, the Lesotho Congress for Democracy (LCD), the Popular Front for Democracy (PFD), the Marematlou Freedom Party (MFP), the Basotho Congress Party (BCP), the National Independence Party (NIP), and the Lesotho People's Congress (LPC).

It is also worth noting that the post-2012 polls coalition government inherited a system in which there have been widespread cases of corruption, but no action taken by its predecessor to correct the situation. The Public Accounts Committee Report to the Eighth Parliament[21] exposes massive cases of corruption across the whole public service and recommends that those responsible be held accountable; particularly the chief accounting officers. Nothing was done about this report. The coalition government got locked up in internal feuds, which ultimately led to its untimely demise. Whether or not this report will be followed up, especially when it covers the period during which the senior partners in this coalition government were in government, is a moot point.

In concluding this section, it is worth indicating that the issue of political will to combat corruption is complex in the context of Lesotho and seems to depend on who is the head of government at the time. Only two cases involving senior bureaucrats with limited political power (Masopha Sole and Matlamukele Matete) have been closed, while those involving powerful politicians are repeatedly postponed. It was under the first coalition government led by Thomas Thabane that prosecution of high profile politicians began, although it did not increase the budget of the DCEO. These processes have, however, either been stalled or have been moving at a snail's pace, with some cases perpetually postponed in the courts – perhaps for technical reasons rather than political interference. The DCEO director-general dismissed the theory of political interference in the work of the agency, though. He said:

> As corruption busters, we in our respective countries, we know we are regarded as endangered species, especially we heads of these units. That is because every time you try to go for government authorities, you are quickly threatened with redeployment, if not dismissal. ... So far I must tell you that we have not, as the DCEO, encountered such instances that we can really say our investigations and cases were hindered due to political interference. We just have cases of individuals trying to resist through proper channels of the law and at the end of the day, there is only one winner, the DCEO. We hit wherever we want without fear or favour. We are ready to take down anyone involved in crime, no-matter their status. We have a government that has undertaken to fight corruption and it has shown this by increasing our budget for this financial year. For the first time, we are able to improve our forensic unit through the budget.[22]

---

21 Public Accounts Committee of the Eighth Parliament (2015) Report on the Auditor General's Report for the Financial Year 2008/2009.
22 Ntsukunyane L (2015, 6–12 December) DCEO ready to take down 'anyone'. *Sunday Express*. p. 4.

The statement is instructive, although of course it may also be regarded as the usual way a serving public officer would react when interviewed publicly. Taken for what it says, the statement indicates an increase in budgets for the DCEO, although this has not done much to give the agency the muscle it need to carry out its legal mandate (see Table 1).

C. International and legal framework

Commitment to international instruments

Given the devastating effects of corruption on societies, efforts have been made at all levels to combat corruption at all levels. The first of these efforts is the United Nations Convention Against Corruption (UNCAC). The convention seeks to:[23]

> a) Promote and strengthen measures to prevent and combat corruption more efficiently and effectively;
> b) Promote, facilitate and support international cooperation and technical assistance in the prevention of and fight against corruption, including its asset recovery; and
> c) Promote integrity, accountability and proper management of public affairs and public property.

Chapter 2, article 5(1) of the convention commits state parties to develop corruption preventive measures. It provides that state parties shall:

> Develop and implement or maintain effective, coordinated anti-corruption practices that promote the participation of society and reflect the principles of the rule of law, proper management of public affairs and public property, integrity, transparency and accountability.

Article 6(1) of the convention specifically commits state parties to establish anti-corruption bodies thus:

> State parties shall ensure the existence of a body or bodies, as appropriate that prevent corruption by such means as:
> a) Implementing anti-corruption policies and where appropriate overseeing and coordinating the implementation of those policies;
> b) Increasing and disseminating knowledge about the prevention of corruption.

---

23 Chapter 1, article 1. Available at https://www.unodc.org/documents/brussels/UN_Convention_Against_Corruption.pdf [accessed 30 September 2016].

These bodies must be independent in order to be effective in the discharge of their mandate. In this connection article 6(2) of the convention commits state parties to:

> Grant the body or bodies ... necessary independence, in accordance with the fundamental principles of its legal system, to enable the body or bodies to carry out its or their functions effectively and free from any undue influence. The necessary material resources and specialised staff, as well as the training that such staff may require to carry out their functions, should be provided.

Secondly, the AU also adopted its own anti-corruption instrument: the African Union Convention on Preventing and Combating Corruption (2003). The AU also expresses its concern about corruption and its 'devastating effects on the economic and social development of the African peoples' and thus seeks through this convention to:

1. Promote and strengthen the development in Africa by each state party, of mechanisms required to prevent, detect, punish and eradicate corruption and related offences in Africa;
2. Promote, facilitate and regulate cooperation among the state parties to ensure the effectiveness of the measures and actions to prevent, detect, punish and eradicate corruption and related offences in Africa;
3. Coordinate and harmonise the policies and legislation between state parties for the purposes of prevention, detection, punishment and eradication of corruption on the continent;
4. Promote socio-economic development by removing obstacles to the enjoyment of economic, social and cultural rights as well as civil and political rights; and
5. Establish the necessary conditions to foster transparency accountability in the management of public affairs.

Under Article 5(3) of the AU convention, state parties undertake to establish, maintain and strengthen independent national anti-corruption authorities or agencies. This undertaking is further reiterated under article 20(4) thus:

> The national authorities or agencies shall be allowed the necessary independence and autonomy, to be able to carry out their duties effectively.

State parties further undertake under the same article to:

> Ensure that national authorities or agencies are specialised in combating corruption and related offences by, among others, ensuring that the staff are trained and motivated to effectively carry out their duties.

At the Southern African level, the Southern African Development Community (SADC) adopted its own anti-corruption instrument, The Southern African Development Community Anti-Corruption Protocol (2001). The purpose of the protocol, as provided under article 2, is to:

a) Promote and strengthen the development, by each of the state parties, of mechanisms needed to prevent, detect, punish, and eradicate corruption in the public and private sector;
b) Promote, facilitate and regulate cooperation among the state parties to ensure the effectiveness of measures and actions to prevent, detect, punish and eradicate corruption in the public and private sectors; and
c) Foster the development and harmonisation of policies and domestic legislation of the state parties relating to the prevention, detection, punishment and eradication of corruption in the public and private sectors.

Unlike the UN and the AU anti-corruption instruments, the SADC protocol does not expressly commit state parties to establish anti-corruption agencies. However, the government of Lesotho established its own agency too, with a mandate to combat corruption, which is assessed in this report against the above international standards.

Lesotho's commitment to these instruments is partial. According to Ramokhoro[24] Lesotho ratified the UN convention, the AU convention, and the SADC protocol in 2005, but has not domesticated them. There is no formal domestication process undertaken, except in the case where laws are amended due to being outdated. It is not the problem of anti-corruption alone, but the country at large. Domestication is a country-wide challenge, though there have been ratifications without reservation, and reports are done where needed.

Regarding other conventions, the DCEO is part of the anti-money-laundering group, working under the auspices of the Eastern and Southern African money-laundering group and conventions on organised crime, which came before the UNCAC.[25]

Regarding communication relating to international conventions, Lesotho has been attending conferences of state parties under the UNCAC and other countries reporting on these issues. In 2015, the government was invited and attended the sixth session of the conference of state parties in St Petersburg, Russia from 2 to 6 November 2015. A peer review or kind of assessment was undertaken where all state parties participated in reviewing and being reviewed by their peers. Lesotho reviewed Mauritius and Nigeria, while Lesotho was reviewed by Botswana and another country from outside the region.

Under the AU convention, Lesotho hosted an AU mission from the AU board on corruption. They assessed Lesotho's implementation of the AU convention. This was in

---

24 Interview with Mr Litelu Ramokhoro, Director-General for Training and Public Education, Maseru, 7 September, 2015.
25 Ibid.

2012/13. In addition, for the first time, a Lesotho citizen, Advocate Sefako Seema, the chief anti-corruption prosecutor, sits on the AU board on corruption.[26]

At SADC level, Lesotho is an active member of the Southern African Forum Against Corruption (SAFAC), which is an informal anti-corruption initiative formed in the late 1990s. It functions as a lobbying mechanism for SADC leadership to make treaties against corruption, including the SADC Protocol Against Corruption. This protocol was adopted by the SADC summit in about 2003. In 2005, the protocol entered into force, but it has not been implemented for unclear reasons.[27]

Legal framework

Lesotho's legal framework for the prevention of corruption is made up of several pieces of legislation. The first is the Public Procurement Regulations (2007) which, in summary, establishes thresholds for the use of public procurement methods, bid evaluations and contract management. The regulations in particular establish a procurement unit which:

> Shall be an individual or a group of individuals authorised to carry out public procurement composed of ministries, district councils, state owned legal entities, any other bodies covered by public law, or any project implementing authority to carry out public procurement.[28]

The procurement unit is empowered to select contractors and enter into contract with them, guided by several factors such as: comparing price quotations obtained from a minimum of three suppliers or contractors; the evaluation of quotations on open bidding principles; advertising of tenders made in the mass media or the Contract Bulletin of the government in either one or both official languages; objective methods of bids evaluation and award of contracts made known to all bidders and results published.[29]

The regulations further provide for exceptional procurement procedures[30] under conditions in which there is 'concern as to the degree of completion that can be secured or there is genuine emergency'. Under these conditions the minister of finance can grant a waiver. This exceptional procurement procedure applies under three conditions:

a) The requirement concerns a new contract that is directly relevant to a completed contract, and the added value of the additional work being given to the same contractor outweighs any potential reduction in costs that may be derived through a competitive tender;

b) The requirement can only be secured from the single source, this may be due to ownership of exclusive design rights or patents; and

---

26 Ibid.
27 Ibid.
28 Legal Notice No. 1 of 2007, Public Procurement Regulations, 2007.
29 Ibid.
30 Ibid: section 8.

c) There must be convincing and accurate reasons in a) and b) for completion to be avoided.

These regulations do not seem to be useful in terms of preventing corruption. Some of the cases of grand corruption indicate that the regulations were disregarded by those accused of corruption (such as Metsing and Matete's cases).

The second is the Money Laundering and Proceeds of Crime Act, No. 4. (2008) which exists, as defined under its general objectives for establishing an anti-money laundering authority and a financial intelligence unit:

> To enable the unlawful proceeds of all serious crimes to be identified, traced, frozen, seized and eventually confiscated; and to require accountable institutions, namely, legal practitioners, accountants and financial institutions, to take prudential measures to combat money laundering.

Section 16(1) provides that these institutions must have adequate identification and verification of all their customers be they natural persons, businesses or legal entities. Customer verification is also required under section 16(2):[31]

a) Where a customer is carrying out an electronic funds transfer;
b) Where there is suspicion of a money laundering offence or the financing of terrorism; or
c) Where the accountable institution has doubts about the veracity or accuracy of the customer identification and verification documentation or information it had previously obtained.

This act has been fairly successful in that the banks were able to provide information to the DCEO about suspicious monies deposited into their customers' accounts, such as that of Metsing.

The National Assembly Electoral Act (2011), section 70(2), regulates funding of electoral campaigns by making it mandatory for all political parties to declare to the Independent Electoral Commission (IEC) all funds or donations in the region of USD 15 000.[32] Whether this provision serves its intended purpose or is effectively enforced is not clear. No cases of this nature have been reported. But this does not mean they do not exist.

Lesotho still does not have access to information laws. The Access and Receipt of Information Bill (2000) has not been passed into law, despite all efforts by the media and key stakeholders to push for this.[33]

---

31 Ibid.
32 This is based on USD 1:M 14.
33 Kapa MA (2013) *Lesotho: Political Participation and Democracy.* Johannesburg: Open Society Foundations. p. 45.

Other than these laws, the DCEO was not established by an act of parliament and not by the national constitution. The Constitution of Lesotho (1993) does not even talk about corruption explicitly. Instead, the DCEO was established under a specific statute, the Prevention of Corruption and Economic Offences Act No. 5 (1999) (henceforth referred to as the principal law).

Given that Lesotho has not been able to sufficiently capacitate the DCEO, it is better to have one anti-corruption agency rather than many. The country already fails to provide the required resources for the agency to carry out its legal mandate. Establishing more than one agency would serve no purpose since these would compete for already meagre resources.

Structurally, the DCEO falls under and reports to the ministry of justice, thus potentially limiting its independence. However, in an attempt to at least guarantee some degree of independence, permanence and continuity, the directorate has been provided for under the Prevention of Corruption and Economic Offences Amendment Act, (2006) (henceforth referred to as the amendment act). Section 4 thereof provides that the directorate:

a) Shall be a juristic person, having perpetual succession, capable of suing and being sued in its own name and performing acts as are necessary for, or incidental to, the execution of its functions.
b) Shall not be subject to the direction or control of any person or authority in the exercise of its functions except in accordance with this act.

The legal bases on which the DCEO was built has evolved, by way of the amendment act, in ways that enhance its powers. The amendment was effected to enhance the status of the directorate by, inter alia, granting it a legal persona status;[34] expanding its membership at the top level by establishing the offices of the director general and two deputy directors general;[35] establishing a directorate board for appointments, promotions and general conditions of service of staff of the directorate other than the director general;[36] and extending the powers of the directorate to investigate the private sector.[37]

The DCEO's existence has not been threatened in any way so far. No other institution has been established to carry out similar functions to those of the directorate and its budget has been increasing steadily over the years (see Table 1 on page 121).

---

34 Prevention of Corruption and Economic Offences Amendment Act (2006) section 4(1).
35 Ibid: section 4(2).
36 Ibid: section 5.
37 Ibid: section 8.

D. Institutional framework
Staff

In terms of the section 5 of the amendment act, the directorate membership contains a directorate appointment and promotion board which is responsible for appointments, promotions, and conditions of service of all staff, except the director general. This board comprises:

a) A member of the judicial service commission nominated by the chairman of the judicial service commission, who is its chairman;

b) The principal secretary responsible for the ministry to which the directorate may be assigned;

c) A senior official to be appointed by the minister responsible for the public service;

d) an eminent person from the private sector who has a track record and extensive knowledge and experience in management; and

e) The director general, who shall be secretary.

The members of this board are appointed by the minister by a notice published in the gazette. Below the board, there is the director general, who is appointed by the prime minister for a term of not less than five years. He/she must be someone, who has been admitted as a legal practitioner under the Legal Practitioners Act (1983), or should have such other qualifications as the minister may prescribe.

The director-general is responsible for the general direction, discipline and administration of the DCEO. The director-general also has powers (under section 3A(4) of the amendment act) to appoint and promote support staff. When the amendment act came into effect, all staff who were employed by the directorate full-time were allowed to terminate their service with the general public service and serve under the directorate in terms of section 31 of the amendment act. His/her terms and conditions of employment are determined by the minister of justice, in consultation with the minister of finance and the minister of public service, after receiving recommendations from the board. Below the director general, the amendment act provides for two deputy directors general, who are appointed by the board for a period of not less than five years, under section 4. However, the reality on the ground is that these two posts have not been filled. There are two senior officers below the director general: the director for public education and corruption prevention and the director of administration; whose positions, together with those of all other staff of the directorate, are permanent.[38]

The amendment act had anticipated that the directorate would grow structurally such that there would be a need to have two directors general, one for administration and the

---

38 Follow-up telephone interview with Mr Litelu Ramokhoro, director of Public Education and Corruption Prevention, 22 September 2015.

other for operations. This has not happened. The directorate has grown at a disappointing rate; from a staff complement of five at inception in 2003 to only 62 in 2015, thus rendering the notion of two directors general redundant. Especially under the current situation in which the government is under pressure from the International Monetary Fund (IMF) and the World Bank (WB) to arrest the escalation of wage bill.[39] Although the amendment act does not prescribe or show the criteria for appointments of all other staff members of the directorate, these appointments are normally based on generally assumed public service criteria of non-partisanship, impartiality, neutrality and competence. The main consideration is the general merit principle applicable to the entire public service.[40]

The director general, as the head of the directorate, has a fixed five-year renewable term. This gives him/her relative security of tenure in that he/she cannot be removed easily. This in terms of section 4(3) which reads:

> A person holding the office of director may be removed from office only for inability to exercise the functions of his office whether arising from infirmity of body or mind or any other cause or for misbehaviour and shall not be removed except in accordance with the provisions of this section.

To have him/her removed is an elaborate process involving prior investigations by a tribunal appointed by the prime minister in terms of section 5 of the principal law. It is this tribunal that can recommend his/her removal to the prime minister. The tribunal itself should be composed of a chairman and not less than two other members, selected by the chief justice from among persons who hold or have held high judicial office.[41] The members of the DCEO are not, however, protected by any immunity against criminal proceedings for acts committed in the exercise of their duties.[42]

In the event that there is a vacancy in the office of the director-general or any other senior members of the DCEO, acting arrangements are made in terms of section 7(2) of the amendment act. This provides that the prime minister may appoint any competent person from the directorate in acting capacity until the return of the incumbent. In fact, the director of public education and corruption prevention acted twice after the contracts of incumbents expired and before their replacements could be made.[43] The acting arrangement is in line with the directorate's ordinary operation, in that the person who has in fact acted in the office of the head of the institution is the senior most person and second in position to the head himself.

---

39 Ibid.
40 Interview with Mr Litelu Ramokhoro, director for Training and Public Education, Maseru, 7 September 2015.
41 Section 4(5) of the principal law.
42 Follow-up telephone interview with Mr Litelu Ramokhoro, director of Public Education and Corruption Prevention, 22 September 2015.
43 Ibid.

The DCEO has some degree of authority over its human resources. It has its own board (of appointments, promotions and general conditions), which is charged with the responsibility of handling all staff-related matters. However, the challenge is that it uses the general public service rules and regulations, which are 'cumbersome and difficult to implement if disciplinary cases are held'.[44] The directorate does not have its own code of conduct regulating, among other issues, ethical standards for staff; it needs simple regulations of its own. These are contained in the pending amendment bill, which provides for standing orders and regulations.[45]

Regarding conflict of interest, however, the amendment act has a provision under section 14(1). This reads:

> A member or an employee of public or private body commits the offence of corruption if he or she or an immediate member of his or her family has a direct or indirect interest in a company or undertaking with which the body proposes to deal, or he or she has a personal interest in a decision which that body has to make and he or she, knowingly, fails to disclose the nature of the interest, and votes or participates in the proceedings of the body relating to the dealing or decision.

Staff of the directorate undergo regular specialised training under the auspices of the commonwealth secretariat unit in Botswana. This unit serves all commonwealth countries in Africa. The directorate has its own training plan, which is actually a requirement of the government. Besides which, the 2015/2016 budget also has provision for specialised training in forensic investigations.[46]

The remuneration package for members of the directorate is slightly better than that of other ministries of the government. Staff salaries are a notch higher than the ordinary public service salaries structure but not enough to attract and retain most qualified workers with the integrity to resist corruption. This has led to the directorate experiencing high staff turnover. In the words of the director general:

> To fight corruption is not easy. You fight people with resources and who are ready to bribe if opportunity comes up. We need competitive conditions of service.[47]

The DCEO competes with the private sector for competent investigators who have undergone specialised training. They leave for the banks and other parastatal agencies.[48]

---

44 Ibid.
45 Ibid.
46 Ibid.
47 Interview with Mr Borotho Matsoso, DCEO director general, Maseru, 14 September 2015.
48 Ibid.

Mandate, investigative and prosecutorial powers

The DCEO has a clear mandate in terms of prevention, sensitisation, and education of the public in the fight against corruption. Its constitutive legislation, Prevention of Corruption and Economic Offences Act No. 5 (1999), spells out this mandate thus:

> To provide for the establishment of a directorate on corruption and economic crime; to make provision for the prevention of corruption and confer power on the directorate to investigate suspected cases of corruption and economic crime matters connected therewith or incidental thereto.

In addition, this mandate is broken down into specific functions of the directorate under section 6. According to this section, the directorate shall, inter alia, receive and investigate any complaints alleging corruption in any public body; educate the public against the evils of corruption; and undertake any other measures for the prevention of corruption and economic offences. The amendment act enhances this mandate under section 8 by amending the principal law and expanding the jurisdictional scope of the powers of the directorate, thus enabling it to cover even the private sector.

The directorate, through its director general, is mandated under section 28 of the amendment act to submit annual reports to the minister on or before 21 March each year, or at the date that may be allowed by the attorney general. The minister is obliged to table such a report before parliament. This is an improvement from the provisions of the principal law since this had only provided that the directorate submits a report to the minister, without saying what the minister had to do with the report thereafter. However, the amendment act still does not stipulate any time frames in terms of when, after getting the report, the minister has to table it before parliament. In fact, the minister has yet to table any report before parliament and the law does not say what should happen under these circumstances. This said, the directorate delivers mid-year reports to the economic cluster committee of parliament, when called upon to report. Other than this formal reporting system, the directorate reports to the public what is suitable for public consumption through its public relations office. These public reports normally include cases that are taken to court for conviction.[49]

The directorate operates from the capital city of the country, Maseru, where it only has office spaces at two locations. It has no physical presence in the other nine administrative districts of the country. It has, over the years, relied largely on the state-owned media to popularise itself. This means the complaints reception mechanism in the fight against corruption is centralised. The informers are legally protected under section 50 of the principal law and under section 27 of the amendment act. The latter provides that:

---

49 Interview with Mr Litelu Ramokhoro, director for Training and Public Education, Maseru, 7 September 2015.

> A person shall not be held or deemed to have breached a disciplinary code of conduct, contract, oath of secrecy, a binding declaration of an undertaking he or she might have made by virtue of his or her office or status, if he or she divulges to the director-general, or an official of the directorate an act of corruption committed.

There is a channel to give citizens feedback on their complaints. There is also a report centre where reports are made on cases of corruption through telephone, personal visits and also anonymously. Complainants can seek feedback regarding their complaints and get feedback depending on the nature of the cases and the stage of their processing. The DCEO cannot and does not disclose information about sensitive cases which are still under investigation, lest they get spoilt.[50]

The directorate has a clear mandate in terms of investigation under section 6 of the amendment act; but it does not, on its own, have mandate to prosecute suspected offenders. This is carried out through the director of public prosecutions in terms of section 43 of the principal law. This provides that the director general shall refer matters for which he believes there is need for prosecution, no prosecutions will be done without a written consent of the director of public prosecutions. However, the director of public prosecutions has delegated his powers to the DCEO so that it does its own prosecutions using its own prosecutors. It is only special and high profile cases that the DPP has to scrutinise. The prosecution process and its pace depend largely on the DCEO itself. The system works smoothly, as the two institutions work very well.[51] The DCEO does not necessarily have criteria for pursuing cases per se. It pursues cases based on their relative simplicity and/or complexity. As such, it deals with 'simpler' cases whose completion rate is substantially higher.

Financial resources

The DCEO is responsible for its budgetary planning process and its financial resources. The ministry of finance issues a call circular on an annual basis, instructing all government ministries and departments to submit their budget estimates; the DCEO also prepares and submits its own to the budget controller with all supporting documents or reasons in support of it. The ministry of finance then determines how much the directorate gets, depending on the availability of funds and justification provided. The resources do, to some degree, correspond with the requirements expressed by the directorate, but are not adequate to allow for the efficient accomplishment of its mission. Other than getting its budget primarily from the public purse, the directorate also gets some funding from Lesotho's development partners. It gains access its financial resources once the budget has been approved.[52]

---

50 Follow-up interview with Mr Ramokhoro, Maseru, 6 October 2015.
51 Ibid.
52 Interview with Mr Borotho Matsoso, DCEO director general, Maseru, 14 September 2015.

It does have some degree of managerial autonomy relating to other aspects than the budget, but it does not have full autonomy and efficient control over its finances. Matsoso bemoaned that the DCEO have to follow the notorious public service red-tape when, for example, it needs to transfer funds to pay for some of their operations. Thus, the agency is fighting for autonomy so that it gets subvention from the government to make it easy for it to determine its own affairs. According to Matsoso, the DCEO has to be fully autonomous so that it can be flexible in its operations and move away from the public service way of doing things. This is particularly imperative, according to him, given the nature of the many phases of corruption which change over time.

The DCEO does have a degree of absorptive capacity, although it does not always finish its budget. This is because of the red tape, which in some cases requires a tender even for fairly small expenditure. In the 2014/2015 financial year, the DCEO had budgeted for the renovation of its building, but the work had not started because of the delays caused by the ministry of works, through which the projects have to go. This may lead to the agency failing to have access to the money allocated for that purpose. Ultimately, even when the directorate has done what must be done, delays occur on the side of other actors, who have different priorities to those of the agency.[53]

The general rules of financial transparency apply to the DCEO to deter both mismanagement of resources and abuse of power. Given that it draws its budget from the public purse, the auditor general is authorised by law to conduct auditing of all resources of the agency. In addition, the agency has its own internal audit mechanism, which is also used to ensure compliance with all rules of financial transparency. The auditing procedures focus on how the resources of the directorate are utilised and not on efficiency.[54] Independence of the agency is as yet unattainable; the closer concept, which is being used and sought, is autonomy.

The DCEO has been receiving funding from government since its establishment, as demonstrated below.

Table 1: Budget allocations for the DCEO, 2010/2011–2015/2016[55]

Fiscal Year	Amount in Maloti	% increase
2010/2011	8 450 075	
2011/2012	8 076 104	-4.42
2012/2013	9 593 723	18.8
2013/2014	11 399 192	18.8
2014/2015	15 575 095	36.6
2015/2016	22 919 281	47.2

53 Ibid.
54 Ibid.
55 Original, derived from interview with Mr Litelu Ramokhoro, Director for Training and Public Education, Maseru, 7 September 2015.

Except for the 2011/2012 fiscal year, where there was an actual decrease, and 2012/2013 and 2013/2014 fiscal years where there was virtually no change, the budget of the agency increased by 36.6 % in 2014/2015 and by a staggering 47.2% in the 2015/2016 fiscal years. In addition to these allocations, the DCEO can also claim some money for special projects (investigations and consultancies) from a total budget of USD 214 286. This means that, in each year, it has an additional USD 214 286. All things being equal, the variations in budgetary allocations would be interpreted as the indicators of the commitment of the government to fight corruption. Despite all the increases, however, the budget falls far too low in terms of helping the DCEO achieve its legal mandate. For example, its budget in 2012/2013 financial year amounted to only 0.09% against 0.5%, the internationally recommended benchmark for institutions of its nature to operate at full capacity.[56]

Relationship with the stakeholders

This section describes the nature of the relations between the DCEO and its key stakeholders, namely: key public institutions, civil society, the private sector, the media, and Lesotho's development partners. The kind of relationships between the agency and these actors are cordial, collaborative and complementary, though not as strong as they would be expected to be.

Other public institutions

The DCEO generally has good complementary and collaborative relations with all its stakeholders in the public sector, ranging from parliament, the police, auditor general, and the director of public prosecutions. These relations were described by the director general.[57] The directorate gets invitation to attend sessions of the public accounts committee of parliament. This makes it possible for the directorate to get first-hand information from government ministries and departments on how public funds have been used, thus enabling it to pursue cases, should a need arise. Even the parliamentary portfolio committee on law and public safety has been supportive to the directorate, eager to learn more about it.

The DCEO also has complementary and collaborative relations with the Lesotho Mounted Police Service (LMPS) and the Lesotho Revenue Authority (LRA). The three institutions have a tripartite memorandum of understanding. The DCEO and the LMPS share information relating to their respective works, thus enabling them to carry out their respective mandates. They also have a referral system in which each passes on or refers cases relevant to the other after receiving them from the public. The LMPS also seconds its staff to the DCEO; this helps to fill the staff shortages experienced by the latter. This memorandum also helps them to carry out some sensitive operations, which need security, police visibility and keeping evidence such as vehicles. The DCEO would not be able to do all these alone. The DCEO and the LMPS also work together to trap and arrest suspected

---

56 Transparency International (2014) *Overview of Corruption and Anti-Corruption in Lesotho*. Berlin: Transparency International.
57 Interview with Mr Borotho Matsoso, DCEO director general, Maseru, 14 September 2015.

bribers. This complementary and collaborative relationship has been made possible by the historical background of the DCEO. Its founding senior managers came from the LMPS and as such they find it very easy to talk to their colleagues in the LMPS. Similarly, the directorate also has good working relations with the attorney general and the director of public prosecutions.

As for relations with the LRA, the two institutions carry out joint investigations together; with the LRA interested in getting tax and the DCEO pursuing corruption cases. They also share information that is relevant for each other's mandates.

Through this tripartite arrangement, criminals do not escape easily. There is also collaboration and complementarity between the DCEO and the financial intelligence unit (FIU),[58] which is hosted by the Central Bank of Lesotho (CBL). Every financial institution deals with the FIU and the unit shares financial intelligence with the DCEO, the LMPS and other external relevant institutions. The former accountant general, Mr Kenneth Hlasa,[59] points out that the DCEO worked in a collaborative and complementary manner with the office of the accountant-general during his time in office, but notes that the directorate has some challenges, which have to be addressed if it is to do its work as expected.

Civil society

The relations between the DCEO and civil society organisations have also been complementary and collaborative. Representatives of key civil society organisations whose mandates relate to that of the directorate (such as the Transformation Resource Centre [TRC] and the Development for Peace Education [DPE]) confirm this. According to Lenka,[60] being a human rights organisation, which works for justice, peace, democracy, good governance and participatory sustainable development, the TRC has a direct call and mandate for advocating for a corruption free society. The TRC has a close working relationship with the DCEO at two levels. Firstly, the TRC is one of the primary stakeholders in the fight against corruption. It monitors the public sector and exposes corruption whenever it occurs. Secondly, the TRC participates in the development of policy and corruption strategy. It does research on corruption and corruption-related activities. It educates the public about corruption and its effects on the national economy and society at large. It is an independent actor on behalf of the DCEO:

---

58 The Financial Intelligence Unit (FIU) is a central national agency responsible for receiving, requesting, analysing and disseminating to law enforcement and supervisory bodies disclosures of financial information concerning suspected proceeds of crime and alleged money laundering and terrorist financing offences (see http://www.fiu.org.ls/home). It was established under section 14 of the Money Laundering and Proceeds of Crime Act, 2008.
59 Interview with Mr Kenneth Hlasa, accountant general in 2002–2007 fiscal years, Roma, 18 September 2015.
60 Telephone interview with Mr Mabusetsa Lenka, programmes director, Transformation Resource Centre, 21 September 2015.

Particularly where the latter may have political pressure that may hinder it to speak. And when the TRC speaks, it does so objectively with a research-based evidence.[61]

The TRC has been close with corruption cases within the Lesotho Highlands Water Project (LHWP) and very vocal about these, leading to Lesotho being regarded as one of the success stories in the global fight against corruption.

The DCEO also has collaborative and complementary relations with the DPE. According to its co-ordinator, Mr Sofonea Shale,[62] the DPE and the DCEO have relationship at two levels: first at the more general civil society sector, under the Lesotho Council of Non-Governmental Organisations (LCN); and second at the level of direct relations between the two institutions. At the LCN level, the DCEO is often given a platform to address participating civil society organisations at the annual event called NGO Week. The idea, through these interactions, is to raise awareness about corruption and encourage participating organisations to include corruption on the list of social ills they deal with. Shale indicated that, in 2014, the DCEO's director of public education and corruption prevention was highly appreciative of these interactions. He remarked that if civil society could make as much noise about corruption as it does with elections, political conflict and such other issues, corruption would be uprooted easily.

At the level of the two institutions, the DPE complements the work of the DCEO through organising local-level dialogue and raising public awareness on corruption, its causes and the way public officials and political leaders are exposed to corruption, and how it adversely affect service delivery.

On collaboration, Shale went on, the DPE approached the DCEO to support a social audit programme. Under this programme, the DPE wanted to involve communities in exposing corruption around grazing fees in the community councils. The DCEO wrote a letter to the World Bank's Small Grants Programme, supporting the DPE proposal. Through the project, the DCEO would train communities and support the DPE in establishing anti-corruption teams in their own community councils. The outcome of this collaborative effort has yet to be determined.

Besides this, the DPE and the DCEO shared a platform in the governance sub-sector during the formulation of the National Development Strategy Paper. They both advanced a point of co-ordination of relevant public offices (the police fraud division, public accounts committee, and the auditor-general), in fighting corruption. The DPE also participated in the formulation of the DCEO strategic plan.

The DCEO jurisdiction was limited to the public sector at its inception under the principal law. The amendment act includes the private sector and makes it subject to the powers and mandate of the directorate. It provides under section 8(b) that the principal

---

61 Ibid.
62 Telephone interview with Mr Sofonea Shale, co-ordinator, Development for Peace Education, 20 September 2015.

law is amended in section 6: 'inserting the words "or private" immediately after the word "public" wherever it appears'. The directorate also has the mandate and power to seize assets. This is provided for under section 10(1)(b) of the principal law. This gives the officer of the DCEO powers to arrest persons and to 'seize and detain anything which such officer has reason to believe to be or to contain evidence any of the offences' stipulated in the law. Matsoso points out that the DCEO also enforces and can seize unexplained assets under the Money Laundering and Proceeds of Crime Act (2008). The DCEO is in the process of auctioning some of the seized assets so that the proceeds can be deposited in a special account which will help maintain the value of the assets. As indicated under the section on stakeholder relations above, the directorate collaborates with the LMPS on this.[63]

The media
The media has been making the public aware of the activities of the DCEO, especially regarding high-profile cases. Citizens have been following these cases with keen interest. This is not surprising given that such stories sell more than others. All the cases involving high profile individuals have been well covered in the print media, including: the deputy leader of the DC, Mr Monyane Moleleki; former minister of finance, Dr Timothy Thahane; deputy prime minister and leader of the LCD, Mr Mothetjoa Metsing; the former deputy clerk of the national assembly, Mr Matlamukele Matete; and former principal secretary of finance, Mr Mosito Khethisa. Even private radio stations do not miss these cases during their programmes and news bulletins.

Private sector
The private sector does not have clear relationships with the DCEO beyond the formal structure called Business Action Against Corruption. The structure was established in 2012 with a view to, among other activities, create joint private/public anti-corruption programmes. Nothing much has come out of this structure, even though business plays a huge role in corruption by way of paying bribes to secure government tenders and contracts. According to Transparency International 'the private sector has largely been absent from the fight against corruption in Lesotho'.[64]

Development partners
The DCEO/development partners' relationships have also been of a complementary and collaborative nature. According to Mosoeunyane, the development partners collaborate and support Lesotho under an inter-agency strategic plan, where they have agreed to 'delivering as one'.[65] This collaboration and support operate under the broad framework of two documents: the Country Programme Document 2013–2017 and the Lesotho United

---

63 Interview with Mr Borotho Matsoso, DCEO Director-General, Maseru, 14 September 2015.
64 Transparency International (2014) *Overview of Corruption and Anti-Corruption in Lesotho*. Berlin: Transparency International. p. 10.
65 Interview with Mr Thabo Mosoeunyane, UNDP Governance Specialist, Maseru, 30 October 2015.

Nations Development Assistance Plan 2013–2017. Assistance is based on the priority needs of the country as reflected in the National Strategic Development Plan 2012/13–2016/17. The overall development assistance to Lesotho focuses on, for the purpose of this report, governance and accountable institutions. The aim is to 'boost institutional leadership, performance and accountability, citizen participation and mechanisms for maintaining social justice'.[66]

It is in this context that the DCEO got support for two purposes, as outlined below. The first way was that the agency received USD 50 000 from the United States embassy, through the UNDP, to develop and launch the National Anti-Corruption Strategy and Action Plan 2014/15–2018/19 (NACSAP).[67] The NACSAP consisted of two main activities: a national dialogue on corruption and, based on that, the development, endorsement and launch of the NACSAP.

The national dialogue on corruption (on the theme of harnessing political will to fight corruption) was held from 23 to 25 July 2013 in Maseru. The dialogue was jointly supported by the UNDP, the US embassy in Maseru and the EU delegation in Lesotho. It was attended by about 250 stakeholders, drawn from all key sectors: public, private, academia, civil society and the media. More importantly, it was attended by Prime Minister Thabane, Deputy Prime Minister Metsing, and a full cabinet and principal secretaries.[68]

The prime minister gave a key note address which was critical in that it indicated the Thabane-led coalition government's position regarding corruption. In his address, Thabane called on the public to blow the whistle on corrupt individuals abusing the country's resources, and emphasised the key role of fighting corruption in improving the country's development status. He lamented that Lesotho is classified as least developed because of corruption, declaring corruption as one of the worst enemies of the Basotho, second only to HIV/AIDS. He urged the stakeholders to confront and interrogate the phenomenon of corruption in detail, and explore possible strategies to tackling it, including sensitisation of leadership structures at all levels.[69]

Following the dialogue, a situation analysis was developed, which served as an input to develop the baseline for the anti-corruption strategy. A common understanding was created for the direction of the strategy and stakeholders were engaged to support the continuation of the work on the strategy.[70] Building on the national dialogue on corruption, and following consultations and technical work, the DCEO developed the NACSAP, which establishes a coordinated approach for all stakeholders in the fight against corruption. It establishes, among others, a national anti-corruption coordinating mechanism (NACCM), a body responsible for an oversight function of the implementation of the NACSAP. The

---

66 See http://www.ls.undp.org/content/lesotho/en/home/operations/about_undp.html [accessed 18 November 2011].
67 Interview with Mr Thabo Mosoeunyane, UNDP governance specialist, Maseru, 30 October 2015.
68 Thabang Tlalajoe, UNDP programme manager, email message to the author, 16 September 2015.
69 Ibid.
70 Ibid.

strategy provides a standard and systematic approach for both private and public sectors in the fight against corruption in Lesotho.[71]

The NACSAP was produced in 2013/14, and the official launching of the NACSAP by the director general took place on 28 January 2015. There were 92 participants from traditional leadership, local government, the judiciary, the public and private sector, CSOs, media, faith-based organisations and institutions of higher learning. About 500 copies of the NACSAP were printed and distributed to various stakeholders.[72]

The second purpose for which the DCEO received support from development partners was capacity building. This took the form of internal workshops for the public education and prevention of corruption division on: schools anti-corruption programmes, to equip DCEO officers with the necessary knowledge and skills to enable them to do their job effectively; and a study tour by the principal corruption officer and the principal public education officer to Mauritius in a south–south cooperation. The officers were also attached to the Independent Commission Against Corruption (ICAC) of Mauritius in order to get exposure to international best practices. They received training on how the institution carries out its mandate and had working sessions with: the director general; the deputy director of the systems enhancement branch and community relations; and heads of units throughout their engagement. They further had consultations with other stakeholder groups, such as the Women International Association, the district council and the regional youth council. They also visited the University of Mauritius, Lycee Polytechnic and the Mahatma Ghandi Institute, and the ministry of civil service and administration reforms, where they witnessed ICAC induction training for new recruits in the public sector.[73]

On the whole, development partners have supported the DCEO in the development of the NACSAP and capacity-building areas. This assistance notwithstanding, the DCEO is not listed under the institutions that were to receive support, explaining the limited support it seems to have secured.

E. Performance

It is not clear whether the formation of the DCEO was a product of internal pressure from CSOs or external pressure from development partners, or clear political will in the form of a political decision for government to purge its enemies – or any combination of factors. Its constitutive legislation came at a time when Lesotho was effectively under a one-party-dominant system (the Lesotho Congress for Democracy). As such, it would not be possible to establish the directorate to purge government's political enemies. The political will thesis also does not quite explain this move, given that the government only established this agency in 2003 yet the constitutive law was passed in 1999. It is not clear what caused

---

71 Ibid.
72 Ibid.
73 Ibid.

this delay. Could its establishment be a product of donor pressure? This is perhaps the most logical explanation.

The primary mandate of the DCEO can be broken down into four main categories: investigation of cases of corruption, prevention of corruption, prosecution of suspects of corruption, and public education about corruption.[74] The performance of the agency can thus be assessed on its ability to address these categories. The assessment is affected by extremely limited data owing to the poor record system of the agency, which results from the aforementioned chronic capacity challenges. Since its establishment in 2003, the DCEO staff complement has grown extremely sluggishly,[75] leading to serious overload, backlog of cases and low conviction rates. One investigator has to handle about 30 cases per year.[76]

Despite these capacity challenges, the directorate has done a fair amount of work regarding investigation of cases of corruption. According to Transparency International,[77] from 1999 to 2012, the directorate submitted 37 cases for prosecution out of which two received guilty verdicts; while in 2012, it brought 71 cases before the courts, resulting in 16 convictions and two acquittals. On the last week of September 2015, the DCEO received a complaint, investigated it and took it before the courts that same week. The courts are yet to hear the case at time of writing, however. The case involved some police officers who confiscated marijuana, but also extorted money from the suspects, thereby committing acts of corruption.[78] More importantly, the directorate has taken a very brave and unprecedented move in recent years by investigating cases involving very high profile individuals, some while still in public office.

The first case involved the former clerk of the national assembly, who was involved in corrupt activity in procuring (for the national assembly) a heavy duty photocopier for USD 113 481 (about three times its actual price) from Konica Enterprises (Pty) Ltd, trading as Itec Lesotho, which was second accused. The corruption took place between March 2005 and March 2006.

He was convicted and sentenced to seven years in jail by the high court, but appealed the sentence. The court of appeal imposed a fine of:

> [USD 715] or five years imprisonment, plus an additional seven years imprisonment of which three years are suspended for three years on condition that the accused is not convicted of an offence of bribery or corruption under the Prevention of Corruption and Economic Offences Act 5 of 1999 as amended committed during

---

74 See the general objects of the principal law and section 6 thereof.
75 Follow-up interview with Mr Ramokhoro, Maseru, 6 October 2015.
76 Transparency International (2014) *Overview of Corruption and Anti-Corruption in Lesotho*. Berlin: Transparency International. p. 9.
77 Ibid: 8.
78 Ibid.

the period of suspension and in respect of which he is sentenced to imprisonment without the option of a fine.[79]

During the ABC, LCD and BNP coalition government, the DCEO made an unprecedented move in Lesotho's history. It launched investigations against prominent politicians, who were alleged to have committed acts of corruption. What was unprecedented is the fact that these individuals were still in power. In the first of these cases, the DCEO investigated former minister of finance, Dr Timothy Thahane, who faces two counts of corruption. In the first count he is alleged to have made a misrepresentation to:

> The Standard Lesotho Bank that Prime Minister Pakalitha Mosisili and minister of agriculture, Ralechate 'Mokose, had endorsed the Block Farming Project for vegetable farmers of the Temo-'Moho Mpharane Agricultural Association, resulting in a loss of [USD 1 292 328]. This is Thahane's home area. In the second count Thahane is again accused of making misrepresentation to the Standard Lesotho Bank that fuel supplied to Temo-'Moho, worth [USD 434 036], was payable by the financial institution to the suppliers, Engen Lesotho Limited.[80]

He was fired by the post-2012 coalition government.

In the third case, Thahane and former principal secretary for finance, Mosito Khethisa, were accused of defrauding the government of Lesotho of USD 1 361 905. The two are charged with fraud, together with a local company, Civa Innovations Management Pty Ltd. The charges concern a contract for a wool and mohair project, awarded to this company on 29 April 2010 by the government in contravention of the Public Procurement Regulations (2007).[81] The outcomes of this case are still pending.

The fourth case of grand corruption involves the former minister of local government and deputy prime minister, Mothetjoa Metsing. The DCEO had begun investigations between October and November 2013 after receiving a tip-off that Big Bravo Construction (Pty) Ltd was undeservingly and illegally awarded a tender to construct roads in Ha Matala and Ha Leqele villages; and that Metsing, who at that time was the minister of local government and chieftainship affairs, received bribes from the company in order to award the tender to it. Based on that information, the second respondent commenced a discreet and confidential investigation. The investigation revealed that Metsing appointed the deputy principal secretary as his delegate on the evaluation and adjudication panel,

---

79 *Matete v The Crown* (CofA [CRI] 4/2010). Available at www.lesotholii.org/ls/judgement/court-appeal/2010/27 [accessed 27 September 2016].
80 Thahanes' Corruption Case Postponed (2014, 11 November) *Public Eye Online*. Available at www.puliceyenews.com/site/2014/11/11/thahanes-corruption-case-postponed/ [accessed 29 September 2016].
81 Tefo T (2014, 20 June) Thahane, Khethisa back in court. http://lestimes.com/thahane-khethisa-back-in-court/. Available at http://lestimes.com/thahane-khethisa-back-in-court/ [accessed 30 September 2016].

which assessed the tenders. It further revealed that the initial evaluation report had been revised to favour the company.[82]

The DCEO demanded Metsing's bank statements from the Standard Lesotho Bank and the Nedbank, in terms of section 7(1)(c) of the principal law, amended by section 9 of the amendment act. The banks complied with this request. The Standard Lesotho Bank statement indicated that USD 23 429 had been deposited into Metsing's account. Similarly, the Nedbank statement also indicated that USD 8, 428 was deposited.

Metsing challenged this move by the DCEO, arguing that the DCEO and the section of the law empowering it to have access to his personal accounts, violate his right to respect for private and family life, as provided for by section 11 of the constitution. He lost the case in the high court but appealed, and again lost in the court of appeal.[83] This means the DCEO can pursue its case against him.

F. Conclusion

Lesotho established its anti-corruption agency even before international instruments against corruption such as the UN and AU conventions and the SADC protocol were adopted. Although it has ratified all these instruments, the country has not domesticated them. It established the DCEO as a specialised anti-corruption institution through an act of parliament, which has not granted the agency the requisite autonomy to discharge its mandate.

It attempted to separate the staff of the agency from the general public service by establishing the appointment and promotion board. However, the process is not complete; other important issues such as appointment criteria and code of conduct have not yet been development. Crucially, the appointment of director general is still made by the prime minister; this appointment could compromise the director general's autonomy in the discharge of his/her duties, should there be a need to investigate the prime minister or those close to him/her.

The DCEO has delegated powers from the DPP to prosecute corruption cases it has investigated. It does not have powers to independently prosecute corruption cases without the authorisation of the DPP. This arrangement has the potential to cause serious problems, should the two offices have disagreements over some cases.

Looking at the figures of the last six years, the DCEO has been receiving annual increases of its overall budget from the public purse. While this is commendable, the budget of this agency falls far too short of internationally recommended level thus inhibiting it to carry out its mandate effectively.

---

82 *Mothejoa Metsing vs. Director General & others*. Constitutional Case No. 11/14.
83 Metsing fails to stop corruption probe (2015, 8 November) Lesotho *Sunday Express*. Available at http://sundayexpress.co.ls/metsing-fails-to-stop-corruption-probe/ [accessed 30 September 2016].

Lastly, the agency has generally collaborative and complementary relations with all its stakeholders: other public institutions, civil society, and the country's development partners. It has been able to secure some financial support from some of the development partners to carry out some of its important activities; including the development of the NACSAP, an important document for the fight against corruption should it be fully implemented.

Overall, the agency could do more that it has done in the fight against this plague if the following recommendations could be implemented.

G. Recommendations

Legal Reforms

- Lesotho should domesticate the international conventions of corruption it has ratified.
- Parliament should discuss, with a view to enhancing the autonomy of the DCEO, the currently pending bill on corruption and go beyond this by constitutionalising this important national institution to protect it from possible abuse.
- Powers to appoint the head of the agency should be removed from the executive head of government to some oversight structure with close links to parliament, which should also open the appointment process for competition so that the best qualified people can apply and get this post. There is an emerging trend in Lesotho in which public officials, who were appointed by past governments, are replaced by appointees of the new governments.
- Parliament should grant the DCEO full prosecutorial powers so that it does not work under the delegated authority of the DPP.

Institutional reform

- The government should capacitate the DCEO by increasing its annual budget in line with the commitments it has made under the international conventions. It serves no purpose to create an entity like this, give it such a huge and important mandate, and starve it of resources.

Other reforms

- When resources have been availed, the DCEO should embark on the process of decentralisation so that citizens of Lesotho can access it easily.
- The DCEO should also increase its visibility to the public through aggressive public education campaigns to generate public awareness on the evils of corruption and enhance popular will against the scourge.

6
MALAWI

Dr Henry Chingaipe

A. Executive summary

This chapter is a report of the assessment of the Anti-Corruption Bureau (ACB) of Malawi. It is part of a wider effort on assessing and understanding the operational context of anti-corruption commissions in Southern Africa.

The chapter endorses the observations that corruption in Malawi is pervasive and recognised as part of social behaviour especially after the transition to multiparty democracy in 1994. The assessment shows that while the ACB has a comprehensive mandate and a required institutional form, its functioning and performance is limited. The key impediments relate to low levels of operational independence in view of high levels of political interference especially in investigating and prosecuting corruption, inadequate funding of operations partly because of genuine resource constraints but also a perceived motivation to stifle its oversight work by the political executive, several institutional and legal requirements that collectively undermine effectiveness, and staff and institutional capacity gaps.

In view of these constraints, this study observes that the fight against corruption by the ACB amounts to efforts aimed at exciting donors who have been vocal on the issue after revelations of massive looting of public funds at the seat of government, tackling political opponents of the incumbency while fresh malfeasance goes on as groups of political and bureaucratic elites take their turns to feed off the state by appropriating public for private motives or advantages.

The chapter recommends review and amendment of the Corrupt Practices Statute, specialised training for staff, review of recruitment policy and development of staff retention strategy among others.

B. Introduction

One evening in September 2013, the Malawian government's budget director, Paul Mphwiyo, was shot as he drove into his upmarket suburban home in Lilongwe's Area 43. He survived gun wounds. However, the shooting unravelled a chilling story of systematic, highly organised and deep-seated sleaze, fraud, money laundering and corruption in Malawi's public sector, engineered from the seat of government and perpetrated by the very same public officers entrusted to look after public resources. The malfeasance that has come to be known as 'cashgate' validated repeated findings of governance surveys that claimed that corruption in Malawi was endemic and dovetailed with the social fabric such that it is a part of life. Addressing cashgate has been a primary preoccupation of criminal justice agencies since 2013 and the onus has been mostly on the Anti-Corruption Bureau (ACB) – the agency with an explicit legal mandate to lead and execute anti-corruption efforts.

This report presents findings based on an assessment of the capacity of the ACB, showing how the status quo relates to the performance of the bureau in executing its mandate. It is believed that cashgate, the roots of which date back to a few years before 2013, represents the failure of the ACB to uphold its mandate and prevent corruption; and that investigations and prosecution of cases are tangled in a web of the political and economic interests of powerful political, bureaucratic and business elites who exploit its operational framework to undermine its effectiveness. While the current institutional design of the ACB raises public expectations for effective anti-corruption efforts, the outcomes do not deliver. The mandated incentive to institute anti-corruption measures has been accompanied by external incentives to keep those measures weak, thereby perpetuating corruption. Furthermore, efforts toward investigating and prosecuting corruption are co-opted as government strategies for 'tackling political opponents and tickling donors'.[1] These factors result in a half-hearted approach to the fight against corruption. While the ACB has the right institutional form, its functionality is beholden to the interests of the politically powerful and connected – so much so that operational independence, enforcement and accountability for effective anti-corruption remain challenges.

C. State of corruption in Malawi

Public perceptions of corruption

In the aftermath of the cashgate scandal, there is widespread consensus in the country that corruption is endemic. This is reflected through media outlets in nearly all governance assessments and narratives in the public domain. A seminal survey commissioned by the ACB in 2005 found that 90% of Malawians believed that corruption was a serious problem that was badly affecting the delivery of services by public institutions, and 70% believed that corruption had become worse. A following survey in 2010 showed that the proportion of Malawians believing that that corruption had become worse reduced significantly to

---

1   Hall-Matthews DNJ (2007) Tickling donors and tackling opponents: The anti-corruption campaign in Malawi. In: S Bracking (ed.) *Corruption and Development: The Anti-Corruption Campaigns.* Basingstoke: Palgrave Macmillan. pp. 77–102.

50%, probably due to highly organised political rhetoric of zero-tolerance for corruption that President Bingu Muntharika orchestrated during his first term in office.

Afrobarometer findings, covering the period between 2003 and 2014, consistently show that significant proportions of Malawians believe that corruption is pervasive in public offices, including the presidency, as shown in Figure 1.

Figure 1: People's perceptions of the involvement of public offices in corruption

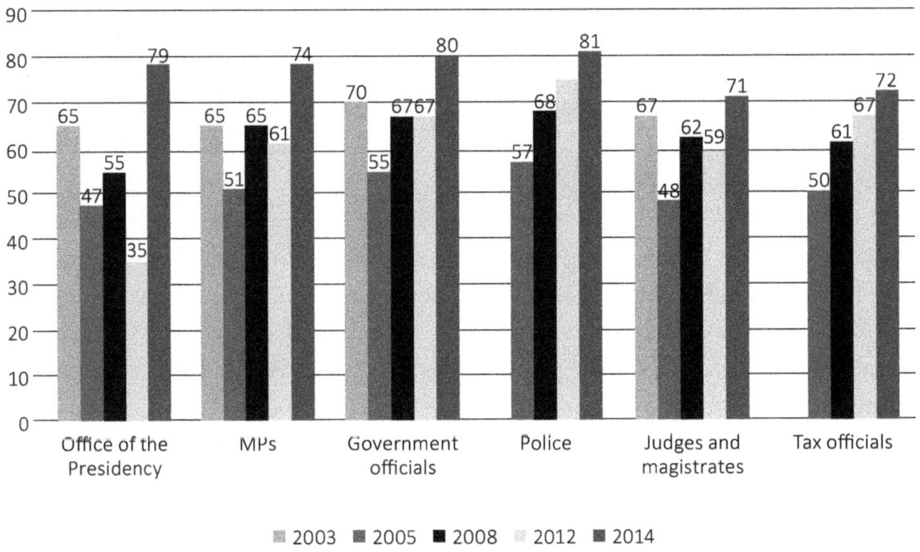

Source: Afrobarometer survey results for rounds 1–5, 2003–2014.

Assessments by external institutions corroborate local findings on the perceptions of the prevalence of corruption in the country. For instance, the corruption perception index for Malawi, as measured and published by Transparency International, shows that Malawi's score has gone from 30 to 37 between 2010 and 2014 on a scale where zero is most corrupt and 100 is most clean.[2]

The financial intelligence unit (FIU) estimated that Malawi lost over K20 billion between 2009 and 2013, through looting of cash at the treasury by public officers.[3] On the other hand, the national audit office report revealed that between 2009 and 2012 Malawi lost or mismanaged K90 billion.[4] According to PricewaterhouseCoopers, the external

---

2   Transparency International (2014) *Corruption Perception Index 2014: Clean Growth at Risk*. Available at http://www.transparency.org/news/pressrelease/corruption_perceptions_index_2014_clean_growth_at_risk [accessed 12 September].
3   Chapalapula T (2013, 17 October) K20 billion lost in Capital Hill scam. *The Daily Times*.
4   Munthali E (2013, 23 October) Audit shows K90 BN stolen under DPP: Payments made without documentation. *The Nation* newspaper.

auditors who were contracted by government to audit its accounts between January and December 2014, over K577 billion could not be accounted for, and later after further analysis and verification, the unaccounted for figure is K236 billion.[5] Other studies and audits on local government have also shown that cashgate is not limited to the central government. It is an equally serious affair in local councils.

Conceptualising and defining corruption in Malawi

There are many understandings or definitions of corruption. Some of the leading definitions that resonate with common Malawian discourses of corruption include the following:

- 'Corruption designates the practice of using the power of office for making private gain in breach of laws and regulations normally in force.'[6]
- 'Corruption is behaviour which deviates from the formal duties of a public role because of private regarding (personal, close family, private clique) pecuniary or status gains; or violates rules against the exercise of certain types of private regarding influence.'[7]
- 'A public official is corrupt if he accepts money or money's worth for doing something that he is under a duty to do anyway or one that he is under a duty not to do, or to exercise a legitimate discretion for improper reasons.'[8]
- 'Corruption is behaviour which deviates from the norms, rules and duties governing the exercise of a public office or role for purposes of private gain or influence. It may do this by ignoring prohibitions against certain actions, or by fulfilling obligations to act, or by exercising legitimate discretions to act, as long long as it does so for private advantage or private motives.'[9]
- Corruption is 'the misuse of public powers, office and authority for private gain through bribery, extortion, influence peddling, nepotism, fraud, speed money or embezzlement'.[10]
- Corruption is 'an abuse of entrusted power by politicians and civil servants for private gain'.[11]

---

5 Chimjeka R & Nhlane S (2016, 9 July) Inside K577BN Forensic Audit. *The Nation* newspaper. Available at http://mwnation.com/inside-k577bn-forensic-audit/ [accessed 13 September 2016].
6 Heidenheimer AJ (ed.) (1978) *Political Corruption: Readings in Comparative Analysis*. New Brunswick NJ: Transaction Books. p. 346.
7 Nye JS (1967) Corruption and political development: A cost-benefit analysis. *American Political Science Review* LX 1(2): 416.
8 McMullan M (1961) A theory of corruption. *Sociological Review* 9: 183.
9 Szeftel M (1982) Political Graft and the spoils system in Zambia: The state as a resource in itself. *Review of African Political Economy* 24: 85.
10 UNDP cited by Matsheza P & Kunaka C (2000) *Anti-Corruption Mechanisms and Strategies in Southern Africa*. Harare: Human Rights Research and Documentation Trust of Southern Africa (HRRDTSA). p. 19.
11 Langseth P et al. (1997) *The Role of a National Integrity System in Fighting Corruption*. Washing DC: The Economic Development Institute of the World Bank.

- It is a broad phenomenon which 'while being tied particularly to the act of bribery is a general term covering misuse of authority as a result of considerations of personal gain, which need not be money'.[12]

For the functioning of the ACB, however, it is the legal definition of corruption that is important. These definitions are found in the Corrupt Practices Act (1995) and the Penal Code (2003). The Penal Code defines official corruption, extortion by public officers, favouritism and abuse of office or false claim as forms of corruption punishable by law.[13] According to the Corrupt Practices Act (CPA) of Malawi, corruption is related to:

> The soliciting, accepting or obtaining, or to the giving, promising or offering, of a gratification ... by way of a bribe or other personal temptation, enticement or inducement.

Also:

> Gratification means any payment, whether in cash or kind, and includes any rebate, bonus, deduction or percentage, discount, commission, service, forbearance, assistance, protection or any other material gain, benefit, amenity, facility, concession or favour of any description, and any fee, reward, advantage or gift, other than a casual gift.[14]

It is worthwhile to note that Malawi's legal definitions of corruption leave out nepotism and cronyism as forms of corruption, even though these are often cited in social and political discourses as being at the epicentre of malfeasance in the public sector. It means nepotism and cronyism cannot be prosecuted under the act as crimes of corruption.

The political economy of corruption in Malawi

Corruption in Malawi essentially thrives because of a huge deficit of willingness among political leaders and government to define and enforce the necessary ethical standards, systems and practices that would promote integrity in the public sector and general society. As Figure 2 shows, enforcement and compliance with regulations has consistently been very low. This means that approaches to fighting corruption that focus on tightening the law will simply add to the statutes without any guarantee of results. Similarly, the control

---

12 Bayley DH (1966) The effects of corruption in developing nations. *Western Political Quarterly* 19(4): 719–732.
13 Under sections 90–95 of the Penal Code (2003), official corruption and extortion or acceptance of improper reward by public officers is a misdemeanour punishable by imprisonment for three years. Public officers receiving property to show favour commit acts or omissions punishable by six months in prison. Those who acquire or hold private interests directly or indirectly in public property shall be guilty of a misdemeanour and given imprisonment for one year. Abuse of office is a felony punishable by three-year imprisonment.
14 Corrupt Practices Act (2004) Laws of Malawi, Chapter 7:04. Zomba: Government Printer. p. 4.

MALAWI

of corruption has persistently been low, despite the adoption of a populist slogan of a zero-tolerance on corruption in 2005 by President Bingu wa Mutharika and the institution of a National Anti-Corruption Strategy (NACS)[15] in 2008 by the ACB. The NACS established a national integrity committee (NIC) comprising leaders from eight sectors of the Malawi political economy: the executive, the legislature, the judiciary, civil society, the private sector, traditional leaders, the media and faith-based organisations. The NIC was mandated to champion the establishment of the national integrity system (NIS), which has suffered a common Malawian disease whereby institutional form and institutional functionality do not always converge in desired outcomes.

Figure 2: Indicators for anti-corruption, regulatory quality and rule of law

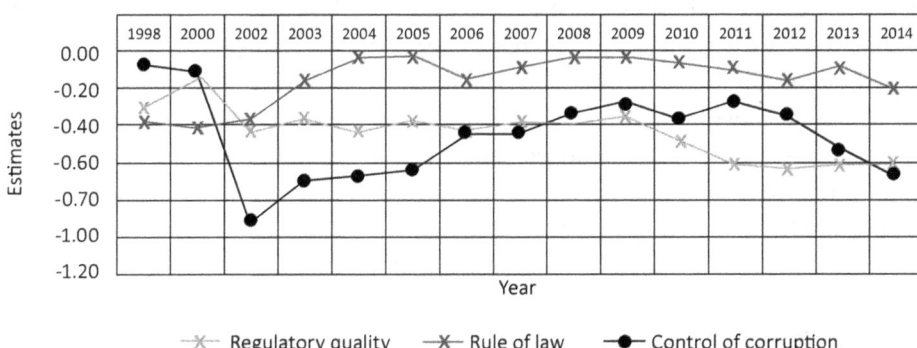

Source: World Governance Indicators 1998–2014.

Corruption in Malawi has become part of a wider pattern of social behaviour especially after the transition to multiparty democracy in 1994. In a multiparty setting, it is seen as a means of upward social mobility and therefore contributes to a process of class formation and restructuring.

The struggle for the control of the Malawian state is less for political reasons than for economic reasons:

> The state is a resource in itself, an avenue for upward mobility and a source of wealth for those with access to the state so that they can acquire resources, opportunities and advantages for entering private sector or enhancing their capital accumulation.[16]

---

15 The NACS was launched in 2008 as one way of achieving the government zero-tolerance policy against corruption. Seven years down the line, the policy seems to have been abandoned as it is rarely referred to by government and other leaders in the public forums.
16 Szeftel M (2004) Political Graft and the spoils system in Zambia: The state as a Resource in itself. In: G Mohan & T-Z Williams (eds) *The Politics of Transition in Africa*. ROAPE Publications.

Corruption thrives mostly because political and bureaucratic elites ignore prohibitions against certain actions, or act in favour of appropriating resources from the state for personal or group interests.

Furthermore, the configuration of political and bureaucratic power revolves around the president, whose economic and political interests, as evidenced by a series of cashgate scams from 2005 to the present, ensure that oversight institutions such as the ACB and auditor general are tamed to retain incumbency. Generally, all agencies of the state mandated to check and punish malfeasance and corruption are part of a larger bureaucracy which gravitates around the president as 'an appointing authority', and the tendency has been to appoint persons deemed compliant and sympathetic to the president's personal interests or the interests of his close associates and party members. The appointees then understand that they hold office and enjoy its privileges on account of the president, and that it is their main role to secure and protect the interests of the president through the mandates of their offices. Thus at any point in time, the political and bureaucratic elites appropriate the spoils of office in ways that attract corruption. This is because access to the state provides them with opportunities to facilitate corrupt transactions and to protect each other from the law, while using their positions of oversight to pursue those that are out of grace with the ruling establishment, or the president himself.

D. Civil society, donors and media engagement

Malawi is historically characterised by state control, a monopoly on public media, and a weak civil society. Civil society and the media, however, have evolved from a culture of silence to a culture of political activism. These have been popular institutions during the democratic transition that began in 1993. In short, 'Malawi's process of democratisation started as a popular movement; a social protest against a political regime that failed to meet the expectations of its people.'[17] Civil society, as 'the realm of organised social life standing between the individual and the state' is necessary for democratic accountability because it is

> an aggregate of institutions whose members are engaged primarily in a complex of non-state activities – economic and cultural production, voluntary associations and household life – and who in this way preserve and transform their identity by exercise all sorts of pressures or controls upon state institutions.[18]

In Malawi, the media operate under a reasonable legal framework. In particular, the Communications Act (1998). The act establishes the Malawi Communications Regulatory

---

17 Ott M, Phiri K & Patel N (eds)(2000) *Malawi's Second Democratic Elections: Process, Problems and Prospects*. Zomba: Kachere Series. p.89.
18 Keane (1988) cited by Chirwa in Sachikonye LM (ed.) (1995) *Democracy, Civil Society and the State, Social Movements in Southern Africa*. Harare: SAPES. p.90.

Authority (MACRA) with powers to issue licences and regulate both public and private media institutions in the country. It promotes open access to information; efficiency and competition among media personnel; fostering the development and operation of media institutions in accordance with international standards; and it works independently. However, the president appoints some of its associated members, including the chairman of MACRA.[19] Since 1994, some cases of corruption have been exposed through the media, and corruption suspects have been named and shamed. The media and civil society have been characterised by a vocal condemnation of corruption, coupled with demands to see it being dealt with. To this end, the media have raised public awareness through information dissemination about corruption. Generally, publicity can contribute powerfully to accountability, especially where information about misdeeds has been concealed, but accountability itself requires penalties beyond publicity – at the very least, the capacity to remove an office holder from office. Without political or legal sanctions, publicity can remain at the level of mere allegations which, the powerful often find ways to manage. What is known, however, is that the right to know is linked inextricably to accountability. Informed appraisal of government by the public, press and parliament is a difficult, perhaps even impossible task if government activities and decision-making processes are obscured from public scrutiny.

Electronic media

The electronic media comprises both public and private radio stations, as well as several private TV stations. Among the radio stations, the most influential are the Malawi Broadcasting Corporation (MBC) and the privately owned Zodiak Broadcasting Station. The MBC is a public institution and operates under the direction of an MBC board, headed by a chairman appointed by the president, in consultation with the public appointments committee (PAC) of parliament. It is the single most pervasive electronic media institution, covering the entire country. However, the MBC has difficulties broadcasting issues of corruption, especially involving senior politicians. While the private media is awash with stories about grand corruption, including electoral fraud, the MBC skips most of them even in its print media reviews. This despite the fact that the Parliamentary and Presidential Elections Act (1993) (PPEA) and the Communications Act (1998) explicitly empower the public media to fairly and equitably cover the electoral process. Political equality requires that all political parties and electoral candidates be treated equally regardless of their social, economic, cultural and political status under section 58 of the PPEA.[20] With respect to the rule of law and use of public resources, all political actors are equal before the law and enjoy equitable access to public resources. The rule of law demands that no one be

---

19 The Communications Act (1998) section 7.
20 The Parliamentary and Presidential Election Act (1993) section 58, promotes political equality when it states that 'every public office and public entity or authority shall give and be seen to give equal treatment to all political parties to enable each political party to conduct its campaign freely'.

above the law and that state power, including that of the Malawi Electoral Commission as a state institution, be exercised in accordance with the law.

Political corruption with respect to public media is rampant in the face of existing legislation. Section 58 of the PPEA promotes political equality when it states that 'every public office and public entity or authority shall give and be seen to give equal treatment to all political parties to enable each political party to conduct its campaign freely'. Section 87(1)(b) of the Communications Act states that:

> The MBC shall provide public broadcasting services in accordance with the following principles – the encouragement of free and informed opinion on all matters of public interest; [d] respect for human rights, the rule of law and the Constitution of Malawi; (2) [a] function without any political bias and independently of any person or body of persons; [b] support the democratic process; ... [d] provide balanced coverage of any elections.

To buttress this provision institutionally, section 45(1) of the act states that:

> MACRA shall regulate the provision of broadcasting in Malawi in the manner which it considers is best suited ... to ensure equitable treatment of political parties and election candidates by all broadcasting licenses during any election period.

The unfortunate part is that the private media is also caught up in the jaws of corrupt political elites who are the owners of those media houses.

Print media

It is not difficult to note that the print media in Malawi is much freer to tackle corruption than electronic media. Almost all the cases of corruption that have come to light in the country trace their exposure to the print media, namely: President Muluzi's K1.7 billion cashgate; President Bingu Mutharika's K577 billion cashgate; President Joyce Banda K40 billion cashgate; the education scam; the maize scam; the Land Rover scam, and numerous others trace their exposure to the print media.[21] However, the numerical scope of the print media in Malawi is limited. It is difficult, therefore, to expect significant impact on corruption through the use of the media because most of the people are illiterate and too poor to afford and read newspapers and magazines. Besides, government has attempted to muzzle the print media by denying them business.

---

21 See, for example, Banda PS (2002, 1 November) Apex Land Rover Case Resurfaces. *The Nation*; Langa J (2002, 19 November) Ministers named in grain sale scam. *The Nation*; Munthali G (2004, 22 October) Malawi drops on corruption rank. *The Nation*; Mwase L (2004, 18 October) K187 million scam: Mpinganjira exposed *The Weekly Chronicle*; Nzembe D (2002, 28-29 September) Government, Anti-corruption Bureau React to Corruption Survey. *The Weekend Nation*; Chapalapata M (2003, 10 March 2003) Corruption worse in Malawi – World Bank. *The Nation*; Mwenenguwe R (2002, 8 January) Corruption: great challenge for Malawi. *The Nation*.

While a free press 'captures the transparency of the system' and that 'by increasing transparency, freedom of press reduces the informational problem in the political system, and increases accountability',[22] political incumbents in Malawi have monopolised state media, and systematically used it to castigate their political rivals (especially during electoral campaigns) perpetrating cycles of corruption. In earnest, although there is a plural media in the country, ownership of media houses remains largely skewed in favour of individual politicians, sons of politicians or political parties.[23] Thus, some of the information reaching the public through this means is either inaccurate or simply politically motivated. Although there is freedom of press in Malawi, 'in reality, the owners of the media intervene daily in the operations of the journalists under their employ' and 'government itself is the largest media owner, which can undermine the independence of the media'.[24] Although section 36 of constitution guarantees freedom of press, there are still 'oppressive laws'[25] in Malawi that obstruct free flow of information and, therefore, transparency and accountability.

Political economy of access to information

Information is power. It can make or break governments. Historically, the predominant political culture in Malawi has been characterised by the marginalisation of groups and individuals that are perceived to be oppositional in the access to public goods and services. With respect to public information, such marginalisation is manifested in resistance and suspicion on the part of custodians of public information towards requests for access to that information submitted by individuals and groups that are perceived to be oppositional. There have been efforts by civil society to put pressure on the government, politicians and decision-makers in order to promote access to information. Unless there is consistent pressure from the stakeholders, the government will not grant access to information. The media outlets must be utilised in delivering the campaign materials to the public. A well-designed media strategy could be the best way to maintain the pressure. Members of the campaign team should avoid issuing contradictory and ambiguous statements to the public.

Despite constitutional provision for access to information (ATI), Malawi has a wide range of statutory provisions that prohibit the disclosure of some types of public information to members of the public. The uncertainty created by the continued existence of restrictive legislation sometimes makes it hard for public officials to know exactly how

---

22 Lederman D et al (2001) Accountability and Corruption: Political Institutions Matter. Washington DC: World Bank, University of Chicago. p. 17.
23 Ott M, Phiri K & Patel N (eds)(2000) *Malawi's Second Democratic Elections: Process, Problems and Prospects*. Zomba: Kachere Series. p. 164–170.
24 Langseth P et al. (1997) *The Role of a National Integrity System in Fighting Corruption*. Washing DC: The Economic Development Institute of the World Bank. p. 21.
25 Some of these oppressive media laws have been inherited from the one-party state and include section 39 of the Police Act which prohibits police from disclosing any information on an ongoing investigation without due authority; section 60 of the Courts Act (cap 3:02) which allows courts to hear cases in camera; section 4 of the Protected Flags, Emblems and Names Act (cap 18:03, section 4[1]); sections 5 and 8 of the Protected Places Act (cap 14:04), the Army Act (cap 12: 01); sections 60, 89 and 366 of the Criminal Procedure and Evidence Act (cap 18: 01); Makossah P (2004, 26 August) Kasambara will lobby for media. *The Nation*.

much to disclose. If one law tells them to release information but another tells them they will be prosecuted for any unauthorised disclosures, officials will most likely err on the side of caution and continue to withhold information. In his study, Kanyongolo[26] (2012) has cited 22 acts of parliament which have provisions that act as barriers to accessing information. These laws must be subjected to judicial challenge for inconsistency with the constitutional guarantee of the right to access public information. Such statutes include: Banking Act (1989), Capital Market Development Act (1990), Competition and Fair Trading Act (1998), Corrupt Practices Act (1995), Criminal Procedure and Evidence Code (1967), Defence Force Act (2004), Employment Act (2000), Malawi Revenue Authority Act (2000), Malawi Bureau of Standards Act (1972), Mental Treatment Act (1948), Money Laundering, Proceeds of Serious Crime and Terrorist Financing Act (2006), National Assembly (Powers and Privileges) Act (1957), Official Secrets Act (1913), Political Parties (Registration and Regulation) Act (1993), Preservation of Public Security Act (1960), Presidential and Parliamentary Elections Act (1993), Protected Places and Areas Act (1960), Public Audit Act (2003), Reserve Bank of Malawi Act (1989), Science and Technology Act (2003), Treaties and Conventions Publication Act (1984), Veterinary and Para-Veterinary Practitioners Act (2001).

Delays in the enacting and implementation of the ATI legislation is also rooted in the perceived fear that the media would use the laws as a gun to force government to disclose classified information. First, the ATI legislation has throughout been championed by the media, and the question is, in whose interest are they doing so? The government and the public servants are suspicious of the motives of the private media, which has been in the forefront of this campaign. Second, most of the private media houses are owned by people who are politically aligned to different political groups. Third, information is power such that government is always afraid that once the media has full access to public information, the government may lose its clout and political muscle. In other words, it is argued that the media in Malawi has not shown the requisite responsibility in the way it handles sensitive information. Some of them are alleged to be agents of opposition politicians. With this perception, it be wise to use the media as a vehicle in public awareness programming about ATI as opposed to having them taking front seat.

E. International and legal framework
Status and general legal framework
Malawi ratified the United Nations Convention Against Corruption (UNCAC), the Africa Union Convention on Combating and Preventing Corruption (AUCCPC), and the SADC Protocol Against Corruption. The UNCAC was ratified on 4 December 2007, the AUCCPC on 26 November 2007, and the SADC Protocol Against Corruption on 2

---

26 Kanyongolo E (2012) Obstacles to access to information in Malawi. *MISA Research Report*.

September 2002.[27] Despite the ratification of the conventions, however, there appears to be minimal or no dissemination of their contents to the members of the public. Nevertheless, the essence of the conventions is adequately covered in the anti-money laundering and corruption laws of Malawi. Hence, despite lack of publicity of the international conventions, the Malawian anti-corruption and anti-money laundering laws are vehicles through which the conventions are domesticated and implemented locally.

The current constitution was enacted at the dawn of multiparty democracy in the mid-1990s. In agreement with democratic principles of good governance, the constitution provides for the creation of public bodies for promoting accountability, financial probity and transparency, so as to safeguard public resources. This provision created a background for the establishment of public bodies for the promotion of good governance and respect of human rights. These bodies are: the Malawi Human Rights Commission, the Law Commission, office of the ombudsman, the ACB, and more recently the FIU. It is, however, important to note, that the constitution does not directly mention corruption, nor does it directly establish the ACB.

The constitutional shortfall notwithstanding, Malawi has made some notable strides in enacting laws that can assist in combating and preventing corruption. In 2014, the government established an assets declaration office under the Assets Declaration Law that requires politicians, senior public officers, and officers in public bodies vulnerable to corruption to declare their assets upon assuming office and every year thereafter. Effective enactment of this would deter political leaders and senior public officials from abusing their official powers to acquire wealth illegally from the public coffers. However, an important factor for success is missing: the enactment of the Access to Information Bill needs to be expedited in order to make acquisition of wealth really transparent. While civil society organisations and the media advocate for the passing of the bill in parliament, progress made by the government and the legislature is so far unconvincing.

Legal and policy anti-corruption framework
Specific anti-corruption law
Malawi has a specific law against corruption, namely the Corrupt Practices Act (CPA). Section 4 creates the ACB, which is mandated, among other things, to 'take necessary measures for the prevention of corruption in public bodies and private bodies'. The measures, in particular, include:[28]

- Examining the practices and procedures of public and private bodies in order to discover corrupt practices and revise methods of work;
- Advising public bodies and private bodies on ways and means of preventing corruption, and on changes of methods of work to ensure effective performance of their duties;

---

27 Researched by Obert Chinhamo and Alouis Munyaradzi of the Anti-Corruption Trust of Southern Africa.
28 Corrupt Practices Act (2004) Laws of Malawi, Chapter 7:04. Zomba: Government Printer. p.8.

- Disseminating information on the evil and dangerous effects of corruption;
- Enlisting and fostering public support against corrupt practices;
- Receiving complaints, reports, or other information of alleged or suspected corruption;
- Investigating alleged or suspected offences under the act and any other law disclosed in the course of investigating corruption; and,
- Prosecute any offence under the CPA (subject to the directions of the director of public prosecutions [DPP]).

Based on the CPA, the ACB established three operational functional areas: corruption prevention; enforcement (investigations and prosecutions); and public education.

The CPA captures a broad range of offences. It defines corrupt practice as meaning three things:
- The offering, giving, receiving, obtaining or soliciting of any advantage to influence the action of any public officer or any other person in the discharge of the duties of that public officer, official, or other person;
- Influence peddling; and
- The extortion of any advantage.

According to the CPA, 'influence peddling' refers to the influence that people in positions of authority exert on their subordinates in order to obtain an advantage; 'extortion of an advantage' refers to charging a fee for a service that is supposed to be offered free, or where compensation is allowed, charging more that the right fee. An advantage, on the other hand, is defined as:

> any benefit, service, enjoyment or gratification, whether direct, and includes a payment, whether in cash or kind, or any rebate, deduction, concession or loan, and any condition or circumstance that puts one person or class of persons in a favourable position over another.[29]

The CPA criminalises benefiting from failure to declare conflict of interest too. It is also worth noting that the act empowers the ACB, upon obtaining a warrant from a court of law, to search and seize property, freeze banks accounts and issue other restraining orders on property suspected to be tainted with proceeds of crime. The CPA thus compliments the money laundering law. Nevertheless, this broad scope notwithstanding, the CPA does not adequately protect informers and it lacks provisions on corruption associated with electoral matters.

---

29 Corrupt Practices Act (2004) Laws of Malawi, Chapter 7:04. Zomba: Government Printer. p.4.

F. ACB institutional framework

Status and autonomy

The ACB was established by the CPA, not the constitution. Consequently, the constitution does not guarantee or safeguard the existence of the ACB. Parliament can repeal the act and abolish the ACB, without necessarily going through the rigorous process of changing the constitution. Section 4(3) of the act provides that the ACB, 'shall exercise its functions and powers independent of the direction or interference of any other person or authority'. However, the ACB is not free from external influence. Administratively the ACB is under the ministry of justice and reports to parliament annually. The appointment and removal of the director and deputy director has always been contentious. Currently, in accordance with the act, the state president appoints and removes the director and the deputy director.

The NACS provides strategies for enhancing the capacity of the ACB, one of which is to review the act so that recruitment of the director and the deputy director should be done 'competitively through interviews', and their removal should be 'in a manner that is transparent and that safeguards the integrity of the office of the director'. Yet, seven years down the line the act has not been reviewed and the fate of the director and deputy director remains in the hands of the president. The director and the deputy therefore must dance to the tune of the executive or else risk being fired. This has been evidenced by the fact that, except on rare occasions, every new government has fired the director and appointed another. During its 18-year life span the ACB has had seven directors, and only two of the directors had a deputy. Hence, in its current state, the ACB is destabilised, incapacitated and skewed towards serving the interests of the incumbent government and not necessarily the desires of the public.

There is hope though. According to the 2012–2017 Strategic Plan, the ACB intends to enhance its independence by reviewing the CPA to address issues of the appointment of the director and deputy director, and lobby for the empowerment of an independent body to oversee the bureau's activities.

Appointment of other members

A review of the ACB staff establishment was undertaken in 2010. It was found that, generally, the ACB enjoys good conditions of service. Acknowledging that there had been an increase of 43 in 1997 to of 115 in 2010, the review nevertheless recommended a further addition of 117 positions, making a total of 232, a rather drastic increase of 102%. The main justification for this increase was the adoption of the NACS, which added considerably to the workload of the bureau; it will not be able to meet the challenges of NACS implementation without additional capacity. The department of human resource management and development in the office of the president (DHRMD) and cabinet (OPC) agreed that this increase would be effectuated over a five-year period, as of the 2010/2011 budget year.[30] However, the financial crisis and the public service recruitment freeze put an effective stop to staff expansion. At the end of 2011, there were still 116 vacancies. This state of affairs had no doubt hampered the operational effectiveness of the bureau.[31] It is worth noting that the ratio between operational and support staff is extremely skewed in favour of the latter. About half of the staff members have support functions, which is highly ineffectual and untenable in the long run. Still, this ratio has persisted for many years. Apart from counting the numbers of staff in operational and support functions to determine a ratio, it would be more appropriate to consider the ratio in salary terms. The pay differential between a senior staff such as the director on the one hand, and a driver or similar on the other, is huge. For example, according to the department of public service management, the pay differential between the two was 26:1 in August 2010.

It is important to note that the other members of ACB staff are recruited by the director. The ACB is free to recruit from the job market according to its requirements. However, the recruitment is determined by the DHRMD, which is under the OPC. Several times, the DHRMD has disagreed on the human resources needs of the ACB and this has resulted in the frustration and demotivation of officers. Officers would like a more open staff establishment that allows quick movement along the ranks through promotions, but this is not the case currently. There are officers who have stayed on entry grade without getting a promotion for 15 years, due to a narrow staff establishment. All the operational staff for the ACB, apart from assistant prosecutors, must have at least a university degree. The ACB thus has quality staff. University degrees notwithstanding, there is no regulation pertaining to the compatibility of education background and job requirements. Every investigator, for example, must have a degree, but the field of qualification is not specified. The strategic plan recognises the problem of misalignment of educational qualification and the job; thus, one of its strategic goals is to review and implement recruitment and promotion policy for investigators.

This challenge of lack of alignment notwithstanding, the ACB values specialised training, especially for the investigators. The ACB has a training plan that is controlled internally. Every operational officer of the ACB is required to attend this mandatory training. However, the training is skewed towards investigations. The mandatory competence training is a basic course that prepares investigators to collect documentary evidence, safely keep exhibits, interview witnesses and suspects, and take statements. The training, however, does not adequately prepare investigators to handle more complex cases involving finances and use of computers. As the strategic plan puts it:

> Although the bureau has consistently met its targets in the area of investigations, there are skill deficiencies in finance and e-related fraud and corruption, as well as to tackle increasing sophistication of corrupt offenders.

---

30 'Report on the Review of the Anti-Corruption Bureau Establishment, Salaries and Terms and Conditions of Service: Discussion Note' [not dated draft mimeo].
31 Nyondo J, Chingaipe H & Nyirenda S (2011) *Democratic Accountability Sub-Sector Capacity Assessment* (Draft Report). Lilongwe: Republic of Malawi. p. 17.

Such training is not easy to come by and no one in the ACB has had the luxury of having serious training on financial crimes and computer forensics. There is hope, however: the plan mentions training of officers in forensics and the establishment of a forensics unit within the ACB before 2017.

Corruption prevention, unlike investigations, is broad and encompasses an array of creative programmes. While corruption prevention officers are trained in basic investigations, there is a problematic lack of specialised corruption prevention training in Malawi. Specialised training can only be accessed outside the country and requires substantial funding and commitment from the bureau. As a result, such training is spread thin and wide. Consequently, the corruption prevention officers are ill equipped to implement effective anti-corruption programmes, despite the fact that corruption prevention is a primary function of the ACB. Section 10(1)(a) of the CPA mandates the ACB to 'take necessary measures for the prevention of corruption in public bodies and private bodies'. The ineffectiveness of corruption prevention may, to a large extent, explain the proliferation of corrupt practices in public institutions, despite the ACB being in existence for close to two decades.

The ACB receives technical support from its development partners, in particular the UK's Department for International Development (DfID). Currently, the DfID has supplied two advisors to provide technical support, especially in the prosecutions of the cashgate cases. The technical advisors are seasoned lawyers from the UK. Their main task is to analyse cases and guide investigators and prosecutors on how to handle them in order to ensure an increased conviction rate in court. As the plan acknowledges, there is a high rate of acquittals which suggests gaps either in investigations or prosecution skills. Thus resources (time and money) are put to waste. In 2012, the ratio of convictions against acquittals stood at 51:49. It is worth noting that the ACB has always had a technical advisor from the DfID and the effectiveness of the current advisors are yet to be measured. It is most likely that the inefficiencies in the prosecution of cases cannot be attributed to the presence or lack of a technical advisor alone, but rather to the quality of investigations, scarcity of prosecutors and the efficacy of the courts.

Staff ethics, conduct and capacity

The ACB has a code of conduct and ethical behaviour that applies to every member of the ACB, whether employed on a permanent or temporary basis. Section 18 of the CPA empowers the director to make standing orders which aim to prevent the abuse or neglect of duty, and uphold the efficiency and integrity of the ACB. The code forms a part of the standing orders and recognises that:

> The work of the bureau would be seriously undermined if any of its officers acted in a manner which the bureau itself or any member of the community found reprehensible in public institution of this nature.

Among other provisions, the code encourages the ACB to strive to carry out its functions promptly and with the highest standards of diligence, objectivity, professionalism and fairness; without undue infringement of people's liberty and privacy; and with strict observance of the right to property in accordance with the constitution. In addition, the code aims to make the ACB responsive and accountable to the community it serves, eliciting public support in the fight against corruption and thus promoting and maintaining confidence in the public service.

The code is an important tool for aligning staff behaviour towards the achievement of the objectives of the ACB. Being an enforcer of corruption legislation, staff integrity is an essential characteristic for the ACB. The code thus has a provision on financial and other private interest disclosures, and declarations of conflicts of interest. As the code sternly puts it, 'there must be no opportunity for an officer's personal interests, associations and activities (financial or otherwise) to conflict with the proper exercise of an officer's duties'. Consequently, all officers are required to make disclosures of personal particulars prior to commencing duties with the ACB. The director may also, at any time, require an officer to make a disclosure about all financial interests. The code also requires investigators and other officers to declare a conflict of interest if, during the course of an investigation or any other duty, the officer encounters information which involves people, organisations, or activities in which the officer has a personal interest. This provision safeguards the conduct of officers and promotes public trust in the ACB. The ACB officers are exposed to temptations as they investigate individuals or companies involved in grand corruption worth millions of kwacha, hence the need to clearly spell out expected conduct.

Remuneration of officers

The ACB is generally better remunerated than the mainstream civil service. All officers of the ACB are on three-year contract, subject to renewal upon successful performance. As contract employees, they receive a gratuity calculated as 25% of gross pay at the end of each contract, and they are not on pension. According to the conditions of employment, ACB salaries must always be higher than the salaries in the civil service. When there is an increase in civil service salaries, ACB salaries must be increased with a larger percentage to make the ACB attractive. In addition, the salaries are supposed to be increased when there is an increase in the cost of living. The conditions of service were crafted with the intention to recruit and retain the best quality staff. However, the reality is different. The ACB recruits quality staff and fails to retain a large number of them due to the government's reluctance to actually implement the conditions of service.

In the 2014/2015 financial year, the government implemented an average of a 70% increase in salaries for civil servants, parliamentarians and other politicians, but gave the ACB no salary increase. The government argued that it was implementing a harmonisation policy for salaries in the public service so that officers on the same grade receive the same pay regardless of the department they are working in or nature of work. This policy is in conflict with the ACB conditions of service. The policy also didn't address the fact that ACB officers are on contract and not entitled to a pension. Consequently, the officers staged industrial action in December 2014, demanding a 70% increase. The government increased the salary by 10% and requested the officers to call off the strike and give negotiations a chance. Five months down the line the negotiations did not materialise and in May 2015 the officers resumed the strike, which resulted in an increase of 9%. While the government might have genuine financial problems due to the pull-out of donors and other economic factors, the lack of application of the harmonisation policy to ACB remuneration appears to defy logic, and may demonstrate government unwillingness to have an effective anti-corruption drive.

Responsibilities and mandate

The core mandate of the ACB comes from section 13 of the constitution. The section emphasises the need for government to deliberately put in place mechanisms that would

> guarantee accountability, transparency, personal integrity and financial probity and which by virtue of their effectiveness and transparency will strengthen confidence in public institutions.

It was this particular constitutional provision that empowered parliament to enact the CPA that creates the ACB and mandates it to perform its three operational functions: public education, corruption prevention and law enforcement.

The ACB is mandated to prevent, investigate and prosecute corrupt practices. This is achieved through four departments: corruption prevention, public education, investigations and prosecutions. Each department is headed by a director who reports to the director general. The positions of director general, deputy director general and directors, however, do not appear in the law. These are new positions, created administratively, intended to create room for promoting officers. Under the old establishment, corruption prevention and public education were sections under one division, headed by a chief corruption prevention officer. Similarly, the investigation division was headed by a chief investigations officer and the prosecutions division by an assistant director. Overall, investigations, public education, and corruption prevention reported to the assistant director for operations. The new positions, though approved by the DHRD under the OPC, are yet to be incorporated into the CPA.

Public education department

The CPA under section 10 (1)(a) empowers the ACB to disseminate information on the dangers and evils of corruption, and enlist and foster public support in the fight against corruption. The provision empowers the ACB to educate people to reject, resist and report corruption practices. This function is the focus of the public education department, which fulfills its mandate through:

- Conducting public sensitisation programmes;
- Producing and distributing the ACB newsletter;
- Organising and facilitating press conferences;
- Producing and distributing information, education and communication (IEC) materials;
- Developing and maintaining a resource centre;
- Establishing and maintaining cooperation with clients and role-players;
- Establishing anti-corruption clubs in communities and schools;
- Participating in the annual trade fairs to punt anti-corruption messages;
- Conducting public debates;
- Observing International and National Anti-Corruption Day; and
- Producing electronic media programmes.

Despite an array of elaborate programmes, ineffective public education seems to be a major hindrance in combating corruption in Malawi. The programmes glitter on paper but the implementation faces a lot of challenges. The 2010 Corruption and Governance Survey revealed that most people are not conversant as to what constitutes a corrupt practice and they do not know how they can report it.

Corruption prevention, research and intelligence department
The ACB under section 10(a) of the CPA is responsible for:

i. Examining the practices and procedures of public bodies and private bodies in order to facilitate the discovery of corrupt practices and secure the revision of methods of work or procedures which in the opinion of the bureau may be prone or conducive to corrupt practices;

ii. Advising public bodies and private bodies on ways and means of preventing corrupt practices, and on changes in methods of work or procedures of such public bodies and private bodies compatible with the effective performance of their duties, which the bureau considers necessary to reduce the likelihood of the occurrence of corrupt practices.

This provision is the background for the creation of the corruption prevention, research and intelligence department, which fulfills its madate through:
- Reviewing legislation and policies to prevent fraud and corruption;
- Teaching basic investigation skills to officers involved in investigative institutions (such as auditors);
- Developing ethical codes of conduct for institutions;

- Conducting prevention of fraud and corruption workshops;
- Conducting work-systems-analysis and reviews;
- Collecting intelligence on suspected corruption offenders; and
- Developing anti-corruption policies for institutions.

Currently, the department is coordinating the implementation of the NACS for the creation of a national integrity system in the eight sectors, as identified in the strategy.

The department is vital to the ACB simply because 'prevention is better than cure'. However, the department is understaffed inspite of its big workload. As the strategic plan acknowledges, the department is overwhelmed by requests from institutions to assist in the implementation of corruption prevention programmes. The plan therefore encourages the devolution of corruption prevention functions to other institutions such as civil society and private consultants, while the ACB maintains a facilitative role.

Investigations department
The investigations department draws its mandate from section 10 of the CPA. The director is empowered under section 11 to authorise any officer of the bureau to conduct an inquiry into suspected or alleged offences. It makes corruption a criminal offence, punishable by a maximum of 12 years in prison. This is in contrast with section 90 of the Penal Code,[32] where corruption is deemed a misdemeanour and therefore not treated as a serious offence. Section 11(1)(a) states that all complaints reported to the ACB should be authorised by the director before an investigation is instituted. As a result, the ACB has put in place a complaints review committee, which comprises heads of departments to review all complaints and make recommendations to the director for action. The director only authorises an investigation on complaints that involve some element of corruption.

Section 11(1) empowers the director to authorise, in writing, any officer of the ACB to:
- Conduct an enquiry or investigations into alleged or suspected offences under the act;
- Require any public officer or any other person to answer questions concerning the duties of any other public officer or other person and order the production for inspection of any information and materials relating to the duties of the public officer or such other public officer or other person;
- Require any person in charge of any office or establishment of the government, or the head, chairman, manager or chief executive officer of any public body or private body to produce or furnish any document or certified true copy of any document which is in his/

---

[32] Cases under the Penal Code are prosecuted by the police and the director of public prosecutions. However, the ACB is empowered by the CPA to prosecute any case under any law if the case is discovered in the process of investigating corruption.

her possession or under his/her control considered necessary by ACB investigations;
- Require any person including any public officer to provide information or answer any question in connection with an inquiry or investigation by the bureau; and
- Do or perform such other acts or things as are reasonably necessary or required for the exercise of the functions of the ABC and the performance of his duties.

Under section 11(2),

> the director, the deputy director or other officer of the bureau authorised in writing ... shall have:
> a) Access to all books, records, returns, reports and other documents relating to the work of the government or any public body or private body;
> b) Access at any time to the premises of any government office, public body or private body, or to any vessel, boat, aircraft or other vehicle whatsoever, and may search such premises or such vessel, boat, aircraft or other vehicle if he has reason to suspect that any property corruptly acquired has been placed, deposited or concealed therein.

Under the CPA, there are many instruments that are used in the process of conducting investigations. Some of the instruments are:
- Use of notice to furnish documents: The director signs this notice, demanding the head of a particular department, ministry, bank or any institution to produce documents within a specified period of time. Failure to comply constitutes an offence under the act.
- Use of restriction notice: Issued to prevent a suspect from disposing of associated evidence. To protect the evidence, the director issues the notice on the property and nobody is allowed to deal in any way with the property without the written consent of the director. Failure to comply constitutes an offence under the act.
- Non-compliance with the bureau's orders and directions: Any person who contravenes or fails to comply with any order, direction, notice, requirement, or demand of the ACB issued, given or made under the act, is guilty of an offence and liable to a fine of K50 000 (USD 112) and imprisonment for two years.

Arrest and search
The ACB has the power to arrest a suspect who has committed or is about to commit an offence, or search a suspect if it perceives that the result will be pertinent for investigations

or prosecutions. The bureau must first, however, obtain a warrant from the magistrate. This requirement is designed as a control to prevent the ACB from abusing its powers. But, in instances where the ACB needs to act swiftly, the requirement is a stumbling block. In such cases, sometimes the ACB has resorted to using the police, who have powers to arrest and search without obtaining a court warrant. In the strategic plan, the ACB lobbies the government to review the CPA in order to remove the requirement of a warrant to arrest and search.

Prosecutions department
The prosecutions department of the ACB has the mandate to prosecute all cases. However, before any prosecution against corruption offences can commence, the ACB must get consent from the DPP, in accordance with section 42 of the act. This consent is supposed to be granted within 30 days. If the DPP withholds consent to any prosecution, he/she is required to provide reasons, in writing, devoid of any consideration for the withholding of the consent other than those of fact and the law and in addition to providing reasons to the director, inform the legal affairs committee of parliament of the decision within thirty days. This provision aims to provide checks and balances, and prevent the possible abuse of power by the ACB. However, some sections of society view the requirement as one that hampers the ACB, and one that politicians can manipulate to their advantage by way of influencing the DPP to deny consent on cases involving people in authority. Consequently, the strategic plan provides for lobbying government to remove the requirement to obtain consent from the DPP before prosecuting corruption cases under the CPA.

The public relations office
The public relations office is attached to the director's office. It promotes the image of the bureau and consists of one officer. The ACB established the office in order to work effectively with the media. The office periodically issues press releases, attends to media inquiries and holds press conferences.

A situational analysis during the development of the strategic plan revealed that the office is more reactive than proactive. According to the plan, therefore, there is need to build the capacity of the office so as to effectively create a positive public image for the ACB, fostering support for its performance. The 2010 Governance and Corruption Survey revealed that the public is not convinced by the strategy used to combat corruption. This reflects negatively on the image and effectiveness of the ACB. To an extent, this negative attitude is due to perceptions that the public relations office should manage. As such, building the capacity of the office will go a long way to improving the ACB's public image.

Financial resources

Government funding
The government, through the treasury, is responsible for providing financial and other resources to the ACB. The treasury sets ceilings on each vote in the national budget.

Annually, the bureau has its own ceiling that must be adhered to when drawing up the budget. Usually, the ceiling is not enough for meeting the operational and administrative costs; as a result, sometimes the ACB requests special funding based on emerging needs. The cashgate investigations, for example, are sometimes funded outside the ceiling because of the increased funding required. The special funding notwithstanding, the ACB faces acute resource constraints which is compounded by erratic funding. Sometimes months pass without funding, and once the funding is in, most of it goes towards administrative costs such as rent, electricity, water and car servicing. The table below shows the ACB planned budget against actual funding for the past three financial years.

Table 1: ACB Government funding for the past three financial years

	Planned budget		
Financial Year	**2012–2013**	**2013–2014**	**2014–2015**
Amount in Kwacha	433 680 569.00	449 312 513.00	1 066 483 315.00
USD equivalent	885 062.39	916 964.31	2 176 496.56
	Actual funding		
Financial Year	**2012–2013**	**2013–2014**	**2014–2015**
Amount in Kwacha	420 098 894.00 (96%)	334 139 672.00 (74%)	775 291 829.00 (73%)
USD equivalent	85 344.68	681 917.70	1 582 228.22

Source: Anti-Corruption Bureau account records.

Donor funding

The ACB has relied heavily on development partners for its operational budget for the past 16 years or so. Normally, donors would fund the ACB through a funding-pool under the arrangement termed common approach to budgetary support (CABS). However, the CABS is now defunct due to donors withdrawing after the cashgate scandal. The DfID withdrew its financial support, but maintained its technical support through advisors to the director on investigations and prosecutions.

The Royal Norwegian Embassy (RNE) and Irish Aid, however, did not withdraw their financial support to the ACB. The RNE is currently supporting the capacity development of the ACB to investigate financial and computer-related corruption through the establishment of a forensic unit. The operation of the unit requires staff training on computer forensics and purchasing equipment, including computer software for analysis. This has not yet been done. Irish Aid on the other hand, is supporting investigations of corrupt practices related to the Farm Input Subsidy Programme (FISP).

The table below shows the breakdown of development partners' financial contribution to ACB programmes.

Table 2: Development partners' funding

	Programme supported	Period	Budgeted	Funded
Irish Aid	Implementation of the NACS	Oct. 2012–Sept. 2013	95 202 000.00	91 947 968.00
	Farm Input Subsidy programme	Jan. 2014–Sept. 2014	138 864 000.00	141 726 489.18
	ACB Strategic Plan	Current	90 204 887.00	37 538 735.92
DfID & RNE	ACB Strategic Plan	May 2013–Mar. 2014	385 196 871.02	365 116 675.00
RNE[35]	Capacity Development Programme	Oct. 2014–Sept. 2015	230 658 693.00	92 184 688
Total			**K709 467 758.02**	**K457 064 643.00**

Source: Anti-Corruption Bureau account records.

Management of finance

The ACB has some autonomy on how its financial resources are managed. Normally, requisitions for government funds are prepared by departments and submitted to the director for approval. Upon approval, the requisitions are submitted to the accounts section, which is under the support services department for processing. The accounts section prepares vouchers, which are then sent to the accountant general's department in the ministry of finance. This arrangement reduces the efficiency of the process. On average, it takes about two weeks from the date of requisition for a cheque to be prepared, and when the cheque is deposited in the bank, it takes a further three to four days to be cleared as the cheque is usually closed for security reasons. The requisitions for development partners' funds, however, are quick and convenient. The ACB maintains accounts in commercial banks and all the account signatories are senior ACB personnel.

The ACB, like many other public bodies, has an internal audit office that reports directly to the director. The office has one officer, whose role is to audit the financial systems and advise management on ways of ensuring prudent financial management. In addition, the account books are subjected to external audit by the national audit office periodically, to ensure strict adherence to the Public Finance Management Act and treasury instructions on the management of public finance. The quest for financial transparency and accountability does not end at internal and external audits, though. Development partners normally hire external consultants to conduct end-of-project evaluations that include financial evaluations, in accordance with agreed-upon project terms of reference.

---

33 The RNE programme is currently running and the funded amount represents half of the funding. The other half is expected to be released soon.

Relationships with the public and other stakeholders

The ACB maintains vital relationships with some key government agencies. Though an autonomous agency, administratively the ACB is under the ministry of justice. In addition, the director is required to report to parliament annually on the performance of the ACB, and justify funding. This requirement notwithstanding, some sectors of society believe that there is still need for a body to control the ACB, to protect it from political influence and ensure an effective and efficient delivery of service. These sentiments are reflected in the NACS:

> The executive needs to ensure that the ACB functions efficiently, effectively and professionally. This will be done through the establishment of an independent body to monitor activities of the ACB. The overseer will ensure that the ACB functions without political interference, and that it submits reports to parliament as stipulated in the Corrupt Practices Act.

The NACS's provision is echoed in the strategic plan which states that, in order for public confidence in the fight against corruption to increase, the ACB intends to lobby for the legal empowerment of an independent body to oversee its activities. Such lobbying, however, would be more effective if it came from external interested partners like civil society organisations. The ACB seems to have a conflict of interest. Hence, it remains to be seen if the ACB can successfully lobby for an independent body.

The police

On an operational level, the ACB has a cordial relationship with the Malawi Police Service. The close relationship between the police is clearly spelt under section 36(3) of the CPA which states:

> Any police officer or officer of the bureau may, if authorised by warrant issued by a magistrate, search any person arrested for an offence under this act and take possession of all articles found upon such person which the police officer or officer of the bureau believes upon reasonable grounds to constitute evidence of commission of an offence by such person under this part.

Hence, the police sometimes assist the ACB to arrest and search, also providing holding cells for suspects before taking them before the court of law. In addition, the police assist the ACB through providing security during arrests, searches and property seizures, since ACB officers do not carry fire arms.

Currently, the police are working hand-in-hand with the ACB on the prosecution of cashgate cases. This good working relationship, if enhanced, can greatly improve the fight against corruption and related offences in Malawi. However, there are major challenges that affect this relationship. Many a time, ACB has arrested some 'bad apples' in the police. The engagement of some police officers in corrupt practices and subsequent arrests by the ACB creates a tension that refuses to ease.

Judiciary

The ACB relies on the judiciary to prosecute corruption cases. The NACS acknowledges that weakness in the judicial system leads to public loss of trust in its capacity to compel the executive and legislature to adhere to the rule of law and promote good governance. According to the NACS, a weak judiciary is a recipe for the institutionalisation of political corruption and abuse of human rights. As such, for the judiciary to assist effectively in fighting corruption, the NACS encourages it to, among other things, ensure the efficient and speedy handling of corruption cases, and ensure that magistrates and other judicial officers are familiar with the CPA and are trained in handling corruption issues.

The importance of amicable relationships between the judiciary and the ACB cannot be over-emphasised. The judiciary is vital for issuing warrants of arrest, searches and property seizures. As it stands, the effectiveness of the ACB hinges on the efficiency of the judiciary. Nevertheless, when it comes to public perception, the delay in prosecuting cases seems to be solely attributed to the ineffectiveness of the ACB. The prosecution of the cases once they are in court, however, is largely controlled by the judicial officers. While on the one hand, the ACB is incapacitated by a shortage of qualified lawyers, the backlog in the court system does not help matters. Hence, in order to improve the working relationship between the ACB and the judiciary, there is an urgent need to not only build the capacity of prosecutions within the ACB, but also the capability of the courts to quickly process corruption cases. As provided in the strategic plan, capacity building can be partly achieved through familiarising magistrates with the CPA, and through the creation of a special court to deal with corruption cases.

Other stakeholders

The ACB maintains informal relationships with other case-handling institutions. Where there is need (for instance when a complaint does not necessarily hinge on corruption and can best be handled by other agencies), the ACB shares the information on the case with a relevant agency such as the ombudsman, or the Malawi Human Rights Commission,

However, the relationship with civil society organisations, traditional leaders, the media, and the private sector is guided by the NACS. These are deemed important economic sectors in combating corruption; thus, their roles and responsibilities are clearly outlined in the NACS. Organisations in these sectors are represented by a person nominated to the national integrity committee who champions the implementation of the national integrity system. According to the NACS, the representatives are supposed to guide organisations in their respective sectors on how to roll out the integrity system and report progress to the integrity commission. While the NIC is functional, its relevance and effectiveness in guiding the fight against corruption is yet to be seen and measured.

Similarly, the effectiveness of the sectors that the NIC represents on combating corruption and complimenting the efforts of the ACB is not yet known.

Civil society
The NACS highlights the important role of the civil society in safeguarding democracy and empowering people to actively participate in the affairs of the state, and advocating policy reforms in order to promote the fight against corruption. According to the NACS, civil society should:
- Educate the masses through public campaigns on the evils of corruption and on how to resist, reject and report corrupt practices to authorities;
- Lobby the executive and the legislature to establish relevant frameworks for promoting transparency, integrity, accountability and service delivery in the public service;
- Monitor and evaluate activities of all the branches of government;
- Publicise and denounce corrupt practices through peaceful demonstrations and other acceptable activities; and
- Demonstrate visible transparency and accountability in the way they conduct their business.

Civil society, however, appears to be in a deep slumber, despite having a representative on the NIC. In accordance with the provisions of the NACS, one would expect that civil society would be in the forefront, demanding thorough investigations and prosecutions of the looters of billions from the state coffers, but this is not the case. While civil society has, in many cases, fiercely advocated for issues of national interest (such as the rights of minority groups), they have conspicuously remained silent on the corruption-fighting front. There is, therefore, urgent need to wake up civil society so that it takes up its role of mobilising the public against corrupt practices in the public sector.

The media
The ACB relies on the media to disseminate messages on corruption. As the NACS puts it, the media is an important tool for promoting public involvement in the fight against corruption. The NACS calls for a professional and effective media capable of soliciting the support and involvement of the public in implementing anti-corruption measures. The NACS spell out the roles of the media in fighting corruption as:
- Disseminating information on corruption from various stakeholders to the public;
- Investigating, publicising and denouncing corrupt practices;
- Intensifying investigative journalism on corruption in order to uncover and denounce suspected and actual corrupt practices; and

- Monitoring and evaluating the activities of various stakeholders to ascertain the effectiveness of their programmes.

As partner of the ACB, the media has made good progress. Both the electronic and print media have been in the forefront informing the public of corrupt practices and corruption cases in courts. The cashgate cases, in particular, have received a lot of attention from the media. In some cases, the ACB has successfully generated investigations from media reports and successfully prosecuted the culprits. Nevertheless, despite the huge success of the media in reporting corruption, there is need for more investigative journalism training in order to build the capacity of journalists to investigate and report corrupt practices.

International agencies

The ACB enjoys cordial relationships with some international organisations in its battle against corruption. The relationships range from capacity building of the ACB through secondments and conferences to issues related to mutual legal assistance. In particular, the ACB works with International Police (INTERPOL) on aspects of investigations and arresting of suspects. In addition, the ACB sends its officers on secondment to sister institutions in the regions such as the Zambian Anti-Corruption Commission, and participates in conferences organised by the Southern African Forum Against Corruption (SAFAC) on best practice. In the light of the cashgate scandal, the United Nations Office on Drugs and Crime, in collaboration with the Assets Recovery Interagency Network of Southern Africa (ARINSA), organised training of ACB officers on money laundering and asset tracing, to facilitate the seizure of property tainted by money-laundering crimes.

These relationships notwithstanding, more support is needed if the ACB is to be effective in dealing with financial crimes where they involve analysing computer-generated information.

Donors

The relationship between the government and development partners is currently affected by the looting of billions from the treasury through fraudulent payments. The development partners have withdrawn direct support to the national budget until the financial system becomes watertight and no longer prone to abuse. The withdrawal of aid has adversely affected the ACB, which mainly depended on such aid for its operations. The ACB's traditional development partner, the DfID, has withdrawn financial aid, but maintained technical aid through technical advisors on cashgate cases. However, Irish Aid and the Royal Norwegian Embassy are still providing financial aid to the ACB. Despite the support from other development partners, the withdrawal of the DfID funding has left the ACB financially constrained and this has affected its operations.

G. Performance

The general performance of the ACB is not satisfactory and there is huge room for improvement. The ACB has not effectively prevented corruption in the public sector as evidenced by the massive looting of money from the government treasury through dubious contracts. Despite the establishment of the NIS, corruption remains the scourge that deters development in Malawi. Public education on corruption appears to be deficient, as evidenced by the 2010 Corruption and Governance Survey results that revealed that most people do not know what constitutes corruption, or where and how to report cases. Moreover, the quality of investigations is questionable, considering that there is only a small conviction rate.

The ACB client service charter sets high standards by stating that 'we will investigate any alleged or suspected offence under the Corrupt Practices Act'. However, this appears to be too ambitious. Though the investigations department mostly meets planned targets, there is a large backlog of cases. Due to financial and resource constraints, the ACB has a case prioritisation matrix that allows only those cases with higher financial value and public interest to be investigated.

The quarterly and annual reports of the ACB are factually sound, but most of the information gleaned from these reports is process-orientated or simply narrates a host of activities. Some of them record outputs, but the information provided is rarely at even medium-term outcome level, let alone at long-term impact level. The challenge of measuring results at outcome and impact level has been raised repeatedly in meetings with donors and in annual reviews.[34] The main point is that the monitoring and evaluation capability of the ACB is grossly inadequate. An anti-corruption agency simply cannot assess its own performance over time unless it has a set of measurement tools. The bureau has been exceedingly slow in responding to such criticism and, in effect, persisted in mere activity reporting, with scant attention being paid to outcome and impact indicators.

It was only in 2011 that a monitoring and evaluation unit was established, albeit with limited staff. There is a strong and urgent case for strengthening the unit. It is conceded that the task of the unit is very challenging, but without an ability to report results, the very legitimacy of the bureau is jeopardised. In other words, reporting results is not primarily a matter of satisfying the donors. It is central to the accountability and continued existence of the bureau. Its strategic plan is not worth much if the ACB cannot account for its results, be it to the donors, the government or the general public. The table below indicates the seriousness of the problems of investigations and prosecutions of cases by the ACB.

---

34 Forster R, Kambalame D & Otieno G (2008) *Annual Review of DfID Malawi's Anti-Corruption Bureau Support Programme 2007–2008*. Lilongwe: DfID; and Hechler H & Parkes B (2010) *Annual Review of DfID/RNE Malawi's Anti-Corruption Bureau Support Programme*. Oslo: Norwegian Agency for Development Cooperation.

Table 3: Investigations and prosecutions statistics

Year	2006/2007	2007/2008	2008/2009	2009/2010	2010/2011
Cases referred for prosecutions	68	95	128	152	108
Prosecutions completed	16	21	20	25	34
Convictions	10	9	9	10	18
Acquittals	5	8	7	12	3

Source: Management International (2012) *The Strategic Plan for the Anti-Corruption Bureau 2012–2017: Promoting a Culture that is Intolerant to Corruption*. Blantyre: Malawi Anti-Corruption Bureau.

Strengths

Despite its short comings, the ACB has strengths that can be exploited to promote the fight against corruption. The anti-corruption legislation in Malawi is reasonably enabling as it allows the ACB to prevent, investigate and prosecute offenders. Moreover, the definition of what constitutes corruption is broad and hence criminalises many malpractices both in the public and the private bodies. So, in this sense, the ACB is strongly empowered.

The internal operations of the ACB are well guided by the existence of the bureau's standing orders that provide standard operating procedures for all ACB officers. The standing orders contain instructions on how to interview witnesses and suspects, as well as the expected behaviour of investigators and other officers of the ACB. As such, it is a good tool for aligning staff performance with the objectives of the ACB.

The ACB can also enhance its good working relationship with the police and other external agencies through the establishment of task teams to handle certain specialised investigations. Financial investigations involving tax invasion, for example, can be jointly handled with the fiscal police and Malawi revenue authority investigators who are experts on such matters (as suggested in the strategic plan).

On issues of corruption prevention and public education, the ACB has an upper hand due to the availability of survey results that reveal areas needing attention.[35] The ACB can prioritise and focus its corruption prevention functions on the key institutions identified through the surveys, such as the road traffic department, the immigration department, traffic police and public procurement entities.[36] In addition, the revelations that people are not aware of what constitutes corruption or how to report it to the authorities can be used as a basis for providing information for the development of an effective communications strategy for the ACB.

---

35 Several surveys have been conducted to map corruption perceptions in Malawi the most notable ones being: Millennium Consulting Group & IFES (2006) *Governance and Corruption Baseline Survey Report 2006*. Blantyre: GoM and; Chinsinga B, Kayuni H & Konyani S (2010) *Governance and Corruption Survey 2010*. Blantyre: Zomba: Centre for Social Research, University of Malawi.

36 The 2010 Corruption and Governance Survey highlighted procurement as the most corrupt area in the public service.

The ACB currently has four offices in the four regions of Malawi. Such decentralisation could be a major strength, especially if the regional offices can be empowered through staff capacity building initiatives and the provision of adequate financial resources. These offices can act as a focal point for effective public education, corruption prevention, investigations and prosecution of corrupt practices at regional level. However, ACB management is concentrated at headquarters. The regional offices are headed by either a principal or senior officer, and hence they do not yield enough power for resource bargaining. In the absence of directors at the regional offices, the decentralisation rhetoric of the ACB appears to be hollow.

The key strength for the ACB, however, is its staff. Most operational staff members have at least a bachelors degree. A good number have masters degrees. Given adequate and relevant training and motivation, the ACB could have a highly competent workforce. But, this is not currently the case.

Weaknesses

The ACB lacks the relevant staff capacity and motivation. The conditions of service are generally good. There are provisions of house ownership, motor vehicle loans and other motivating factors that, if implemented, can help the ACB to retain its most competent staff members. However, the conditions of service are good only on paper. Since its inception, no-one has benefited from the house ownership scheme or a car loan.

The ACB is generally understaffed, and the conditions of service are not implemented comprehensively. Currently, the operational staff contingent stands at 126. However, only 70 positions are filled. The best-equipped department in terms of filled positions is that of corruption prevention: out of 15 established positions, 12 are filled. The reality on the ground, however, is not good. Those 12 officers are supposed to serve the whole nation, acting as desk officers for over 30 institutional integrity committees formed in the eight sectors identified in the NACS. To make matters worse, the officers are not well-trained in corruption-prevention issues. Consequently, the strategic plan provides for the migration from a hands-on approach to a more facilitative approach, where the officers' roles will be more about providing technical support and monitoring activities, while actual implementation is devolved to other actors such as civil society organisations and private consultants. Whether this approach will be adopted has yet to be seen.

As can be deduced from the table, the prosecution department is the most affected by staff shortages. Of the 34 established positions, only 12 are filled. Moreover, most positions are filled with paralegals not adequately trained in law. The problem is compounded by the high resignation rate of qualified lawyers from the department as the result of unsatisfactory working conditions.

Table 4: Staff per operational department against filled positions

Designated positions				
Public education	Investigations	Prosecutions	Corruption prevention	Total
14	63	34	15	126
Filled positions				
Public education	Investigations	Prosecutions	Corruption prevention	Total
8	38	12	12	70

Source: Management International (2012) *The Strategic Plan for the Anti-Corruption Bureau 2012–2017: Promoting a Culture that is Intolerant to Corruption*. Blantyre: Malawi Anti-Corruption Bureau.

Investigation comes second. Of the 63 established positions, only 38 are filled. However, the 38 filled positions include officers in the documentation section and the report centre, who are not directly involved in investigating corrupt practices. The real number of filled positions of investigators, according to human resource records, is 27. The staffing problem is exacerbated by the lack of training in financial and computer related investigations. The understaffing of the investigations department adversely affects the outcomes of the investigations and prosecutions respectively.

The performance of the ACB is also affected by the weaknesses in the CPA. As mentioned elsewhere in this chapter, the act does not adequately protect whistleblowers. On the other hand, the requirement to obtain consent from the DPP before prosecuting corrupt practices creates opportunities for politicians to manipulate the process, whereas the requirement to obtain a court warrant before arresting and conducting searches reduces the efficiency of the investigations and prosecutions of suspected offenders.

The major weakness affecting performance, however, is the lack of financial resources. While there has been sustained financial support from the government, the amounts are barely adequate for implementing comprehensive public education and corruption prevention programmes, let alone for carrying out effective investigations and prosecuting cases. The payment of rent and utilities like electricity and water leaves barely enough for operations. The withdrawal of the DfID from directly funding the activities of the ACB has exacerbated these financial problems.

H. Conclusion

The importance of the ACB to the socio-economic development of Malawi cannot be over-emphasised. The economy needs the ACB to prevent the diversion of public resources for selfish gain at the expense of national development. The exposure of massive looting of money from the government treasury underscores the critical need for an effective anti-corruption drive to reverse the trend and bring culprits to justice. On the other hand, the looting reveals the weaknesses of the Malawi national integrity system, in particular the ACB itself.

The CPA weakens the capacity of the ACB to deliver on its mandate in several ways:
- The act gives too much power to the state president in the appointment and dismissal of the ACB director and the deputy director. Although the appointment is confirmed by parliament, the act empowers the president with exclusive powers for removing the director from office at will. The requirement to seek consent from the DPP, while crafted with noble intentions, is prone to abuse by politicians seeking to protect personal interests.
- The requirement of a warrant before arrest and search reduces the efficiency and effectiveness of investigations and prosecutions. There is the increased possibility of information-leaking as officers are trying to get court warrants, inadvertently warning suspects to destroy evidence before arrest or search is conducted.
- Lastly, the act does not strongly protect whistleblowers and thus fails to promote reporting corruption to the ACB, as informers fear reprisals from criminals.

The internal capacity of the ACB also leaves a lot to be desired. With only 12 under-trained corruption prevention officers, Malawians cannot expect effective corruption prevention in the public sector. The problem is exacerbated by the fact that the ACB uses a hands-on approach in the implementation of corruption prevention programmes. Similarly, the public education function needs revitalisation as it appears to lack focus, resulting in the decreased reporting of corrupt practices to the ACB. On the investigations front, the shortage of staff and inadequate training in financial and computer-related crimes grossly affects investigation success. There is need for more qualified prosecutors if the ACB is to secure more convictions. As for the prosecutors, they appear to lack motivation and opt to resign for greener pastures.

Finally, the withdrawal of financial support from the traditional donor, the DfID, coupled with erratic and meagre funding from government, appears to be the major challenge facing the ACB. The financial woes do not only affect the operations. Officers are unmotivated as a result of a stagnant salary and the unwillingness of the government to fully implement the conditions of service. With a demotivated workforce, the future of the anti-corruption drive in Malawi looks bleak.

I. Recommendations

On the basis of the foregoing analysis, this section offers recommendations as follows:

- The CPA should be reviewed to provide for the appointment of the director and deputy director based on merit, and through competency-based interviews. The act should also make the term of office secure by providing for the removal of the director and the deputy through parliament and not unilaterally by the president as it is currently.
- The act should be amended to provide for the establishment of an independent body such as a commission or board of governors to oversee the functions of the ACB. The body will safeguard the independence of the bureau and ensure its effective performance.
- The requirement for seeking consent from the DPP and obtaining warrants from a magistrate before arrest and search should be amended to ensure speedy and efficient operations of the ACB.
- The ACB should institute rigorous training for its officers in all its operational areas. The training courses should be tailor-made for corruption prevention, public education, investigations and prosecutions.
- The ACB should review its recruitment policy in order to start recruiting people with critical academic backgrounds relevant to each operational department. For example, the ACB can start recruiting people with audit backgrounds into the corruption prevention department and accountants into the investigations department.
- The ACB should expedite the creation of a forensic unit in order to counter the financial and computer-related crimes that are on the increase.
- To enhance the effectiveness of investigations, the ACB should adopt a taskforce approach by teaming up with other institutions with investigations mandates. In particular, the ACB can team up with the fiscal police and the Malawi revenue authority to increase the chances of successfully prosecuting financially corrupt practices.
- The capacity of the corruption prevention department should be enhanced with more staff, and the functions should be gradually devolved to other institutions while the department takes a more facilitative role.
- Based on the corruption and governance surveys, the ACB should develop a comprehensive communications strategy for reaching out to the public. Due to the shortage of staff in the public education

department, some public education functions, such as public rallies, should be devolved to consultants and grassroots civil society organisations.
- The ACB should lobby for parliament and government to increase their funding. There is simultaneously a great need to attract other possible donors to support its operations both financially and technically through the provision of capacity-building initiatives.

7
MOZAMBIQUE

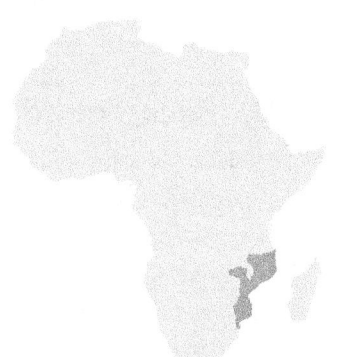

A. Executive summary

Mozambique boasts a robust legal framework for combatting corruption, comprising:
- Principles to promote the right to information;
- Measures to protect whistleblowers;
- A code of conduct for public servants;
- Rules and procedures for programmes;
- Managing, implementing and controlling public resources;
- Regulation for hiring of public works; and
- Provision of public goods and services.

The problem, however, is in the implementation of this framework. The country's political and technical environment has not been conducive to the implementation of anti-corruption legislation. There is poor political will to fight corruption and most of the institutional and legal achievements are due to donor interventions.

The Central Office for Combatting Corruption (COCC), established in 2005, lacks powers for prosecution, limiting its mandate to a more investigative and preventative role. To make matters worse, the COCC lacks the mandate to initiate its own investigations, only acting on audit reports from the administrative court, the general inspectorate of finance and internal audits of state institutions, and complaints from individuals. The establishment of formal mechanisms (such as memorandums of understanding) for cooperative relationships with other public institutions involved in crime prevention and investigation, would be greatly beneficial.

From a political point of view, the fact that the attorney general officer and his deputies (who in turn govern the COCC) are all appointed and removed by the president of the republic; this lack of autonomy puts the effectiveness of the COCC into question.

In alignment with the limitations surrounding the performance of the COCC, the public image of this agency is that it is focuses on petty corruption, and can't handle big cases of corruption involving the political elite. Civil society organisations (CSOs), donors, opposition parties and the media all share this perception.

B. Background

With the establishment of a democratic rule of law in 1990 and the signing of the General Agreement of Peace in 1992, Mozambique launched a challenge to fight absolute poverty, to consolidate peace and democracy, and to increase economic development.

Today, approximately 25 years later, the economy of Mozambique is marked by an impressive average GDP growth of 7.4% each year. Although agriculture is the largest sector in the economy, the extractives industry is the main cause of the growth. In addition, according to some studies, this growth will continue over decades as new reserves of natural resources such as gas, oil and other minerals are being discovered.

However, despite these economic achievements, the country remains very poor, with over half the population living below the poverty line,[1] it is highly dependent on donor budget support. According to the 2014 United Nations Development Programme (UNDP) report:

> In Mozambique, 70.2% of the population are multidimensionally poor while an additional 14.8 % are near multidimensional poverty. The breadth of deprivation (intensity) in Mozambique, which is the average of deprivation scores experienced by people in multidimensional poverty, is 55.6%. The [multidimensional poverty index], which is the share of the population that is multi-dimensionally poor, adjusted by the intensity of the deprivations is 0.390.[2]

In the area of democracy, Mozambique has been a good example in Africa, holding elections every five years, as established by the constitution. The last general election took place in 2014, where three political parties (Frelimo, Renamo and the Mozambique Democratic Movement) won seats in the parliament. Frelimo candidate Felipe Jacinto Nyusi won the presidency of the country, running his term from of 2015–2019.

Despite regular elections taking place every five years since 1994, the post-electoral conflict and intolerance between the parties still prevail, resulting in cases of armed conflict. An illustration of this is the military conflict between the government and the armed forces of Renamo, from 2012 to 2014; mainly due to disagreements over the outcome of the last electoral review, and dissatisfaction regarding the level of compliance with the general peace agreement.

In the field of governance, there is a noticeable deterioration of quality in recent years. According to the Mo Ibrahim index (2015), Mozambique has shown a weakening overall governance score (-2.2) since 2011.[3] The scale of this deterioration places the country as one of the ten largest fallers in overall governance over this time, accompanying countries such

---

1   Instituto Nacional de Estatística (2009) *Relatório Preliminar Do Inquérito Sobre Indicadores Múltiplos*, 2008. Maputo.
2   UNDP (2014) *Sustaining Human Progress: Reducing Vulnerabilities and Building Resilience*. New York: UNDP.
3   Mo Ibrahim Foundation (2015) Ibrahim Index of African Countries: Mozambique. Available at http://mo.ibrahim.foundation/iiag/downloads/ [accessed 13 September 2016].

as Libya, Guinea-Bissau and Mali, alongside Cabo Verde and Botswana. This decline is the largest seen within Southern Africa.

Political economy of corruption

As stated above, Mozambique still has a high dependency on foreign aid, despite the rapid economic growth experienced since the early 2000s. In fact, in 2013, Mozambique was 178th out of 189 countries on the human development index.[4] According to the same report, about 70% of the Mozambican population are multidimensionally poor and the rest are close, living on below USD 1 a day.

On the other hand, while dependency on foreign aid is still high, this is starting to decrease. According to economist João Mosca,[5] the state budget is substantially supported by external resources through donations or foreign aid. In specific terms, there are cases in the budget, mainly in the area of public investment, where about 80% of the investment comes from external resources. It is important to mention, however, that from 2014 to 2015, there was a 6.8% reduction in external donations, covering only 25% of the overall state budget.

Economically, Mozambique has seen rapid economic expansion over the past 20 years, with an average annual GDP growth rate of 7.4%. This is mainly as a result of big infrastructural projects and, more recently, the booming natural resources industry. According to the 2015 International Monetary Fund (IMF) projections, the oil and gas sector is going to contribute to about 50% of the national GDP.

However, this rapid economic growth has, so far, had only a moderate impact on poverty reduction and the distribution of wealth; poor governance and corruption being the critical hindrance. In fact, as pointed out in the 2015 Mo Ibrahim index report:

> Since 2011, Mozambique has shown a weakening overall governance score (-2.2). The scale of this deterioration places the country as one of the ten largest fallers in overall governance over this time period, accompanying countries such as Libya, Guinea-Bissau and Mali, alongside Cabo Verde and Botswana. This decline is the largest seen within Southern Africa.[6]

To make matters worse, corruption is on the rise. According to the corruption survey commissioned by the United States Agency for International Development (USAID) in 2009,[7] over 20 years, corruption in Mozambique spread rapidly, reaching every sector and level of the government. The recent data from the corruption perception index of

---

4 UNDP (2014) *Sustaining Human Progress: Reducing Vulnerabilities and Building Resilience.* New York: UNDP.
5 Mosca J (2012) Economia Moçambicana na Visão de João Mosca. Available at http://jorgejairoce.blogspot.co.za/2012/05/economia-mocambicana-na-visao-de-joao.html [accessed 11 October 2016].
6 Mo Ibrahim Foundation (2015) Ibrahim Index of African Countries: Mozambique. Available at http://mo.ibrahim.foundation/iiag/downloads/ [accessed 13 September 2016].
7 USAID (2009) Mozambique Democracy and Governance Assessment.

Transparency International ranks Mozambique as one of the most corrupt countries in the world today, at 112 out of 168.[8]

The dynamics of corruption in Mozambique are attributed to the high influence of the political elite on the economy and business. This political climate is heightened by Frelimo, the ruling party since independence in 1975. According to the Bertelsmann Foundation's transformation index,[9] the Mozambican democratic state is poor because of the abusive dominance of the ruling party. This index points out the tendency of the state party and economic elite toward self-enrichment, leading to high levels of corruption. [10]

The comingling of politics and business is a reality in Mozambique. According to the Centre for Public Integrity (CIP), business is migrating towards promising areas such mineral resources and energy, taking advantage of the weaknesses in legislation related to conflict of interests. The CIP's analysis of 589 companies with investments from the Mozambican government, noted that the local political elite hold interests in almost all business areas. One of the consequences of this is that the country remains the hostage of individuals, instead of creating a national development agenda.[11]

In early 2015 a scandal of unclear business erupted; known as the EMATUM Case, it involved the state and members of the political elite. Although the total business investment was about USD 850 million, it has only been declared that USD 350 million was invested. Where the remaining USD 500 million ended up is unclear.

The political environment is conducive to this sort of behaviour due to the weakness of the legislative and judiciary system, apathy of citizens, and poor access of information. To worsen this situation, in the last two years the brutal assassination of two judges and a lawyer have exposed the vulnerability of justice system, intimidating judges and lawyers to in the performance of their role.

C. State of corruption in Mozambique

Corruption appears as one of the major scourges undermining the efforts towards development of the country. As pointed out by the Inter-Ministerial Commission for Public Sector Reform (CIRESP)[12] the social and economic cost of corruption is intense and affects the most

---

8   Transparency International (2015) Corruption Perceptions Index 2015. Available at http://www.transparency.org/cpi2015 [accessed on 19 September 2016].
9   Bertelsmann Foundation (2012) Mozambique Country Report. Transformation Index. Available at https://www.bertelsmann-stiftung.de/en/publications/publication/did/transformation-index-bti-2012/ [accessed 11 october 2016].
10 Sousa G & Vieira C (2012) Estudo alemão aponta limites da democracia em Angola e Moçambique. Available at http://www.dw.com/pt/estudo-alemão-aponta-limites-da-democracia-em-angola-e-moçambique/a-15828126 [accessed on 19 September 2016].
11 Issufo N (2012) Elite empresarial de Moçambique está ligada ao poder politico. Available at http://www.dw.com/pt/elite-empresarial-de-mo%C3%A7ambique-est%C3%A1-ligada-ao-poder-pol%C3%ADtico/a-16019516 [accessed on 19 September 2016].
12 Inter-Ministerial Commission for Public Sector Reform (Comissão Interministerial da Reforma do Sector Público [CIRESP]) (2006) *Anti-corruption strategy 2006–2010*. Maputo.

vulnerable layers of population unfairly and disproportionally. Corruption hinders private sector development, reduces foreign investments, and puts in risk the continuation of external aid and international cooperation. It seriously reduces the level of trust of the citizens in government and state institutions. It affects the legitimacy and legality of administrative acts of the government system, as well as the effectiveness and concrete results of public policies.

According to the 2009 USAID corruption survey,[13] over the last 20 years, corruption in Mozambique had spread rapidly, reaching every sector and level of the government. The scale and scope of corruption reached alarming levels, posing risks to the country's nascent democratic government.

Referring to the sectors most affected by corruption:

> The police is perceived to be the sector most affected by corruption (scoring 4,3 on a 1 to 5 scale) in Transparency International's Daily Lives and Corruption survey, followed by public officials and political parties (4,0), education (3,9), judiciary and the business sector (scoring 3,0).[14]

Studies conducted in Mozambique suggest the following as the underlying factors of corruption:
- Highly polarised political context with a single party-party dominance and lack of checks and balance;
- The merging of elite political and economic interests;
- Limited rule of law and lack of recourse for corrupt behaviours;
- Reputed links between corruption and organised crime;
- Lack of transparency and access to information;
- Weak accountability mechanisms;
- Popular tolerance of corruption and fear of retaliation;
- Politicised and ineffective bureaucracy; and
- Social legacies.

World Bank governance indicators (which assess the change in corruption levels over time and against other countries) show that from 2011 to 2014, the level of corruption in Mozambique remained unwaveringly high.

The impact of these levels of corruption on the quality of public services provisions are obviously negative. The 2009 USAID corruption survey also states:

> On a daily basis, citizens experience petty administrative corruption at police checkpoints, health institutions, schools and government offices. Even more serious grand corruption and state capture exist at higher levels of government.

---

13 USAID (2009) Mozambique Democracy and Governance Assessment.
14 Martini M (2012) *Overview of Corruption and Anti-Corruption in Mozambique*. Berlin: Transparency International.

These involve the pilfering of substantial sums from the public coffers and fostering damaging misconduct and abuses, for example, favouritism and nepotism in public appointments and procurements, conflicts of interest and insider dealing that benefit friends, relatives and political allies, and political party and electoral decisions that reduce democratic choices and citizen participation. More troubling are the allegation of linkages between corrupt government officials and organised crime.

Both petty and grand corruption affect all sectors of development. Here it is important to mention, that according to the CIRESP,[15] there is no light or heavy corruption, all manifestations of corruption are bad for a country's development. Grand corruption benefits the minority, with resources that would otherwise generate economic growth and reduce poverty. Petty corruption is only small if considered in isolation; multiplied by thousands or millions of cases, however, it's a disaster.

D. Institutional and legal framework

Institutional and administrative achievements

The condemnation of the malpractices related to corruption in the public sphere is clearly identified in political speeches of the first president of Mozambique, Samora Machel, just after independence in 1975. However, significant and systematic steps to combat corruption were only taken in the early 2000s.

The launch of the Public Sector Reform Strategy in 2001 served as a very important starting point for a more comprehensive approach to the fight against corruption. The ten-year strategy (2001–2011) included critical components for the fight against corruption; such as financial management and accountability measures to improve the management of public finances and enhancing good governance in combatting corruption. This latter component laid ground for the establishment of the Anti-Corruption Unit in 2003.

In 2004, the government conducted the first national research into governance and corruption, which informed the design of the Anti-Corruption Strategy. This was followed by the adoption of an action plan to implement the strategy in the five sectors considered critical and vulnerable: education, health, justice, finance and the interior. Good governance was also one of the pillars of the Poverty Reduction Strategy of 2006–2009.[16] Under this pillar, the government seeks to develop the following interventions aimed at promoting good governance: strengthening of the COCC; implementation and dissemination of the anti-corruption law; gathering of information and promotion of research on governance and corruption issues; preparation of the implementation of the first national Anti-Corruption

---

15 Inter-Ministerial Commission for Public Sector Reform (Comissão Interministerial da Reforma do Sector Público [CIRESP]) (2011) *Estratégia Global de Reforma do Sector Público 2001–2011*. Maputo.
16 Ministério da Planificação e Desenvolvimento (2009) *PARPA II-Relatório da Avaliação de Impacto: pesquisa sobre o combate a Corrupção.*

Strategy 2006–2009. The first strategy also fell under the umbrella of one of the key components of the Government Master Programme of 2005–2009.

In addition to that, the country has witnessed achievements in institutional dimensions. In fact, in 2005 the government created the COCC to replace the less effective Anti-Corruption Unit. The COCC came as a specialised body to handle matters related to corruption within the attorney general's office.

Legal framework achievements

> **Box 1. Relevant anti-corruption laws**
>
> **Law 6 of 2004 of 17 June** (an anti-corruption act) comprises fundamental norms for the control of corruption, be it passive or active. It applies to both the public and private sector. In general, it provides for most of the malpractices that are typified as corruption.
>
> **Penal Code**, a very important legal package to be considered when referring to anti-corruption laws. It comprises very important articles that discourage and penalise malpractices, such as bribery and corruption by public servants, corruption by members of the judiciary and active corruption.
>
> **Decree No. 30/2001 of 15 October** defines the operating rules of public administration services. These include the establishment of the principles that must guide the conduct of agents and organs of public service.
>
> **Law No. 9/2002 of 13 February** creates the state financial management system, aiming to establish and harmonise rules and procedures of programming, management, implementation and control of public resources, allowing for effective and efficient use and production of information in public institutions.
>
> **Law No. 26/2009 of 29 September** establishes the principle of mandatory preventive, simultaneous and successive supervision of acts and administrative contracts, and public spending by the administrative court.
>
> **Decree No. 15/2010 of 20 April** approves the regulation of hiring of public works contracts, supply of goods and provision of services to the state.
>
> **Law No. 15/2012 of 14 August** (whistleblower protection law) establishes special measures of protection, primarily around hiding and obscuring the identity of the whistleblowers.
>
> **Law No. 16/2012** (public probity law) brings important articles to avoid conflict of interest of public servants. It limits the public servants for duplication of job contract in the state.
>
> **Law No. 34/2014 of 31 December** (right to information law): establishes principles that public service must ensure in order to promote the exercise of the right to information, including the parameters of disclosure, transparency and legal proceedings.

From a legal point of view, even though the Mozambican legal framework has introduced some specifications of corruption in the criminal code of 1886, it was only in the 2000s that significant progress had been made in the development of anti-corruption laws. The main achievement in this respect has been the passing of the anti-corruption act as the first systematised and specific law focused on corruption. However, this legislation was not sufficient to cover all related aspects. It did not include key aspects of international conventions and other corruption practices in the public service, such as: illicit enrichment, traffic of influence, limitation of mandates, public probity and money laundering.

In 2012, the lack of substantial results lead to pressure from donors, who wanted to see more effective reforms of the act. As a result, the government came out with a new, richer anti-corruption package. From this package (which later would be adjusted into specific legislation), it is worth highlighting the public probity law, which has encountered some resistance in its implementation, and the whistleblower protection law which was a major milestone for the identification of cases of corruption through public reports.

In 2014, parliament also passed a right-to-information law, enriching the legal basis for combatting corruption. The draft law was tabled by a group of CSOs in the national assembly in 2007, and garnered attention from other CSOs and the media, given their strategic roles gaining access to critical information.

International anti-corruption commitments

Mozambique has ratified important international conventions and instruments against corruption. Among these, are included the SADC anti-corruption protocol, ratified by Resolution No. 33/2004 of 9 July; the African Union Convention on Preventing and Combatting Corruption, ratified by Resolution No. 30/2006, of 23 August; and the United Nations Convention Against Corruption, ratified by Resolution No. 31/2006, of 26 December.

Apart from above, the country has joined various regional and global organs against corruption, namely: the Association of Anti-Corruption Agencies in Commonwealth Africa; the Southern African Forum Against Corruption (SAFAC); and the AU Advisory Board on Corruption.

Accordingly, the COCC attends the annual meetings promoted by SAFAC in order to review the progress of the region's efforts to combat corruption. It has also joined initiatives organised by the Association of Anti-Corruption Agencies in Commonwealth Africa, the 32nd International Symposium organised by Cambridge University, conferences organised by the International Associations of the Anti-Corruption Agencies, the International Anti-Corruption Academy as well as other initiatives by the UN and the SADC.

E. Central Office for Combatting Corruption (COCC)

The COCC, as mentioned previously, was established in 2005 within the attorney general's office as a unit subordinated to that office. Chapter II(8) of Decree No. 22/2005 provides that

> the Central Office for Combatting Corruption is an organic unit of the attorney-general of the republic, responsible for investigating crimes of corruption and illicit economic participation and acting on the instruction of the respective processes.

Although not specifically pre-empted by the constitution, the establishment and functioning of the COCC is regulated by provisions in the anti-corruption act, as well as Law No. 22/2007 of 1 August and Decree No. 22/2005 of 22 June.

Since its establishment, the COCC has been carrying out activities focused on two areas of work.
- Criminal prevention, focusing on carrying out civic education lectures with multidisciplinary participation, involving state officials, students, private sector institutions and civil society organisations (CSOs).
- Investigation of corruption crimes and illegal economic participation, by inspectors and crime investigation police assigned to the COCC.[17]

COCC establishment status

Although the law does not specifically provide for the autonomy of the COCC, a degree of autonomy is implied by the provision that establishes autonomy of the attorney general. This autonomy is ensured in article 2(1) of Law 6/89 which states: 'the attorney general of the republic enjoys autonomy in relation to other bodies of the state, pursuant to this law'.

However, the COCC is highly subordinated to the attorney general. The director is nominated and reports to the attorney general as established in Decree No. 22/2005. As pointed out in the 2007 Global Integrity Report: 'the COCC is not fully independent as appointments to the office are made by the attorney general, who himself is appointed by the president of the republic'.[18] In addition to the power of nominating the director and staff, the attorney general, according to the internal regulations department of the COCC, also has the power to direct and preside over its meetings.

Regarding its composition, the COCC consists of four main organs: the director, the department of investigation and proceedings, the registry and the secretariat.[19] Although the director does not have power to appoint its members, he proposes nominations of judges, justice officials and staff of the central and provincial offices to the attorney general.[20]

From the point of view of staff qualifications and mandates, the anti-corruption act clearly establishes that, in addition to the judges, the COCC can integrate contract workers who comply with the specific requirements of integrity, impartiality and experience.

The responsibilities and powers of the COCC

Article 19(2) of the anti-corruption act mandates important responsibilities to the COCC, including:
- Conducting inquiries and investigations about complaints and reports of corruption;
- Promoting penalties through judicial authorities for declaration of assets;
- Promoting preparatory instructions;
- Promoting evidence searches;

---

17 Procuradoria Geral da República (PGR) (2011) *Plano Estratégico do GCCC (2011–2014)*.
18 CIP (2007) *Informe do PGR mostra fraquezas no Sistema Nacional de Integridade*. Maputo: CIP.
19 Articles 10 and 16 of Decree no. 22/2005.
20 Article 11(1)(e).

- Ordering the detention of indicted individuals and submitting them to judges for criminal proceedings; and
- Accessing, without prior notice, public administration institutions, government bodies, and municipality administrative services for the purposes of investigations.

According to article 2, the scope of action of the COCC applies to directors, officers or employees of the state or local municipalities, as well as public companies, private companies with participation in the state, or company concessioners of public services. However, despite these competences, the COCC lacks power to officially prosecute any case investigated by them.[21]

Human resources

For any anti-corruption body to be effective, it should have autonomous control of its budget, good infrastructure, and above all, be well equipped with qualified staff. Assessing the capacity of the COCC based on these three components, the institutional diagnosis carried out in 2011 highlighted the constraints on financial and human resources, and infrastructure.

From 29 employees hired, including the director, the magistrates and the investigators, not more than 40% were qualified people. The agency complained of a shortage of investigators in relation to the number of judges. This was aggravated by the lack of qualifications among the staff, as most only had basic education or a pre-university degree.

Of the 62 positions available, only 34% were occupied. The positions least occupied were those of investigators, law clerks, magistrates and professional technicians. An important aspect to note is that most of the staff are seconded from other agencies.

As of 2014, however, there had been some significant progress towards institutional development.[22] Quantitative and qualitative improvements were noted in human resources, with the number of staff increasing from 29 members in 2011 to 48 in 2014. Within this figure, there are 13 magistrates and four professional technicians. It is also important to mention that there is a total of 100 employees in the central and provincial offices.

Infrastructure

As for infrastructure, the most important achievement has been the construction of a separate building for the COCC in 2011, with support from China. However, it should be noted that the Chinese government is not known for their commitment to democracy and the values and practices of good governance.

---

21 Martini M (2012) *Overview of Corruption and Anti-Corruption in Mozambique.* Berlin: Transparency International.
22 Procuradoria Geral da Republica (2014) Discurso do Procurador, Augusto Raul Paulino, Na Abertura da II Sessão Ordinária do Conselho Coordenador de PGR.

Financial resources

Regarding budgetary planning, the COCC is very dependent on the attorney general. In accordance with article 23 of Decree 22/2005, the expenses of the COCC are covered by the state budget and are an integral part of the funds allocated to the attorney generals' office. The costs of the provincial offices are supported by government provincial budgets. The high subordination to the attorney general limits the COCC's power and autonomy, making it vulnerable. For example, in 2008, the opposition in the parliament criticised the 45% reduction of the budget allocated to the COCC. According to the opposition parties, this fact showed clearly that there was no political will to fight corruption.

However, in addition to the funds from the state budget, there are other sources of funding such as donations by international development partners. Here it is important to point out that donations are also channelled through the attorney general.

F. Other national state and non-state bodies

National state bodies

Financial intelligence unit

The *Gabinete de Informação Financeira de Moçambique* (GIFiM), established under Law No. 14/2007 of 27 June, is the Mozambican financial intelligence unit. It is a state body, with a national scope, that is unincorporated and has no judicial capacity, only administrative autonomy. It falls under the supervision of the council of ministers. The statutory functions of the GIFiM consist of the collection, analysis and dissemination of information to the competent authorities relating to financial and economic activities that are likely to constitute acts of money laundering and related crimes.[23]

To comply with its duties, the GIFiM can request information from entities that are required to report operations that may constitute crimes referred to in the law.[24] They may exchange and/or transmit other information to other authorities and they may exchange information with their foreign counterparts at either's initiative.[25] Although the GIFiM was officially established in 2007, it only started functioning in July 2011.

The institutional coordination of the GIFiM is safeguarded by a coordinating council, consisting of the prime minister, who chairs it; the ministers of finance, interior and justice; the attorney general of the republic; and the directors of the Bank of Mozambique. The GIFiM is headed by a director, who is assisted by a deputy director, both of whom are appointed by the prime minister under the advisement of the coordinating council. Taking this into account, it is unclear whether the institution is truly autonomous.

---

23 Article 2, N°1 of Law n°14/2007.
24 Law N° 14/2007, article 2, paragraph 2a.
25 Law n° 14/2007, article 2, paragraph 2c.

Justice ministry

Presidential Decree No. 1/2012 of June 26, defines the ministry of justice's current attributions and competences, which include:
- Legally advising government;
- Contributing to the technical preparation of legislation;
- Promoting respect for legality;
- Promoting civic and legal education of citizens;
- Establishing institutional coordination mechanisms and extended network with justice administration bodies.

Criminal investigation police

The criminal investigation police are integrated into Mozambique's national police force. However, neither the law governing the national police nor its organic statutes refer to them as a police unit. Rather, it mentions a national directorate of criminal investigation.

The duties of this national directorate are:
- The prevention and investigation of criminal acts;
- Conducting preparatory activities for criminal proceedings in accordance with the law;
- The realisation of steps required by the judicial authorities and prosecutors;
- Conducting surveillance of establishments that are suspected of criminal activity (or the assistance thereof), or the use of gains from criminal activity; and
- Inspection, from an operational point of view, of the organs that are directly dependent on the directorate.

Office of the attorney general and the superior council of the public ministry magistrate

The public prosecutor's office consists of the following bodies: the attorney general's office; the assistant attorney general's office; the COCC; the attorney provincial office; the provincial office for the fight against corruption; and the district attorney.

The public prosecutor's office is a hierarchically organised magistracy, headed by the attorney general of the republic, who is responsible for:
- Representing the state before the courts;
- Defending interests that are determined by law; reviewing legality and the duration of detentions;
- Directing the preparatory instructions of criminal procedures;
- Exercising action against criminal activity; and
- Ensuring the protection of minors, absentees and the incapacitated.

Justice ombudsman

The ombudsman plays an important role, both directly and indirectly, in the prevention and the combatting of corruption in public administration. It is the main body responsible for the protection of citizens' rights and the defence of legality and justice in public administration. The ombudsman is independent and impartial and cannot be persecuted, investigated or detained for the recommendations or opinions it provides, or the acts it commits in exercising its activities.

The ombudsman has jurisdiction over activities undertaken by:
- Public administration on national, provincial, district, local and municipal levels;
- Defence and security forces;
- Public institutions;
- Public companies and service providers;
- Companies with a considerable amount of public capital; and
- Companies that exploit resources in the public domain.

Administrative court

The administrative court is ranked higher than the tax and customs courts, as defined by article 228 of the constitution. The organisation of the administrative court is regulated through Law No. 25/2009 of 28 September. The organisation, functioning and procedures of the department of public revenue and expenditure, of both the national and the provincial administrative courts, is regulated by Law No. 26/2009 of 29 September. According to article 4 of the law, the administrative court has the following competences:
- Checking the legality of the administrative acts, and the implementation of regulations issued by the public administration, which do not fall under the responsibility of the tax and customs courts;
- Reviewing the legality of public expenditure and deciding on/placing responsibility for financial infringement; and
- Judging actions related to disputes arising from legal and administrative relations.

Judicial courts and the superior council of the judiciary

The organisation of courts is designed in article 223 of the constitution, where it provides for the supreme court, the administrative court and the judicial courts (civil and criminal). Apart from these, the constitution provides for the existence of administrative courts for labour, tax, customs, maritime issues, arbitration and community.

The supreme court is the highest body in the hierarchy of the courts, ensuring a uniform application of the law.[26] The supreme court operates in sections and in plenary,[27] is knowledgeable on the appeals law, and assesses the decisions of the superior appeal court.

Specific individuals warranting special privileges (such as parliamentarians, members of the cabinet and state council) who are defendants in criminal proceedings will appear before the supreme court instead of the criminal court.

The superior council of the judiciary is the disciplinary and management body of the judiciary and is responsible for, amongst other duties:[28]

- Proposing names to the president for the appointment of supreme court judges;
- Executing all acts related to appointing, assigning, transferring, promoting, retiring, discharging, appreciating professional merit and taking, disciplinary action of/towards judges;
- Considering professional merit of and taking disciplinary action towards other justice officials without compromising the disciplinary jurisdiction of judges;
- Processing (prosecuting) and judging any suspicions raised against one of its members in proceedings that are under its control;
- Ordering regular and special inspections as well as surveys and investigations of the courts;
- Approving the internal regulations of the superior council of the judiciary;
- Assessing the annual budget of the superior council of the judiciary; and
- Giving an opinion and/or recommendations on the judicial policy, either on its own initiative or at the request of the president, the national assembly or the government.

Non-state bodies

Private sector and anti-corruption efforts

The emergence and development of the private sector in Mozambique, after almost ten years of restrictions imposed by the socialist regime,[29] has always been linked to the political elite. In fact, the process of privatisation, guided by the structural adjustment

---

26 Article 225 of the Constitution.
27 Article 227 of the Constitution.
28 Article 128 of Law No. 7/2009.
29 After independence in 1975, for either ideological and practical reasons, Mozambique nationalised most of the companies that were inherited from the colonialists. In fact, government adopted a socialist orientated regime, based on a centralised and planned economy. In addition, the former colonialist's owner had abandoned most of the companies, which meant that the state had to take care of them. The remaining private operators were obliged to comply with the state's economic plan, which administratively defined a lot of conditions, which included the areas and milestone of production.

programme, has been highly politicised. Most of the companies have been given to people connected to the ruling party. Among these groups, the veterans of the liberation struggle benefited the most.

Today, almost 25 years after privatisation, the links between the private sector and political elite are still strong. According to Martini, 'the current president has extensive business interests'.[30] For instance, an assessment conducted by USAID in 2009 states that:

> The desire by the head of state to appoint entrepreneurs and others friendly to business interests was a characteristic of the early years of the Guebuza government. The ability to attract lucrative investment opportunities from the private sector be they a new cell phone company, extractive mining industries, or deep sea petrol exploration, all were seen to be attributes of the early Guebuza executive branch appointees who were expected to demonstrate loyalty to the chief of state.[31]

In this context, characterised by patronage and clientelism between the private sector and the government, corruption finds a good environment for its reproduction. According to the Bertelsmann Foundation:

> The current system relies on patronage and personal relationships with members of the ruling party. ... According to the business community, particularly small and medium size enterprises, corruption and bureaucracy remain the main impediments to their operations.[32]

In fact, because of all these constraints, also including lack of transparency, Mozambique is not well positioned on the World Bank ease of doing business index (127 out of 189 in 2014) and global competitiveness index (133 out of 144 in 2015).[33]

When assessing the COCC's mandate to control corruption in the private sector, we easily note that it is limited. The anti-corruption act only opens a window of action for the office to investigate the private sector when their business is linked to a public entity.

Although there is room for collaboration with the private sector, the COCC has not been maximising it. For example, there should be more collaboration with the commercial banks to trace bank activity, and with the mobile phone companies to trace calls.

---

30 Martini M (2012) *Overview of Corruption and Anti-Corruption in Mozambique.* Berlin: Transparency International.
31 USAID (2009) Mozambique Democracy and Governance Assessment.
32 Bertelsmann Foundation (2010) Mozambique Country Report. Transformation Index. Available at https://www.bertelsmann-stiftung.de/en/publications/publication/did/transformation-index-2010-2/ [accessed 11 October 2016].
33 World Bank (2015) *The Worldwide Governance Indicators.* Washington DC: World Bank Group.

Civil society organisations and anti-corruption efforts

The Mozambican Constitution of 1990 laid the grounds for the promotion of active citizenship in a democratic framework. It established, among other rights, the liberty and right of free association.

Since then, the country witnessed a rapid growth in number and intervention of civil society organisations. According to a CSO survey, carried out by the FDC, there were more than five thousand CSOs registered and operating in Mozambique.[34]

Actually, the role and nature of CSO interventions has shifted and diversified over time. From mere emergency humanitarian assistance associations, CSOs have reinforced their role and engaged in new areas, such as the defence of civic rights, and the enhancement of good governance and democracy.

Donor funding has been a key factor in shaping these interventions over time. In the early 1990s, many donors were investing their funds in humanitarian assistance with a focus on the health sector, HIV/AIDS eradication and peace reconciliation.

Box 2. CSOs chasing transparency in a tuna-fishing company

In 2015, a group of 14 CSOs, including the Budget Monitoring Forum (FMO), joined the voices of contestations surrounding the public debt accrued in the establishment of the new tuna fishing company, EMATUM, in 2013. The FMO published a very critical position paper, assessing the implications of the debt on social services provision. The paper included recommendations, such as the government's need to disclose the EMATUM contract, and for the COCC to proceed with investigations into criminal acts in the negotiations and setting up of the tuna company

It is worth noting that the position paper came after a parliamentary session, held in June 2015, which dented the commercial viability of the tuna fishing company. In this session, Mozambique's political opposition labelled the EMATUM case as the greatest financial scandal since independence and has called for the attorney general to arrest the former president of the republic and minister of finance, who established the company, calling for a need to end the 'endless impunity'.

Source: FMO (2015) *Análise do impacto da dívida da EMATUM nas contas públicas nacionais*. Maputo: FMO.

In the 2000s, with the adoption of the Poverty Reduction Strategy Programme (PARPA), donor funding took a new direction, aiming at funding CSO initiatives focused on advocacy, and monitoring/evaluation of public policies.

However, despite this shift in approach to intervention, only a few CSOs have been active and vocal on the prevention and suppression of corruption in Mozambique. The Public Integrity Centre (CIP), and Action Aid Mozambique are featured as the most active in this domain.

The CIP adopts an approach of publicly and regularly putting pressure on the state to act against corruption, even in pending cases of high profile corruption involving the political elite. It has also established a database to track members of the political elite's business interests.

---

34 FDC (2008) *Indice da Sociedade Civil*. Maputo: FDC.

Action Aid Mozambique has taken a different approach. Lately, together with its provincial-partners, it has been carrying out a series of one-week anti-corruption campaigns, coinciding with the celebrations of International Anti-Corruption Day. These campaigns consist of activities and messages targeted at raising public awareness of the effects of corruption on the quality of health and education services.

The fact that only a few CSOs publicly raise issues of corruption was likely a large contributing factor to the 2010 State of the Union Continental Report[35] ranking of CSOs in Mozambique as less effective (in terms of consistently and courageously raising issues of corruption) than those in Ghana, Kenya, South Africa and Nigeria.

The same source noted a need for CSO peer support, mentoring and capacity-building. There is a need to expand the number of CSOs tracking progress in combatting corruption in the country. Another area that should be strengthened is the cooperation between CSOs and the COCC, taking into account that the former can raise issues or provide information to assist corruption investigations by the latter.

Currently, the COCC establishes relations with CSOs on two main occasions: in prevention, when CSOs are involved in civic education lectures carried out by the COCC; and when both parties attend annual planning meetings involving government and its programme aid partners. Cooperation between CSOs and the media should also be strengthened on the grounds that media coverage would potentially boost the impact of both of their actions.

Media and anti-corruption efforts

The media in Mozambique operates in a legal context characterised by freedom of press, freedom of expression and rights of access of information, guaranteed by the constitution and operationalised by the Press Act 17/91 of 3 August and the right to information law (Law No. 34/2014 of 31 December).

Since 1991, with the approval of the press act, the Mozambican media has grown in number and diversity. According to the 2014 Friedrich Erbert Foundation report on the media, the media had grown by 0.3% since 2010.[36] Today, apart from the public media, there is a proliferation of private media too: television, radio, print media, electronic media and social media.

In spite of this growth, the media sector faces various constraints on its functioning and independence, with political interference being the main constraint.

According to the same source,[37] the quality of news content in the media is still not satisfactory. This situation is clear in issues related to politicians, as well as complaints of government malpractice. The main reason is attributed to the fact that the press, especially the state press, is not protected from political interference.

---

35 State of the Union (2010) *State of the Union Continental Report 2010*. Continental Advisory Research Team.
36 Friedrich Erbert Stiftung (2015) *Barómetro Africano do Média: Mozambique 2014*. Available at http://library.fes.de/pdf-files/bueros/africa-media/11361-20150521.pdf [accessed 13 September 2016].
37 Ibid.

According to *Reporters Sans Frontières* (Reporters without Borders), press freedom indices, press freedom in Mozambique has fallen from 66 in 2012 to 79 in 2014, indicating growing self-censorship in a climate of increasing restriction.[38]

Despite all these constraints, the private media has been one of the most vocal actors in the struggle against corruption. Important corruption cases in Mozambique are identified and reported by the media and, in some cases, the media has put pressure on government to take action through the COCC to investigate and prosecute cases of corruption. This is evident in cases such as the mismanagement of funds at the National Institute of Social Security, the Mozambican Airports Company (see Box 3), and the recent and ongoing case of the Mozambican Insurance Company. In these particular cases the newspapers *Savana, Zambeze, Canal de Moçambique* were the most vocal.

In addition, *Jornal Dossier e Factos*, an independent magazine, has also been very active. STV, Miramar and TIM have been the most visible television presences in exposing corruption cases to the public.

Actually, the relationship between the COCC with the media is provided for in article 5(2) of Dispatch No. 1/G/PGR/2014. This mandates the director of the COCC to liaise with the media for regular reporting, and to use the media to identify cases that need to be investigated. In fact, in 2012, the COCC publicly committed to organising monthly media briefings to report on the state of affairs regarding their current corruption cases.

However, despite the relative openness of the COCC to the media, many journalists still complain about the quality of information in these briefings, stating that the office normally brings irrelevant cases of petty corruption. The cases of grand corruption remain secret and mostly unsolved.

International development partners

Since the early 2000s, the prevention and suppression of corruption has been incorporated as one of the government's key objectives in its political and economic programmes, as stated in the government's five years plans of 2005–2009 and 2010–2014.

The fight against corruption has also been part of discussions between the government and development partners, termed G-19. The theme falls under the pillar of good governance in the memorandum of understanding on state budget support (2009–2014).

Annually, there is a joint review that takes place between the government and development partners in which both parties assess the status of three anti-corruption indicators, namely: number of cases of corruption identified; number of cases prosecuted; and the effective implementation of the anti-corruption legislative package.

Donors have been exerting pressure to enhance transparency and accountability in Mozambique. For instance, in an interview conducted in 2012 by *O Pais* newspaper,[39]

---

38 Data culled from the Reporters Sans Frontières website, https://rsf.org/fr/ [accessed 11 October 2016].
39 Belmiro J (2012, 29 June) A corrupção é um problema muito grande e visível em Moçambique. *O Pais*. Available at http://opais.sapo.mz/index.php/entrevistas/76-entrevistas/20918-a-corrupcao-e-um-problema-muito-grande-e-visivel-em-mocambique.html [accessed 11 october 2012].

the former Swedish ambassador, Ulla Andrem, stated that the most concerning issue in Mozambique is the lack of transparency, linked to a lack of disclosure of details related to big investment contracts, especially at this time of natural resource discovery.

In general, donor pressure is behind the adoption of the country's anti-corruption reforms, as well as the prosecutor general taking up several high-profile corruption prosecution – including those of two former ministers, and convictions in several other cases involving parastatal officials and provincial government offices.

Despite this perception, G-19 donors still claim that corruption is widespread in the country and that the government should do more to reduce it, by more effectively implementing the anti-corruption package and other existing laws.

In 2014, the attorney general's office and the European Union signed a four million Euro funding agreement to support the institutional development of the attorney general and the COCC. This support falls within the scope of an existing partnership between the EU and the attorney general which aims to promote a more balanced system of governance by strengthening the mechanisms of checks and balances between state institutions, and the administration and effectiveness of justice.

On this occasion, the head of the EU delegation in Mozambique expressed his expectations by saying that only a strong and independent attorney general, subject to democratic control, can ensure the fulfilment of its mandate: observance of the law, control of legality, and the fight against corruption.

G. Performance and effectiveness of the COCC

Effectiveness in handling corruption cases

Data provided by the attorney general's report in 2014 shows that about 906 cases related to corruption were opened that year. From this number, 597 are directly linked to corruption cases. During this period, the COCC handled 239 trials (40% of the total). This data demonstrates an increase in the cases handled.

According to the 2014 attorney general report:

> Looking at the numbers of the cases related to corruption, speculation, misappropriation of funds on public goods, and illicit business participation, since 2008 there were about 4 142 cases handled, 1 318 prosecuted and 508 judged.

When assessing data from the previous years extracted from attorney general reports by the CIP, there is an increase in the number of cases opened and handled by the COCC. An important aspect of the results shown in the table below is that from 35 in 2005, the number of cases increased by more than 100 by 2012. According to projections, it is expected that the number of cases will reach more than 200 in the coming years.

As demonstrated by the CIP:

Assessing the statistics on the performance of the [COCC], from 2005 onwards, it appears that, annually, the number of cases tried by the agency has shown a growing trend, which means greater capacity in the handling of corruption cases. However, from another perspective it suggests that the agency has not yet reached the level of reduction of occurrence of cases of corruption, given the fact that there is no significant decrease in the number of cases to be tried.[40]

Table 1. COCC performance data

Year	Cases received or handled	Pending cases from previous years	Number of cases for prosecution	Cases actually prosecuted
2005	331	None	331	35
2006	100	171	271	21
2007	75	296	371	44
2008	430	0	430	107
2009	309	151	460	135
2010	322	167	489	174
2011	323	185	508	162
2012	209	167	376	151
2013	227	168	395	114

Source: CIP (2014) Controlo da corrupção não foi prioridade na agenda da governação no período 2005–2013. Maputo.

Although the data presented in the table shows an increase in the number of cases handled by the COCC, it is important to note that, from a qualitative point of view, there is not a massive improvement. The most significant cases of big corruption raised by the press have not been resolved and there appears to great reluctance to prosecute these cases properly.

As shown by the CIP,[41] the common practice of anti-corruption institutions 'has always been to bring to public attention the cases considered petty corruption, involving lower-ranking officials in the public administration'. An elucidating example is what happens with the monthly statistics reports from the COCC, initiated in 2015, in which the major cases of corruption involving leading political and administrative figures are not listed.

Examples of the cases of grand corruption not mentioned in the briefings are given in boxes 3 and 4 below.

---

40 CIP (2014) *Controlo da corrupção não foi prioridade na agenda da governação no período 2005 – 2013.* Maputo.
41 CIP (2015) *Informe do(a) Procurador(a) – Geral da República pouco esclarecedor e sem referência a medidas concretas visnado o controlo e combate à corrupção.* Maputo: CIP.

> **Box 3. Case Aeroporto de Moçambique**
>
> In 2011, the supreme court sentenced to jail Diodino Cambaza, then chairman of the board of directors of the Mozambique Airport Company, for the misuse of state funds and goods, estimated at 1.3 million Euros. António Munguambe, former minister of transportation and communication, was also involved and got charged and sentenced to jail for having unduly benefitted from 22 000 Euros and a luxury car, between 2005 and 2008.
>
> This case resulted in a COCC investigation after anonymous complaints were made by Airports of Mozambique workers in 2008.
>
> In the end, however, António Munguambe's penalty was reduced from 16 to four years, and Diodino Cambaza's from 22 to 12 years, a decision related to the fact that the penalty bands applied to judge the former defendants are not applicable to public companies.

> **Box 4. Political leaders involved in Illegal export of timber to China**
>
> In late January 2013, the British Environmental Investigation Agency published an extensive report in which they exposed the illegal export of timber, involving under-invoicing by Chinese companies operating in the province of Cabo Delgado.
>
> According to the report, the agriculture minister, Jose Pacheco, and former agriculture minister, Tomas Mandlate, facilitated this illegal activity and received commissions from the companies.
>
> After a lot of pressure from the press, the COCC initiated an investigation. In 2014, it declared both leaders innocent of timber trafficking, ignoring all the evidence.
>
> This decision decreased public trust in the neutrality of the COCC.

Effectiveness of reporting systems cases

The system (an anonymous telephone hotline) for reporting cases of corruption was established in 2008. In the past five years, 1 958 cases of corruption have been reported, of which 109 led to criminal proceedings and the arrest of 120 individuals in the act of receiving money resulting from acts of corruption. Such individuals were public officials and agents who deal daily and directly with the public, including traffic police, customs officers, nurses, as well as officials from civil identification and immigration services.[42]

Challenges

As stated above, the COCC is subordinate to the attorney general's office and its mandate is mainly to conduct inquiries and investigations into corruption practices; it has no powers to prosecute corrupt practices. This is considered a weakness that puts the effectiveness of this agency into question. The lack of this critical competence restrains the impact of its contribution to combatting corruption.

The second weakness is the fact that it has no mandate to initiate its own investigations, so the agency can only act after receiving suspicious audit reports from administrative

---

42 Moçambique: detidos 120 suspeitos de corrupção nos últimos 5 anos. *Portuguese Independent News Network*. Available at http://portugueseindependentnews.info/2014/12/10/mocambique-detidos-120-suspeitos-de-corrupcao-nos-ultimos-cinco-anos/ [accessed 11 October 2016].

courts and the general inspectorate of finance, internal audits of state institutions, and complaints from individuals.

A third factor is the lack of inter-institutional mechanisms for coordination and articulation. Inter-institutional cooperation would be beneficial for the provision and interpretation of additional information necessary for investigations.

Given that the Anti-Corruption Strategy has defined five priority areas to focus on (education, health, justice, security and finance), the COCC has established cooperation with the following public institutions:

- The administrative court: in obtaining external audit reports from public institutions;
- The criminal investigation police: as a supportive body;
- The general inspectorate of finance: in performing inspections and audits of public institutions and public enterprises;
- The ministry of public works and housing: regarding the request for experts for the evaluation and interpretation of documentation related to public works;
- Registrations services: in providing information concerning property and vehicle ownership, and company registration;
- The national directorate of migration: in confirming the authenticity of documents issued; and
- The financial information office of Mozambique: in providing information on suspicious financial activity.

However, it has been noted that there is still a need for planning and coordinating prevention actions, as well as establishing mechanisms for coordinating activities to prevent corruption with other public institutions through establishment of memorandums of understanding.[43]

In some corruption reports and press, the COCC has been portrayed as focused on petty corruption cases and not providing information on progress related to big corruption cases that have taken place in the past ten years.

H. Conclusion

Mozambique boasts a robust legal framework for combatting corruption, resulting from incremental anti-corruption reforms that took place after the approval of the anti-corruption law. Anti-corruption legislation has gradually evolved to add relevant crimes in public service, including the embezzlement of public funds, influence peddling, money laundering and illicit enrichment.

---

43 Procuradoria Geral da República (PGR) (2011) Plano Estratégico do GCCC (2011–2014).

In this context, 2012 can be held as a legislative milestone when parliament passed two of the five elements of a package of further anti-corruption reforms, namely the law on public integrity and the whistleblower protection law (Law No. 15/2012 of 14 August) to address conflict of interest issues involving public officials.

In 2014, parliament also passed the right to information law, securing the legal basis for combatting corruption after the draft law was tabled by a group of CSOs in the national assembly in 2007.

Despite the gains witnessed in the legislative domain, there is a general perception that corruption is still widespread. This perception has lead us to think that the country's key problem lies in law enforcement. When assessing the country's political and technical environment, we found that law enforcement has been insufficient for the implementation of the anti-corruption legislative package.

In practice, the COCC lacks powers for prosecution, limiting its mandate to a more investigative role. To make matters worse, it lacks a mandate to initiate its own investigations, and therefore, as stated above, only acts based on audit reports from the administrative court, the general inspectorate of finance and internal audits of state institutions, and complaints from individuals. This is counter-productive.

Formal mechanisms for coordination and articulation with other public institutions have also not been established. It has also been noted that there is still a instigating corruption-prevention activities, as well as establishing mechanisms for coordinating activities to prevent corruption with other public institutions, especially those involved in combatting crime.

From a political point of view, the fact that the attorney general and his deputies are all appointed and removed by the president of the republic means that they are all accountable to that office, putting the effectiveness of the COCC into question.

It is not hard to understand the public perception that donor pressure has been behind the adoption of the country's anti-corruption reforms, as well as the prosecutor general taking on high-profile corruption prosecutions.

I. Recommendations

To strengthen the effectiveness of the COCC in the struggle against corruption, there is a need to develop a holistic approach to intervention with multi-stakeholder collaborations. In addition to that, there is a need to develop action plans which include quick wins to serve as a basis for long-term impact. In more specific terms:

- The legislation should provide for more autonomy for the COCC. In fact, the COCC should function relatively independently. Its director should be recruited via public tender based on merit and, once recruited, should remain in the post (according to his performance) for the duration of a term fixed by law. This would reduced the power of the attorney general over the COCC, who should not appoint

or remove COCC staff. The director should report directly to the minister and parliament.
- In dealing with corruption cases, COCC staff are exposed and vulnerable to organised crime groups; they should be provided with a special security status.
- It is necessary to invest more in the expertise and professionalism of COCC staff and related institutions. There is also a need to strengthen the development of a coordinated and comprehensive anti-corruption programme.
- CSO interventions should adopt a more comprehensive approach that prioritises transparency and citizen oversight of government. They should engage in more civic education, advocacy, and monitoring, while holding the government accountable. CSOs can play an important role in pressuring the state to improve the implementation of the legal framework for preventing and combatting corruption.
- CSOs should also consider:
  - Diversifying the number of CSOs that monitor the performance of the COCC, the administrative court and the general inspection of finance;
  - Creating cooperation and joint memoranda between anti-corruption CSOs and state auditing and inspection institutions;
  - Conducting annual performance assessments of state auditing and inspection institutions;
  - Raising citizen awareness about the impact of corruption on the economic and social development of the country, involving the media, theatre groups, singers and community leaders;
  - Conducting and disseminating studies on the culture and behaviours that favour corruption practices.
- The country's high dependence on donor support leads to pressure for transparency and good management of their funds. Therefore, more pressure for reforms and monitoring of the implementation of anti-corruption regulations should be among the donors' priorities. In addition, donors should increase support to CSOs to enhance their role of watchdogs of budget management.

8
NAMIBIA
Prof. Lesley Blaauw

A. Executive summary

Corruption in Namibia has become a national issue of great economic consequences for the country. In an attempt to reverse the consequences of this corruption, the Anti-Corruption Commission (ACC) was established in 2003, yet only became operational in 2006. Prior to the establishment of the ACC, the task of fighting corruption in Namibia was assigned to the office of the ombudsman. Realising that corruption has indeed become endemic in Namibia, President Pohamba vowed to root it out. In fact, his ascend to the highest office in Namibia was marked by a proclamation of zero tolerance for corruption. However, his pronouncement to the public and the Namibian parliament that he would make public the findings of the commissions of inquiry commissioned by his predecessor, President Sam Nujoma, didn't come to fruition.

The need to address the challenges of corruption as a developmental issue for Namibia was necessitated by what transpired in the 1990s: government corruption involving a number of ministers, necessitated the establishment of various commissions by president Nujoma. However, at the time of writing, none of the findings of these committees were ever made public. The commitment of the ruling party to fight corruption became an issue of public debate during the formative years of the ACC. Most opposition members expressed dissatisfaction with the way in which government handled corruption in the early 2000s. Despite the negative perception from politicians, the general public were optimistic about the formation of the ACC and its operations.

The ACC was established in 2003 by an act of parliament as an independent body. It was made a constitutional body in 2010. The director and deputy-director of the ACC in Namibia is appointed by the president of the republic on recommendation by the national assembly. The Anti-Corruption Act (ACA) does not spell-out the required qualifications for both the director and deputy-director, but since inception these positions are occupied by qualified lawyers. The removal of the head of the ACC is done through an extensive process by the president. The legal framework that underpins the fight against corruption only changed incrementally in the late 2000s. For example, constitutional changes were affected only in 2010. The legal basis of the ACC was strengthened to support other institutions and laws aimed at fighting corruption. Constitutionally, the ACC has the power to prevent, report and investigate incidences of corruption. It does not, however, have the authority to prosecute offences in its own name. It is capable of, and empowered to, investigate incidences of corruption in both the public and private sectors.

Despite the tightening of the legal loopholes which provided the fertile ground for corruption, high-level corruption manifests itself through tendering and irregular issuing of licences and bribery to issue them, procurement (at various ministries and at local level), and investment schemes. Kickbacks and non-declaration of conflict of interest are common features in many corruption allegations. Recent legal challenges by those accused of corruption suggest the need to tighten the loopholes in national law and to ensure convergence with other agencies involved in the fight against corruption. Also, in an effort to strengthen the effectiveness of the ACC, there is a need to ensure laws are passed that will protect whistleblowers, provide access to information and compel public office bearers to disclose their interests and assets. Moreover, there is a need for the ACC to become more pro-active in the review process of legislation such as the Public Procurement Bill. Namibia's failure at a national level is also reflected at the regional, continental and international levels.

Despite its commitment to extra-territorial treaties on corruption, the country's failure to extradite two criminals means that it is not fulfilling its duties beyond the boundaries of the country. This, by and large, is a product of the absence of a national framework for the prevention of corruption. Other legal impediments hampering the fight against corruption are the absence of a law protecting whistleblowers, the absence of a law on access to information and a complete disregard for conduct where these exist. Given this state of affairs, it is not surprising that the ACC has failed dismally. The commission has been able to only contribute to the successful conviction in fewer than 40% of cases thus far. Indeed, this lack of success has in recent years led to the perception that government, and by extension the ACC, is not doing enough to fight corruption. A recent survey conducted by Afrobarometer, suggests that more than two-thirds of the respondents feel that government and the agencies established to fight corruption are not doing enough. Not surprisingly, the same study suggests that the media has been most effective in highlighting incidences of corruption in Namibia.

Positive developments about the ACC include: an increase in its budget over the years; its ability to engage both the public and the private sectors; its attempts at raising awareness about the impact of corruption; and successful staff recruitment and retention. The ACC has also been able to decentralise its operations by establishing two regional offices in the north and in the Erongo region of the country. There is still a need to establish one in the south. Financial independence, and the fact that the ACC has not been able to use the resources allocated to it optimally, pose a threat to its financial security. The precariousness of its financial situation is exacerbated by projections that government revenue will decrease considerably in the short to medium term. Also, the appointment of the director and deputy director by the president after nomination by the national

assembly undermines its autonomy. For the ACC to improve its effectiveness and enhance its legitimacy, it will have to do the following:
- The loopholes in legislation, which prevent the Namibian government from fulfilling its obligations to international bodies, should be closed;
- Given that members of the Namibian parliament have disclosed their interests only twice since independence, legislation should be implemented to indicate the intervals at which parliamentary disclosures must take place;
- The Public Service Act must be amended to make it compulsory for management in the public service to annually declare its assets and interests;
- The Namibian government must introduce a code of conduct for the extractive industries;
- The mismatch between cases reported and those actually pursued suggests that the ACC should implement focused public education programmes to highlight when and on what grounds members of the public should report cases to the ACC;
- Government should also enact legislation that provides for a national strategy to fight corruption; and
- Legislation needs to be put in place to guarantee citizens access to information.

B. Introduction

Namibia has a long history in fighting corruption. During the colonial period, in particular under apartheid rule, the only focus in this regard concerned the issue of bribery. Nico Horn and Isabella Skeffers[1] contend that the legal limitation of the Anti-Corruption Amendment Act of 1985 was that it protected public servants from prosecutions. As such, the law did not ensure the proper criminalisation of corruption. Apartheid South Africa not only protected white public servants from prosecution, but also excluded the majority of Namibians from serving the public. The politics of cultural, economic, political and social exclusion provided, by and large, the context against which contemporary Namibia should be measured. Indeed, in the aftermath of independence, the protection of public servants in general, and the political elite in particular, shaped the contours of the fight against corruption. This suggests that in the post-independent period: 'Corruption takes place in a grey zone of activity populated by politicians, holders of high offices, parastatals and members of their families'.[2] The nature of the political system and the dominance

---
1 Horn N & Skeffers I (2010) The Fight against Corruption in Namibia. In: M Hannam & J Wolff (eds) *Southern Africa: 2020 Vision, Public Policy Priorities for the Next Decade.* London: e9 Publishing.
2 Bertelsmann Stiftung BTI (2014) *Namibia: Country Report.* Gütersloh: Bertelsmann Stiftung. p. 12.

of the ruling party, the South West Africa People's Organisation (SWAPO), seems to circumscribe the efforts of corruption fighting agencies.

By some accounts, Namibia is considered a one-party dominated state.[3] This is borne out by the national assembly elections held in 2014. SWAPO won the national assembly elections in 2014, taking 80% of the vote. In this context, legislative power is subsumed by executive dominance. This has consequences for the proper functioning of the legislature. Moreover, while the judiciary is seen as independent, Peter Von Doepp has noted that: 'Namibia's courts have not been asked to adjudicate cases that have gone to the heart of the ruling party's power and interests'.[4] Reflecting on the impotence of the opposition, the ineffectiveness of the legislature, the lack of accountability from the ruling party and the general dominance of SWAPO in the political life in Namibia, André du Pisani posits that: '… democracy is often at the mercy of party interests – both political and economic – and the political elites'.[5] This highlights the issue of an independent and effective anti-corruption strategy. Moreover, given the high levels of unemployment and poverty, the need to address the issue of corruption as a developmental challenge, becomes more urgent.

The Namibian constitution came into force on the eve of the country's independence as the supreme law of the land. Consequently, the constitution is the ultimate source of law in Namibia and attaches great weight to the division of powers and responsibilities among the executive, legislature and judiciary. It is the latter branch of government that plays a pivotal role in anti-corruption efforts in Namibia. In a generic sense, corruption can be defined as the misuse of authority as a result of considerations of personal gain, which need not be monetary.[6] In the context of Namibia, it is instructive to also point out that the different typologies of corruption, as outlined by Simplice Asongu,[7] find particular reference. Asongu asserts that the following three types of corruption aptly capture the African condition:

> Firstly, incidental corruption is characterised by petty bribery and involves opportunistic individuals or small groups. In this context, corruption is the exception rather than the rule. High-level private sector actors and senior officials seldom bother with such theft. Secondly, systematic corruption is organised, not

---

3 Du Pisani A (2013) The politics and resource endowment of party dominance in Namibia: The past as the present and the future? In: Nicola de Jager and Pierre du Toit (eds) *Friend or Foe? Dominant Party Systems in Southern Africa.* Cape Town: UCT Press; Melber H (2013) Namibia: Cultivating the liberation gospel. In: R Doorenspleet and L Nijzink (eds) *One-Party Dominance in African Democracies.* Boulder: Lynne Rienner Publishers; Melber H (2014) *Understanding Namibia: The Trails of Independence.* Auckland Park, South Africa: Jacana Media.
4 Von Doepp P (2009) *Judicial Politics in New Democracies: Cases from Southern Africa.* Boulder: Lynne Rienner Publishers. p. 116.
5 Du Pisani A (2013) The politics and resource endowment of party dominance in Namibia: The past as the present and the future? In: Nicola de Jager and Pierre du Toit (eds) *Friend or Foe? Dominant Party Systems in Southern Africa.* Cape Town: UCT Press. p. 134.
6 Mbaku JM (2007) *Corruption in Africa: Causes, Consequences and Cleanups.* Plymouth UK: Lexington Books.
7 Asongu S (2012) *Fighting Corruption in Africa: Do Existing Corruption-Control Levels Matter?* Munich: Munich Personal RePec Archive.

necessarily institutionalised or pervasive but recurrent. It usually involves large gains which are often subject to popular scandals. While it is entrenched and functions with a large number of officials, intermediaries and entrepreneurs, this form of corruption originates from high-level civil servants that recognise and exploit the illegal ventures and opportunities in government departments and agencies. Thirdly, systemic corruption is pervasive, institutionalised (perhaps accepted, but not necessarily approved), and built into the economic and political institutions. It occurs and flourishes in situations where public sector wages fall below a living-wage. In contrast to systematic corruption, it involves all levels of employment.[8]

The Namibian ACC defines corruption as any conduct which amounts to but not limited to:
- Influencing the decision-making process of a public officer or authority, or influence peddling;
- Dishonesty or breach of trust, by a public officer, in the exercise of his duty;
- Inside dealing/conflicts of interests; and
- Influencing peddling by the use of fraudulent means.[9]

As in most African states, corruption in Namibia is seen as a developmental and social issue that places a serious constraint on economic growth and poverty reduction, among others. In the aftermath of independence in 1990, corruption was, understandably, not a priority area for a newly elected government confronted with the challenge of overcoming the legacy of racially based economic and political segregation.[10] While pronouncements about the lack of tolerance for corruption were made by former president Sam Nujoma, various scandals were unearthed, especially by the print media in the 1990s. Ironically, top government officials and the political elite under investigation during this time were either promoted or, in some instances, the findings of commissions of inquiry went unpublished.[11] This prompted efforts in 1997 to design legislation geared towards addressing corruption and promoting ethics.[12] The table below shows that corruption has been a serious concern for government since the early 2000s.

---

8 Ibid: 6-7.
9 Anti-Corruption Commission (2014) Annual Report. p. 9.
10 Nico Horn and Isabella Skeffers posit that: 'Corruption as a threat to the Namibian nation has a long history in Namibia. During colonial rule Namibia shared South African Roman Dutch common law. Consequently, the common law crime of bribery was always part of our law. Unfortunately, common law bribery covers an extremely limited sphere of corruption. Only public servants can be bribed in terms of this crime, and the crime did not cover actions of agents on behalf of their principals. This situation changed with the coming of the Anti-Corruption Ordinance and later the Anti-Corruption Amendment Act of 1985.' Horn N & Skeffers I (2010) The Fight against Corruption in Namibia. In: M Hannam & J Wolff (eds) *Southern Africa: 2020 Vision, Public Policy Priorities for the Next Decade.* London: e9. p. 104.
11 *The Namibian*, 29 May 2001, Anti-corruption law 'still in the pipeline' (2001, 29 May). *The Namibian*.
12 Horn N & Skeffers I (2010) The Fight against Corruption in Namibia. In: M Hannam & J Wolff (eds) *Southern Africa: 2020 Vision, Public Policy Priorities for the Next Decade.* London: e9 Publishing.

Table 1: Summary of Namibia's performance on the Transparency International (TI) Corruption Perception Index (CPI), 2002–2014

	02	03	04	05	06	07	08	09	10	11	12	13	14
TI CPI Score	57	47	41	43	41	45	45	45	44	44	48	48	49
No. of countries	102	133	146	159	163	180	180	180	178	183	178	177	175
Ranking	28	41	54	47	55	57	57	61	56	56	57	58	57	55

Source: Transparency International.

The above survey measures perceived levels of public sector corruption, a considerable problem in Namibia as indicated by scores below 50. With the exception of 2002, this has consistently been the case. Other indicators include the Afrobarometer survey for 2008, which suggests that perceptions of corruption are high for the police (42%). Disturbingly, the survey also indicates that: 'A sharp increase of 15% in perceived corruption of national government occurred between 2005 and 2008'.[13] The ACC carried out its own Urban Corruption Perception Survey in 2011 to deal with issues including perception of corruption, reporting corruption, and the institutional image of the ACC. The survey revealed the following: 54.3% of respondents perceived corruption to be high in Namibia, 17.7% indicated that it is moderate, while 3.4% perceived it as low.[14] Surveys conducted since 2006 reveal that the perception of corruption and the government's ability to deal with it has decreased significantly. For instance, a survey conducted in 2008 reveals that 54% of respondents positively supported government efforts in fighting corruption. By 2012, this perception was down to 43%.[15] A more recent survey (2014) suggests that corruption in Namibia is on the increase: 63% of respondents say that corruption has increased and 56% feel that government is doing a poor job in curbing corruption.[16]

C. State of corruption

The politics of corruption

Corruption, money and politics

The interface between money and politics as the driving forces for the politics of corruption in Namibia surfaced during the formative years of independence under President Nujoma. The 'borehole scandal' was revealed in early 1993, implicating the justice minister Ngarikutuke Tjiriange, prisons minister Marco Hausiku, deputy environment minster

---

13 Institute of Public Policy Research (2009) *Perceptions of corruption in Namibia. Afrobarometer Briefings.* p. 3.
14 Lindeke B (2013) *Results from the Afrobarometer Round 5 Survey in Namibia.* Windhoek, Namibia: Institute of Public Policy Research. Afrobarometer Briefings.
15 Ibid.
16 Tjirera E (2015) *Namibians see increased corruption; business executives now top list of 'most corrupt'.* Windhoek, Namibia: Institute for Public Policy Research.

Nangolo Ithete, deputy finance minister Rick Kukuri, Okavango governor Ambrosius Haingura and the Southern African Development Community (SADC) executive secretary, Kaire Mbuende. Despite the appointment of a commission of inquiry, whose findings were not released, all top officials implicated were exonerated by the Namibian Cabinet in 1994.[17] During the same period, the permanent secretary of foreign affairs was accused of nepotism for awarding a contract for the supply of luxury cars to his wife.[18] Another major scandal involved the fraud and bribery claims during the upgrading of the Katutura Single Quarters in the late 1990s under the Nujoma presidency. Another case involved a 'wedding gift' for the Minister of Fisheries and Marine Resources Abraham Iyambo, who received NAD 140 000 from fishing companies to underwrite his wedding.[19] The president defended Iyambo by suggesting that these fishing companies made donations voluntarily, so the minister remains innocent. While several presidential commissions of inquiry were initiated under the Nujoma regime, none of the investigations to establish corruption, the abuse of government property, and the misappropriation of government funds have ever been opened to public scrutiny.[20] This prompted an opposition parliamentarian to suggest that the ruling party, SWAPO, has been condoning corrupt practices since the 1990s.[21]

In 2004, newly elected President Pohamba declared zero tolerance for corruption in Namibia as a key element of his administration's agenda, and accelerated the establishment of the ACC. He also twice promised parliament and the public that he would made public the presidential enquiries; a promised never fulfilled.[22] Corruption continued its upward spiral. Indeed, a recent Afrobarometer survey suggests that the perception of corruption in Namibia is increasing. The survey points out that: 'almost two-thirds (63%) of respondents … say that corruption has increased in Namibia over the past year, and a majority (56%) say that government is doing a poor job combating corruption'.[23] Namibia hosts an international business community with strong historical ties with Angola, Europe and South Africa. It also hosts a rapidly growing Chinese business community. These foreign business relations in combination with the easy accessibility over land (long and porous borders, limited capacity for effective control of cross-border movements of citizens and

---

17 Namibian borehole scandal (1995, 19 May) *Mail & Guardian*.
18 According to the National Society for Human Rights, the value of these Mercedes' was estimated at USD 3.8 million.
19 Melber H (2003) Of big fish and small fry: The fishing industry in Namibia. *Review of African Political Economy* 30(95): 142–149.
20 In the early 2000s, Nujoma instituted a number of commissions of inquiry into perceived corruption in the state-owned enterprises sector: These were the following: (i) Commission of Inquiry into Activities, Affairs, Management and Operations of the Social Security Commission (2002); (ii) Commission of Inquiry into Activities, Affairs, Management and Operations of the Roads Authority (2002); and (iii) the Commission of Inquiry into Activities, Affairs, Management and Operations of the former Amalgamated Commercial Holdings (Pty) Ltd and the former Development Brigade Corporation (2004). See Links F & Haimbodi M (2011) *Building Integrity: Corruption and the Construction Industry*. Windhoek, Namibia: Institute for Public Policy Research.
21 Dentlinger L (2005, 26 October) Namibia: MPs 'named and shamed' over corruption. *The Namibian*.
22 Lindeke B (2015) *Presidential Power and Performance in Namibia: The First Quarter Century*. Windhoek, Namibia: Namibia Media Holdings.
23 Tjirera E (2015) *Namibians see increased corruption; business executives now top list of 'most corrupt'*. Windhoek, Namibia: Institute for Public Policy Research. p. 1.

goods), also make the country vulnerable to illicit businesses, which move in and out along the same routes. These avenues, however, are not the primary concern. Corruption relates to government in that corruption is viewed as posing the biggest threat to the Namibian economy. High-level corruption manifests itself through tendering and irregular issuing of licences, and bribery to issue them; procurement (at various ministries and at local level); and investment schemes. Kickbacks and non-declaration of conflict of interests are common features in many corruption allegations.

Table 2: Selected corruption cases in Namibia, 2000–2012 (proven and still pending in court)

Social Security Commission (SSC) channelled NAD 30 million through Avid Investment, a special purpose vehicle set up to receive and launder money.
Offshore Development Corporation (ODC) lost NAD 100 million in a fraudulent investment scheme involving Great Triangle Investments
NAD 120 million lost from the ministry of finance; the government and the city of Windhoek incurred further costs for subsidies and grants for land, road, electricity and water infrastructure, and for repairing environmental damage caused by the Ramatex company.
Namibia Liquid Fuel (NLF): Namibia state oil corporation, Namcor, awarded a profitable contract to the NLF, a joint venture with senior government officials as major shareholders; proved to be not illegal but public perception was that it was unethical.
Government Institution Pension Fund (GIPF): An estimated NAD 1.8 billion lost through investments in Development Capital Portfolio.
Nutech: A bribery scheme that secured a USD 55.3 million contract (at inflated prices) to install 13 Nutech scanners in return for kickbacks to Teko trading ('Namibian consultant').
NamPower: The national power utility awarded a tender to Xaris Energy to set up a 250-megawatt power plant. The KPMG Consortium which advised NamPower was supposed to be paid NAD 2 million for the provision of commercial and technical services, but instead was paid more than NAD 34.5 million.

Source: Auditor general.

The endemic nature of corruption in Namibia became an issue for the office of the auditor general mid-2000, when the deputy director suggested that a lack of accountability, transparency and financial discipline had led to rampant corruption and the abuse of state resources, where 20% of people on the payroll of the ministry of education in 2004 were ghost workers.[24] As Table 2 illustrates, there have been various cases of corruption involving a number of high-placed public officials. The functioning of the public procurement system has facilitated corruption in Namibia. Frederico Links noted that:

> In recent years, tenders awarded ranging from a multi-million-dollar oxygen supply contract for the ministry of health, a tender for NAD 75 million offices for the ministry of lands, and the supply and laying of railway tracks for a northern

---

24 Maletsky C (2005, 12 May) Top Government bean counter spills some beans on corruption. *The Namibian*.

Namibia railway extension, to a lucrative hostel catering contract with the ministry of education, have ended up in litigation over allegations of irregular awarding of these tenders.[25]

Under the pretext of black economic empowerment (BEE), the tender system has exacerbated corruption in Namibia; tender exemptions are often advanced as the way to empower the previously disadvantaged. For instance, during the financial year 2012/13, a total of NAD 13.9 billion worth of tenders were approved by the tender board.[26] Tenders that enjoyed exemption privileges during the financial year amounted to NAD 9 billion.[27] Projects under the Targeted Intervention Programme for Employment and Economic Growth (TIPEEG) worth NAD 1.1 billion were granted exemptions. BEE 'tenderpreneurs' continue to benefit from tender exemption. Indeed, both the number and value of tender exemptions have increased over the last few years. Many BEE managers have become business tycoons who influence parliamentary decisions and lobby for legislation that will ultimately secure their wealth.[28] This has led Brigitte Weidlich to conclude that: 'BEE is not about empowering certain groups. It is about empowering individuals who have business ideas and need information and capital to take off'.[29]

Corruption related to the exploration of Namibia's natural resources (farming, fishing, and mining concessions) is another a source of concern. The granting of exclusive processing licenses (EPLs) or mining licences has become a lucrative venture for those with political connections and access to the highest office. In June 2011, the Brazilian oil and gas prospector and miner, HRT Petroleum threw a party at which former president Sam Nujoma, senior politicians, and those with political connections were present.[30] One of the beneficiaries of these political connections is Knowledge Katti. In early August 2012, in a much publicised visit to the office of both the former president, Hifikepunye Pohamba and former prime minister, Nahas Angula, Katti unveiled the facilitation of a NAD 50 million bonus payment to the state-owned oil company, the National Petroleum Corporation of Namibia (Namcor) by another Brazilian oil and gas exploration company, Cowan Petroleo e Gas SA, of which Katti is a partner in exploration activities off the country's southern coast.[31]

---

25 Links F (20110) Corruption Prevention: Strengthening Systems Procedures and Practices. Windhoek: Hanns Seidel Foundation Namibia. Available at http://www.hss.de/fileadmin/namibia/downloads/FredericoLinks_CorruptionPrevention.pdf [accessed 18 November 2016]. p. 3.
26 Tender exemptions continue unabated (2013, 13 May). *The Namibian*.
27 Ibid.
28 All Africa (2010) *Privilege and Poverty – Liberation's Limits*. September 2016.
29 Weidlich B (2010, 27 May) Politics and economic are bedfellows – Shangula. *The Namibian*.
30 Links F (2012) *On A Slippery Slope: Corruption and the Extractive Industries in Namibia*. Windhoek, Namibia: Institute for Public Policy Research.
31 The political connections and ability to influence decisions stretch beyond the president and members of the executive. In June 2012 it was reported that Namibia's petroleum commissioner, Immanuel Mulunga, had been the recipient of large sums of money through suspicious transactions involving an exploration holder. His job, amongst others, is to advise the minister of mines and energy on the awarding of licences in this sector. *Insight Magazine* reported that Mulunga received on separate occasions payments of almost NAD 2 million between 2009 and 2010 from license holder Katti. In one instance, the Financial Intelligence

The connection between politics and money, and its influence on advancing corrupt practices is also discernible in the construction industry. Two cases worth mentioning took place during different phases of the construction process. The first involves the financing of the expansion construction project by state-owned Namibian Ports Authority (NamPort). The NAD 2 billion project was for the construction of a new terminal at NamPort's Walvis Bay port. Prior to awarding the tender to the Chinese, the NamPort board and senior members of the company accompanied by officials from the ministry of works (responsible for awarding government tenders), met with Chinese officials in China. Ultimately, the Chinese were awarded the tender over traditional trading partners Japan and others (approximately 20 companies bid) in Western Europe.[32] The second involves the University of Namibia (UNAM) and occurred during the pre-qualification and tendering phases. The procurement panel of UNAM awarded, in controversial circumstances, a NAD 80 million contract for the construction of student accommodation to a company in which the university's council vice-chairperson Dr Ndeutala Angolo-Amutenya held a stake. Apart from servicing the university, Dr Angolo-Amutenya is also the permanent secretary in the office of the president.[33]

Box 1: Weaknesses and misunderstandings

The Anti-Corruption Act No. 8 of 2003 suffered a potential setback in 2010. In a verdict by Judge Marlene Tommasi of the high court, the definition of what constitutes a corrupt practice was challenged by defence counsels and led to the acquittal of Nama Goabab and Abraham George on corruption charges. In S v. Goabab and Other, the accused were charged with contravening section 43(1), read with sections 32, 43(2), 43(3), 46 and 49 of the ACA – corruptly using office for gratification.

In her judgement, Tommasi argued that:

> given the history of the offence in Namibia and the legality principle, I conclude that the provisions of section 43 (1) should be interpreted strictly. The narrow interpretation thereof can only be that this provision relates to the corruptee and the corresponding provision for the corruptor is contained in section 38 of the ACA. It follows that the state needed to prove that gratification was obtained from another person i.e. that the public officer who allows himself to be corrupted (the 'corruptee') was required to be corrupted by a corruptor. The evidence adduced does not support the commission of the offence since there was no corruptor.

Judge Tommasi concluded that the state has not succeeded to adduce evidence that the accused committed the offence referred to in the main counts of contravening section 43 (1) of the ACA. This led to a not guilty verdict on the main counts on which the accused were charged. Whether this is a weakness in the act or an over-strict interpretation remains to be seen. The judgement faces an appeal in the supreme court. However, any such loophole could be a boon for defence lawyers who could use it to question the correctness of judgements and sentences already handed down and delay current cases.

Another case in point that led to the state losing a corruption case involves a professional blunder on the part of the police. An employee at the ministry of works and transport (MWT) in Swakopmund was charged with allegedly using her position to obtain gratification from members of the public by renting out the rooms of a government house allocated to her, i.e. contravening section 43(1) of the ACA. Due to the illegal involvement of the police, all charges were dropped against the MWT employee. The lawyer

---

Centre at the Bank of Namibia picked up a direct payment of NAD 80 000 from Katti into Mulunga's local bank account. See Business unbecoming (2012, 10 June) Insight.com.na. Available at http://www.insight.com.na/business-unbecoming/ [accessed 18 November 2016].

32 Links F & Haimbodi M (2011) *Building Integrity: Corruption and the Construction Industry*. Windhoek, Namibia: Institute for Public Policy Research.

33 Ibid.

Box 1: Weaknesses and misunderstandings (cont.)

representing the accused argued that: 'the police were not authorised to conduct and execute search warrants in terms of the ACA', and that the whole search at the house and the arrest were outside the scope of the police as they were not appointed as investigators under the act and that they were not part of the ACC. In his verdict, the presiding magistrate stated that it was clear that the police had to be authorised by the ACC, and that the police are not recognised as investigative officers or special investigating officers under the anti-corruption law, as they are not appointed by the ACC director. Thus, it follows that the whole investigation and search related to the case for which the accused was charged under the act was not within the powers of the police and therefore *ultra vires* and illegal. Clearly, communication between the police and ACC was lacking, with the police failing to understand very basic differences in the mandates of the two law enforcement agencies. Encouragingly, the ACC identified professional rivalry as one of its 17 strategic issues on which the ACC Strategic Plan 2010-2014 is based.

> External professional rivalry can result in organisational paralysis. Initiatives can be frustrated into staleness in the pursuit of self-interest and self-image. Some organisations may feel threatened or feel that their position and influence has been usurped by the commission and may not have the commitment towards the need to interact and work with the commission.

Box 2: ACC nabs corrupt police officers

An increasing number of police officers, who are mandated to enforce the law and curb criminality, are implicated in corruption, especially in abusing their positions for self-indulgence and embezzlement.

Despite repeated warnings from high-ranking security officers, the rot is yet to subside with two high-ranking commissioned police officers of the Namibian police recruitment office, chief inspector Nikanor Ashipala Tweumuna and inspector Anna Maria Klaudia Angula, and a civilian Sackaria Ashipala, arrested by the ACC for nepotism and favouritism this month. The officers were detained in connection with an enduring inquiry into an alleged corrupt appointment of Ashipala, a former police officer, who was discharged from Nampol in July 2012 following his involvement in a case of theft committed in May 2009.

Ashipala, who applied for a position in Nampol's human resource division headed by his brother-in-law in July 2014, reportedly made false representations on his application form by stating that he had no criminal record despite having been convicted of theft and charged with fraud. Inspectors Tweumuna and Angula reportedly manipulated some requirements on the documents to enable Ashipala to qualify for the position. The trio appeared in court where they were granted bail of NAD 5 000 each and the case was remanded to 3 December 2015 for further investigation.

On 22 October the ACC also nabbed a city police traffic officer, sergeant Katrina Elizabeth Auchas, 43, for corruptly using her position to obtain a gratification. The case relates to an iPhone that had apparently been stolen from a vehicle that was involved in an accident on the Gobabis Road on 29 July 2014. Sergeant Auchas allegedly attended to the accident scene. The owner of the phone was traced and identified the phone as his property. Sergeant Auchas appeared in the Windhoek magistrates' court on 23 October and was granted bail of NAD 3 000. The case was remanded to 10 February 2016.

The ACC also arrested two law enforcement officers, Andreas Timotheus Andreas Helao, 26, of Nampol and Alberto Matheus Miguel, 35, of the city police on 21 October for corruptly using their position to obtain gratification. The duo allegedly solicited NAD 3 000 (of which NAD 2 500 was allegedly paid) and a further amount of NAD 4 000 from a person whom they arrested on two different occasions for traffic offences, in order to release his car.

The duo detained the suspect at the Windhoek police station and impounded his vehicle at the city police yard. The suspect was released without charge and paid NAD 2 500 and his car was handed over with an agreement that he will pay the outstanding amount of NAD 500 at a later stage. He was subsequently again arrested for allegedly failing to pay the remaining NAD 500 and his vehicle impounded on a second occasion. Again no charges were brought against him. The police officials then allegedly requested him to pay NAD 5 000 (later reduced to NAD 4 000) in order to release his vehicle.

> **Box 2: ACC nabs corrupt police officers (cont.)**
>
> He then approached the ACC who then set up a sting operation. Helao and Miguel appeared in the Windhoek magistrates' court on 23 October and were released on bail of NAD 3 000 each. The case was remanded to 19 January 2016.
>
> An immigration officer, Alice Namasiku Simaata, 31, was also arrested by the ACC for soliciting a bribe from a South African customer who applied for a work permit. On 25 September the man applied for a work permit for himself and his family through the normal official channels. A home affairs employee then contacted him via SMS to solicit a bribe of NAD 2 000 in order to speed up the approval of the work permit. Simaata was then arrested after receiving the requested NAD 2 000 and handing over the letter of approval.
>
> She appeared in the Windhoek magistrates' court on 19 October on charge of corruptly using her position to obtain gratification. She was remanded in custody and the case postponed 'til 27 January 2016.
>
> Source: Informanté, (2015, 29 October) Available at http://www.informante.web.na/acc-nabs-corrupt-police-officers.16915 [accessed 18 November 2016].

> **Box 3: Conviction of a Zimbabwean**
>
> Press release regarding the conviction of a Zimbabwean in respect of the contravention of certain provisions of the Anti-Corruption Act No.8 of 2003 and the Immigration Control Act No.7 of 1993.
>
> Mr Innocent Mapfumo, a Zimbabwean Citizen, was arrested on 7 July 2008 for being in possession of what then appeared to be a forged passport allegedly corruptly endorsed by certain immigration officials at Ariamsvlei. During the ACC's investigation Mr Mapfumo gave a statement under oath that he never dealt with any of the immigration officials stationed at Ariamsvlei. However, with the evidence collected the ACC managed to establish the opposite. As a result, the ACC opened a separate case against Mr Mapfumo and charged him for having contravened the following laws:
>
> - Section 29(1) (d) of the Anti-Corruption Act, 2003 providing false information to an authorised officer of the ACC; and
> - Section 56(e) of the Immigration Control Act using a permit or document that has been forged or not lawfully issued to enter or remain in Namibia.
>
> On 4 November 2008 Mr Mapfumo was convicted in the Gobabis magistrates' court on the above-mentioned counts and sentenced to a fine of NAD 10 000 or to a period of five years' imprisonment. Two immigration officials, Abraham Willemse and Abrosius Hanabeb, were arrested on 10 July 2008 in connection with the endorsements made in Mr Mapfumo's passport. The trial date in respect of the matter has been set for the 4 December 2008.
>
> Advocate Erna van der Merwe
> Acting director: Anti-Corruption Commission

D. Civil society, donors and media

Civil society has always been at the forefront in the fight against corruption. In 2001, head of the office of the ombudsman Bience Gawanas, urged civil society to start a campaign against corruption as it was becoming obvious that the Namibian government was too slow in putting in place a co-ordinated anti-graft programme.[34] Rick Stapenhurst,[35] states that

---

34 Amupadhi T (2001, 30 May) Civil Society key to change urged to take action against corruption. *The Namibian*.
35 Stapenhurst R (2000) *The Media's role in Curbing Corruption.* Washington: The World Bank Institute.

the media can act as an antidote against corruption in both tangible and intangible ways. Tangible functions are performed when:

> visible outcomes can be attributed to a particular news story or series of stories – for instance, the launching of investigation by authorities, the scrapping of a law or policy that fosters a climate ripe with opportunities for corruption, the impeachment or forced resignation of a crooked politician, the firing of an official, the launching of judicial proceedings, the issuing of public recommendations by a watchdog, and so on. Intangible effects, by contrast, by contrast can be characterised as those checks on corruption which arise from the broader social climate of enhanced political pluralism, enlivened public debate and a heightened sense of accountability among politicians, public bodies and institutions that are inevitably the by-product of a hard-hitting, independent news media.[36]

The print media has, over recent years, increased its coverage of corruption. In a study conducted for the Namibia Institute for Democracy (NID), it was revealed that: 'Cases reported came to 240 cases in 709 news stories compared to only 92 cases reported on in 682 printed news stories between 2004 and 2006'.[37] *The Namibian* topped the list – as it has done since 1990 – producing 247 news articles on corruption during the 12-month period reviewed; an average of 20 articles a month. The Afrikaans daily *Republikein* came second with 192 corruption stories, and the government daily, *New Era*, third with 114 stories. A weekly paper, *Informanté*, came fourth with 79 stories, followed by the German daily *Allgemeine Zeitung* with 50 reports, while the *Windhoek Observer* covered 21 corruption cases and the *Namibia Economist* with 12 stories. Offences receiving most coverage were: embezzlement of funds (49%) abuse of power (26%), conflict of interest (13%) and bribery (6%).[38] In a recent survey, respondents suggested that the media is doing a good job (75%) in exposing corruption in Namibia.[39] In addition to newspapers, *Insight Namibia*, a monthly magazine, publish a section called 'Corruption tracker and access to information'. Two non-governmental organisations, The Namibian Institute for Democracy (NID) and the Institute for Public Policy Research (IPPR), also publish regularly on corruption.

E. International and legal framework
Commitment to international conventions on corruption

Namibia has ratified several regional, continental and international anti-corruption instruments. The country signed the Southern African Development Community (SADC)

---

36 Ibid: 3.
37 Weidlich B (2008, 4 January) Corruption on the increase. *The Namibian*.
38 Ibid.
39 Tjirera E (2015) *Namibians see increased corruption; business executives now top list of 'most corrupt'*. Windhoek, Namibia: Institute for Public Policy Research.

Protocol Against Corruption on 14 August 2001 and the Namibian parliament ratified it on 27 April 2004. The protocol aims to encourage the development of anti-corruption mechanisms at national level, promote cooperation in the fight against corruption among governments, and harmonise anti-corruption legislation in the region.[40] Namibia is also a member of the Southern African Forum Against Corruption. The African Union (AU) Convention on Prevention and Combating Corruption came into force on 5 August 2006. Namibia signed the convention on 9 December 2003 and the Namibian parliament ratified it on 27 April 2004. The convention aims to strengthen the development of anti-corruption mechanisms; facilitate and regulate cooperation among government; and develop and harmonise policies and domestic legislation relating to corruption.

Namibia is also a signatory to two United Nations conventions on corruption. The United Nations Convention Against Transnational Organised Crime came into force internationally on 29 September 2009. Namibia signed the Convention on 13 December 2000 and ratified it on 16 August 2002. The United Nations Convention Against Corruption came into force on 5 August 2006. Namibia signed the convention on 9 December 2003 and parliament ratified it on 27 April 2004. A study by the Institute for Public Policy Research reveals that: 'Namibia came up short of the standards and benchmarks set out in chapter 3 articles concerned illicit enrichment, disqualification from public office, the protection of witnesses, experts, victims and reporting persons and the consequences of acts of corruption'.[41] Shortcomings in Namibian law, despite constitutional provisions to the contrary, as it relates to transnational organised crime are: extradition; transfer of sentenced persons; mutual legal assistance; law enforcement cooperation; joint investigation; and special investigative techniques.[42] To bring Namibian law in conformity with the UN conventions, a number of issues will have to be addressed, including: designing a whistle-blower protection law, an access to information law, an effective law on the declaration of assets by parliamentarians; and developing a national framework to counter-act corruption.

Legal framework for preventing and combatting corruption

The Constitution of Namibia which was adopted in 1990, did not specifically set up an anti-corruption agency, but rather established an office of the ombudsman vested with myriad functions, including a duty to investigate complaints about corruption. Debate on the drafting and establishment of an independent anti-corruption law started in the late 1990s. The second chamber of government, the national council initially rejected the establishment of the ACC.[43] The ACA was passed in 2003. The constitutional amendments

---

40 Carr I (2009) Corruption, the Southern African Development Community Anti-Corruption Protocol and the principal-agent–client model. *International Journal of Law in Context* 5(2): 147–177.
41 Institute of Public Policy Research (2013) *More Namibians unhappy about the government's effort to fight graft despite having confidence in the Anti-Corruption Commission.* Afrobarometer Survey. Windhoek, Namibia: Institute of Public Policy Research. p. 26.
42 Ibid: 37.
43 Hamata M (2002, 15 February) Former AG backs NC rejection of ACC. *The Namibian.*

removed the power to investigate corruption from the functions of the ombudsman.[44] These functions were assigned to the ACC, established in 2006 in terms of section 2 of Anti-Corruption Act No.8 of 2003. The constitution was amended in 2010 to incorporate anti-corruption measures.[45] The ACC was established as an independent body.[46] It is, however, also a government agency as outlined in the Public Service Act No.13 of 1995. Article 94A of the constitution provides that:

- The state shall put in place administrative and legislative measures necessary to prevent and combat corruption;
- There shall be established by an act of parliament an ACC with its powers and functions provided for in such act;
- The ACC shall be an independent and impartial body;
- The ACC shall consist of a director, a deputy director and other staff members of the commission;
- The national assembly shall appoint the director of the ACC and the deputy director upon nomination by the president; and
- The director of the ACC and the deputy director shall be appointed for a period of five years and their qualifications for appointment and conditions and termination of service shall be determined in accordance with an act of parliament.

Anti-Corruption Act No.8 of 2003

This act provides for the powers and functions of the commission to:
- Receive, initiate and investigate allegations of corruption;
- Decide whether an allegation should be investigated and whether the investigation should be conducted by the commission or another authority;
- Consult, cooperate and exchange information with other bodies or authorities that investigate corrupt practices;
- Gather evidence and investigate corrupt practices;
- Make referrals to the prosecutor general in instances where there is evidence of a corrupt practice;
- Take measures to prevent corrupt practices in public and private bodies; and
- Conduct public education on combating corrupt practices. This is done by:

---

44 Blaauw L (2009) *Promoting the Effectiveness of Democracy Protection Institutions in Southern Africa: The Case of the Office of the Ombudsman in Namibia*. Johannesburg: Electoral Institute for Southern Africa.
45 The Namibian Constitution Second Amendment Act of 2010
46 Anti-Corruption Act, 2003

- Advising public and private bodies on ways of preventing corrupt practices,
- Educating the public on the dangers of corruption, and
- Enlisting and fostering public confidence and support in combating corruption.

The following laws are specifically concerned with and aligned to the ACA.

Prevention of Organised Crime Act No.29 of 2004
This act addresses the combating of organised crime, money laundering, racketeering, smuggling of migrants, trafficking in persons and criminal gang activities in Namibia and elsewhere. The act also allows for the seizure of property used in offences and profits made, which is then transferred to a Criminal Assets Recovery Fund and used to fund crime prevention activities. The highest profile case to date under this act involves the former Chief of the Namibian Defence Force, Martin Shali, who had USD 359 526.27 held at Standard Chartered Bank, Lusaka, Zambia, seized under section 51 of the Prevention of Organised Crime Act.[47]

Financial Intelligence Act No.13 of 2012
The main purpose of this act is to combat money laundering by imposing a duty on accountable institutions to report certain transactions to the Bank of Namibia. A recent study reveals that, in the case of Namibia, most financial activities take place outside the formal financial system. Tax evasion – at an estimated 9% of GDP – is by far the largest source of ill-gotten money in Namibia and is clearly a challenge for the authorities. Money laundering is often described as a three-stage process of 'placing' (introducing illegal profits into the financial system), 'layering' (engaging in a series of conversions and movements to distance the funds from the source), and 'integrating' (re-entering the funds in the legitimate economy). Fifty-one percent of Namibia's adult population is 'financially excluded'.[48]

Criminal Procedures Act No. 25 of 2004
The constitutional powers and legitimacy of the prosecutor general are complemented by this act, which gives the prosecutor general the prerogative to institute criminal proceedings with regard to offences that fall under the jurisdiction of the Namibian courts.

---

47 Shalli to lose money in Zambian bank account (2013, 14 October) *The Namibian*. Available at http://www.namibian.com.na/index.php?id=115228&page=archive-read [accessed 18 November 2016].
48 Yikona S, Slot B, Geller M, Hansen B & el Kadiri F (2011) *Ill-Gotten Money and the Economy: Experiences from Malawi and Namibia*. Washington: The World Bank.

Companies Act No. 28 of 2004

This act regulates the establishment, operation and judicial management and liquidation of companies. The act obligates a director of a company to disclose a direct or indirect interest in a proposed contract entered into by the company or a contract already entered into by the company. Failure to do so constitutes a criminal offence. The same is true for officers of the company who have been authorised to enter into a contract on behalf of the company. The act also deals with the offence of insider trading, the practice of dealing in securities of a company with the intent of profiting on the strength of information not yet disclosed to shareholders. Despite the existence of the act, a recent survey suggests that respondents view business executives as the most corrupt in Namibia, overtaking government officials and the police.[49]

Electoral Act No. 5 of 2014

Chapter 4 of the act makes extensive provision for increased transparency and accountability in political party financing and addresses 'vote buying' in section 181. The act regulates foreign, domestic and public funding of political parties, prescribes audits of political party finances and highlights sanctions for non-compliance. Commenting on the legislation, Frederico Links and Clement Daniels[50] note that Namibia has made significant progress in the adoption of anti-corruption legislation since 2000. Despite this remarkable progress, they caution that: '...there appear to be some loopholes in the enforcement of a general anti-corruption legislative framework because of overlapping roles and functions between the ACC, the Namibian police and the office of the prosecutor general'.[51]

The Namibian constitution does not provide for an express right of citizens to gather information on legislation. Indeed, Namibia is among the 14 African states whose constitutions have protected the right to information within the broader context of the right to freedom of expression.[52] Karen Mohan[53] contends that access to information in Namibia is limited by a number of factors. She points out that:

> The current legislative framework is not conducive to facilitating the right of citizens to access information by virtue of the fact that there is currently no access to information law in place in the country... Namibia's legal environment is predominantly skewed in favour of promoting secrecy, with apartheid legislation, such as the Protection of Information Act 1982, still awaiting repeal.[54]

---

49 Tjirera E (2015) *Namibians see increased corruption; business executives now top list of 'most corrupt'*. Windhoek, Namibia: Institute for Public Policy Research.
50 Links F & Daniels C (2012) *Protected Disclosure: Informing the Whistleblowing Debate in Namibia*. Windhoek, Namibia: Institute for Public Policy Research.
51 Ibid: 3.
52 Maina H (2012) *Access to Information: Disclosure vs Secrecy*. Windhoek, Namibia: Institute for Public Policy Research.
53 Mohan K (2012) *Sunlight is the best disinfectant: Why Namibia needs access to information*. Windhoek, Namibia: Institute for Public Policy Research.
54 Ibid: 1.

Moreover, while legislation is readily available to all citizens, there are a number of problems that citizens have to overcome to access such information. Sam Amoo and Isabella Skeffers assert:

> information on legislation... is still very difficult for most Namibians to use effectively: the official language in Namibia is English and, therefore, all acts of parliament are printed in that language. The problem with this is that the majority of the Namibian population lives in rural areas, where most of them do not speak or read the English language. In addition, the acts are not available in braille.[55]

This undermines the good governance and accountability that are essential elements of any democracy. Moreover, the lack of legislation also weakens the institutional framework of Namibia.

The ACC receives oral or written complaints from members of the public and other institutions. Complaints may be submitted in person, by post or mail or fax to the ACC. The ACC has also developed a website through which complaints are submitted. With the exception of section 52(4) of the ACA, legislation on whistle-blower protection in Namibia is non-existent. This section of the act states that no action or proceedings, civil or criminal in nature may be instituted or maintained by any person or authority against any informer or person who has assisted the commission in an investigation into alleged or suspected offences under this act. However, the absence of constitutionally-sanctioned legislation means that becoming a whistle-blower in Namibia could be the road to ruin.[56]

While the legislation outlined in the legal framework, along with other legislation relating to both politicians and others in positions of particularly state-owned enterprises, make provision for respective codes of conduct, the enforcement of these are not underpinned by political will. Ellison Tjirera posits that: 'Namibia's approach to the disclosure of assets and interests on the part of officials wielding considerable power across the various branches of the state could best be described as *laissez faire*'.[57] This is because the existing legislation provides only for the legislature to fulfil requirements of disclosure. The requirements for disclosure by members of parliament are contained in the Powers, Privileges and Immunities of Parliament Act No. 17 of 1996. Despite the existence of legislation, members of the national assembly, the highest body of the legislature, have only declared their interests twice: in 2003 and 2009. This suggests that members of the national assembly have been allowed to contravene the existing code of conduct with impunity. Other branches of government are not compelled to adhere to requirements

---

55 Amoo S & Skeffers I (2008) *The Rule of Law in Namibia*. Windhoek, Namibia: Konrad Adenauer Stiftung. p. 26.
56 Links F & Daniels C (2012) *Protected Disclosure: Informing the Whistleblowing Debate in Namibia*. Windhoek, Namibia: Institute for Public Policy Research.
57 Tjirera E (2012) *Asset Disclosure in Namibia: The need for reform and enforcement*. Windhoek: Institute for Public Policy research.

for regular disclosure. In an attempt to reverse this culture of *laissez faire*, the president of Namibia declared his assets on 25 May 2015, a move that is unprecedented in the country.

F. Prevention and Combatting of Corruption Bureau

Agency staff

The director and deputy director of the ACC are appointed by the parliament following a nomination by the president. Their tenure is a renewable five-year term. The current director Paulus Noa and his deputy have been at the helm of the ACC since its inception. Recently, the national assembly has given permission for Noa and his deputy to be re-appointed for another five-year term. The re- appointment of the two was not without controversy. Three law-makers who have been investigated by the ACC, suggested that the powers of the commission be curtailed. The current attorney general, Sacky Shangala, has been investigated by the ACC twice: for his role on how he changed the catering contracts of the education, and after receiving NAD 55 million in three years as a co-owner of Namibia Liquid Fuel, which scooped a state-owned oil deal in 2004 worth NAD 4 billion. Fisheries Minister Bernard Esua and Education Minister Katrina Hanse-Himarwa were also investigated by the ACC and also opposed the re-appointment.[58] In addition, the ACC has a staff component of 49.

Recruitment of agency staff and tenure

The director and deputy director of the ACC are appointed by parliament following a nomination by the president. Their tenure is a renewable five-year term. These two appointments are made by the president based on the following two considerations:
- They are of good character and of high integrity; and
- Possess knowledge or experience relevant to the functions of the commission.[59]

All other staff members are appointed according to the provisions of the Public Service Act.

Security of tenure

The appointment of the director or deputy director may be terminated if they:
- Fail to comply with a condition of their appointment;
- Are unable to perform office functions, by reason of mental or physical infirmity;
- Fail to perform efficiently the duties of their office; or
- Have been found guilty of misconduct.

---

58 Immanuel S (2015, 13 November) Noa's ark sails on. *The Namibian*.
59 Anti-Corruption Act No.8 of 2003.

The above are the factors to be considered before termination. However, before termination, the president must notify the chief justice, who after consultation with the Judicial Commission established under article 85 of the Namibian constitution, must within 30 days appoint a board to inquire into the matter and submit a report and recommendation to the president. The act does not indicate what other criteria, skills or expertise these two members of the board should possess. During that period in which the matter is before the board for consideration, the president may suspend the director or deputy director, but the suspension lapses if the board recommends to the president that the appointment should not be terminated. The board must investigate the matter in accordance with such rules as the board may make conforming to the rules of natural justice, and submit its recommendations to the president within 30 days. If the board recommends for the director or deputy director to be removed from office, the president must communicate those findings to the national assembly within fourteen days if the national assembly is in session and, if the national assembly is not in session, within 14 days after its next session.[60] All other members of the commission are permanent employees appointed according to conditions regulated by the Public Service Act.

Agency staff ethics, conduct, capacity and remuneration

The remuneration associated with the office should be commensurate with the responsibility and the required qualifications. This salary bracket not only reflects the level on which the commission eventually conducts investigations, it also guards against corruption and justifies the rule that, generally, the director and deputy director are not allowed to generate income other than the remuneration which is granted in their functions as a director/deputy director. The provisions of the Public Service Act in relation to requirements for appointment, tenure of office, conditions of service suspension and dismissal from office do not apply to the director and deputy director in so far as they are inconsistent with the provisions of the ACA. All other staff members are remunerated according to the provisions of the Public Service Act.

Investigative and prosecutorial powers

The directorate of investigation and prosecution has the core responsibility to:
- Receive, analyse and process reports of corrupt practices;
- Investigate allegations of corrupt practices in both private and public bodies;
- Arrest and arraign suspects in corruption or other related cases;
- Compile case dockets for submission to the prosecutor general (PG) for decision;
- Liaise with prosecutors to ensure successful prosecution of corruption and related cases;

---

60 Anti-Corruption Act No.8 of 2003.

- Testify in criminal courts and at disciplinary hearings; and
- Enforce the ACA.[61]

Figure 1: Cases during the financial year 2013/2014

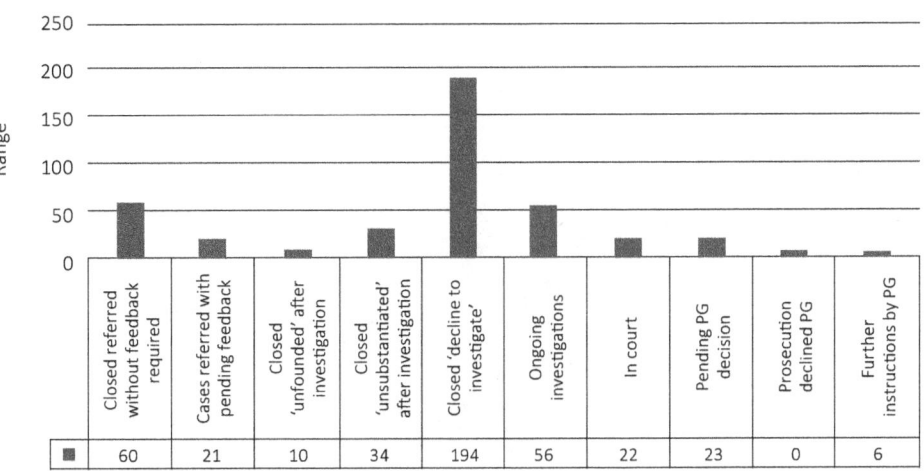

Source: ACC (2014) Annual Report 2013/14.

According to the ACC Annual Report 2013/14, 435 reports of alleged corrupt practices were received. These were dealt with accordingly:
- 194 cases were closed as authorisation to investigate was declined.
- 60 cases were referred to the relevant institutions to deal with. This normally is done in instances where the cases do not fall within the mandate of the ACC because they are purely administrative, but should be brought to the attention of the institution. Such cases are closed without any feedback.
- 21 cases were referred with a request for feedback. In such instances, the cases normally have merit, but the institution should investigate reports and provide feedback to the ACC. The ACC on receipt of such feedback will take a decision whether further investigation is warranted or close the case as unfounded or unsubstantiated.
- Ten cases were regarded as unfounded after investigation as they were found to be false or without merit.
- In 34 cases, after investigations were conducted, the allegations could not be substantiated on the available evidence.
- In 56 cases investigations are on-going, 22 cases are in court and 23 are pending awaiting the prosecutor general's decision.
- The prosecutor general declined to prosecute in nine cases.[62]

---

61 Anti-Corruption Commission (2014) *Annual Report 2013/14*. Windhoek, Namibia: Government printers.
62 Ibid.

Since the ACC does not have prosecutorial powers, 60 cases for the period under review were referred to the prosecutor general.[63] Figure 2 illustrates the origin of reports of corruption.

Figure 2: Cases by entity

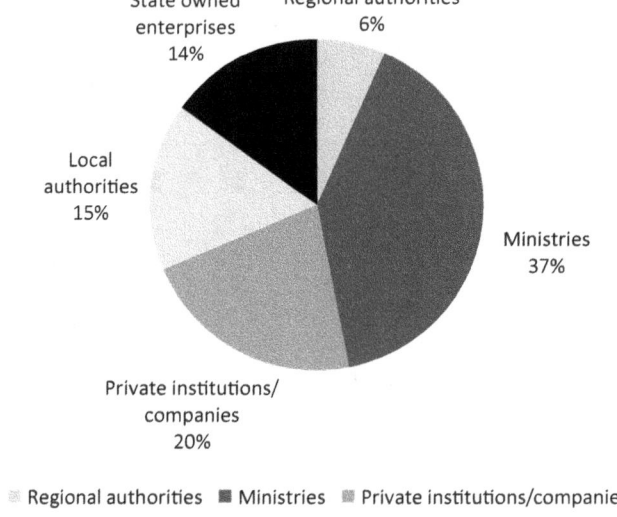

Source: ACC (2014) Annual Report 2013/2014.

Public feedback mechanism and witness protection

Perceptions about the effectiveness of anti-corruption agencies (ACAs) are crucial in shaping opinions about how the country is doing in fighting corruption. An IPPR study suggests that: 'Perceptions of corruption always exceed the actual experience of corruption, but the status of corruption fighting agencies is a mitigating factor in public perceptions'.[64] While the same survey reveals that 54% of the respondents viewed the ACC as a neutral body performing its duties within the confines of the law, there is a caveat to this perception. Increasingly, the legitimacy of the ACC is undermined by the perception that the politically well-connected are beyond its reach. Indeed, 44% of Namibians interviewed are of the opinion that the ACC only goes after petty offenders and tends to ignore the politically well-connected. The accountability and legitimacy of the ACC is however reinforced by the perception of 51% of respondents that it does not discriminate in its pursuit of perceived acts of corruption.[65]

---

63 Ibid.
64 Institute of Public Policy Research (2013) More Namibians unhappy about the government's effort to fight graft tax despite having confidence in the Anti-Corruption Commission. *Afrobarometer Survey*. Windhoek, Namibia: Institute of Public Policy Research. p. 2.
65 Ibid.

Seizure, forfeiture, recovery of assets and mutual legal assistance

The Prevention of Organised Crime Act No.29 of 2004 (POCA) is the legal instrument used to force forfeiture of ill-gotten gains. Numerous cases involving both criminals and high-placed officials illustrate the seriousness with which this act is applied. In the case of David Swartz, a known drug dealer, the state was successful and was granted permission by the high court to seize the property of Mr Swartz.[66] Namibia, as a signatory to the UN Convention Against Transnational Organised Crime, is legally bound to ensure international cooperation with fellow signatories of this convention, that is: mutual legal assistance. However, the failure of the Namibian government to amend domestic law in conformity with the convention means that the country has not been able to fulfil its international obligations. The case of Hans Juergen Koch illustrates its failure on extradition. Namibia's extradition procedures are long and drawn out. Koch, a German national was arrested in 2002. He committed 203 fraud crimes, to the value of NAD 440 million, faced four charges of tax evasion involving the equivalent of NAD 24 million, and four charges of falsifying documents. These crimes were committed between 1978 and 2000. Koch, who came to Namibia during the 1990s, became a Namibian citizen in 2002. After an extradition hearing in the high court, Koch approached the supreme court, which ruled that the Extradition Act had not been followed properly.[67]

Financial resources

At its formation the ACC was allocated a budget of NAD 1.5 million for the 2004 financial year from the national budget.[68] There has been an upward allocation to the ACC from the national budget every year. The allocations for 2011 and 2012 must be viewed against the background of money allocated for the construction of a new head office for the ACC. Also, in subsequent years, the process of decentralisation which saw the establishment of two regional offices contributed to an increase in budget. Apart from this capital expenditure, the growing budget allocation of the ACC is an indicator of its development and relevance in Namibia. Despite this increased allocation annually, the ACC is still heavily underfunded if national comparisons are made. The table below illustrates the growth in the allocations to the ACC over the years. The ACC is expected by law to submit to the auditor general annual reports of how it managed its budget during a financial year. The financial report of the ACC is than tabled in parliament annually.

---

66 *David Swartz Case* No. A 334/2011, High Court of Namibia.
67 A similar case involved the Israeli citizen, Jacob Alexander who is wanted in the United States on 35 criminal charges relating to alleged stock market fraud. Because Namibia does not have an extradition agreement with the US, Alexander was not extradited. See Institute of Public Policy Research (2013) More Namibians unhappy about the government's effort to fight graft despite having confidence in the Anti-Corruption Commission. *Afrobarometer Survey.* Windhoek, Namibia: Institute of Public Policy Research.
68 Dentlinger L (2005, 26 October) Namibia: MPs 'named and shamed' over corruption. *The Namibian.*

Table 3: Budget of the ACC

Financial year	Total budget	ACC's budget	%
2015	67 080 000 000	53 248 000	0.08
2014	60 100 000 000	54 792 001	0.09
2013	47 600 000 000	48 581 000	0.10
2012	40 150 600 000	50 303 000	0.13
2011	36 713 197 341	63 406 576	0.17%
2010	27 574 641 000	36 786 000	0.13%
2009	23 933 341 000	26 983 000	0.11%
2008	21 133 668 000	14 144 000	0.07%
2007	16 625 641 000	11 258 000	0.07%
2006	13 677 120 000	6 579 000	0.05%

Source: Auditor General Reports

Table 4: Donations received by the ACC from development partners

Financial year	Name of the donor	The purpose of the donation	Nature of the donation
2009	United Nations Democracy Fund (UNDEF)	Support to the ACC for the implementation of the ACA	USD 245 000
2009	Hanns Seidel Foundation Namibia(HSFN)	Establishment of a website for the ACC	NAD 45 000
2010	Hanns Seidel Foundation Namibia(HSFN)	Reproduction of the ACC pocket book	NAD 30 000
2011	Hanns Seidel Foundation Namibia (HSFN)	Reproduction of the ACC pocket book	NAD 30 000
2012	African Development Bank	To fund the Southern Africa Forum against Corruption (SAFAC) annual general meeting	NAD 179 849.50
2012	Freedom House Southern Africa (FHSA)	To finance the Encase Forensic phase 2 training for six ACC officers	The money was paid by the donor directly to the service provider
2013	United Nations Development Programme (UNDP)	To fund the development of a national Anti-Corruption Strategy Plan	USD 20 000 was paid directly to the company
2013	Commonwealth Secretariat	To pay for the perception survey in Namibia	NAD 141 050
2013	National Planning Commission	Office equipment donated by the government of the People's Republic of China	Office equipment donated
2014			

Sources: Auditor General's Reports.

In addition to government funding received by the ACC, it has also received financial resources from development partners like the United Nations Development Programme (UNDP), amongst others. Table 4 illustrates the amount of money that the ACC received over the past few years, the purpose of the money and the partner responsible for the money.

Relationship with the public and other stakeholders

The ACC has a directorate of public education and corruption prevention, the core responsibilities of which are:

- To educate the public on the evils of corruption and foster ethical values. This is done through training and integrity related workshops that are tailor-made to meet the needs of target groups.
- To identify weaknesses and shortcoming in the systems, practices and policies of public and private bodies and advise on the changes to be effected thereto in order to prevent the occurrence of corruption.
- To design projects and conduct surveys to assess the public opinion and perception on corruption as well as to make recommendations on better prevention of corruption.

In an effort to raise public awareness on the risks of corruption, the ACC held seminars and workshops with various stakeholders such as the public and private sectors, youth groups, traditional leaders and church leaders as well as various non-governmental organisations. The objectives of these workshops and seminars include: to sensitise the stakeholders on the dangers and evil of corruption, and equip them with relevant information on corruption.[69]

Relationship with private sector

While no formal agreements exist between the ACC and the private sector, the organisation also continuously attempts to raise awareness about the impact of corruption on this sector. Interestingly, a recent survey by the IPPR suggests that the private sector is now seen as the most corrupt institution in Namibia.[70]

Reporting mechanism and public perception

The ACC has a hotline for reporting corruption. In an attempt to reach the far corners of the country and in line with government objective, the ACC has also established three regional offices. People can also report corrupt practices by using the email address provided by the ACC. It also has a website which allows citizens to report incidences of corruption. Public perception of corruption since the inception of the ACC has varied. Not surprisingly, public perception of the ACC – and indeed, government efforts to reduce corruption – is dwindling, as Table 5 illustrates.

---

69 Anti-Corruption Commission (2014) *Annual Report 2013/14*. Windhoek, Namibia: Government Printers.
70 Tjirera E (2015) *Namibians see increased corruption; business executives now top list of 'most corrupt'*. Windhoek, Namibia: Institute for Public Policy Research.

Table 5: Public perceptions of corruption (2006–2014)

	2006	2008	2012	2014
Very well	50	51	43	34
Very badly	40	41	56	65

Source: Tjirera E (2015) *Namibians see increased corruption; business executives now top list of 'most corrupt'*. Windhoek, Namibia: Institute for Public Policy Research.

Performance

The table below shows the performance of the ACC since its establishment. Since its inception the ACC has received favourable ratings from both the public and a panel of experts. For example, a survey conducted among a panel of experts by Global Integrity in 2007, showed that the experts gave the ACC 89 out of 100 for its effectiveness and 63 for its accessibility.[71] Afrobarometer surveys conducted between 2006 and 2008 illustrate the confidence the public had in the ACC during that period. Tjirera and Hopwood note that: 'Those adjudging government's efforts as positive grew from 50% in 2006 to 54% in 2008, while the percentage of those who had a very negative view went down from 22% to 15%.'[72] The Afrobarometer survey conducted in 2012 reflects a growing negativity towards the government, and by extensions the commission in its fight against corruption. While the survey reveals that the agency still enjoys some legitimacy (54%), a more disturbing finding is that the ACC only goes after the proverbial small fish as opposed to those that are politically-connected.[73] The Afrobarometer survey conducted in 2014 also suggests that perceptions of corruption are increasing among the general public. Ellison Tjirera points out that: '…almost two thirds (63%) of respondents the Afrobarometer 2014 survey say that corruption has increased in Namibia over the past year and a majority (56%) say that government is doing a poor job of combating corruption'.[74] As Figure 3 and Table 6 illustrate, the ACC has not been very successful in contributing to securing convictions and prosecutions. For instance, during its first five years of existence, the ACC has only been able to contribute to 38 convictions.[75] Table 6 illustrates that the ACC has not been able, at any given year, to secure more than 20% of all cases reported. It has also been unable to close more than half of the cases reported. Also significant is that the number of cases reported to the ACC has decreased significantly since 2011.

---

71 Global Integrity (Global Integrity report 2007: Key Findings. Available at https://www.globalintegrity.org/wp-content/uploads/2013/08/KeyFindings2007.pdf [accessed 18 November 2016].
72 Tjirera E & Hopwood G (2011) *The ACC in Action: What does the track record say?* Windhoek, Namibia: Institute for Public Policy Research.
73 Lindeke B (2013) *Results from the Afrobarometer Round 5 Survey in Namibia*. Windhoek, Namibia: Institute of Public Policy Research. Afrobarometer Briefings.
74 Tjirera E (2015) *Namibians see increased corruption; business executives now top list of 'most corrupt'*. Windhoek, Namibia: Institute for Public Policy Research. p. 1.
75 Tjirera E & Hopwood G (2011) *The ACC in Action: What does the track record say?* Windhoek, Namibia: Institute for Public Policy Research.

Figure 3: Performance of the ACC

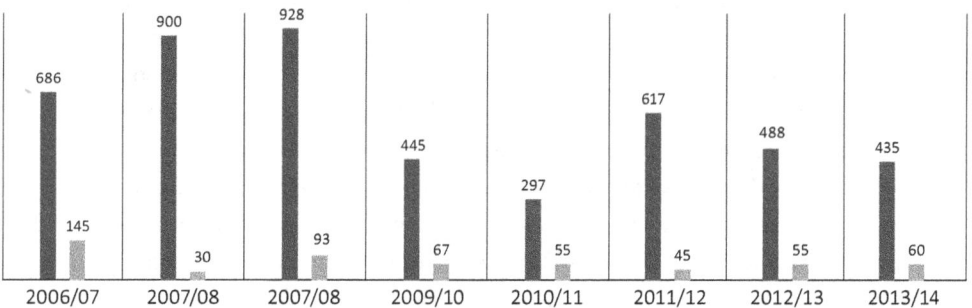

■ No. of reports received ■ No. of cases referred to PG

Source: ACC, Annual Reports.

Table 6: Cases referred to the prosecutor general

Proportion of cases referred to PG/pursued								
Year	2006/07	2007/08	2008/09	2009/10	2010/11	2011/12	2012/13	2013/14
%	21%	3%	10%	15%	19%	7%	11%	14%

Summary of cases received by the ACC since 2006/2007 financial year up to the end of 2013/2014 financial year	No. of cases
Case status	Closed 1987
Referred without feedback	1186
Unsubstantiated after investigation	593
Unfounded after investigation	440
Ongoing investigation	216
In court	191
Prosecutor general declined to prosecute	73
Convictions	70
Acquittals	34
Pending referred with feedback	26
Pending prosecutor general decision	24
New reports awaiting decisions by director	17
Cases returned by prosecutor general with instructions	7
Total	**4864**

Source: ACC, Annual Reports.

G. Conclusion

The preceding pages illustrate that Namibia seems to have a problem with reducing and eliminating corruption. The history of colonialism continues to cast a shadow on efforts to fight corruption. This is, in part, a result of the inability of the state to tackle the structural factors that continue to promote colonialism. Corruption exists at both elite and lower levels, while the formation of the ACC has heightened expectations that Namibia would be able to win the fight against corruption. For example, in 2006 and 2008, an Afrobarometer survey showed that more than two-thirds of the population believed that the country would overcome corruption. This optimism was replaced with pessimism as revealed by the 2012 and 2014 surveys. More than half of the population is now convinced that government and its agencies are not doing enough to fight corruption. This negative perception stems from the intimate relations between politics and money, and how only the proverbial small fish are pursued at the expense of the politically-connected. The inability of the country to address corruption as a developmental issue is also intimately related to the lack of political will by those who are in control of the body politic.

The legal loopholes and the interface between politics and money suggest that the fight against corruption is a challenging one. The media has been instrumental in the fight, yet the ACC still faces considerable challenges. The low level and the small number of cases resolved do not auger well for the anti-corruption body. Its future success is contingent on increasing the level of awareness of the impact of corruption in both the public and private sectors. In addition, the success of the corruption body is also contingent on it ensuring that loopholes recently identified through the various court challenges are closed through the amendment of legislation. Namibia also needs to bring its domestic law in compliance with the various regional, continental and international legal conventions it has signed. For example, there is a need to change the law on extradition to bring it in line with international requirements. Domestically, there still exists an absence of a law on whistle-blowing, access to information, and an effective law on the declaration of assets by public officials in powerful positions. Ultimately, the success of the ACC is predicated on both its own ability to show increased activism and support from the general population.

H. Recommendations
Policy and legal reforms
- The loopholes in legislation that prevent the Namibian government from fulfilling its obligations to international bodies should be closed. For instance, the extradition law is not in conformity with the UN conventions to which Namibia is a member. Simplified extradition procedures and deadlines aimed at expediting the extradition process need to be addressed in existing legislation.
- Given that members of the Namibian parliament have disclosed their interests only twice since independence, legislation that indicates the intervals at which parliamentary disclosures must take place should be implemented. This should be used as a guide for developing particular

codes of conduct and asset declaration systems for the legislature, different tiers of government and other public agencies.
- The Public Service Act should be amended to make it compulsory for those in public service management to declare their assets and interests annually. There is currently also no comprehensive policy and legal approach to conflict of interest. There should be a national law that clearly sets out the principles that should govern a sound conflict of interest policy.
- The Namibian government must introduce a code of conduct for the extractive industries.
- Government should also enact legislation that provides for a national strategy to fight corruption. This would require that all key stakeholders (state and non-state actors) should be involved in the implementation phase of the national anti-corruption strategy.
- Namibia should develop and introduce access to information legislation based on the principles of the African Union's model law on the issue. The country should also consider adding access to information to chapter 3 of the constitution as a fundamental right.

Institutional reforms

- Capacity and resources of the ACA for increasing and disseminating knowledge about the prevention of corruption should be increased. No other agency has this mandate.
- The ability of the ACC to be an effective preventative entity is weakened by is lack of research capacity. There is a need for government and other stakeholders, both private and public, to ensure that the capacity and resources of the ACC are augmented.
- The relationship of the ACC to other bodies engaged in the fight against corruption needs clarifying. Moreover, the appointment of the director and deputy-director of the ACC should be made by the national assembly and not by the president as is currently the case.
- The ACC should establish a directorate of corruption prevention to be dedicated to researching systems, procedures and practices that will best enable Namibia to reduce corruption (currently the directorate is merged with that of public education).

Other reforms

- The mismatch between cases reported and those actually pursued suggests that the ACC should have focused public education programmes that highlight when and on what grounds cases should be reported to the ACC.

- Public awareness should be sustained and increased through the publication and distribution of brochures and pamphlets.
- No public conference has ever been held on the evil and dangers of corruption. This needs to happen on a regular basis. Such conferences should quantify the monetary losses to corruption and its impact on development programmes nationally.

9
SOUTH AFRICA
Dr Ralph Mathekga

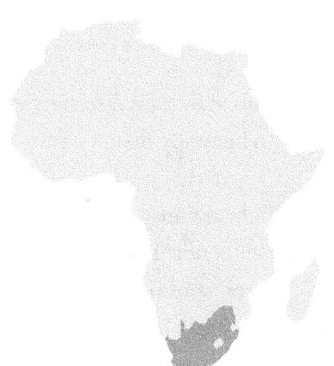

A. Executive summary

The fight against corruption in South Africa perfectly coincides with the process of state formation and nation-building in the post-apartheid era. The history of apartheid is a dark space for South Africa, where the majority of people were not recognised as citizens; they were only seen as 'subjects' by the state. This relationship brought with it a peculiar point of contact between the state and the majority of the people. The state related to the people only by way of policing them. It was a regulatory relationship. These people did not have any legitimate claims against the state; neither did the state recognise its obligation towards the majority, apart from policing them and ensuring that law and order prevailed.

The end of the apartheid system redefined the relationship between the state, government, and the people. The people were to become an embodiment of the state. A new set of obligations between the state and citizens were identified and included in the constitution. Human dignity was to be at the centre of this new relationship.

Citizenship entails that citizens are consulted regarding the management of public resources and the broader implementation of policies. With the democratic dispensation in South Africa came the need for government to fully account to the people. Citizens are obligated to demand that accountability and also to play their part in respecting the institutions of democracy. Corruption is corrosive to this relationship; a relationship that is still in its formative years, following the collapse of apartheid just over a decade ago.

In order for citizens to develop an open relationship with the institutions of democracy, corruption should be fought against because its proliferation and survival negatively affects the manner in which citizens relate with institutions of democracy. Corruption is inimical to democratic consolidation; it undermines it.

It is clear that South Africa is losing much-needed resources to corruption, as it undermines the stability of institutions such as the prosecution authority, otherwise known as the Directorate of Priority Crime Investigation (DPCI). Weak leadership in such institutions undermines the broader criminal justice system in the country. There is a need for political leaders to demonstrate their commitment to ensuring the stability of these institutions. Most importantly, political leaders have to begin to partner with the general public and civil society organisations (CSOs) in the fight against corruption. Citizens need to be made aware of the corrosive effects of corruption on their institutions and livelihoods.

At this point however, some political leaders in South Africa seem to believe that the fight against corruption should be managed in a way that does not raise suspicions among the general public regarding the extent of the scourge. This needs to be overcome in the interest of involving broader society in anti-corruption efforts.

South Africa has credible institutions of accountability that could repel corruption, but they are subverted in the interest of political expediency. There is an emerging trend among government departments to ignore the findings of the public protector. This will have a long term impact on the credibility of the entire institution of democracy.

There is a viable anti-corruption institutional framework; what is lacking is the commitment to respect those institutions and allow them to carry out their function as provided for in the constitution. The 2014/2015 Afrobarometer survey indicates that citizens' approval of democratically elected leaders in South Africa is on the decline due to increasing incidents of corruption – a clear indication of the impact that corruption can have on democracy. If corruption is not uprooted, democracy will be deemed a poor means to achieve societal wellbeing.

B. State of corruption in South Africa

South Africa is experiencing a significant rise in corruption, particularly in the public sector. The 2014 Transparency International Index ranks South Africa 67th out of 175 countries when it comes to corruption.[1] It has been stated that in the last 20 years, South Africa has lost R700 billion to corruption.[2] That is equivalent to more than half of the annual budget.

It was reported in 2013 that 'almost half (47%) of South Africans who came into contact with government paid bribery'.[3] The 2013 Transparency International Survey indicates that South Africans believe that public sector corruption is getting worse. It was also reported in 2013 that South Africa is losing R25 billion a year in corrupt government procurement practices.[4] The national treasury's 2015 supply chain management (SCM) review raises concerns over the 'negative effects of inefficient public sector SCM, particularly in the procurement phase of the chain'.[5] Perennial violation of supply chain

---

1 SA ranked 67th in corruption index (2014 12 March) *City Press*.
2 R700 billion lost to corruption in South Africa (2015, 28 January) *BusinessTech/SAPA*. Available at http://businesstech.co.za/news/general/78489/r700-billion-lost-to-corruption-in-south-africa/ [accessed 4 October 2016].
3 Ibid.
4 Corruption Watch (2013, 5 April) Dodgy procurement costs R25bn every year. *Moneyweb*. Available at http://www.moneyweb.co.za/archive/r25bn-lost-every-year-to-dodgy-procurement/ [accessed 4 October 2015].
5 National Treasury (2015, 28 January) Public Sector Supply Chain Management Review. p. 21. Available at (http://www.treasury.gov.za/publications/other/SCMR%20REPORT%202015.pdf [accessed 4 October 2016].

guidelines has become a norm in the public service. The treasury report also points to price distortion; the practice of over-charging for goods and services.

The previous public protector, Advocate Thuli Madonsela, stated that corruption in South Africa is becoming 'aggressive'.[6] 2015 saw revelations of major scandals in the public sector and within state owned entities such as the Passenger Rail Association of South Africa (PRASA), South African Airways (SAA), and Eskom. It is because of general mismanagement in those institutions that the public approval of political leaders is reported to be declining. The 2014/15 Afrobarometer survey indicates that:

> South Africans are generally dissatisfied with their elected leaders' performance in the past year. President Zuma and local government councillors receive the lowest approval ratings (only 36% of respondents 'approve' or 'strongly approve'), followed by MPs (42%), while provincial leaders enjoy the highest levels (53%).[7]

Corruption is not limited to the public sector, though; the private sector is also involved. Among some of the case showing the interface between private and public sector corruption is the case of collusion between construction companies in the 2010 World Cup stadium procurement. The competition commission found that companies 'held meetings to rig profit margins on the construction of six stadiums ahead of the soccer tournament'.[8] The case was not, however, dealt with as a corruption matter, but as a collusion matter. This shows an uneven approach to corruption in the private sector as opposed to that in the public sector.

There is no clear picture regarding the state of corruption in the private sector in South Africa. It has the resources and complex communication machinery to obscure perceptions of corruption. The state of corruption in the private sector could only be measured through its involvement in public procurement, in which it has increasingly regular interactions with the public sector. There is a need for thorough research on the subject.

Political economy of corruption

Corruption has become part and parcel of politics in South Africa in two distinct ways. Firstly, corruption has an influence on politics in the country in that it is resorted to as a means to attain political influence; such as in instances where political processes are infiltrated through patronage. Secondly, corruption has an impact on the effectiveness and legitimacy of state institutions, including those of democracy. In the case of South Africa, where institutions of democracy are still in their formative stages, intense proliferation of

---

6 Interview with AT Madonsela, Public Protector. Pretoria, 3 December 2015.
7 Lekalake R (2015). *South Africans increasingly dissatisfied with their elected leaders' performance*. Cape Town: Afrobarometer.
8 Cohen M & Bhuckory K (2014, July 22). Government wants more payments from colluding World Cup builders. *Mail & Guardian*. Available at http://mg.co.za/article/2014-07-22-government-wants-more-payments-from-colluding-world-cup-builders [accessed 4 October].

corruption competes with legitimate institutions of democracy as channels for distributing resources.

The experience in South Africa shows a disturbing trend in which political elites accused of corruption and impropriety attack the state institutions tasked with investigating the acts. This has the potential to undermine the legitimacy of institutions of democracy and accountability, which have also been used to fight political battles under the pretext of fighting against corruption. This enfeebles genuine investigations into corruption. The conflict between former president, Thabo Mbeki, and then ANC deputy president, Jacob Zuma, has left the impression that, at times, state institutions can be used to wage political battles and that anti-corruption institutions are conveniently available for such a task.

The emergence of the Economic Freedom Fighters (EFF), amidst allegations of tender irregularities against founding leader Julius Malema, is another such case. Irrespective of the merits of the allegations that are often raised regarding the issue, the effect of such narratives on the legitimacy of state institutions is irrefutable. The idea that corruption is a 'western thing'[9] leads to the conclusion that the institutions of democracy, particularly those that are responsible for ensuring accountability and fighting against corruption, are also western tools that are conveniently used to undermine some leaders. The effect of this viewpoint is more pernicious in a setting such as South Africa where institutions of democracy have not yet become stable or cemented. Let us first observe how corruption infiltrates democratic processes and then we will later deal with how it affects the legitimacy of democratic decisions.

One of the fundamental presumptions of democracy is that the processes for making decisions should be fair, open and accessible to all. This essentially entails that players should have similar amounts of resources when they compete for political power. The quest to buy political influence has become one of the main drivers for corruption in South Africa. It is well understood that competition for political positions within the African National Congress (ANC) is one of the key drivers of corruption in the country. The ruling party is plagued by this problem not because the party is inherently corrupt but because of its dominance in the national, provincial and local spheres of government. The ANC is largely represented in major areas of society where decisions are made regarding the distribution of resources. The type of corruption that would emerge in this kind of exposure has come to be characterised also as flowing from the 'sins of incumbency'. According to ANC national executive committee (NEC) member Joel Netshitenzhe, reflecting on the challenges the ANC has been confronting:

> We need to reflect on the issue of whether the 'sins of incumbency' can be dealt with merely as an internal organisational issue! This is because ... these sins affect – as we heard during the course of this week – infrastructure spending

---

9   Du Plessis C & Du Plessis C (2012, 24 October) Zuma wanted charges dropped because corruption is a 'western thing'. *City Press*. Available a http://www.news24.com/SouthAfrica/Politics/Zuma-wanted-charges-dropped-because-corruption-is-a-Western-thing-20141012 [accessed 4 October 2016].

and payment for work done; delivery of text-books to poor children; quality of legislation passed by parliament.[10]

As an incumbent political party responsible for the distribution of state resources, the ANC finds itself plagued by corruption resulting in corrosion of internal processes within the party, on one hand, and also corrosion of the principle of fairness in the broader political spectrum in South Africa on the other. Besides the influence of corruption on internal processes, the ANC is also facing allegations that it has used state resources to enrich itself as a party in order to fund its elections campaigns. This affects procurements in the public service and may increase the price of procuring goods in the country. For example, the ANC's relationship with Hitachi has recently come under scrutiny, where the party is alleged to have improperly benefitted from procurement relating to the construction of the Medupi power station. Through its investment arm, Chancellor House, the ANC secured a stake in Hitachi Africa which has been awarded USD 5.6 billion to build boilers in the Medupi power station in Limpopo province.[11]

Hitachi was subsequently investigated by the US Securities Exchange Commission (SEC) regarding allegations that the company's partner in the Medupi power station deal was merely a front for the ruling ANC. Hitachi Japan agreed to pay a settlement fee of USD 19 million the SEC.[12] Although Hitachi did not agree that it has an improper relationship with the ANC-owned Chancellor House, its decision to pay a fine to the SEC is a demonstration that the company is aware that its relationship with the ANC investment arm is not beyond reproach.

The SEC's investigation into the matter also raises concerns about South Africa's own anti-corruption machinery. It raises the suspicion that local anti-corruption institutions are subdued by the influence of the ruling party. Despite years of allegations of impropriety regarding the relationship between Chancellor House and Hitachi Africa, there has not been a single investigation into the matter within the country. Following the SEC investigation, the opposition parties are pushing for a local investigation into the matter. The question that needs to be asked is whether the Hitachi saga is the tip of an iceberg or just an isolated case.

It is difficult to answer this question because information regarding private funding to political parties is not available in South Africa, so one cannot assess how much funding is flowing through vehicles such as Chancellor House. Nor is it clear how many such partnerships exist out there.

Lack of regulation on party funding serves as an incentive for corruption. It makes it difficult for citizens to gain information regarding who fund parties, to know how to make

---

10 Netshitenzhe J (2012, 15–21 June) Competing identities of a national liberation movement. *ANC Today*. Available at http://www.anc.org.za/docs/anctoday/2012/at23.htm#art2 [accessed 4 October 2016].

11 Wild F (2015, 5 October) From Hitachi deal with arm of ANC to power cuts. *Bloomberg*. Available at http://www.bloomberg.com/news/articles/2015-10-05/from-hitachi-s-deal-with-arm-of-south-africa-s-anc-to-power-cuts [accessed 4 October 2016].

12 Ibid.

sense of some policy decisions that have been made by the ruling party, or to understand the policy stance assumed by opposition parties. This means that their voting decisions are largely uninformed. If citizens are not aware of how political parties are funded, they cannot be in a position to fully interrogate parties and assess in whose interest parties are making policy decisions. Even more immediate is that the system incentivises political parties to influence procurement processes by awarding tenders to companies that would, in turn, make financial donations to those respective parties. This amounts to kickbacks, and there is no regulation that allows for tracking of private donations to political parties.

The two dominant political parties in South Africa, the Democratic Alliance (DA) and the ANC, have both resisted releasing information about their private funders. The issue of political parties influencing funders also came to fore in the period leading up to the May 2014 general elections, where secret funders were alleged to have had a hand in the 'short-lived merger between the DA and Mamphela Remphele's Agang'.[13] It was conceded then that donors were exerting pressure for the merger to take place, potentially forcing parties in a direction that might not be preferred by voters and members of those parties. The latest bid for regulation of party funding failed when the constitutional court dismissed application to force political parties to reveal their private funders in September 2015.[14]

There are different ways in which the political economy of corruption plays out in South African politics. Corruption affects the functioning of politics in varying and interesting ways. The perverse effect of corruption in South Africa is such that it is somehow possible for perpetrators to launch an attack on anti-corruption efforts. It is worth asking why it is possible in South Africa, or perhaps in Africa in general, for politically connected elites to launch a political project on the basis of an attack against anti-corruption initiatives. This consideration should elucidate on how better to frame anti-corruption initiatives in post-colonial Africa.

South Africa has thus far experienced two interesting cases where individuals who were accused of corruption have actually exploited the allegations to sustain political projects, using anti-corruption institutions as political tools to drive the western agenda. When Jacob Zuma was accused of corruption, not only did his popularity within the country rise, he also launched a successful political project through which he became the president of the ANC and subsequently of the country. What made his campaign successful was that he cast himself as the victim of political conspiracy, targeted by western infiltrated institutions.

The second interesting case relates to corruption charges against former ANC Youth League president, Julius Malema. After the public protector's report implicating Malema's companies in tender irregularities in Limpopo Province, Malema crafted a political project

---

13　Davis R (2014, 28 July) Who funds our political parties. *Eye Witness News*. Available at http://ewn.co.za/2014/07/28/OPINION-Rebecca-Davis-Who-funds-our-political-parties [accessed 4 October 2016].

14　ANC welcomes Constitutional Court ruling on part funding (2015, 30 September) *The Citizen*. Available at http://citizen.co.za/794822/anc-welcomes-constitutional-court-ruling-on-party-funding/ [accessed 4 October 2016].

that defined itself against the use of state institutions to pursue political battle. Malema's court appearances have drawn many supporters and sympathisers,[15] irrespective of the fact that he faced corruption charges. This says something deep about the relationship between citizens in a post-colonial dispensation and institutions of democracy. It is one thing to stand on the 'presumption of innocence until proven guilty', it is quite another to actively support alleged perpetrators of corruption. Furthermore, this highlights the challenge that anti-corruption institutions might be seen as too distant from the people, and are hence unable to invoke sympathy from the people as they carry out their functions – further evidence of the general ambivalence regarding anti-corruption also demonstrated by some leaders.

When questions were asked relating to former police commissioner Jacky Selebi's relationship with known drug dealer Glen Agliotti, Selebi responded that Agliotti 'is my friend, finish and klaar'.[16] Either the commissioner did not respect or fully understand what is required of him as a police commissioner, or he did not respect the legitimacy of the police services as an institution whose responsibility is also generally to fight against corruption. Selebi was finally convicted of corruption in 2010 and sentenced to 15 years in jail, after Agliotti testified against him in court.

The questions of 'friendship' and integrity of leaders also came up in the relationship between President Jacob Zuma and his then financial advisor Shabir Shaik. Shaik was convicted of two counts of corruption and one count of fraud. Shaik has also made payments to Jacob Zuma, which implicates Zuma in corruption. The prosecution authority has since decided not to prosecute Zuma; a decision that is still under review. Zuma has maintained throughout the matter that the two were friends and the payments were 'loans' merely meant to assist Zuma, and not intended to solicit favours.

The ongoing maladministration within state owned entities such as South African Airways is in indication of the growing networks of corruption and patronage in the public sector. Corruption has plagued many state owned entities, such as the electricity supplier Eskom, the port agency Transnet, PRASA, and the SABC, for example. These agencies are experiencing leadership turbulences and financial mismanagement as they remain the weakest link when it comes to policy implementation in the country, particularly given that they largely remain host to 'networks of patronage'.[17]

While there are efforts to fight corruption in South Africa, the anti-corruption narratives within society still allow for corrupt elements to find refuge among communities. This is because the anti-corruption drive is still distant from ordinary communities; it is still seen as

---

15 Tlhabye G (2015, 1 June) EFF group hold night vigil for Malema. *Independent Online*. Available at http://www.iol.co.za/news/crime-courts/eff-group-holds-night-vigil-for-malema-1865757 [accessed 4 October 2016].
16 De Waal M (2010, 12 October) From hero to zero, the Jackie Selebi story. *Daily Maverick*. Available at http://www.dailymaverick.co.za/article/2010-10-12-from-hero-to-zero-the-jackie-selebi-story/#.V_OMUvl97IU [accessed 4 October 2016].
17 Donnelly L (2015, 6 November) State loses patience with parastatals. *Mail & Guardian*. Available at http://mg.co.za/article/2015-11-05-state-loses-patience-with-parastatals [accessed 4 October 2016].

an initiative driven only through government bureaucracy – a technocratic initiative with no bearing on real life. Anecdotal evidence shows that South Africans despise corruption, as they often take a public stance against corruption, including during service delivery protests in local government. However, it still remains unclear as to whether the general public in South Africa has generated a strong anti-corruption narrative which ought to be demonstrated in the manner in which they assess leaders through voting. There is no evidence yet indicating that an average voter in South Africa uses integrity as a criterion for electing leaders, in both local and national elections.

Among some of the issues troubling the ANC in post-apartheid South Africa is the dispensing of patronage through the party's deployment policy. The ANC's framework of fielding officials in key government positions has raised concerns regarding the poor quality of skill sets and integrity among some of those deployed. Because the decisions regarding deployment of senior officials is made within the party, following their own internal processes, criticisms have emerged that individuals are selected on the basis of their political connections and support within the party instead of skills and qualifications. This has been identified as a major factor that affects both the integrity and effectiveness of the public service. The problem is starker at local government level, where corruption seems to be thriving. It has been argued that 'during the transitional period in the early 1990s, the ANC found itself with the realities of insufficient number of properly trained cadres to fill the administrative posts'.[18] The ANC relied on the skills provided by former public servants who served under apartheid 'homelands'. This resulted in former administrators extending their networks of patronage to the local communities, some of which remain entrenched.

Local government structure in South Africa is experiencing systemic instabilities due to poor performance. Besides the lack of skills, corruption undermines the ability of municipalities to deliver services to communities. Politicisation of municipalities, coupled with increased proliferation of patronage, poses a serious challenge to municipalities. Despite the existence of laws such as the Municipal Finance Management Act (MFMA), municipalities continue to experience maladministration and financial impropriety.

Country context: dual approach towards anti-corruption

South Africa has a highly decentralised anti-corruption framework. This has implications for both the evolution of the anti-corruption institutions and the way in which the effectiveness of these institutions can be assessed. The legal provision for the institutional makeup of anti-corruption institutions in South Africa poses a challenge for assessing their effectiveness. In a sense, there is no single institution that is solely responsible for fighting against corruption; the responsibility is with a network of institutions designed to function in a way that they each contribute towards anti-corruption as an outcome. This will be

---

18 Ndletyana M, Makhalemele PO & Mathekga R (2013) *Patronage Politics Divides Us: S study of poverty, patronage and inequality in South Africa.* Johannesburg: Real African Publishers, p. 36.

thoroughly explained since this should serve as a basis for understanding and assessing anti-corruption initiatives in the country.

South Africa's constitution does not directly or explicitly provide for the set-up of anti-corruption laws or institutions. The constitution does, however, provide that South Africa is bound by international agreements, once such agreements have been approved by resolution in both the national assembly and the national council of provinces (NCOP).[19] Therefore, the obligation for South Africa to establish effective anti-corruption institutions and laws at national level derives directly from the country's assenting to the international conventions against corruption, and not directly from the constitution. Among the international conventions that provide for anti-corruption bodies is the United Nations Convention Against Corruption (UNCAC), which South Africa ratified in 22 November 2004.[20] South Africa is also a signatory to the Southern African Development Community (SADC) Protocol against Corruption, ratified in 2003.

By assenting to these conventions, South Africa then became obligated to establish specific instruments and also pass specific laws aimed at addressing corruption, as prescribed by those conventions. The obligation to establish a specific set of institutions prescribed by the conventions automatically became constitutional obligations in the sense that the constitution prescribes compliance with international agreements entered into by the republic. The constitution does not, however, directly or explicitly prescribe adoption of national legislations or formations of institutions specifically tasked to fight against corruption. This was clarified in the constitutional court case of *Glenister vs. the President of the Republic of South Africa*,[21] where it was delivered that the constitution does not prescribe the form of an anti-corruption institution, neither does the constitution prescribe where such an institution or institutions should be located within the state bureaucracy.

Before South Africa ratified international conventions against corruption (in 2003 and 2004 respectively), the country already had anti-corruption institutions in place. However, those institutions were not specifically mandated to fight against corruption; they were generalised crime fighting and accountability institutions. Therefore, there are two channels through which corruption can be effectively fought against in South Africa: by utilising generalised institutions whose effective function would also expose and combat corruption-related activities; and/or, by utilising specialised anti-corruption institutions adopted pursuant to prescriptions by international agreements against corruption.

It is therefore important to consider the question of how this schema would affect the functioning of the fight against corruption. Two important points can be made here. Firstly, it is necessary to consider whether a specialised anti-corruption initiative with focused institutions and laws would improve the fight against corruption in the country. For the purpose of analysis in this paper, this would be termed 'a centralised approach' to

---

19 Constitution of Republic of South Africa, Act 106 of 1996, section 231.
20 United Nations Convention Against Corruption. Signature and Ratification Status as of 21 September 2016. Available at https://www.unodc.org/unodc/en/treaties/CAC/signatories.html [accessed 4 October 2016].
21 *Glenister vs. President of the Republic of South Africa and Others* (CCT 48/10) (CC March 17, 2011).

fighting against corruption. The second point relates to assessing a decentralised approach towards anti-corruption, where anti-corruption institutions are not solely concerned with corruption, but on general acts of illegality, dishonesty, fraud, etc.

In assessing the effectiveness of anti-corruption institutions in South Africa, this paper argues that South Africa has both centralised and decentralised approaches towards fighting against corruption. A decentralised approach is seen in the functioning of institutions such as: the courts in their normal deliberations in rolling out justice; the office of the public protector; the DPCI, otherwise referred to as the Hawks; and the Special Investigating Unit (SIU).

These institutions have been in place before South Africa ratified international anti-corruption agreements (the UNCAC, and SADC Protocol against Corruption). It is interesting, therefore, to identify the institutional regime and laws that were adopted following ratification of international agreements. Even more interesting, is how assenting to the anti-corruption conventions has influenced the functioning of generalised institutions of accountability and the criminal justice system in a way that effectively constitutes a fight against corruption, without necessarily adopting a single anti-corruption 'bureau'.

The exercise of distinguishing pre-ratification anti-corruption experience from the post-ratification experience in South Africa is an important basis for understanding the anti-corruption architecture in the country. This also helps to address the question as to which approach works better for South Africa, where the general institutional framework is still evolving and experience is growing, regarding the actual application of anti-corruption instruments.

The manner of operation of pre-ratification institutions did not necessarily remain entirely the same after post-ratification, focused legal instruments and specified institutions came into the picture. As we will see in the case of South Africa, there are 'turf wars' between the pre-ratification institutions and post-ratification instruments (including the legal system). In this regard, the side-by-side existence of multiple anti-corruption institutions creates a complex chain of accountability, obfuscating the issues at hand as attention is devoted to which institutions have more authority in pronouncing on corrupt conduct.

Perhaps the Nkandla issue, involving expenditure of public funds at President Jacob Zuma's private home, is a case in point. The Nkandla case shows how multiple probes by different institutions have resulted in contradictory findings on the same issue. It has been argued that the institutions seem to be 'working against each other'.[22]

Before outlining South Africa's anti-corruption legal framework, it is necessary to illustrate the two approaches to corruption that have thus far been expressed in the country. This is also to outline the source of authority for institutions whose function contribute towards the fight against corruption.

---

22 Interview with AT Madonsela, Public Protector. Pretoria, 3 December 2015.

Figure 1. Institutional architecture of anti-corruption initiatives

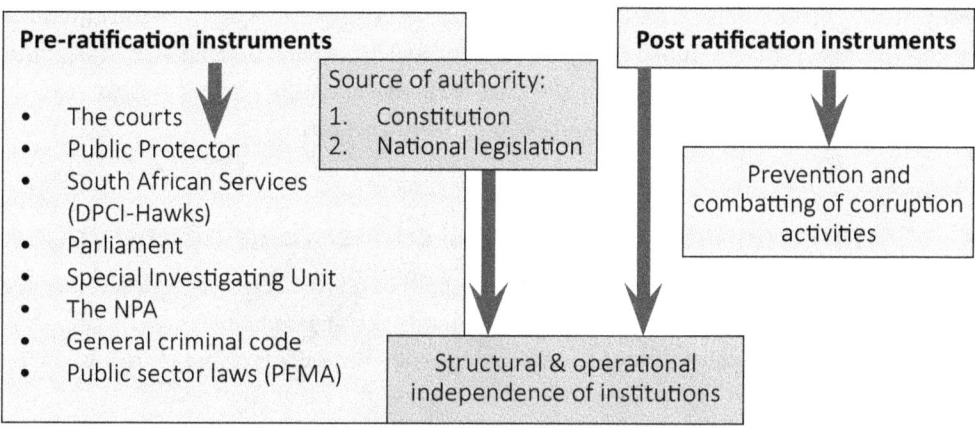

The above schema illustrates that South Africa has both a centralised approach towards the fights against corruption and decentralised anti-corruption machinery which derives from the democratic framework – both give rise to different kinds of obligations to fight corruption.

The locally derived institutional framework relies on its own internal checks and balances and may as such be unduly influenced by local political dynamics upon which its effectiveness relies. When that happens, as will be demonstrated in the chapter, the international instruments are then invoked as a way of assessing the efficacy and integrity of the local anti-corruption institutional framework.

The international conventions against corruption are expressed locally in two different ways. Firstly by directly dealing with corruption-related activities; for example, in court cases where the instruments' own regulations are invoked and South Africa, as a signatory, is obligated to follow. The constitution provides that international conventions entered into apply directly.[23] The international conventions against corruption also apply indirectly through influencing local anti-corruption laws, and the structural and operational autonomy of local anti-corruption instruments. For example, some of the bodies whose other functions are understood as aimed at combatting corruption attain their independence and operational autonomy by way of invoking international conventions against corruption. International conventions demand some degree of independence which is enjoyed by anti-corruption bodies (including those that investigate priority crimes).

Suffice it to add the third element through which anti-corruption initiative may work in South Africa, however – through constitutional provisions for integrity, accountability and carrying out public affairs within the state in a dignified and open manner. South Africa's constitution provides for a generalised anti-corruption framework which is intrinsic to the

---

23 Constitution of Republic of South Africa, Act 109, 1996, chapter 14.

institutional framework in the country. The principle of separation of powers is also laden with anti-corruption ethos or 'checks and balances'. The establishment of parliament as a forum for accountability also serves this purpose. Further, the creation of constitutional institutions, such as the public protector, also provides a safeguard and remedy against corruption. However, it is important to note that those institutions are not specifically devised to focus on corruption; it is only one of their functions.

C. Commitment to international conventions on corruption

In order to ensure global uniformity when it comes to combatting corruption, there are international instruments that stipulate that signatory countries implement certain tools in fighting against corruption. The international instruments are important for the following notable functions:

- To ensure a uniform approach towards anti-corruption;
- To ensure that the anti-corruption instruments constantly adapt to the changing forms of corruption; and
- To ensure that the local anti-corruption measures are not subverted by local political dynamics.

It is instructive to see how international anti-corruption instruments have shaped local anti-corruption initiatives in South Africa. The aim of this exercise is to explore if there is synergy between generalised anti-corruption measures as embedded in the justice and accountability system on one hand, and the centralised institutional framework as deriving from the international anti-corruption instruments on the other. This chapter will ultimately map out the interface between the two approaches in the case of South Africa. Lack of clarity as to which institution is responsible for dealing with particular instances of corruption may result in duplications that produce varying and conflicting results, therefore undermining the effectiveness of anti-corruption efforts in the country.[24]

Parallel to the generalised accountability framework runs a centralised anti-corruption regime in South Africa. This regime is directly provided for by the international anti-corruption instruments to which South Africa is a signatory. It is important to identify the specific manner in which this anti-corruption approach shapes local institutions. It is also worth noting that the institutions based on global anti-corruption conventions at times clash with the functioning of the locally derived, generalised accountability framework.

As previously stated, South Africa is a signatory to the UNCAC and the SADC Protocol against Corruption. It is pursuant to these instruments that South Africa passed different pieces of legislation, notably the Prevention and Combatting of Corrupt Activities Act 2004 (PACCA). The law focuses specifically on corruption-related activities by

---

24 Pereira PG, Lehmann S, Roth A & Attisso K (2012). *South Africa Anti-Corruption Architecture.* Switzerland: Basel Institute on Governance.

criminalising specific conducts both in the public and private sector.[25] The PACCA is an addition to existing laws that generally address some corruption-related activities. The distinct character of the PACCA, however, is that it focuses specifically on conducts related to corruption as opposed to the generalised criminal code that may incidentally address some of corruption-related activities.

Some corruption-related activities were prosecuted before the enactment of PACCA in 2004. For example, former ANC member of parliament, Tony Yengeni, was convicted of fraud in 2003 for receiving a 50% discount on a luxury vehicle.[26] Yengeni was convicted because he failed to register the benefit in parliament. While his conduct insinuates his involvement in corrupt activities, Yengeni was not convicted of corruption. This incident shows that even before a specified anti-corruption law (PACCA) was enacted, the generalised accountability mechanism (including the code of ethics for parliamentarians) also functioned in a way that also deals with acts of misconduct and dishonesty, i.e., corruption. However, the enactment of the act signalled something quite interesting and different in terms of South Africa's approach to anti-corruption, and it is important to outline the background to how the law came into being. This will also elucidate how the act relates to the entire anti-corruption institutional architecture in South Africa.

The enactment of the PACCA heralded the creation of a focused and specialised anti-corruption institution within the public service in South Africa. This also resulted in the formation of multi-stakeholder forums focused specifically on anti-corruption. The department of public service and administration (DPSA), responsible for developing a regulatory framework for the public service, was to be at the forefront of the creation and coordination of the anti-corruption institutional architecture in the public service. As a result, government ministers responsible for the national anti-crime-prevention strategy were tasked to work on an anti-corruption strategy in 1997.[27] That was followed by an anti-corruption conference held in November 1998; this focused on issues such as the definition of corruption, the necessary anti-corruption architecture and also 'restoring ethos in the public service'.[28] This step would begin to shape the national anti-corruption strategy which was to focus on coordination of anti-corruption measures in South Africa. This process is distinct in the sense that it was specifically aimed at isolating corruption vis-a-vis the common conducts of malfeasance or misconduct. Therefore, specialised anti-corruption machinery was evolving in line with the international conventions on anti-corruption instruments as ratified by the country. At times, however, the anti-corruption

---

25 Loxton D (n.d.) *South African Chapter of Global Legal Insights Bribery and Corruption*. Available at http://www.werksmans.com/wp-content/uploads/2013/07/South-African-Chapter-of-Global-Legal-Insights-Bribery-and-Corruption-First-Edition.pdf [accessed 4 October 2016].
26 Quintal A (2003, 20 February) Parliament to move against 'crook' Yengeni. *Mail & Guardian*. Available at http://mg.co.za/article/2003-02-20-parliament-to-move-against-crook-yengeni [accessed 4 October 2016].
27 Sangweni SS (2005, 29 July) Overview of Anti-Corruption Programmes and Strategies in South Africa. Address at the Free State Provincial Anti-Corruption Summit, Bloemfontein, 29 July 2005.
28 Ibid.

tools that evolved pursuant to ratification instruments seem not to enjoy local support from political leaders, though CSOs do support this anti-corruption stream.

D. Civil society, donor and media engagement

The creation of a specialised anti-corruption bureaucracy in South Africa was also aimed at demonstrating a stakeholder-relations approach towards anti-corruption. Unlike the generalised anti-corruption approaches of the criminal justice system, the judiciary and the broader accountability framework, the specialised approach included members of CSOs, government leaders, labour unions, the business sector, the public service and also the broader empathisers. Opting for this approach, the 'national consensus' on corruption resulted in the first national anti-corruption summit held in 1999. Key to this approach is the coordination of a set of activities and initiatives that would specifically focus on anti-corruption in the country. The challenge with this centralised multi-stakeholder approach towards anti-corruption is that the burden of coordination is akin to the 'tower of babel'.

Much time and effort is dedicated towards coordination and deciding on who is responsible for which activities. Further intensifying institutional commitment towards anti-corruption, the National Anti-Corruption Forum (NACF) was created in June 2001 'as the formal mechanism to bring the public, business and civil society sectors together to fight corruption in all aspects of our society'.[29] The NACF held the second anti-corruption summit in March 2005. South Africa's centrally coordinated approach towards anti-corruption culminated in the formation of the Anti-Corruption Task Team (ACTT) in 2011.[30] The task team was responsible for the coordination of anti-corruption activities across different government structures, as well as the related challenges.

> **Box 1: Anti-corruption institutions**
>
> The national task team is not working. Stakeholders are too far apart. The first there years of its existence, the task team spent it on setting up infrastructure. The task team also duplicated some of the institutional infrastructure that was in place. When the time for reporting its activities came, it became clear that the task team was not functioning adequately at all.
>
> Source: Commercial Crimes Unit, N. (2015, August 25) Anti-corruption institutions. R Mathekga, interviewer.

Government has also been accused of being half-hearted when it comes to supporting the ACTT. Besides the fact that the task team is seen as an advisory body that lack powers of origination, the task team is made up of government agencies: the DPCI, the South African Revenue Services (SARS); the SIU; the National Prosecuting Authority (NPA);

---

29 Ibid.
30 Pereira PG, Lehmann S, Roth A & Attisso K (2012). *South Africa Anti-Corruption Architecture.* Switzerland: Basel Institute on Governance.

and the Assets Forfeiture Unit (AFU).[31] The effectiveness of the body as an anti-corruption initiative has been seen as dependent on the good will of government. The ACTT is largely dominated by cabinet ministers (the executive branch of government).

According to the civil society organisation Corruption Watch, some members of civil society (such as a lawyers from the Watch) 'sit on one of the committees of the anti-corruption task team and [add] a voice to the forum'.[32] There is also a process underway aimed at setting up a civil society forum to involve non-government organisations (NGOs) in the task team. The anti-corruption task team 'is not meant to be a representative forum, it's meant to be a forum for government agencies to strategise on cases involving corruption'.[33] It is also understood that there is international pressure on South Africa to be seen as taking a strong stance against corruption, according to Corruption Watch.

Opposition party leader and Western Cape premier Helen Zille claimed in January 2015 that 'government has dismantled the anti-corruption task team',[34] a step which, according to Zille, is a clear demonstration of a lack of commitment towards fighting against corruption. In response to this, the presidency stated that her assertion was 'incorrect and baseless'.[35] This shows mistrust between government and the opposition parties, and also CSOs regarding the configuration of the ACTT in particular and the centrally coordinated anti-corruption framework in general.

For the purpose of this report, however, it is important to note that anti-corruption institutions established pursuant to international conventions often function in way that ensures just compliance with international order. Thus, such bodies do not reflect a genuine commitment towards anti-corruption. They also suffer an inherent coordination fatigue which has detrimental impacts on their effectiveness.

The key concern with a centrally coordinated anti-corruption framework in South Africa is that it is located within the executive branch of government and hence becomes overly subject to the whims of the executive. If the executive branch of government is weakened at a point in time, so will the efforts towards anti-corruption. The performance of this institutional infrastructure in South Africa is quite dissatisfactory. The conviction rate by the task team speaks volumes regarding the effectiveness of the initiative. In the progress report in 2013, the task team reported that '42 convictions were recorded'[36] since its formation. This reporting is specifically said to be a 'dishonest exercise' because some of the cases attributed to the ACTT were actually finalised outside and before its establishment. One of the cases which the 'progress report' attributes to the task team (*the State vs. Mokoena*) was in court before the task team was established. 'The case was not

---

31 Pereira PG, Lehmann S, Roth A & Attisso K (2012). *South Africa Anti-Corruption Architecture*. Switzerland: Basel Institute on Governance.
32 Interview with L. Johannes on the effectiveness of the anti-corruption Task Team, August 2015.
33 Ibid.
34 Anti-Corruption Team dismantled – Zille (2015, 26 January). *News24* online. Available at http://www.news24.com/SouthAfrica/News/Anti-corruption-team-dismantled-Zille-20150126 [accessed 15 July 2015].
35 Anti-Corruption Task Team in tact. Pretoria (2015, 27 January). *SA News*.
36 Commercial Crimes Unit, N. (2015, August 25) Anti-corruption institutions. R Mathekga, interviewer.

supposed to be counted in 2013 task team progress report'.[37] In 2014, the ACTT has only recorded a 23% conviction rate.

Poor coordination and poor communication among government agencies represented in the task team also has a detrimental effect on the effectiveness of the forum.

> **Box 2: The Specialised Commercial Crime Unit**
>
> Rapid shifts in strategies among members of the task team is a source of problems. For example, the South African Police Service (SAPS) suddenly created what they refer to as 'projects' on cases of corruption. Before this, the SAPS used to work together with the specialised crime unit in the NPA. According to this 'project' approach, what are seen as ordinary corruption cases are now to be referred to detectives at various police stations. This results in situations where detectives are preoccupied with common criminal cases instead of focusing on high level corruption cases.
>
> The shift in strategy by the SAPS has also disturbed the good relationship between the SAPS and the specialised crime unit within the NPA. Before this shift, the SAPS used to engage in guided investigations together with the unit. This worked because corruption cases are complex and they require intense cooperation between the SAPS and the NPA. The entire task team is marred be 'turf wars' between different agencies. The high turnover of leadership across the agencies also poses a risk when it comes to effectiveness of the task team.
>
> Source: Commercial Crimes Unit, N. (2015, August 25) Anti-corruption institutions. R Mathekga, interviewer.

As at the time of publication, the South African Police Service (SAPS) is without a fulltime commissioner. Police Commissioner Riah Phiyega has been suspended pending a commission of enquiry into her fitness to hold office.[38] The NPA has been embroiled in controversies surrounding its leadership. President Jacob Zuma's appointment of Menzi Simelane as a the director of public prosecution was set aside by the constitutional court in 2012 when it was ruled that Simelane was not fit to hold that office.[39] The court ruled that Zuma's decision was found to be irrational because Simelane was deemed not to be a person of sufficient integrity to lead the institution.

This left the NPA without a permanent head until President Zuma appointed Mxolisi Nxasana to the head of the prosecution body in August 2013. Nxasana's tenure was soon surrounded by allegations that he failed security clearance because he did not disclose that he had in the past faced criminal charges related to murder.[40] President Zuma subsequently requested a commission of enquiry into the matter of Nxasana's fitness to hold office. Just before the commission initiated its work, Nxasana resigned. The president then appointed Shaun Abrahams to lead the prosecution authority.

---

37 Ibid.
38 Hunter Q (2015, 14 October) Zuma suspends police commissioner Riah Phiyega. *Mail & Guardian*. Available at http://mg.co.za/article/2015-10-14-zuma-suspends-police-commissioner-riah-phiyega [accessed 19 November 2016].
39 *Democratic Alliance vs. President of the Republic of South Africa* (CCT 122/11) (CC 5 October 2012).
40 Evans J (2015, 11 May) Zuma shuts down inquiry into NPA boss Mxolisi Nxasana. *Mail & Guardian*. Available at http://mg.co.za/article/2015-05-11-are-mxolisi-nxasanas-skeletons-ready-for-inspection [accessed 19 November 2016].

Another institution key to the task team is SARS. In a similar manner to the NPA and the SAPS, SARS has also had a fair share of leadership instability and credibility challenges. SARS has been at the centre of controversy, leading to the resignation of Commissioner Magashula. Magashula resigned in 2013 following a probe into 'allegations of impropriety against him'.[41] Some of the allegations at the centre of the probe include improper hiring of a female staffer and also allegations of an improper relationship with a convicted drug dealer. President Jacob Zuma subsequently appointed Thomas Moyane as SARS commissioner in September 2014. Moyane's tenure did not immediately restore the credibility of the once respected government agency. SARS continues to be embroiled in controversies following revelations that the agency formed a rogue spy unit which carried out clandestine spying activities on some politicians in the country in contravention of the law.[42]

The controversies surrounding the key agencies that are supposed to drive the ACTT demonstrate two important things. Firstly, that a centralised approach towards anti-corruption runs into difficulties particularly when it is configured in ways that overly subjects it to the control and whims of the executive. Secondly, that the creation of centralised or specialised anti-corruption forums pursuant to the international conventions against corruption may effectively bring about malicious compliance; thus erecting institutions while undermining their leadership and rendering them ineffective. A close observation of the ACTT shows this trend.

The challenges relating to the effectiveness of a centralised anti-corruption instrument are not unique to South Africa, though. Heilbrunn observes:

> Anti-corruption commissions are especially problematic when political leaders are only responding to demands from international donors. In such countries, policymakers can ignore domestic demands for reform and enact minimal reforms to satisfy external agents. This minimum may be nothing more than the establishment of an anti-corruption commission, an office of the ombudsman, or an anti-fraud unit without enabling legislation, competent staff, or a budget.[43]

This shows that if the anti-corruption institutions are not anchored by local demands, they are bound to be merely perfunctory and ineffective. Heilbrunn argues further, and cynically, that:

> An anti-corruption commission is a manifestation of a policymaker's desire to renege on any stated commitment to reform. It is all too often nothing more than a token effort without the difficult reforms.[44]

---

41 SARS boss Oupa Magashula resigns after probe (2013, 12 July) *Business Day*.
42 Sole S (2015, 15 May) Rogue' SARS unit spied for Zuma. *Mail & Guardian*. Availale at http://mg.co.za/article/2015-05-14-rogue-sars-unit-spied-for-zuma [accessed 19 November 2016].
43 Heilbrunn J (2004) *Anti-Corruption Commissions: Panacea or real medicine to fight corruption*. Washington DC: International Bank for Reconstruction and Development/The World Bank. p.1.
44 Ibid.: 2.

An important instrument that is utilised to keep such anti-corruption commissions subverted is that they are not independent from the executive. The ACTT fits this explanation perfectly. While South Africa is not a donor-dependent country, the country's legitimacy as one of the recently founded democracies depends on its demonstration that the country believes in international instruments.

Because of the drive to ensure that the new democratic state is not an international pariah, South Africa formally subscribes to most of the international peace and good governance instruments, including the anti-corruption ones. Implementation of the commitments identified in those institutions remains weak. To put it bluntly: at times, the executive makes efforts to undermine such conventions as they are seen as irritations.

Like any other system that is centralised, a centralised anti-corruption system would obviously suffer a single point failure. The main threat to the effectiveness of a centralised anti-corruption system is that it relies on the will of the executive, at least as configured in South Africa. Recent experience with the task team in South Africa indicates that the executive has not provided the stable leadership required for the effectiveness of bodies such as the ACTT. If the executive is not fully committed to anti-corruption, or views it with ambivalence, that might constitute a single point failure for the entire anti-corruption framework.

The question that needs to be raised is whether South Africa is experiencing a single point failure when it comes to anti-corruption initiatives. The answer is no. This is because the country's decentralised anti-corruption institutional machinery can be relied upon. It is therefore necessary to outline the legal framework that constitutes the decentralised anti-corruption machinery.

E. Legal framework

Public Finance Management Act (1, of 1999)

The Public Finance Management Act (PFMA) was enacted with the aim to regulate the use of public finance in South Africa. The law is provided for in the constitution to enable and ensure 'transparency and expenditure control in each sphere of government'.[45] The PFMA provides for standards and norms that need to be observed when it comes to the use of public resources. The law also provides a regulatory framework for procurement of goods and services in the public sector. Together with the constitution, the PFMA allows for the national treasury to instate an additional regulatory framework that might be necessary to ensure efficient and transparent management of public resources. While the PFMA is located within the public service, the law provides for a regulatory framework that also needs to be followed by the private sector when engaging with the public service.

---

45 Constitution of the Republic of South Africa, Act 109.

Promotion of Access to Information Act (2, of 2000)

The Promotion of Access to Information Act (PAIA) has been hailed as an important tool when it comes to ensuring transparency and accountability in South Africa. The law applies to access to 'records held by official or independent contractors of public or private bodies'. The legislation provides for requests for information that would otherwise not be publicly accessible. It is, however, important to note that the effectiveness of the law also depends on willingness within the public service to comply timeously.

In a recent attempt to advance regulation of private funding of political parties, CSOs argued in the constitutional court that parliament has failed to pass legislation that allows for access to information regarding private donations to political parties. Opposing the initiative by the CSOs, parliament argued that PAIA has been passed to provide access to such information. The CSOs argued that PAIA was not sufficient in this regard. The court ruled that they should then rather challenge the constitutionality of PAIA.[46] PAIA might be useful when it comes to accessing records held by public and private institutions under certain circumstances; it is also clear that the reach and effectiveness of PAIA would be extended as it is being implemented. There is a possibility to assess the law in terms of the extent to which it contributes towards access to information about private funding of political parties.

Prevention and Combatting of Corrupt Activities Act (12, of 2004)

Prevention and Combatting of Corrupt Activities Act (PCCA) is South Africa's first post-apartheid corruption focused legislation. The preamble of the PCCA draws on the values stated in the constitution: 'human dignity, equality and freedom'. The preamble also invokes South Africa's commitment to anti-corruption conventions (such as SADC Protocol Against Corruption and the UNCAC); the act would therefore complement other existing legislations that are in place to deal to crime and acts of dishonesty.

The PCCA has been used in the conviction of former police commissioner Jacky Selebi in 2010, and continues to be used in complex commercial crimes cases in the country. It directly applies to the public and private sectors.

Municipal Finance Management Act (56, of 2003)

The Municipal Finance Management Act (MFMA) applies to financial regulations within municipalities, and to national and provincial organs of states in their dealings with the finances of the municipalities. The powers exercised by municipalities under this act are delegated from the national treasury, as provided for in the constitution. The MFMA also stipulates the planning and budgeting process that need to be followed. Section 11 of the act provides for supply chain management, stipulating that each municipality must have and implement an SCM policy in line with act. In most cases, however, municipalities fail

---

46 Sources of party funding to remain private—court rules (2015, 30 September) *Mail & Guardian*. Available at http://mg.co.za/article/2015-09-30-sources-of-party-funding-to-remain-private [accessed 19 November 2016].

to adhere to this provision. If complied with, the MFMA sets out an extensive and perhaps exhaustive framework for the management of public finance within municipalities.

The above sets of legislation are among some of the laws whose implementation effectively constitutes the generalised anti-corruption machinery in South Africa. In addition to these laws, there are others that also deal with acts of dishonesty and theft. It is important to observe how a complex interface of various laws and institutions of accountability constitute a decentralised anti-corruption architecture in SA.

Historical development of institutional framework

South Africa has a complex anti-corruption machinery, including institutions such as the judiciary and the public protector. The evolution of these institutions is due to the notion of separation of powers and the general mechanism of constitutional democracy. However, these institutions would not be effective in their attempts to address corruption had South Africa not acceded to international and regional anti-corruption instruments. For the purpose of this study, there are two identifiable anti-corruption mechanisms running parallel to each other, at times in support of each other and at times running into conflict with each other.

The first is a centralised approach towards anti-corruption, as explained in the above section. The other mechanism includes the accountability process spread across different institutions such as the public protector, the judiciary, the auditor general and parliament. These institutions separately function in a way that contributes towards anti-corruption as an outcome. It is important to explain how these institutions operate independently, albeit towards a common goal of a transparent accountable governance model.

The principle of constitutional democracy, in the context of South Africa, envisages the institutional framework whose proper functioning would eliminate corruption. This avenue for fighting against corruption needs to be outlined in the context of South Africa because it represents another institutional approach to anti-corruption. It is also necessary to outline how this institutional framework has thus far functioned in the case of South Africa.

The Constitution of South Africa does not explicitly provide for the separation of powers between the executive, legislature and the judiciary. The constitution does, however, provide for the institutional framework that recognises the principle of separation of powers. In outlining the function of the judiciary, the constitution states that it is the 'supreme law of the republic'. This means that all laws should be compliant with the constitution. It states also that the legislative authority is vested with a parliament.[47] Section 85 of the constitution provides that the executive authority of the republic lies with the president, who is the head of the executive.

The relationship between the three branches of government is rather delineated in the constitutional provision for the role and authority of the courts. It states that 'the judicial

---

47 Constitution of the Republic of South Africa, section 43.

authority of the republic is vested in the courts', which 'are independent and subject only to the constitution and the law'.[48] This is where the principle of separation of powers is nearly explicitly expressed. It is, however, explicitly stated that 'no person or organ of state may interfere with the functioning of the courts'.[49] This provision provides for judicial review – one of the cornerstone of accountability in a constitutional democracy. Judicial review is a system whereby the courts have powers to review decisions or complaints relating to decisions made by government or individuals.

Under constitutional democracy:

> The courts ... are charged with determining the allocation of constitutional authority and resolving conflicts that might be brought before the courts as different institutions struggle to ensure that there is legal accountability for government failures as well as individual malfeasance.[50]

The institutional design envisioned in the constitution provides 'checks and balances' and it is the first line of accountability and strengthening of democracy. In line with this principle, it provides for specific types of institutions and enactments under which practices such as corruption would be fought against.

From this point of view, the constitution sees accountability as integral to strengthening democracy. More specific institutional design is subsequently provided for in the form of institutions mandated to 'strengthen constitutional democracy in the republic'.[51] Among the institutions provided for in this section are the offices of the public protector and the auditor general. It further provides that these institutions should function in a way that they are 'independent and subject only to the constitution and the law'.

In an ideal world, the principle of constitutional supremacy, together with a separation of powers and the formation of constitutional institutions, would suffice as a framework for fighting against corruption. If the courts have authority to pronounce on the administration of the law, then there seems to be no loophole for interference regarding the functioning of this framework in combatting corruption. Due to the complexity of malfeasance and the complex nature of democracy, there are other institutions that need to be in place in order for this ideal chain of accountability to function toward the goal of a society with integrity. Those are institutions whose formations are provided for explicitly in the constitution (e.g. the public protector) and their authority is clearly stipulated.

Therefore, the constitution provides for the formation of the NPA, a single prosecuting authority which has the powers to institute criminal charges on behalf of the state.[52] It also provides that national legislation should be passed to ensure that the prosecuting

---

48 Section 165.
49 Section 165(3).
50 Klug H (undated draft) Separation of powers, accountability and the role of independent constitutional institutions.
51 Constitution of the Republic of South Africa, section 181.
52 Section 179.

authority 'exercises its functions without fear, favour or prejudice'.[53] This critical provision enjoins the adoption of legislation that would ensure the prosecution is independent. If the legislation, or any section of the legislation, that establishes the prosecution authority does not allow for independent functioning of the entity, that would be unconstitutional. While prosecutorial independence does not necessarily denote accountability,[54] it is the basis for the foundation of accountability when it comes to decisions on whether to prosecute certain cases or not.

It is worth noting at this point that the prosecution authority in South Africa is located within the executive.[55] However, the functioning of the prosecution is reviewable outside the executive, through the courts. This has had implications on the fight against corruption in the country. As these lines are written, there is a review process underway in the courts regarding whether the decision by the prosecution authority to drop corruption charges against Jacob Zuma was reasonable and defensible.[56] The NPA decided back in April 2009 not to proceed with charges of corruption against Zuma because of 'political interference' with the prosecution process. The court has yet to decide on the matter.

Another institution of significance is the police services, whose formation is provided for under section 205 of the constitution. The political accountability of the police services is under the minister of police, a member of the executive. The minister is ultimately accountable to parliament. The minister's decision to hire and dismiss senior managers within the police, including the accounting officer, is subject to oversight by parliament.

Other national institutions contributing toward the broader anti-corruption initiative include:
- The Office of the Public Protector;
- The Directorate for Priority Crime Investigation (DPCI);
- The Assets Forfeiture Unit;
- The Auditor General;
- The Independent Police Investigative Directorate; and
- The Financial Intelligence Centre.

All these institutions either account to parliament or to the executive. Some of the institutions simultaneously account to the executive and also to parliament. The national treasury's 2015 public sector SCM report refers to the above institutions' responsibility

---

53 Section 179(4).
54 Schönteich M (2014, April) *Strengthening Prosecutorial Accountability in South Africa*. Pretoria: Institute for Security Studies.
55 De Villiers W (2011) Is the prosecuting authority under South African law politically independent? An investigation into the South African and analogous models. *Journal of Contemporary Roman-Dutch Law* 74: 248.
56 Thamm M (2015, June) Zuma corruption charges: Lead NPA prosecutor throws weight behind DA 'spy tapes' court challenge. *Daily Maverick*. Available at http://www.dailymaverick.co.za/article/2015-06-10-zuma-corruption-charges-lead-npa-prosecutor-throws-weight-behind-da-spy-tapes-court-challenge/#.WC_kx7J97IU [accessed 19 November 2016].

to 'detect and combat corruption'.[57] The core function of these institutions is not to fight against corruption. They each have own set of outputs, but repelling corruption is one of the effects of their functions. The institutions mentioned above can be referred to as constitutive of a decentralised approach towards anti-corruption.

As indicated earlier, the constitution provides for the public sector to be framed in a way that ensures integrity, accountability and efficiency. The constitution also ensures the principle of separation of powers, where the conduct of the executive is subject to oversight by parliament and also review by the judiciary, where necessary. The notion of constitutional supremacy, according to which 'law or conduct inconsistent with it is invalid, and the obligations imposed by it must be fulfilled',[58] is the most prolific safeguard to ensure that organs of state, government departments and other public institutions operate in a way that ensures integrity and efficiency.

The line of accountability generally provided for in the constitution ensures that corruption does not proliferate; or where it takes place, that there is institutional recourse. Given the understanding that corruption is predominantly embedded in other common acts of malfeasance that are prohibited by the law, it is arguable that the first and foremost anti-corruption initiative is the general body of institutions aimed at dealing with illegal conducts, coupled with those aimed at ensuring general accountability. This refers to a 'system of justice and accountability'.[59] Where a system of justice and accountability exists and functions appropriately, misconduct – generally referring to violation of laws, regulations, and internal policies[60] – would not thrive.

A generalised approach towards corruption is also identifiable in the legislation where the general laws promoting integrity, prohibiting malfeasance and misconducts can be found in the constitution, common law and statutes. The criminal law prohibits fraud, while company law prohibits conduct that leads to unfair or unjustifiable enrichment, for example. A conglomeration of these sets of laws effectively prohibit conduct involving corruption. That said, countries cannot rely on the generalised approach to malfeasance as the only instruments in the fight against corruption.

Each and every country would have some form of generalised institution for addressing misconduct and malfeasance. A monarchy, for example, would have its own chain of accountability, as opposed to a constitutional democracy. A constitutional democracy with a presidential system would bear a different set of accountability institutions from that of a proportional representation system. Electoral systems together with different systems of government would result in the adoption and use of different mechanisms of accountability, resulting in differentiated abilities to deal with misconduct and malfeasance. Even more

---

57 National Treasury (2015, 28 January) Public Sector Supply Chain Management Review. p. 21. Available at (http://www.treasury.gov.za/publications/other/SCMR%20REPORT%202015.pdf [accessed 4 October 2016].
58 Constitution of the Republic of South Africa, Act 106 of 1996, section 2.
59 Diamond L (2002) Horizontal accountability and corruption control. *Economic Reform and Good Governance: Fighting Corruption in Transition Economies*. Beijing. p.12
60 KPMG (2006) Fraud Risk Management: Developing a strategy for prevention, detection, and response. p.4. Johannesburg: KPMG.

interesting is that these systems would produce different results in different country settings, at different points in time.

Therefore, if a country's system of accountability were to be the only one relied upon in the global fight against corruption, the initiative would yield results that are too diverse, making it difficult to benchmark the anti-corruption initiative globally. There are no international instruments setting out which instruments of democracy should be adopted to ensure a better accountability system. This shows that the concept of democracy is quite broad and its application may result in varied institutional arrangements. Some countries would opt for a parliamentary sovereignty system as a viable approach to ensuring accountability, given their specific circumstances. Others may opt for a constitutional supremacy system. No system is superior to the other; they depend on a range of other factors to function optimally.

South Africa has a generalised anti-corruption approach which is rooted in the country's system of governance, as provided for in the constitution and ancillary legislations. This represents one of the approaches towards anti-corruption in the country. The other approach, which may run parallel to the generalised approach is the one provided for through the international anti-corruption instruments.

Stability and functioning of accountability institutions

Despite serious challenges regarding implementation, international instruments have been applied in line with the local laws. South Africa effectively avoids centralisation that is based on the sudden realisation that an international instrument exists. The ANC maintains that the party has historically taken a stance against corruption, often dismissing the criticism that it is has become corrupt. In response to a CSO-led march against corruption held in September 2015,[61] the government lamented the very idea of the party harbouring corruption. The ANC continued that the party has been fighting against corruption and it is rather sinister that the party has come to be been seen as synonymous with it. The same attitude has been displayed in relation to the anti-corruption approach of the international conventions where they are, at times, seen to be reproachful of local commitment to anti-corruption.

The constitution embraces the idea of an accountable public sector characterised by high levels of integrity. This requires a dispersal of responsibility across different institutions. Chapter 9 of the constitution provides for the formation of the office of the public protector, whose function is to 'strengthen constitutional democracy'.[62] This is an interesting institution, located within the broader accountability machinery in South Africa.

Office of the Public Protector

The constitution provides that the public protector has the power to 'investigate any conduct in state affairs, or in the public administration in any sphere of government, that is alleged

---

61 Tandwa L (2015, 14 September) Zuma lets a skirt think for him – anti-corruption protesters. *News24*.
62 Constitution of the Republic of South Africa, Act 108 of 1996, chapter 9.

or suspected to be improper or to result in any impropriety or prejudice'.[63] The public protector also has the power to take 'appropriate remedial action'.[64] Although not directly responsible for investigating corruption, the public protector is part of a web of institutions whose function contributes towards anti-corruption. The powers of the public protector derive from the constitution and also from the national legislation. The Public Protector Act provides for 'matters incidental to the office of the public protector as contemplated in the constitution'.[65]

The constitution therefore provides for the enactment of the national legislation which regulates and guides the office of the public protector. However, the national legislation should be in compliance with the constitution, which directly provides for the powers of the public protector. This means that if an act of parliament abrogates the powers accorded to the public protector in the constitution, such an act would therefore be deemed unconstitutional. That the powers of the public protector are provided for in the constitution effectively provides a safeguard for its independence, and implies that its powers may not be limited or encroached upon through national legislation. The constitution further states that the office of the public protector 'must be accessible to all persons and communities'.[66]

The public protector is appointed for a non-renewable period of seven years. The constitution provides that the president of the republic is responsible for appointing the public protector, who should be a 'fit and proper' person.[67] The process of appointing the public protector also involves recommendation by the national assembly. The public protector may be removed from office on the basis of misconduct, incapacity or incompetence. The national assembly does this through a two-thirds majority vote. This means that the public protector cannot be removed solely by the president. The Public Protector Act (113 of 1998) states that the public protector has to be someone who is admitted as an advocate or an attorney. The public protector is expected to possess the same level of integrity and qualification as 'a judge of the high court'.[68] The public protector is also remunerated at the same level as a high court judge.

The office of the public protector is accountable to the national assembly and reports its activities to parliament. The institution also attains its budget from parliament. In 2014 the office of the public protector operated on a R200 million budget, which, according to the public protector, was not proportional to the workload of 40 000 cases handled that year.[69] The increasing workload of the office of the public protector may account for the increasing level of confidence the public seems to have in the office. It can even be argued that the office

---

63 Section 182(a).
64 Section 182(c).
65 Public Protector Act 113 of 1998, preamble.
66 Constitution of the Republic of South Africa, Act 108 of 1996, section 182(4).
67 Constitution of the Republic of South Africa, Act 108 of 1996, Section 193(1)(b).
68 Public Protector Act 113 of 1998, section 1A.
69 Mokone T (2014, 23 October) Madonsela: No funds, no public protector. *TimesLive*. Available at http://www.timeslive.co.za/thetimes/2014/10/23/madonsela-no-funds-no-public-protector [accessed 19 November 2016].

of the public protector carries a disproportionately high load of complaints on government conduct because of the perception that the office is effective in investigating the complaints.

Since she was appointed to head the office in 2009 until the end of her tenure in October 2016, Madonsela handled high profile investigations involving high ranking politicians in the country. Among some of the notable cases was the investigation into the R1.60 billion leasing of building to the SAPS, under former police commissioner Bheki Cele. The investigation centred on procurement practices followed by the SAPS with regard to the leasing of the building.[70] The case served as a demonstration that the office of the public protector was entering a new era following the poor performance of her predecessor, Lawrence Mushwana. Madonsela found in the SAPS leasing agreement that procurement procedures were flawed and in violation of the PFMA. Cele was found guilty of maladministration and he was subsequently dismissed from his position.

In 2011, the public protector made findings into allegations of abuse of travel and accommodation privileges by the then minister of cooperative affairs and traditional affairs Sicelo Shiceka. Madonsela found that Shiceka 'had acted improperly, unlawfully and dishonestly in abusing travel privileges'.[71] President Jacob Zuma responded by dismissing Shiceka from his cabinet post.

The public protector also handled a high profile investigation into a Limpopo-based company, On-Point Engineering. The investigation revealed a complex web of tender-rigging practices within Limpopo Province's public works department. Investigations were triggered by allegations that companies related to Julius Malema, the then ANC Youth League president, were involved is massive tender-rigging activities in the province. The public protector found evidence of fraud, maladministration and enrichment at the expense of state resources in the manner in which On-Point was awarded tenders.[72] Recommendations were made that criminal investigations had to be undertaken by the Hawks on the company's operations.

Throughout the experience of the office of the public protector, the two cases that stand out the most are the ones relating to investigations into expenditure on the security upgrade by the president in his Nkandla private home, and the investigations of allegations of maladministration at the SABC. The two cases respectively provide test-cases in relation to the extent of the powers of the office of the public protector. Both cases also reveal interesting points regarding the nature or configuration of South Africa's anti-corruption institutional infrastructure.

In both cases, parliament has been used as an avenue to sidestep findings by the public protector. The process used to effectively set aside the public protector's finding is not an illegal one. It is rather a process that indicates the risks that come with decentralised anti-corruption

---

70 Marvelous Madonsela: Five cases that put the Public Protector in the spotlight (2014, 3 September) *DailyVox*. Available at http://www.thedailyvox.co.za/marvelous-madonsela-five-cases-that-put-the-public-protector-in-the-spotlight/ accessed 19 November 2016].
71 Molele C (2011, 28 October) Dismissal 'shatters' ailing Shiceka. *Mail & Guardian*. Available at http://mg.co.za/article/2011-10-28-dismissal-shatters-ailing-shiceka [accessed 19 November 2016].
72 Public Protector (2012). *On the Point of Tenders*. Office of the Public Protector.

initiatives. Where multiple agencies are involved, that may occur in a way that the institutions undermine each other instead of furthering the commitment against corruption. Again, this may unfold democratically. When this happens, corruption thrives and the broader anti-corruption drive is derided. This may also demonstrate the conflict between local political machinery and the commitment to the international instruments against corruption.

Following allegations of maladministration and corporate governance deficiencies at the SABC in 2011, the public protector carried out an investigation into the matter. The findings were presented in a report titled 'When Governance and Ethics Fail'.[73] The allegations include the irregular appointment of the then acting CEO at the SABC, Hlaudi Motsoeneng, as well as the allegation that he does not poses a matric certificate, contrary to the claim he made in his curriculum vitae. It was further alleged that Motsoeneng increased his salary package from R1.5 million per annum to R2.4 million per annum in a single year. The public protector found that the appointment of Motsoeneng as the acting CEO at the SABC, and his increase, were irregular.[74]

Regarding allegations that Motsoeneng irregularly increased staff salaries, substantially increasing the salary bill for the SABC, the public protector found that the conduct amount to maladministration. To this, the public protector recommended that the SABC suspend Motsoeneng and institute disciplinary action against him. As the constitution and the Public Protector Act provides, the public protector has the powers to undertake remedial action.

Opposition party, the DA, approached the Western Cape high court to petition for the SABC to implement the public protector's recommendations. It was clear that the SABC was reluctant to implement the remedial action and there was no indication that it intended to approach the court to review the findings by the public protector.

The DA therefore found it appropriate to approach the court and seek relief regarding implementation of the remedial action. In ruling on the matter regarding the powers of the public protector the Western Cape high court ruled that:

> The findings of the public protector are not binding and enforceable. The court stated however that when an organ of state rejects those findings or remedial action, that decision itself must not be irrational.[75]

That the powers of the public protector are not similar to a court order and yet cannot be ignored implies an avenue to deal with the finding of the public protector besides implementing those finding or having the findings reviewed by a court; the latter being an avenue recognised both in the Public Protector Act and the constitution. By stating

---

73 Public Protector (2014) *When Governance and Ethics Fail.* Pretoria: Public Protector.
74 SABC must discipline Motsoeneng-Thuli Madonsela (2015, 17 February) *Politics Web.* Available at http://www.politicsweb.co.za/documents/sabc-must-discipline-hlaudi-motsoeneng---thuli-mad [accessed 19 November 2016].
75 Madonsela's counsel in Motsoeneng case under spotlight (2015, 18 September) *eNCA.* Available at https://www.enca.com/south-africa/madonsela-recommendations-motsoeneng-case-under-spotlight [accessed 19 November 2016].

that remedial action by the public protector cannot be ignored, is to provide some form of review mechanism or engagement with the findings of the public protector besides reviewing the findings in court.

The main question therefore is whether the constitution intended to provide a 'negotiation clause' on the remedial action proposed by the public protector. If so, how does this impact upon the role of the public protector as a custodian of public resources? An interesting question is whether the framers of South Africa's constitution intended that acting upon the public protector's finding is discretionary. Despite the reasoning that the powers of the public protector are not similar to that of the court, the judge ruled in this case that the SABC should implement the proposed remedial action. Thus, the SABC should suspend Motsoeneng and undertake disciplinary action against him.

The SABC subsequently approached the supreme court of appeal (SCA) and challenged the decision that Motsoeneng has to be suspended. In considering the matter, the SCA dismissed the Western Cape court's reasoning that the powers of the public protector are not as binding as a court order.[76] The supreme court delivered that 'the public protector cannot realise the constitutional purpose of her office if other organs of state may second-guess her findings and ignore her recommendations'.[77] Regarding the high court reasoning that the power of the public protector is to make 'recommendations', the supreme court of appeal stated that this approach is 'neither fitting nor effective, [it] denudes the office of the public protector of any meaningful content'.[78]

The reasoning of the SCA adds another pillar of strength regarding the independence of the office of the public protector, preventing any second guessing of its findings. This also says that once the public protector has made findings, there shall be no other parallel process to modify them. The only avenue available is either to comply with the findings in their entirety or approach the court for a review of the findings.

The SCA's judgment on the powers of the public protector shows how the functioning of the judicial process of accountability, made up by various institutions, contribute towards anti-corruption. Larry Diamond emphasises the point that the fight against corruption requires multiple institutions instead of a single-commission approach.[79] Diamond points to three important elements of institutional design required to fight corruption:[80]

- Agencies are needed to monitor conduct and expose wrongdoing;
- A system is needed to assess charges of wrongdoing and punish wrongdoers if they are convicted; and
- A framework is necessary for constituting and insulating watchdog agencies so that they cannot be subverted by the very actors they are supposed to control.

76 *SABC vs. DA* (393/2015) (Supreme Court of Appeal 8 October 2015).
77 Ibid.
78 Paragraph 53.
79 Diamond L (2002) Horizontal accountability and corruption control. *Economic Reform and Good Governance: Fighting Corruption in Transition Economies*. Beijing. p.12
80 Ibid.: 3.

The court in the SABC case has undertaken to protect the powers of the office of the public protector by maintaining that the she does not merely make recommendations, but enforceable remedial action. The constitutional court has a final say on the powers of the public protector in a case to be heard regarding whether President Zuma has to pay back some of the money spent on his private home of Nkandla. The Nkandla report by the public protector is instructive when it comes to understanding a peculiar manner in which anti-corruption mechanisms can be subverted to local politics.

Nkandla dilemma
Following allegations of impropriety and unethical conduct in relation to security installations at the private residence of President Jacob Zuma in Nkandla, the public protector investigated and issued a report in 2014.[81] The complaint related to the R246 million that was spent on Zuma's home. At the centre of the complaint was whether some of the installations were warranted and justifiable as 'security installations', or if there been impropriety and unethical conduct involved. Questions were raised as to whether those who were responsible for spending the public funds did follow the necessary guidelines and laws outlined in the Public Finance Management Act.

The Nkandla expenditure was coordinated by the department of public works, which is responsible for providing housing for government officials. The defence department, the SAPS and the state security departments were involved in making assessments regarding the security needs of the president. The public protector had to investigate who allocated the funds spent in Nkandla and the procurement processes that were followed. The complaint received by the public protector about Nkandla was not centred on corruption, it was rather about excessive expenditure.[82] In her findings, the public protector delivered that some of the installations and construction at Nkandla were not justifiable. This refers to installations such as the swimming pool, cattle kraal and tuck shop.

It was found that the expenditure was excessive and in contravention of the law. According to the public protector, this was due to 'unconditional and unlimited authority for the procurement of goods and services'.[83] The report stated notably that:

> The excessive nature in which the Nkandla Project was implemented went a long way to beautify the president's private residence and to add comfort to its infrastructure, which was not the objective of security measures that had to be implemented for his protection.[84]

It was found that government departments involved in Nkandla installations 'failed dismally' to adhere to procurement regulations, including the PFMA. The most

---
81 Public Protector (2014) *Secure in Comfort*. Pretoria: Public Protector.
82 Interview with AT Madonsela, Public Protector. Pretoria, 3 December 2015.
83 Public Protector (2014) *Secure in Comfort*. Pretoria: Public Protector. p. 404.
84 Ibid.: 407.

interesting part of the findings relates to the responsibilities regarding paying for some of the installations. The public protector found that:

> As the president tacitly accepted the implementation of all measures at his residence and has unduly benefited from the enormous capital investment from the non-security installations at his private residence, a reasonable part of the expenditure towards the installations that were not identified as security measures in the list compiled by security experts in pursuit of the security evaluation, should be borne by him and his family.[85]

It was therefore recommended that, as part of the remedial action, the president (together with the national treasury and the SAPS) should determine the amount that the president had to pay back. The president was to then report to the national assembly on his comments and action on the report.

The findings that the president had to pay back a certain percentage of expenditure on Nkandla had a significant impact on the direction that parliament opted to follow regarding the public protector's report.

As the head of the executive, the president bears the responsibility to protect the public resources. The expenditure in Nkandla demonstrates a lapse in exercising that responsibility. Therefore, it follows that the president has to account and answer to parliament regarding expenditure in Nkandla as a further extension of accountability on the matter. A set of procedures and processes were to be undertaken on the Nkandla report, namely:

- There ought to be investigations by the police and relevant authorities regarding the flaunting of procurement processes and the motive behind excessive expenditure on the project;
- The national treasury together with the SAPS were required to determine a 'reasonable amount' that President Zuma had to pay back on non-security-related installations in Nkandla; and
- Parliament was expected to undertake a process of engaging with the public protector's report as part of its responsibility to ensure accountability in the use of public funds.

These leave no leeway for engaging in a parallel process regarding the public protector's findings. The only process that was provided for was an extension of the findings of the public protector by way of concretising some of the findings/sanction already stipulated in the report.

What was to follow after the public protector's report however was a completely new process which arguably borders on second guessing the public protector's initial findings.

---

85 Ibid.: 437.

Parliament ignored the findings of the public protector and engaged in a new process that amounts to a completely new investigation into Nkandla. Instead of limiting his scope of involvement to the determination of the amount to be paid back, police minister Nkosinathi Nhleko undertook a new enquiry into what constitutes unnecessary installations in Nkandla; an issue that was already settled by the public protector.

In the author's interview with Madonsela for a television show, Straight Talk,[86] she stated that

> The police minister has no authority to enquire as to whether or not the president has to pay a certain amount in relation to Nkandla expenditure; his mandate in relation to this is limited to determining an appropriate amount. The manner in which the Nkandla report was handled is subject to court litigation after the opposition party Economic Freedom Fighters approached the court to force President Zuma to comply with the public protector's office and pay back some of the money spent on Nkandla.[87]

Madonsela successfully asked to join the case as *amicus curiae* (friend of the court).

The Nkandla case demonstrates both the positives and the negatives regarding the shaping of South Africa's anti-corruption institutional framework. The case demonstrates how the system of justice and accountability amounts to an anti-corruption initiative. It is important to note, however, that in the majority of Madonsela's investigations and findings, her office does not utilise the corruption-targeted Prevention and Combatting of Corrupt Activities Act. The public protector largely relies on the Public Finance Management Act – the law that governs the use of public funds in South Africa. She also utilises the national treasury regulations and the procurement guidelines for the departments she investigates. This shows how South Africa has a complex web of ethics laws ranging from those affecting members of the executive to those affecting members of parliament to internal procurement guides within respective departments.

When making her findings, the public protector doesn't really refer to the grand commitment towards anti-corruption. It is mostly when the courts interpret the powers of the public protector that they make this commitment explicit. An example is when the courts provide justifications as to why the office of the public protector should be given sufficient powers to exercise checks and balances on the exercise of executive authority.

The success of the office of the public protector shows how decentralised anti-corruption instruments function. This approach works well in the public service, but falters in relation to corruption in the private sector. The private sector is not subject to a similar

---

86 Interview with AT Madonsela, Public Protector. Pretoria, 3 December 2015.
87 Public Protector to EFF's Nkandla case (2015, 6 October). eNCA. Available at https://www.enca.com/south-africa/public-protector-join-effs-nkandla-case [accessed 19 November 2016].

regulatory framework hence specialised anti-corruption legislation is necessary to deal with malfeasance in the sector.

The Nkandla issue, on the other hand, shows how democratic processes can be used to subvert anti-corruption initiatives in a way that is not illegal. The manner in which parliament dealt with the Nkandla report is a case in point. Most importantly, the Nkandla issue shows how local political dynamics can weigh against anti-corruption initiatives. The ANC-dominated parliament stated that the public protector's report on Nkandla 'misled the nation' as to what actually happened regarding the security installations at the president's private home. Opposition parties in parliament attempted unsuccessfully to 'derail the ANC's push to absolve President Jacob Zuma from repaying any of the R246 million spent on his Nkandla home'.[88]

Parliament is an appropriate channel through which accountability on Nkandla has to be carried out, as part of the broader accountability framework in the country. However, parliament has no right to second guess the findings of the public protector on Nkandla. The only way to challenge the findings by the public protector would be to bring such findings up for review through a court of law. However, in accepting the police minister's report that President Jacob Zuma does not have to pay back any money on Nkandla, parliament has effectively endorsed a report that fundamentally deviates from the public protector's findings. Therefore, parliament effectively reviewed the report of the public protector.

The contentions around the Nkandla debacle reveal one of the weaknesses of South Africa's decentralised anti-corruption machinery. The Nkandla issue shows that the desire to not embarrass the ruling party and its leaders has become a motivation for parliament to absolve the president of liability for the improper Nkandla expenditure.

Under these circumstances, much of the hope then is left to the courts as part of the broader accountability framework. The constitution provides for the separation of powers across different branches of government. Therefore, in principle, it is not favourable for the courts to pronounce on the functions of the legislature. However, the courts are responsible for ensuring that the constitution, as the supreme law of the country, is upheld.

The Nkandla saga could certainly become a matter of different branches of government encroaching upon each other's space. Parliament has sought to protect the head of the executive, the president, from liability. The court ought to pronounce if the process followed by parliament is allowable under the constitution. In this case, the courts remain the last line of defence in the implementation of the public protector's findings and the remedial action.

When adjudicating matters involving the independence and governance of anti-corruption institutions, the courts invokes the international instruments to derive an interpretation that affirms South Africa's commitment towards anti-corruption. This was seen in a case involving the independence of the Directorate of Special Operations

---

88 Hartley W (2015, 19 August) ANC rides roughshod over House on Nkandla. *Business Day*.

(DSO/the Scorpions); which was subsequently replaced by the Directorate of Priority Crime Investigations (the Hawks). In cases involving the operations of these institutions, and an appropriate line of accountability to ensure their independence, the courts work from the international anti-corruption conventions that South Africa is a signatory to. It is therefore important to focus now on how those units, while located within the executive, have functioned and carved their space as anti-corruption institutions.

Directorate of Priority Crime Investigation

The DPCI was formed after parliament passed legislation to dissolve the DSO in 2008.[89] The DPCI was constituted under the SAPS, as opposed to the DSO which was under the NPA. The DSO came into effect through the South African Police Services Amendment Act,[90] which establishes the DPCI within the police service. The act further stipulates that the head of the directorate 'shall be deputy national commissioner, appointed by the minister [of police] in concurrence with cabinet'.[91] Regarding the process of appointing the head of the directorate, the act states that the minister 'shall report to parliament on the appointment of the head of the directorate'. Section 17(d) of the act states the powers of the head of the directorate, that he or she is to 'prevent, combat, or investigate national priority offences, which in the opinion of the head of the directorate need to be addressed by the directorate'.

This means that the DPCI has to exercise full discretion regarding which cases he or she may investigate. Parliament is responsible for providing oversight on the directorate. The directorate attains its mandate from the 'policy guidelines' set out by the ministerial committee.[92] Section 17(b) of the act states, however, that the directorate needs to have 'the necessary independence to perform its functions'. The act has no specific provision regarding the level of independence that the directorate ought to have. This has been the subject of court enquiry – whether the creation of the DPCI, following the dissolution of the DSO, satisfies the constitutional requirement of the establishment of an independent anti-corruption unit.

Unlike the DSO which was located within the NPA, the DPCI is located directly within the SAPS, which is located within the executive branch of government. It was contended that this structure is unconstitutional, on the grounds that the directorate lacks sufficient safeguards for its independence – independence that was guaranteed while the DSO was located within the NPA. In dealing with the question of whether the DPCI has sufficient 'structural and operational' independence, the constitutional court argued that it does not matter whether the directorate is located within the NPA or the SAPS; what matters

---

89 Lewis M & Stenning P (2012, March) Considering the Glenister judgement: Independence requirements for anti-corruption institutions. *SA Crime Quarterly* 39: 12.
90 South African Police Service Amendment Act, no. 57 of 2008. Section 17C.
91 Ibid: section 17C(a).
92 Lewis M & Stenning P (2012, March) Considering the Glenister Judgement: Independence requirements for anti-corruption institutions. *SA Crime Quarterly* 39: 12.

is whether the chain of command and the line of accountability display operational and structural independence.

Judge Moseneke delivered that South Africa's ascension to international instruments on anti-corruption requires that the country establishes an anti-corruption body which will operate with sufficient safeguarding against undue political interference.[93] When the case regarding the independence of the DPCI was heard, it did not relate to any concrete instance of political interference with the function of the DPCI. The contention in the Glenister case was framed in abstraction, and thus not based on actual interference with the functioning of the DPCI. The contention was based on the disbandment of the DSO, which was believed to be located in a way that ensures no political interference, or at least to enjoy safeguards thereof.

A concrete case regarding alleged political interference with the DPCI came in the form of the suspension of its head, Anwar Dramat. Dramat was suspended on 23 December 2014, following allegations that he was involved in the illegal rendition of four Zimbabweans in November 2010.[94] The Helen Suzman Foundation (HSF) approached the court to challenge the decision by the police minister, Nkosinathi Nhleko, to suspend Dramat. There were allegations that Dramat's suspension was to do with his decision to investigate certain cases, including the Nkandla expenditure case. The Dramat suspension saga concretised the issue of the operational independence of the DPCI. If the head of the unit can be 'decapitated' in the way the minister suspended Dramat, that would take away the independence of the DPCI and place it completely at the behest of the minister, as was argued in court.[95]

The legislative provision for the DPCI[96] states that the minister has to report to parliament regarding the appointment of the head of the directorate. This therefore implies that the minister also has to report to parliament regarding the suspension and dismissal of the head of the directorate. According to the act, the head of the directorate accounts to parliament. This shows that parliament has to be involved in the process. The court held that the minister's power to suspend or remove the head is 'subject to the prior start of the proceedings of the committee of the national assembly for the removal ... and passing of resolution calling for the removal of head by a two-thirds majority'.[97]

The independence of the DPCI is also measured in the extent to which the minister can, on his own, suspend and dismiss the head. The role of parliament is to provide checks on the powers exercised by the minister in dealing with the suspension or dismissal of the head. The court's ruling on this matter shows that the minister has to exercise such powers of dismissal by involving parliament. By single-handedly suspending Dramat, and

---

93 *Glenister vs. President of the Republic of South Africa and Others*, (CCT 48/10) (CC March 17, 2011).
94 SAPA (2015, 23 January) Dramat suspension found unlawful (2015, 23 January) *Mail & Guardian*. Available at http://mg.co.za/article/2015-01-23-dramat-suspension-hailed-unlawful [accessed 19 November 2016].
95 Ibid.
96 South African Police Service Amendment Act, no. 57 of 2008. Section 17(c)3.
97 *The Helen Suzman Foundation vs. Minister of Police* 1054/2015 (High Court, 23 January 2015).

by not following a parliamentary process, the court found that the minister of police acted unlawfully and unconstitutionally. The minister's conduct was set aside.

The reasoning provided by the court in the Dramat case is an indication that the courts in South Africa have a clear idea regarding the meaning of 'structural and operational' independence that should be accorded to anti-corruption bodies in the country. The interpretation on this derives from the international conventions on anti-corruption and from the constitution. The legislative framework to establish the anti-corruption institutions is interpreted by the courts with the purpose of emphasising the country's commitment to anti-corruption and the need to realise the constitutional prerogative to establish integrity within the public service.

In the Glenister case,[98] the court drew from the SADC Protocol against Corruption, from which the court derived an understanding regarding the meaning of independence anti-corruption institutions should have. The court in this case also relied on the Organisation for Economic Co-operation and Development (OECD) report.[99] It is upon these instruments that the courts then assessed the validity and effectiveness of the local legislation setting out the formation and operation of anti-corruption institutions.

This shows that, in the case of South Africa, the weakest point of the anti-corruption machinery is local legislation, which seems to be crafted in a way that allows for unchecked executive encroachment. This challenge has been muted by the court's willingness to interpret the law in a way that emphasises the need for anti-corruption institutions to remain independent, both structurally and operationally. The DPCI is still largely located within the executive, although the court derived an interpretation that accords the unit operational independence. The suspension of Dramat also indicated that the location of the DPCI within the executive may also create an unfavourable relationship between the head of the directorate and the minister of police. After the court's decision that Dramat's suspension was unconstitutional and unlawful, he reached a settlement agreement with the minister and resigned from the unit. Unfortunately, the court cannot provide relief that forces the head of the directorate to turn down a settlement payment and return back to the unit.

Special Investigating Unit

The SIU was created by the Special Investigative Units and Special Tribunals Act 74 of 1996. It is tasked to investigate 'serious malpractices or maladministration in connection with the administration of state institutions'. The act allows for the president to establish, through the Government Gazette, any special investigative unit to investigate maladministration. The proclamation must set out the terms of reference for any special investigating unit.

---

98 Glenister vs. President of the Republic of South Africa and Others (CCT 48/10) (CC 17 March 2011).
99 OECD (2008) Specialised Anti-corruption Institutions: Review of Models . Available at https://www.oecd.org/corruption/acn/39971975.pdf [accessed 19 November].

The head of the unit is appointed by the president.[100] The act stipulates further that, when appointing the head of the unit, the president must have regard to 'experience, conscientiousness and integrity'.[101] The head may appoint other persons to the unit that are in his or her opinion fit to serve in that office. The SIU resides within the department of justice, an executive branch of government. Section 11 of the act provides that the minister of justice may:

> After consultation with the heads of such special investigating units and special tribunals as may be in existence at that stage, make regulations regarding any matter not in conflict with this act, which is reasonably necessary in order to promote the efficiency of special investigating units and special tribunals established in terms of this act.

It is the prerogative of the president, as the head of the executive, to refer matters to the SIU and also to constitute special tribunals. Recommendations for a matter to be referred to the unit may be made by other bodies such as a parliamentary committee or the public protector. However, the final decision lies with the president.

The leadership of the SIU has been quite unstable – the case with leadership of the DPCI and the prosecution authority. In November 2011, President Jacob Zuma appointed retired judge Willem Heath to head the SIU. Immediately after his appointment, Heath made allegations that President Thabo Mbeki had orchestrated rape charges against his then deputy, Jacob Zuma, for political reasons. Pressure mounted on Heath following the allegations he made and he subsequently resigned as the head of the SIU only days after his appointment. Heath served the shortest term as head of the SIU, at less than a month. Zuma appointed Advocate Vas Soni to head the SIU in September 2013. Advocate Soni resigned 16 months into the job, stating 'personal reasons'.[102]

In March 2015, President Zuma appointed Advocate Gerhard Visagie as the new head of the SIU. The appointment did not bring reprieve in the eyes of anti-corruption activists such as Advocate Paul Hoffman, who said that the unit 'is a toothless bulldog and [Zuma's] appointment of acting head [Visagie] will not change things'.[103] There is a strong perception that it lacks the necessary independence from the executive to carry out its function as a corruption-busting body. The leadership paralysis at the unit adds to this problem.

There are several high-profile investigations that have been referred to the SIU, among them is the Nkandla case and tender rigging practices in different provinces. Some of the investigations undertaken by the SIU also involve enquiry into 'financial

---

100 Special Investigating Units and Special Tribunals, Act no. 74 of 1996. Section 3.
101 Ibid.
102 Monama T (2015, 3 March) New SIU head 'will not change things'. *Independent Online*. Available at http://www.iol.co.za/news/crime-courts/new-siu-head-will-not-change-things-1825987 [accessed 19 November 2016].
103 Ibid.

maladministration, human resource irregularities, and non-compliance with internal processes'.[104] President Jacob Zuma signed the proclamation for the SIU to investigate these matters in December 2010. The SIU report found:

- An overpayment to the amount of R1.5 million for the construction of sewer and water networks in Soshanguve;[105]
- Self-enrichment in the amount of R70 000;
- Financial mismanagement, with an amount of R200 000 being overspent in fees paid to universities;
- Unauthorised expenditure amounting to R75 million, in violation of section 32(2) of the MFMA;
- Change in scope of the electrical work from the original budgeted amount of R90 292,73 to R28 263;
- Collusion between a senior procurement official within the metro police and seven service providers awarded contracts to the value of R77.7 million between 1 January 2007 and 8 November 2010;
- The receipt of gratification to the value of R16.1 million from the service providers as a result of the corrupt relationship that existed; and
- Four officials identified as having submitted fraudulent qualifications to secure jobs.

These are some of the findings arrived at by the SIU, demonstrating myriad webs of corruption within the City of Tshwane. In relation to this investigation, the unit recommended civil action to recover some of the funds, and also criminal investigations into areas where fraud and criminal activity were suspected.

Perhaps the most interesting case the SIU has handled thus far relates to the expenditure at the private residence of President Jacob Zuma. The Nkandla expenditure is interesting in the sense that it involves the president having to issue a proclamation into an expenditure and procurement involving departments in his cabinet as well as to his private residence. During the public protector's investigations into Nkandla expenditure, President Jacob Zuma signed a proclamation for the SIU to investigate relevant allegations of maladministration and procurement irregularities. The terms of reference for the investigations were set out in the proclamation signed by Zuma on 18 December 2013. The SIU would investigate issues related only to procurement, and not issues relating to the president's responsibility to exercise oversight on the use of public funds.

The investigations by the unit also ran parallel to the public protector's investigations into Nkandla in 2013. As the public protector requested information from ministers in the

---

104 De Lange D (2012, 30 July 30) Massive corruption in Tshwane exposed. *Independent Online*. Available at http://www.iol.co.za/news/politics/massive-corruption-in-tshwane-exposed-1351845 [accessed 19 November 2016].
105 Special Investigating Unit (2012) Interim Report: April-September 2012.

security cluster (the police, defence, state security and justice departments), it was made clear that the ministers did not want to cooperate with the public protector because they preferred investigation by the SIU. If one takes into consideration the fact that the SIU is highly influenced by the executive (also because it requires presidential proclamation to carry out any investigation), it seems clear why the executive preferred such an institution.

Responding to the public protector's request for information relating to the Nkandla investigation, police minister Mthethwa responded through a letter:

> I am concerned that you have now decided to investigate the matter even though a number of processes are underway to deal with the maladministration identified by the task team. In effect, an allegation or suspicion of maladministration no longer exists. The task team has identified maladministration and, therefore, the ministers in the JCPS cluster have decided that a special investigating unit and the auditor-general must conduct a full investigation and audit.[106]

Anti-corruption activists have since identified the SIU investigation into Nkandla as a way to deflect attention from the main issue relating to the president's breach of the ethics code. The DA stated that the 'special investigating unit is using the architect who worked on the R246m upgrade to President Jacob Zuma's private home as a scapegoat'.[107] The DA is suggesting therefore that the process of appointing the SIU to carry out investigations into Nkandla is an attempt to absolve the president from any liability. However, something even more sinister might have been at play regarding the appointment of the unit to carry out investigations into Nkandla: to undermine any investigation by other state bodies that might come up with adverse findings against the president regarding the matter.

Quite often when the president was called upon to respond to Madonsela's report on Nkandla, the president stated emphatically that there were other processes that were underway, the investigation by the SIU, for example. The SIU investigations did find that Zuma had unduly benefitted from Nkandla expenditure, but the report blamed the architect responsible for Nkandla's construction.

Corruption, society and the private sector

South Africa's anti-corruption machinery is still largely framed in a way that understands corruption as a public-sector problem. There is still an unwavering perception that the private sector is inherently corruption free and that where corruption exists in this sector, it is owing to red tape, and policy shortfalls and inefficiencies in the public sector. The narrative around corruption in South Africa is racialised: with blacks in the government

---

106 Public Protector (2014) *Secure in Comfort*. Pretoria: Public Protector.
107 Hartley W (2014, 14 August) SIU painting Nkandla architect as scapegoat – DA. *BDLive*. Available at http://www.bdlive.co.za/national/2014/08/14/siu-painting-nkandla-architect-as-scapegoat-says-da [accessed 4 October 2016].

seen to be corrupt while the largely white private sector is seen to be efficient and clean.[108] The media in South Africa tends to disproportionately report on corruption in the public sector rather than focusing on malfeasance in the private sector.

The consequences of corruption in the private sector are understood as affecting shareholders in private transactions, which could be addressed through corporate governance and the recourse that shareholders have against company executives. Corruption remains a phenomenon that is believed to reside only in the public sector. There is consequently a pressing need to raise awareness regarding the corrosive effect of corruption in the private sector.

F. Conclusion

Since the advent of democracy in 1994, South Africa has made remarkable strides towards building a modern democratic system characterised by a complex set of institutions. The Constitution of South Africa is recognised as one of the most advanced of its kind, and a strong defence for human rights and the idea of dignity. The constitution provides for the principle of separation of powers, which provides 'checks and balances with regard to the exercise of power'. The constitution recognises international law and prescribes that international conventions are binding once entered into by the republic.

The constitution serves as the basis for anti-corruption initiatives in the country. The constitution provides a seamless set of accountability frameworks, adherence to which would ideally repel instances of corruption. Judicial independence is guaranteed under the constitution and the courts also serve an important role in reviewing decisions of the executive. Constitutional institutions, such as the office of the public protector, also provide a useful avenue to conduct checks and balances on the exercise of power in the country. The justice and crime prevention cluster also has instruments whose operation should prevent corruption, such as: the criminal law system, the prosecutorial system and the broader justice system.

All this constitutes a decentralised anti-corruption mechanism. The challenge in South Africa, however, is that the powers to make crucial appointments in key anti-corruption-related institutions is primarily with the executive. As Judge Moseneke stated, it is important for South Africa to consider reviewing the powers given to the president when it comes to appointing key personnel serving in institutions responsible for protecting the nation's integrity.

Further, CSOs need to be more involved in the fight against corruption. It is important for government to accord space for CSOs when it comes to waging the war on corruption.

---

108 Vegter I (2013, 26 November) Do we tolerate private sector corruption? *Daily Maverick*. Available at http://www.dailymaverick.co.za/opinionista/2013-11-26-do-we-tolerate-private-sector-corruption/ [accessed 4 October 2016].

The suspicion between CSOs and government is detrimental to the development of collective efforts towards anti-corruption.

South Africa seems to be shifting towards a point of ambivalence regarding the importance of international instruments and forums when it comes to shaping them and instilling a values system within them. This can be seen in the implementation of some of the provisions provided for in the anti-corruption conventions. The recent decision by the ANC general council to withdraw the country from participation in the international criminal court is a point of concern.

South Africa should use the Open Government Partnership (OGP) membership to bolster its commitment towards good governance and building a more credible public service. The first two OGP Country Action Plans are a missed opportunity for South Africa to show a genuine commitment to the fight against corruption. There needs to be more public awareness regarding the effect of corruption on society. The idea of some of the politicians in the country that 'corruption is a western thing' will generate national ambivalence towards corruption in the country.

G. Recommendations

The anti-corruption machinery is multifaceted and all elements need to be aligned to ensure the effectiveness of the broader initiative. The anti-corruption initiative can be understood as comprising two categories: the legal or institutional framework, and the demand by society. The institutional framework is a technical regulatory regime – including the penal code and the accountability framework – that sanctions corruption-related activities. This is a formal process through which conduct relating to dishonesty, malfeasance and maladministration are processed formally.

The role of societal demand for an anti-corruption initiative includes perceptions regarding the legitimacy of the anti-corruption institutional framework. This is important in the sense that the active populace mediates the political cost of corruption, ultimately empowering citizens to consider corruption as a factor in determining the integrity of leaders. The recommendations for South Africa are therefore classified into these two categories, institutional reform and societal agency.

Institutional reforms

- Government needs to consider using the Open Government Partnership (OGP) initiative to commit to fighting corruption. It should be understood that proliferation of corruption undermines democracy. The OGP is a good tool to set targets to ensure the effectiveness of anti-corruption initiatives within the public sector and should be used to implement mechanisms such as the integrity management system within the public service. The department of public service and administration (DPSA) should lead in this initiative.

- There needs to be stability of political leadership within the justice and crime prevention cluster. The high turnover of senior managers and leadership within these institutions raises concerns regarding their readiness to tackle corruption, among their other responsibilities. Efforts have to be made to restore that integrity of those institutions, the success of which requires that leadership is strengthened and given political support.
- The process of appointment to key positions needs to be rethought. These appointments need to be subject to some form of effective confirmation by parliament, instead of the current process where parliament merely recommends without scrutinising. The power to appoint personnel is highly concentrated within the executive; this places the executive under immense political pressure whenever these institutions confront challenges. Therefore, dispersing responsibility for these appointments would ultimately alleviate the political pressure on the executive.
- Although South Africa has a decentralised anti-corruption machinery, there is a need to create synergy between the collective of institutions within it. According to Advocate Thuli Madonsela, synergy will ensure a common approach towards anti-corruption. At this point, there are varied institutions with differentiated mandates. The approach across these institutions is too fragmented.

Societal agency

- Citizens need to be made more aware of the impact of corruption on their daily lives. The current level of awareness is poor and results in public ambivalence. Civil society organisations should enable citizen-participation in anti-corruption forums.
- It is therefore necessary to activate the demand for anti-corruption initiatives among communities. For accountability to happen, it is important to re-emphasise the participation of the general citizenry, particularly at local government level. There needs to be popular will regarding the fight against corruption.

10
SWAZILAND

Ms Maxine Langwenya

A. Introduction

In his speeches from the throne in 2006 and 2012 respectively, the king declared zero tolerance towards corruption. In 2013 the prime minister said that institutions with a mandate to fight corruption will be adequately resourced to enable them to perform, and that 'there will be no refuge for the corrupt'. The Swazi public seems to agree; when polled in 2010 a majority agreed that corruption was at an all-time high.[1]

This report considers the dimensions of corruption in Swaziland through the examination and evaluation of the political as well as the legal environment under which the Anti-corruption Commission (ACC) operates. The research concludes that the king, the prime minister and the public are correct: corruption is a major – and growing – problem in Swaziland. The paper posits that most of the responsibility for this state of affairs rests squarely with those who have the fewest excuses for behaving corruptly: the politically powerful and the economically dominant.

In Swaziland, petty corruption of public officials is neither marginal nor confined to specific sectors, it is also not repressed. It is generalised and common place. Small-scale corruption is part of the landscape. Grand corruption, on the other hand, is practised at the summit of the state by the political elite and directors or chief executive officers in public or parastatal enterprises[2] involving millions of Emalangeni. The reason for both petty and grand corruption is that the country has little or no 'ethic of the public service' and a tradition of the 'public domain', both vital to good governance. Public officials have a sense of entitlement to state resources. In a nutshell, corruption in Swaziland is

---

1   Anti-corruption Poll (2010).
2   *Nathi Dlamini vs. The Commissioner of Anti-Corruption Unit*, Supreme Court Appeal Case No. 44/2009. The appellant, a chief executive officer of the Swaziland Telecommunication Corporation (a government parastatal) was arrested for corruption, it being alleged that he refused to furnish the Anti-Corruption Commission with information pertaining to the formation of a company called Horizon Mobile Limited, New Payphone Installation, ADSL Project and New Generation Network Project. According to the company's memorandum of association, the appellant owned 99 shares on behalf of the SPTC and his lawyer owned one share. He approached the court seeking that his arrest be declared unlawful. The court did not agree.

fuelled by the massive employment and promotion of unproductive civil servants; the bankruptcy of the employer-state; the irresponsibility and cupidity of the political elite; and the underpayment of civil servants, which has forced them to take on outside work to supplement their salaries.

The political economy of corruption

According to Trading Economics: 'Swaziland is the 69th least corrupt nation out of 175 countries, according to the 2014 Corruption Perceptions Index reported by Transparency International. Corruption Rank in Swaziland averaged 88.40 from 2005 until 2014, reaching an all-time high of 121 in 2006 and a record low of 69 in 2014. Corruption Rank in Swaziland is reported by the Transparency International'.[3]

Corruption is prevalent within the bureaucracy as companies and private entities pay public officials to sidestep regulations. The police, the ministry of finance, the ministry of commerce, industry and trade, and the department of customs and excise have long been implicated in corrupt practices. Corruption has also been prevalent in the government procurement and tendering processes. For instance, in 2011 Polycarp Dlamini, former general transport manager of the Central Transport Administration (CTA) was convicted of defrauding the government after he admitted to authorising payments worth up to SZL 12 million to a private company for services that were never rendered[4]. On another level the public accounts committee (PAC) was informed that SZL 1.6 million was paid to service providers for the maintenance of a machine that was neither broken nor in use at the Swaziland Broadcasting and Information Service (SBIS)[5]. The PAC was informed that the officer who authorised the bogus job cards had since been promoted and transferred to another government department. This type of behaviour is common, albeit covert and therefore difficult to monitor, as goods and services are undersupplied or rerouted for personal use. The results of grand corruption are evidenced by the increase in wealth of high civil servants and officers of state. It has been suggested that Swaziland has no fewer than 31 millionaires who are junior government officials.[6]

In 2005, the then minister of finance, Majozi Sithole, stated that 'the twin evils of bribery and corruption have become the order of the day in the country ... the economy is dying gradually because of this practice, and the citizens are placed under a heavy yoke'.[7] The minister estimated that corruption was costing the Swazi economy approximately SZL 40 million a month. Poor people, who suffer as a result of corruption, took the

---

3 Swaziland Corruption Rank 2005–2016. Available at http://www.tradingeconomics.com/swaziland/corruption-rank [accessed 3 November 2016].
4 *R vs. Polycarp Dlamini* High Court Case No 403/2011: neutral citation 403/11) (2012) SZHC 12 March 2012.
5 Sukati S (2015, 12 May) The PAC unearths E1.6million fraud at SBIS. *The Swazi Observer*. Available at http://www.observer.org.sz/news/72751 [accessed 3 December 2015].
6 Vandome C et al. (2013) *Swaziland: Southern Africa's Forgotten Crisis*. London: Chattam House. Available at https://www.chathamhouse.org/sites/files/chathamhouse/home/chatham/public_html/sites/default/files/20130900SwazilandVandomeVinesWeimer.pdf [accessed 26 September 2016].
7 See Simelane H (2012) The Swazi monarchy and the poor performance of the Swazi anti-corruption agency, 2006–2009. *Journal of Asian and African Studies* 47(4): 424.

minister's statement as confirmation of the extent to which the country was being driven to bankruptcy through corrupt activities. The corrupt public officials thought the minister was exaggerating the extent of corruption while academics were sceptical of the statement as the minister did not provide a basis for his assertion. The minister's statement was significant in so far as it highlighted the fact that the economy of the country was being undermined by corrupt activities. The current Minister of Finance Martin Dlamini says government has put in place measures to fight corruption, yet it has made little progress in prosecuting and punishing corrupt people.

In the past, ministers have been found by a Parliamentary Select Committee to have acted in a manner that is tantamount to theft of state property. The ministers had allocated to themselves, and subsequently 'bought', land belonging to the state at ridiculously low prices without competing with other would-be buyers. The matter was never pursued by the ACC and it eventually died down.

In 2015 judge Mpendulo Simelane stated that he had been approached by the former minister of justice, Sibusiso Shongwe and told that judges could and should make money from cases over which they presided. The then minister of justice is said to have the asked the judge to preside in a case of wealthy business people who were suing the Swaziland Revenue Authority for goods they had imported. The minister is said to have told the judge that the business people were willing to pay approximately SZL 2 million for help in winning the case. Shongwe suggested that Simelane should preside in the case and explained how the SZL 2 million would be shared between the parties. Simelane and Shongwe were subsequently arrested by the ACC and charged with corruption, but charges were subsequently dropped against Simelane. Simelane remains on suspension while Shongwe is presently out on bail. This case illustrates how the Swazi justice system was abused to settle political scores and make it complicit to actions of corrupt public officials.

B. Legal and institutional framework

International legal instruments

Swaziland is a signatory to the African Union Convention on Preventing Corruption and Related Offences and the SADC Protocol Against Corruption; it has also ratified the United Nation's Convention against Corruption in 2012. Swaziland is also a signatory of the OECD Anti-bribery Convention. As with most countries in Africa, Swaziland is quick to sign and ratify international legal instruments yet slow to incorporate their provisions into national law.

The Constitution Act, 2005

The Constitution of Swaziland contains general guidelines for public servants and politicians. It seeks to ensure that those who are in leadership, whether elected or appointed:

- Act in a transparent and accountable manner in their activities and the people they represent;
- Are committed to the rule of law and to administrative justice;
- Adhere to the principles of service for the common good;
- Do not abuse office; and
- Do not engage in conduct that is likely to lead to corruption in public affairs.[8]

There is currently no code of conduct for public servants and politicians.

The Money Laundering (Prevention) Act, 12/2000

This act prohibits money laundering and associated matters. The supervisory authority and the powers associated with enforcing the act are vested in the governor of the Central Bank of Swaziland. The act also makes money laundering an offence for the purpose of any law relating to extradition or rendition of offenders.

The Parliamentary Privileges' Act, 1967, and the Public Accounts Committee Order, 20/1974

The Parliamentary Privileges Act established the PAC. Through the PAC, parliament is empowered to punish for contempt by fine or otherwise and where such fine is not paid, the offender may be jailed. This act, along with the Public Accounts Committee Order of 1974 is used by the PAC to levy fines on public officials found guilty of offences related to misuse of public funds. The challenge is that both legislations have been overtaken by time and the fines they impose are no deterrent as these are limited to SZL 100 and SZL 400 respectively, or a term of imprisonment of up to six months.

The Swaziland Anti-Corruption Policy, 2015

The policy promotes inclusiveness, participation and the collaboration of all stakeholders in fighting corruption. The policy emphasises a sector-wide, broad-based, non-partisan, transparent and participatory approach with the roles and responsibilities of all stakeholders clearly spelt out. The aim is to increase awareness and understanding of the anti-corruption initiative and improve acceptance levels across the public, private and civil society sectors.[9]

The Legal Framework of the Anti-corruption Commission

Swaziland passed its first legislation aimed at combating corruption in 1986.[10] The act applied to any person holding office in a public corporation; local authority; a company, society or voluntary association, or anyone else payable from public funds or from the Swazi

---

8   Section 239 of the Constitution Act, 2005.
9   Swaziland Anti-Corruption Policy, 2015, p. 26.
10 The Prevention of Corruption Act, 1986.

national treasury. It prohibited a corrupt offer or acceptance of a gift or consideration as an inducement or reward for doing or forbearing to do so, or showing or forbearing to show any act, favour or disfavour in an official capacity. The act was not supported by an institutional body to make it operational.

The Prevention of Corruption Act of 1986 was replaced by the Prevention of Corruption Order of 1993; a law that was passed by the king and his council of ministers when parliament was prorogued. The 1993 order created the ACC and mandated it to report to the office of the prime minister. This order was amended through the Prevention of Corruption (Amendment) Act of 1997, to provide for the appointment of the commissioner and two deputy commissioners of the ACC by the king, in consultation with the minister of justice. According to the amendment, annual reports had to be submitted by the commissioner to the minister of justice. The first official launch of the ACC by the prime minister was in 1998. The ACC created by the 1993 order did not have powers to investigate, charge and prosecute corrupt activities involving public officials, companies and public enterprises.

In 2002, the high court declared that the 1993 order was unconstitutional and accordingly set it aside. The operations of the ACC came to a halt as a result of the invalidation of the law that created it. In 2005, the supreme court set aside the high court order and accordingly re-activated the ACC and its operations. The scourge of corruption continued unabated. Various national and international groups and the media increasingly became critical of the growing corruption levels in the country. It was as a result of donors threatening to cut aid to Swaziland that in 2006, parliament passed the Prevention of Corruption Act (POCA) and established an ACC dedicated to fighting corruption through prevention and investigation of corruption as well as educating the public and raising awareness about the need to fight corruption. The POCA re-established the ACC as an independent body and provided for matters incidental to the prevention of corruption. According to the POCA, the ACC only has operational and not administrative independence because it is a government department under the ministry of justice and constitutional affairs. The ACC therefore reports to the justice ministry. The Constitution of Swaziland was passed in 2005 prior to the POCA in 2006. Consequently, the ACC is not a constitutional body. This therefore means that the constitution does not guarantee and safeguard the existence of the ACC. By extension, parliament can repeal the POCA and abolish the ACC without necessarily going through the rigorous process of changing the constitution.

The ACC needs to have a legal framework that ensures independence and helps maintain its autonomy without depending upon the whims of the government. Simultaneously, while independence of the ACC is critical, so too is its own institutional accountability. While independence is essential for it to undertake investigation and prosecution without any fear or favour from other government agencies and politicians, there is a parallel need to ensure that the ACC itself does not become an organisation that is accountable to no one. A system of checks and balances should therefore be introduced so that while its functioning is independent from the executive, it will be overseen by an independent board (with the requisite qualification and experience), the membership of which will be mostly from outside the ACC.

It is often said that the composition of the ACC should be guaranteed in the constitution so that the level of engagement and interaction of its members is not only deemed to be, but also perceived to be, important. There is, however no evidence to support this position. Whether or not the ACC is made a constitutional body will not necessarily result in the enhanced standing of the body. The difference between the two positions is the same.

Other anti-corruption bodies

Commission of Human Rights and Public Administration and the auditor general's office
The Constitution Act of 2005 establishes the Commission on Human Rights and Public Administration (CHRPA) and the auditor general's (AG) office; these being institutions that have an explicit and a tacit mandate to fight corruption. The constitution mandates the CHPRA to 'investigate complaints of … corruption … by a public officer in the exercise of official duties',[11] while the AG has power to audit and report on all public accounts and offices in Swaziland.[12] The AG's office submits reports to the minister of finance who causes those reports to be laid before both chambers of parliament. The 2011 report of the AG reflects that the judiciary purchased supplies in excess of SZL 1 million which were never delivered and 46 laptops, of which only 36 of were distributed to members of the judiciary while ten lap tops were alleged to have been stolen.[13] Audits by the AG are largely ineffective as they are not followed by any disciplinary action where public officials have been found to have mismanaged or misappropriated public funds. Even more telling is that such audits seldom result in any further investigation or prosecutions.

Since its establishment in 2009, CHPRA has not investigated any complaints of corruption by public officers. The reason cited was that the public direct such complaints to the ACC. CHPRA also acts as an integrity commission with the mandate to process asset declarations and enforce the code of conduct of public officials. Notably, the asset declarations are not open to public scrutiny. Further, there is still no code of conduct of public officials.

Public accounts committee
The PAC of the house of assembly is regulated by the standing orders of the house and its duties include that of examining and reporting to the house about accounts of the government tabled by the minister of finance through the AG's report. The PAC conducts its hearings publicly and has unearthed a lot of corrupt practices relating to the embezzlement and mismanagement of public revenue. It has, on several occasions, referred such cases to the ACC for further action.

---

11 Section 164(1)(b).
12 Section 207(3).
13 Auditor General's Report (2011) pp. 216–217.

Directorate of Public Prosecutions (DPP)

The DPP is mandated by section 162 of the constitution to: institute and undertake criminal proceedings against any person before any court (other than a court martial) in respect of any offence alleged to have been committed by that person against the laws of Swaziland; take over and continue any criminal proceedings that may have been instituted or undertaken by any other person or authority; and discontinue, at any stage before judgment is delivered, any criminal proceedings instituted or undertaken by the DPP or any other person or authority. Where the DPP discontinues any prosecution including a private prosecution he may have taken over, the accused person is entitled to a verdict of an acquittal. This may result in a miscarriage of justice if the DPP abuses his prosecutorial powers or where his office is unable to conduct a prosecution due to the technical nature of the matter.

The DPP and the ACC enjoyed a 100% conviction rate in five cases that have been prosecuted since the ACC was re-established in 2008. While the rate of success is impressive, the rate of prosecution is very low. This can be attributed to:

- Limited case law and jurisprudence on corruption cases leading to limited confidence among prosecutors in taking up corruption dockets;
- Limited skills and knowledge of financial crimes among the justice delivery partners; and
- Limited skills in criminal procedure on the part of the ACC investigations team thereby limiting the number of dockets qualifying for prosecution.

Royal Swaziland Police (RSP)

The RSP is responsible for the maintenance of law and order[14] and for preserving peace as well as the prevention and detection of crime and apprehending of offenders. The Police Act of 1957 regulates the police service.

Judicial Service Commission (JSC)

The JSC is a body established by the constitution. It is mandated by the constitution to receive and process recommendations and complaints concerning the judiciary as well as exercise disciplinary control and remove judges and the DPP from office.[15]

Swaziland Public Procurement Regulatory Agency

The Swaziland Public Procurement Regulatory Agency was established by the Procurement Act of 2011. Its functions are to advise government and procuring entities about the procurement laws and all matters relating to public procurement. It has the power to investigate breaches and powers to initiate prosecutions.

---

14 See Section 189 of the Constitution Act, 2005.
15 Section 160(1)(d) &(a) of the Constitution Act, 2005 respectively.

The ACC works with the Swaziland Revenue Authority and the Swaziland Financial Intelligence Unit (SFIU) housed in the Central Bank of Swaziland. There is need to further strengthen – and take advantage of – the information and skills inherent in these institutions in order to ensure effective investigations and productive prosecutions. The ACC should strengthen such partnerships through the signing of memoranda of understanding with the above institutions and bodies.

C. Organisational framework of the ACC

Appointments and dismissals

The commission is headed by the commissioner, who is appointed by the king on the advice of the JSC. The commissioner holds office for a period not exceeding five years, renewable for a single term, on terms as may be determined.[16] The commissioner must qualify for appointment as a judge of the high court.[17] The incumbent, like his predecessor, is a non-Swazi and was appointed in 2013 for a period of five years. The commissioner has two deputies who are also appointed on similar terms. Deputy commissioners must have experience and competence in the conduct of public affairs, as well as academic qualifications and experience in law, economics, accounting and criminal investigation.[18] The commissioner or his deputies may be removed from office by the king if they are deemed unable to perform functions of the office, or for misconduct. If misconduct is alleged, it shall be investigated by the JSC.[19]

It is submitted that the commissioner and his deputies must have security of tenure, ensuring that they are not dismissed for insignificant reasons. If they are accused of acts of misconduct, such must be investigated by an independent committee. A special tribunal chaired by a retired judge must preside over the matter. The JSC is notorious for the unconventional dismissal of judges of the high court.[20] It is recommended that the JSC's role be curtailed in the impeachment of the commissioner, if only to ensure that the commissioner discharges his duties without fear or favour.

The other members of staff are recruited and appointed by the commissioner after consultation with the justice minister.[21] Officers recruited from other government agencies shall be transferred to the commission without prejudice to their accrued benefits.[22] It is an anomaly that, even though the commission has a human resource section whose duty is,

---

16 Section 4(1) and (2) of the Prevention of Corruption Act, 2006.
17 Section 5(1) of the Prevention of Corruption Act, 2006.
18 Section 8(1) of the Prevention of Corruption Act, 2006.
19 Section 8(1) of the Prevention of Corruption Act, 2006
20 In 2012, the chief justice, who is head of the JSC preferred charges against Judge Masuku. The chairman of the JSC refused to recuse himself from the proceedings even though he had preferred charges against Masuku, charges which imputed that Masuku was insubordinate to the chief justice. Judge Masuku was never afforded due process before the JSC.
21 Section 8(1) of the POCA, 2006.
22 Section 8(2) of the POCA, 2006

among others, to recruit staff on behalf of the commission, 'investigating and other officers' should be hired by the commissioner after consulting the minister. This may raise issues of political interference in the work of the commission. The commission should be allowed the latitude to hire its staff without having to consult politicians. The act does not provide for a minimum qualification in operational staff for the commission, nor is there a requirement pertaining to compatibility of education background and job requirements. The nature of corruption is dynamic and requires those tasked with tracking and combatting it to be ahead in the fields of accounting, economics and information technology in order to be able to gather, analyse and store data. It is therefore untenable that investigation officers are not required to have basic qualification in the areas outlined above, or in any other areas for that matter.

The legislation is fairly comprehensive, albeit fragmented and therefore difficult to coordinate and enforce. Notably, none of the laws provide for the protection of whistle-blowers and witnesses. The laws further lack redress for those falsely accused of corrupt practices.

Office space and security

The ACC offices are currently housed at Mbandzeni House, a private building. These offices are leased to the ACC and the government pays the rent. The nature of the work of the ACC is sensitive and requires the provision and enforcement of security measures. This can only be achieved by providing a stand-alone building with dedicated security personnel.

Administration department

The commission has two departments, namely administration and operations. The administration department is headed by a deputy commissioner of administration (DCA), while the operations department is headed by a deputy commissioner of investigations and asset recovery. The latter is divided into three sections: the corruption prevention section, the public education section and the investigation section.

This department is responsible for the effective management of day-to-day operations of the commission, including: finance, information technology, human resources, staff welfare and performance review, among others. The department is now divided into four sections namely: general administration, human resources, information technology and the finance. Each of the sections will be discussed in turn.

General administration

This section is responsible for the maintenance and safety of ACC assets within available resources. It is further responsible for transport management, procurement, budgeting and general office administration, which includes: maintenance of office premises, secretariat, registry, messenger, reception, security, travel arrangement and facilitation of executive meetings. This is in line with the commission's mandate and government general guidelines aimed at providing efficient and effective support services for ACC core operational activities. In collaboration with the accounts section, the section prepared the commission's annual budget estimates for the years 2015/2016 and 2016/2017. The total budget estimates requested for the financial period 2014/2015 were SZL 30 million and the budget was approved at SZL 11 267 343.

Human resources

This section is responsible for the acquisition, development and retention of ACC staff. In particular, the section facilitates:
- The recruitment and selection and training of members of staff;
- The development of a people strategy that will help the ACC secure, motivate and effectively manage its workforce;
- The focus on the structure of staff development programmes; and
- The creation of a conducive work environment including employee welfare and management of issues of satisfactory performance, misconduct and grievances and labour relations matters in an expeditious and fair manner while promoting integrity at all times.

During the period under review, the senior human resource officer, who was on a year's study leave, returned and shortly left to work in another government ministry. The deputy commissioner of investigations and asset forfeiture is presently on precautionary suspension because she is facing corruption-related charges.[23] One officer has been dismissed from the employ of the commission. The staff compliment of the ACC currently stands at 34 employees. This insufficient staff compliment hampers the work of the commission in several ways.

Information technology

This section is responsible for helping the commission to gather, analyse and store data, and host the ACC website. The website is not user-friendly and requires re-designing in order to be interactive.

Resources such as sophisticated and enhanced technology and information technology systems are essential to establishing capability in the collection of information. Personnel with specialised skills and experience are required in order for the commission to function effectively and efficiently. It is recommended therefore that the commission ensures that appropriately skilled persons are employed and that skills development is prioritised and implemented.

---

23 Dlamini W (2015, 23 August) Anti-corruption boss Lillian arrested. *Swazi Observer.* Available at http://www.observer.org.sz/news/75495-anti-corruption [accessed 30 November 2015].

Finance

The ACC operates on a minimum budget. The total annual budget requested for the current year was SZL 30 million, but only SZL 11 370 308 was approved by government. It is submitted that the commission should have financial independence and that funds required for effective functioning should be made available by parliament and not be dependent upon governmental discretion. It should be funded by the government through the consolidated fund. The accounts of the ACC should be subject to audit by the auditor general and its report should be tabled in parliament. This ensures the financial accountability of the ACC. This should be done so that no future government can interfere in the working of the commission and adversely impact its financial independence.

The table below shows the total approved budget, the actual released as well as the actual expenditure, and the variance reflected against each reporting item for the current financial year.

Table 1: Budget and expenditure, 2014/2015

Activity	Estimated (SZL)	Released	Actual (E)	Variance (SZL)	Variance in %
CTA charges	109 5195	109 5195	1 166 884	-71 689	-6.54%
Personnel	761 2863	761 2863	7 599 502	13 361	.18%
Communication and travel	534 478	754 475	686 601	67 874	8.9%
Professional fees	175 8901	1 398 900	1 192552	206 348	14.75%
Consumables and supplies	175 911	315 910	288 033	27 877	.09%
Durable items	90 000	90 000	19 868	70 132	77.92%
Total	**11 267 343**	**11 267 343**	**10 953 440**	**313 903**	**2.79**

Source: 2014/2015 Annual report Anti-corruption Commission, Swaziland, p. 21.

Operations Department

The operations department has three sections: investigation, public education, and prevention.

Investigation

The investigation section is responsible for the investigation of all pursuable reports. In the current year, three investigating teams were set up and headed by a senior investigator. The commission supplemented the shortage of staff within this section by using the inter-agency task team to maximise its efforts. The office of the DPP worked closely with the ACC investigating teams. This year alone, a total of 210 reports were received by the commission compared to 103 complaints in the previous year, reflecting a double increase in the complaints received. Eighty-six complaints were authorised for investigations. A total of 33 were referred to other agencies. Twenty-two cases were investigated and referred to the DPP office.

The table below shows the number of complaints received by the ACC since it became operational in 2008.

Table 2: Complaints received since 2008

Year	Complaints reported
2008/2009	51
2009/2010	201
2010/2011	249
2011/2012	103
2012/2013	78
2013/2014	103
2014/2015	210
Total number of complaints	**995**

Source: 2014/2015 Anti-corruption Annual Report, p. 16.

The following table shows the breakdown of complaints reported to the commission in the year 2014/2015.

Table 3: Type of complaints reported to the ACC, 2014/2015

Type of complaint	Number of cases
Theft	20
Fraud	70
Cheating public revenue	10
Conflict of interest	35
Corrupt activities relating to law officers and public prosecutors	5
Bribery	10
Other (administration, civil and labour-related complaints)	60
Total	**210**

Source: 2014/2015 Anti-corruption Annual Report, p. 16.

The workload of the investigators is high, both in terms of the number and complexity of cases. Currently, there are three senior investigators, four investigating officers, one acting investigator and two assistant investigators – with many positions still vacant. These need to be filled in order for this section to function optimally.

Currently, most personnel in this section come from a law enforcement background and there is need for greater specialisation in anti-corruption technical competencies. Such training will help build investigative and support skills in the commission.

The section has new investigative and support units in line with the commission's new Strategic Plan 2014/2015. The aim is not only to decentralise the work of the commission, but to turn the activity-based roles into results-based roles. The new and additional units are aimed at gearing the investigations section towards the speedy investigation of cases, lifestyle audits and recovery of illicit assets.

Public education

The public education component is mandated by POCA and is aimed at disseminating information on the dangers of corrupt practices on the society and to rally public support towards the fight against corruption. The public education section of the commission has conducted a number of anti-corruption awareness campaigns targeting specific sectors of society. It is disconcerting that the campaigns have not been directed at the sectors of society that are perceived to be more corrupt: the business sector, members of parliament and top government officials.[24] More awareness training should target the groups that are perceived to be most corrupt.

Table 4: Institutions receiving training, 2014/2015

Institution	Number of activities
Royal Swaziland Police	5
Regional education officers (Manzini)	1
Swaziland Electricity Company	1
Swaziland Bankers Association	1
School principal associations	6
Schools inspectors	1
School children and school staff	6
Communities	1
Health workers	5
KOBWA company	1
Lutsango Lwaka Ngwane (women's regiment)	2
Management and board (Swaziland Water Services Corporation pension fund trustees)	1
Completing students and staff of Nhlangano Agricultural Skills Training Centre (NASTC)	1
Teaching diploma students at the Swaziland College of Technology	1

Source: 2014/2015 Anti-corruption Commission Annual Report, p. 11.

---

24 Motau P (2015, 3 December) Business execs, government officials most corrupt. *The Times of Swaziland*. p.10.

In the current year, the commission carried out 33 interactive educational sessions that reached four thousand people. In the current year, the public education section of the ACC collaborated with the national police to finalise and launch the police anti-corruption module that will be used to train recruits during their training at the police college.

D. Mandate and operations

From the preceding section, it can be seen how the ACC operates based on its mandate drawn from section 10 of the POCA. The POCA outlines the following functions of the commission:

    (a) To take necessary measures for the prevention of corruption in public and private bodies including, in particular measures for:
        i) Examining in the practices and procedures of public and private bodies in order to facilitate the discovery of corrupt practices and secure the revision of their methods of works or procedures which, in the opinion of the Commissioner, may be prone or conducive to corrupt practices;
        ii) Advising public and private bodies on the ways and means of preventing corrupt practices, and on changes in the methods of work or procedure of those public and private bodies compatible with the effective performance of their duties, which the Commissioner considers necessary to reduce the likelihood of the occurrence of corrupt practices;
        iii) Disseminating information on the evil and dangerous effects of corrupt practices on the society; and
        iv) Enlisting and fostering public support against corrupt practices;
    b) Receive and investigate complaints of alleged or suspected corrupt practice made against any person, and refer appropriate cases to the Director of Public Prosecutions;
    c) Investigate any alleged or suspected offences under this Act, or any offence disclosed during such an investigation;
    d) Investigate any alleged or suspected contravention of any of the provisions of the fiscal and revenue laws of the country;
    e) Assist any law enforcement agency of the government in the investigation of offences involving dishonesty or cheating of the public revenue;
    f) Investigate the conduct of any public officer which in the opinion of the Commissioner may be connected with or conducive to corrupt practices;
    g) Instruct, advise and assist any person, on the request of that person, on ways in which corrupt practices may be eliminated by that person; and
    h) Do all such things as may be necessary for the prevention of corruption and the furtherance of the objects of this Act.

The mandate of the commission is to prevent, investigate and educate with respect to corruption. The prevention component requires the commission to take necessary measures to prevent all forms of corruption in the country, with particular emphasis on public and private bodies. The POCA gives the commission the mandate to examine the practices and procedures of public and private bodies in order to facilitate the discovery of corrupt practices and secure the revision of their methods of work or procedures which in the opinion of the commissioner may be conducive to corrupt practices. In the year of writing, the department responsible for the prevention of corruption has one staff member. The officer has conducted four corruption risk assessments in public entities in collaboration with other stakeholders. The department responsible for the prevention of corruption was part of a team that reviewed Ghana and Singapore on the implementation of the United Nations Convention Against Corruption (UNCAC). The report has been finalised. The team also undertook Swaziland's self- assessment in accordance with provisions of the UNCAC, and the report is with the justice ministry.[25]

Procedure for handling corruption allegations

All the complaints reported to the commission are channelled to the report centre office. Such complaints are received through the following methods:

- By personal call at the office of the ACC (if the caller might or might not wish to identify himself);
- By telephone (if the caller might or might not wish to identify himself);
- By letter (if the caller might or might not wish to identify himself);
- By telex, fax;
- From information from an officer of the commission; and
- Through the hotline.

The reporting procedure appears to be fairly broad except the commission does not use electronic communication such as email, Facebook or Twitter.

The summary of the complaint must be factual, concise and sufficiently detailed to enable the complaints review committee (CRC) to make a rational recommendation to the commissioner. The complaint will be scrutinised by the senior report centre officer and consider the complaint not to be one of corruption and outside the ACC mandate, they will immediately advise the complainant accordingly. The report centre officer will then register the complaint and send the report to the CRC.

---

25 2014/2015 Anti-Corruption Commission Report. p. 9.

Prosecutorial powers

The commission does not have prosecutorial powers. The power to prosecute rests in the director of public prosecutions (DPP), who may, at any stage, institute criminal proceedings or discontinue same without giving reasons for his decision.[26] The ACC refers its cases to the office of the DPP as it doesn't have the power to prosecute or any in-house prosecutors. The concern is that cases relating to corruption are not prioritised in the court roll. The result is that many cases are pending while others await enrolment. Some of the cases have been dragging on for more than nine years without being finalised, and some of the accused end up dying without getting justice.[27]

Independence

According to the POCA the commission is established as an independent body and its commissioner and deputy commissioners are also independent with respect to their duties. The POCA states that: 'in the performance of their functions in carrying out their duties, the commissioner and the deputy commissioners shall be independent and shall not be subject to the direction or control of any person or authority'.

In discharging its functions, the commission operates as an independent and autonomous institution. This is provided for in section 4(11) of the POCA. Under section 8 of the act, the commission is mandated to appoint such investigating officers and other officers to assist the commission in the performance of its functions. However, in administrative, financial, human resources and supply matters, the commission operates as a government department under existing government regulations.[28]

The commissioner reports to the minister of justice on the administration of the ACC. The commissioner prepares an annual report that is presented by the minister to parliament on an annual basis. The commissioner may, with the exception of his deputies terminate the appointment of an officer of the commission and give reasons but he does not have to consult the minister. In the year of writing, one officer was dismissed from the ACC for contravening the commission's code of conduct.[29] All the staff of the ACC is subject to the laws and regulations of the civil service.[30]

---

26 Section 162 of the Constitution Act, 2005.
27 An example is that of the case involving a former Principal Secretary in the Ministry of Finance who was alleged to have authorised the use of a sum of E50 million for use to train the public to start businesses. The money was alleged to have been squandered by the supposed trainers within a period of two weeks. The 'trainers' were Directors of different companies. In 2007 the Principal Secretary and the directors were arrested and charged with corruption. The case is still pending before court and has not been finalised nine years since the accused were arrested. The former principal secretary is now deceased. The matter was dubbed the '50 million case'.
28 2014/2015 ACC Annual Report, p.18.
29 2014/2015 ACC Annual Report, p.18.
30 Section 9 of the Prevention of Corruption Act, 2006.

Relationships with other stakeholders

Public, private and civil society partnerships
The ACC currently has limited formal relationships with the private sector and civil society. There is need to rekindle the National Anti-corruption Forum (NACF), whose responsibility it is to implement the national anti-corruption strategy and thereby create links between the ACC, the public and the private sectors, including civil society. Such a partnership would, among other things, ensure that there is a shared responsibility in the fight against corruption. Some of the skills that are limited in the ACC and are prohibitively expensive (for instance, financial forensics) are plentiful in the private sector and could be tapped into through such partnerships.

The Media
The media in Swaziland is largely state-controlled. The commission does not have formal links with the media but does use it to spread the information about its mandate. In the year of writing, the commission featured in the state television station, the Swaziland Television Authority (STVA) and on the radio station, the Swaziland Broadcasting and Information Station (SBIS). Print media enquiries increased during the year as the commission made major arrests of high profile people within the judiciary. The print media uncovered allegations of corruption, which were followed on by the commission with positive results.

International organisations and donor agencies
The ACC has partnered with the Southern African Forum Against Corruption (SAFAC), the Association of the Anti-Corruption Agencies in Commonwealth Africa (AACACA) and the Africa Association of Anti-Corruption Authorities (AAACA) and the SADC Anti-Corruption Committee.

New partnerships have also been forged with the Africa Development Bank (AfDB). The ACC signed a memorandum of understanding (MoU) with the AfDB for technical assistance. The commission sent a request to the bank for conducting a diagnostic review in order to ascertain where they can focus their assistance. The bank then sent a needs assessment survey which was undertaken and returned. The commission awaits results.

The United Nations Development Programme (UNDP) works with the ACC. In the year of writing, the UNDP allocated USD 10 000 for quality assurance of the Strategic Plan and the revival of the anti-corruption unit at the office of the deputy prime minister under the ministry of Tinkhundla. For the year 2015, the ACC has collaborated with the Tinkhundla ministry and other stakeholders to pilot initiatives aimed at improving service delivery. The UNDP funds some aspects of the national ACC to be run in one of the regions in Swaziland.

The UNDP also gave technical and financial support to the Commission during the preparation of its 2014–2018 strategic plan.

Challenges

Strengths

The main strength of the ACC is that it has a qualified and experienced commissioner, who has been able to steer it into calmer waters since he took over in 2013. This can be seen from the deliverables that the ACC has managed to accomplish in a record two years; to wit, the ACC strategic plan, policy and annual reports. This is laudable as it ensures that the ACC has a comprehensive and enabling legal framework. The commissioner also has a dedicated staff that has, regardless of poor pay, been able to achieve favourable assessments by international and regional organisations regarding the dropping levels of corruption, however minimal. Given adequate relevant training, the staff the ACC is on course to have a competent workforce.

The ACC has a fairly comprehensive legal framework – barring the POCA of 2006, which needs amending to make provision for the protection of whistleblowers and witnesses.

That the ACC works with a variety of stakeholders and has signed MoUs with some of them is a strength, as collaborating can make for a meaningful impact. In this regard, the commission is able to tap into the assistance of the inter-agency task team whenever there is an investigation and a need to make an arrest.

Weaknesses

The commission does not have secure and decentralised offices. This makes it inaccessible to the majority of people who might want to report acts of corruption by visiting the office. It is consoling that their plans to decentralise the ACC will be implemented in the next financial year.

The biggest challenge is the insufficient budget allocated by government. There is a need to grant the commission independence in budget-related matters. The ACC should be funded from the consolidated fund and be permitted to mobilise resources in order to meet all its programmes.

The shortage of staff – coupled with high staff turnover – is another weakness. Staff members must be incentivised by higher salaries than those of civil servants. Their terms and conditions of service must also be reviewed to provide them with accommodation in government houses.

In the current year, the commission has given assistance to government departments in the formulation of departmental guidelines governing civil service integrity and mapping out tailor-made preventative educational programmes for their staff. The commission has further conducted studies of operational and financial processes in the different government departments and public bodies, and has made recommendations on preventative measures and followed up with monitoring reviews.

The commission also promotes ethics in the private sector and encourages organisations to take preventative measures against corruption. The commission works with other organisations and bodies whose aim is to prevent or fight corruption; it also trains different sectors on the prevention of corruption.

To further the mandate of corruption prevention, the NACF was established in 2007 following a recommendation from the first national civil society/private sector anti-corruption summit held in 2006. The NACF consists of civil society and private and public sector representatives. An MoU for the establishment of the NACF was signed. However, the NACF has been in decline since its inception. It is recommended that efforts be made to reactivate the NACF, as it is only when the commission partners with all stakeholders that it will succeed in its fight against corruption. The aim of the NACF remains to contribute towards establishing a national consensus to fight corruption through the coordination of sector strategies.

The investigation component of the mandate requires the commission to receive and investigate complaints of alleged or suspected corrupt practices. The aim is to enforce the law vigilantly and professionally in order to seek out and eradicate corruption wherever it exists. In that regard, all complaints are referred to the CRC, which determines i) whether the commission has the legal mandate; and ii) the seriousness and financial implications of the complaint. The CRC then advises the commissioner whether or not the ACC should investigate the complaint or refer it to other relevant bodies such as the police. The commissioner then gives the necessary directions and authorises what action is to be taken.

Despite the efforts currently in place, the fight is not without its challenges.

- Although the ACC, law enforcement agencies and oversight institutions refer cases to the DPP, they do so in a haphazard, disjointed and isolated manner. Follow-ups and systematic coordination and collaboration are weak. The establishment of the inter-agency task team is a step in the right direction as it seeks to coordinate the work of the law enforcement agencies:
- As in all government sectors in Swaziland, the law enforcement agencies, the ACC and the oversight institutions do not offer competitive conditions of service. Thus, most institutions have serious capacity constraints and inadequate specialised skills. In addition, the ACC and the other institutions do not have the requisite material resources needed to effectively execute their public service responsibilities;
- There is a lack of transparency and accountability in the exercise of public authority; and
- Unregulated official discretion is prevalent.

E. Conclusion

Corruption continues to undermine socio-economic development as a result of poor governance manifested in the stifling of freedom of expression. In order to make headway in the fight against corruption, Swaziland should firmly commit to the policy of 'zero tolerance'. This policy must permeate Swaziland's political culture, governance, legal system and administration. Where corruption is ingrained and pervasive, especially at the highest political level, its eradication requires more sustained efforts over a long period of time. It is important therefore that the ACC be enabled – and not disabled – to execute its mandate. Enabling the ACC entails allowing it free rein to vigorously pursue corruption by involving the media in bringing information on arrests, indictments, trials and convictions into the public domain.

In a free democratic society, the media plays an important role in exposing corruption by insisting on transparency in governance and ensuring the accountability of administrators. Simultaneously, the ACC needs to maintain its independence and autonomy to be able to deal with corruption impartially, objectively and efficiently. The perception that the ACC is at the beck and call of certain individuals does not help the institution. The ACC should not only be independent and autonomous in theory, it must manifestly be seen to be so through being housed in a stand-alone building and not be under a government ministry. The minister should not play a role in the recruitment of commission staff. Accordingly, the POCA should be amended to remove this provision. The ACC should be given constitutional status to ensure its autonomy.

There are a number of factors militating against the ACC in executing its mandate. First, the POCA fails to promote the reporting of corruption to the commission by not protecting whistleblowers. In the absence of legal protection, informers may fear reprisals from criminals if they report corruption to the ACC. In addition, the law does not enable the media and the ACC to freely access information in the control of public authorities in absence of a law on freedom of information.

The failure to provide the ACC with enough skilled staff and resources to carry out its functions effectively gives the impression that the commission was set up to fail. With less than ten under-trained investigating officers serving the entire country, Swaziland cannot expect effective prevention of corruption in the public sector. The ACC must be decentralised to other parts of the country and not be confined to the capital, Mbabane. For this to happen, the commission needs financial independence. Funds should be made available by parliament and not be dependent upon government discretion. The commission should be paid from the consolidated fund and be allowed to mobilise for funding from external sources in support of its programmes.

The Swazi criminal justice system suffers a crisis of credibility. The rule of law has long been on the precipice. The country must restore the rule of law to ensure that the legal system and the institutional mechanisms available treat all people in a fair and just manner; that acts of corruption committed by the most powerful and influential people in society must be investigated in a professional manner so that justice is delivered.

The fact that the activities of the ACC can potentially infringe upon human rights underlies the need for strengthening the human rights machinery in Swaziland. If adequate checks and balances are not placed on the ACC, it could become politicised and threaten the foundations of the very rule of law that is being proposed to be protected through the ACC.

F. Recommendations

- Domesticate provisions of international legal instruments. The leadership of the country must publicly demonstrate commitment to regional and international conventions by incorporating these in Swaziland's municipal law;
- Anti-corruption laws and regulations should be enhanced and harmonised, and the Whistleblowers Act and the Witness Protection Act should be enforced;
- The inadequacy of transparency of and accountability can be mitigated if government establishes a freedom of information act. Through this act, the government could improve transparency and accountability ratings by allowing the media and other members of society to obtain information. It will enable the media to act as a government watchdog by highlighting corruption within the public sector by means of objective evidence. The constitution guarantees the freedom to receive and communicate ideas and information without interference as part of the right to freedom of expression. A freedom of information act would operationalise the provisions of the constitution;[31]
- The most effective approach to dealing with corruption is for the state to effectively enforce the constitutional provisions for accountability of public officials and to guarantee participatory democracy. This will encourage the participation of civil society in ensuring accountability and transparency of governance. Good governance is a basic requirement for development in Swaziland;
- The ACC must actively market itself to address the perception that it makes arrests only to embarrass people and settle political scores. This requires that its website be updated and be made user-friendly, and that its offices are decentralised. The ACC must make its report public and accessible without charging a fee. The ACC must be more visible for educational purposes, not only when it carries out arrests;
- A properly capacitated ACC is essential to ensure that it can effectively fulfil its mandate. The ACC should be provided with sufficient and consistent funding to enhance its effective functioning. The ACC should also be allowed to mobilise funding from external sources to support some of its programme initiatives. The ACC needs to build its institutional capacity to ensure that appropriately skilled persons are employed and that skills development is implemented throughout

---

31 Section 24 of the Constitution, 2005.

all its departments. Collaboration with international organisations fighting corruption should also be strengthened;

- The vast backlog of corruption cases and financial crimes within the court system can be addressed through the establishment of a specialised commercial court, manned by dedicated personnel and judges. This would help bring about quicker resolution to corruption-related cases; and

- In every national integrity system, the judiciary represents the last wall of defence against corruption and impunity in the society. However, where confidence in the judiciary is at an all-time low,[32] as is currently the case in Swaziland, it creates a pernicious multiplier effect on the rest of society. Public confidence needs to be restored when corruption cases are heard by the ordinary courts. This can be done through laying down suitable rules and procedures for making judicial appointments, and increasing the number of judges in order to expedite all the pending cases and deal with future workloads.

---

32 In April, 2015 certain judges were arrested and cited for corruption-related charges. The former chief justice had a warrant of arrest issued against him by the ACC. One of the judges is still on suspension while the other has been re-instated on the bench.

11
ZAMBIA

Mr Goodwell Lungu

A. Executive summary

Corruption in Zambia is a widespread problem that ranges from petty, to moderate (electoral, political, administrative), to grand or large-scale corruption. Corruption in Zambia has continued to rise despite some improvements recorded on a number of local and international indices such as the Transparency International Corruption Perception Index (CPI) and the Zambia Bribe Payers Index (ZBPI).

The socio-economic and political context of Zambia's economy performed relatively well within the Southern African Development Community (SADC) region despite the decline in the growth rate in 2015. Diversifying the economy away from dependence on copper and the creation of decent jobs are the two overarching policy goals of the government. Improving accountability and strengthening the fight against corruption is also firmly on the government's agenda.

The state of corruption in Zambia reveals that the overall aggregated bribery index for 2014 calculated from 22 public service institutions was 8.5%. However, when compared to the 16 public institutions covered in the 2012 ZBPI, the overall aggregate bribery index in 2014 was 11.9% and in 2012 it was 9.8%. This means that in 2014 the likelihood of paying a bribe to a public institution worsened from 9.8% in 2012 to 11.9% in 2014.

On the other hand, Transparency International CPIs for the past five years from 2009 to 2014 have been showing slight improvements in the perceived levels of corruption in Zambia. In the 2009 CPI, Zambia had an improved score of 3.0 out of 10 points. In 2014 and 2013, Zambia's score improved again to 3.8. Overall, Zambia has been making steady but slow improvements by an average of 10–20%.

Zambia has a number of civil society organisations (CSOs) that have activities on the prevention and suppression of corruption in the country. Key CSOs include: Transparency International Zambia (TIZ), Caritas Zambia (CZ), the Southern African Centre for Constructive Resolution of Disputes (SACCORD) and the Civil Society for Poverty Reduction (CSPR).

Zambia has signed and ratified the African Union Convention on Preventing and Combatting Corruption, the SADC Protocol Against Corruption, and the United Nations Convention Against Corruption (UNCAC). Zambia has domesticated and made most of these anti-corruption conventions part of its substantive laws. These conventions require that they are domesticated into law.

The 1996 Constitution of Zambia guarantees and pledges the accountability of the state in terms of human rights, adherence to the law and use of resources. In particular the preamble reiterates that the citizens 'resolve to uphold the values of democracy, transparency, accountability and good governance'.[1] In line with the constitution, Zambia has enacted a number of pieces of legislation in compliance with these conventions. The key laws include the Public Interest Disclosure (protection of whistleblowers) Act No. 4 of 2010, the Anti-Corruption Act No. 3 of 2012, the Plea Negotiations and Agreements Act No. 20 of 2010, the National Prosecution Authority Act No. 34 of 2010, the Forfeiture of Proceeds of Criminal Act No. 19 of 2010, and the Financial Intelligence Act of 2010.

The Zambian government has made progress to domesticate or implement most of the anti-corruption instruments that it has signed and ratified. Despite this, their actual implementation and compliance has not been very effective. Adopting these instruments was perhaps more of a political step to appear to be in compliance with international trends.

The Anti-Corruption Commission in Zambia (ACC) was established through the enactment of the Corrupt Practices Act No. 46 of 1980. The ACC is not created under the constitution. The independence of the commission is guaranteed under section 5 of the Anti-Corruption Act No. 3 of 2012 and provides that 'subject to the constitution, the commission shall not, in the performance of its functions, be subject to the direction or control of any person or authority'. Despite this, the executive is on record going against such a provision. For instance on 6 December 2012, the late president Michael Chilufya Sata castigated the ACC for not getting permission from him when investigating senior party officials. He explained that, by law, the commission was supposed to get permission from him to investigate any senior party official.

The head of the ACC – the director general – enjoys security of tenure and is also immune or protected from criminal and civil proceedings for acts committed in the exercise of duty.

The ACC has both a centralised and decentralised system of receiving complaints against corruption. The ACC has made public statements assuring informers of their protection. However, there have been very few instances where informers who have reported cases of corruption to the ACC have not ended up being dismissed from their employment.

As for it funding, in 2013 the ACC confirmed that it could not implement some of its planned training activities due to inadequate funding. It was also confirmed that the ACC lacked the presence at district level necessary for it to enhance its accessibility to the public.[2]

---

1 Constitution of the Republic of Zambia, 1996.
2 Anti-Corruption Commission (2013) Annual Report.

The ACC has performed relatively well over the years. For instance, in the strategic plans for 2009–2013 and 2013–2016, one of the commission's strategic objectives was to increase the number of convictions. A number of arrests have also been recorded over the same period. However, respondents on the effectiveness of the ACC argued that the commission needs to achieve more by increasing its investigation and prosecution capacity.

The financial absorption capacity of the ACC in Zambia is quite high. In 2014 the total national budget provision for funding amounted to USD 7 527 245 and the ACC received USD 7 225 994 – 96% of the budgeted amount. In terms of its absorption capacity, by the end of 2014, it was able to utilise USD 6 592 465 (81.40%). By June 2015, however, the ACC had only received funding amounting to USD 2 271 169 out of the total budget provision of USD 6 664 954, representing only 34.08%. This confirms that the ministry of finance does not release ACC funds in full and not always in time.

This report concludes that Zambia has a strong legal framework for the fight against corruption, though the levels of compliance and enforcement are low. It recommends that the ACC in Zambia should upscale and enhance the levels of compliance and enforcement of all anti-corruption laws and regulations in the country. Many analysts argue that the executive's power to appoint the head of the ACC and its commissioners makes it difficult for the commission to operate independently, despite public pronouncement of political will by President Edgar Lungu. It is strongly proposed that the ACC head and commissioners be appointed by an independent body and only ratified by parliament so that its allegiance is not to the president.

B. Introduction

In Zambia, corruption has continued to be a widespread problem. The problem ranges from petty corruption, often perpetrated as a means for supplementing meagre incomes; through to electoral, political and administrative corruption; to grand or large-scale corruption, which involves diverting and illegally privatising public resources, or funds meant for public programmes and projects. Corruption in Zambia has continued to rise despite some small improvements recorded on a number of local and international indices such as the Transparency International Corruption Perception Index (CPI) and the Zambia Bribe Payers Index (ZBPI).

C. State of corruption in Zambia
Socio-economic and political context

Zambia's economy performed relatively well within the Southern African Development Community (SADC) region despite the decline in growth rate. This decline was largely as a result of lower production in the mining sector compared to the year before, as well as slower growth in manufacturing and public services. Agriculture, on the other hand, grew by over 6%. Economic performance is expected to remain strong in the medium term, driven by large investments in infrastructure and a growing public administration and defence sector.

Diversifying the economy away from dependence on copper and creating decent jobs remain the overarching policy goals of the government. Improving accountability and strengthening the fight against corruption also remain firmly on the government's agenda. In 2014 there was some fiscal consolidation with the deficit falling by about 1% from 2013.[3]

Table 1: Macroeconomic indicators

	2013	2014	2015	2016
Real GDP growth	6.7%	5.7%	6.5%	6.6%
Real GDP per capita growth	3.5%	2.5%	3.3%	3.3%
CPI inflation	7%	7.9%	7.6%	7.6%
Budget balance % GDP	-6.7%	-5.5%	-5.1%	-4.9%
Current account balance % GDP	0.7%	0%	0.6%	0.3%

Source: African Development Bank, Organisation for Economic Co-operation and Development, United Nations Development Programme (2015) African Economic Outlook 2015. p. 290.

Zambia's economy remains strong with growth expected to increase above 6% in 2015/16 after a decline in GDP growth from 6.7% in 2013 to 5.7%, due mainly to waning copper production. Inflation is expected to fall below 7% by 2017. Governance and democratic processes continue to gather strength, with the recent presidential by-elections held on 20 January 2015, reinforcing Zambia's status as a peaceful and stable country. Poverty, at over 60%, remains significant despite strong economic performance along the main transport corridors and reduced poverty in the large urban agglomerations.

These economic disparities have provided a breeding ground for corruption. Some analysts have concluded that many citizens have been held hostage by poverty and, in some instances due to desperation in seeking public services, have opted to engage in bribery.

Analysts and respondents agree that the way out of this quagmire is to marshal citizens to call for accountability among civil servants. It is agreed that popular will, in the absence of political will, would result in an effective and responsive anti-corruption drive, particularly in addressing the issue of imprudent use of public services.

The politics of corruption and money in Zambia

Freedom House broadly refers to Zambia as an electoral democracy with democratic institutions and multiparty elections.[4] While there have been improvements in the conduct

---

3 African Development Bank, Organisation for Economic Co-operation and Development, United Nations Development Programme (2015) African Economic Outlook 2015. p. 290. Available at www.africaneconomicoutlook.org/sites/default/files/content-pdf/AEO2015_EN.pdf [accessed 10 November 2016].
4 Freedom House (2013) Freedom in the world: Zambia. Available at https://freedomhouse.org/report/freedom-world/2013/zambia [accessed 9 November 2016].

of elections since the country's transition to a multiparty state in 1991 (including more transparent procedures for voter registration, counting and tabulation), progress has been uneven. Many analysts and CSOs in Zambia believe that there is too much corruption in the electoral process. Politicians benefit from this and are reluctant to commit to fighting corruption as a result. Recent elections have been characterised by an unfair electoral landscape, sporadic violence and intimidation.[5] The 2011 elections were characterised by massive misuse of public resources by the Movement for Multiparty Democracy (MMD). They were labelled 'free' by international observers, but their fairness has been questioned by others.[6] Seventy percent of 2013 Global Corruption Barometer respondents believe Zambia's political parties to be corrupt.[7]

In early 2002, Levy Mwanawasa was sworn in as the third president of Zambia, amid opposition protests over alleged fraud in the 2001 presidential elections.[8] He has been praised for his anti-corruption commitment and largely been credited with having put the fight against corruption high on Zambia's political agenda. This is reflected by the establishment of a task force on corruption, the design of a corruption prevention strategy, and the reinforcement of anti-corruption institutions.[9] Following Mwanawasa's death in 2008, then vice-president Rupiah Banda assumed power after a narrow election win over the main opposition candidate, Michael Sata. His presidency was characterised by restrictions of civil liberties and a mixed anti-corruption record.[10] Banda stepped down peacefully after a defeat by the opposition party led by Michael Sata in the 2011 presidential elections.[11]

There have been instances of grand corruption, embezzlement and abuse of office involving high-ranking officials under the various presidencies in Zambia. For example, former late president Frederick Jacob Titus Chiluba was found liable for defrauding USD 46 million by a UK civil court, but was later acquitted by a Zambian court. Former president Banda was allegedly involved in corruption relating to an oil procurement contract and there are a number of major new cases involving senior members of the Banda administration.[12] A major health scandal broke out in 2009, leading to the suspension of

---

5 Freedom House (2011) Freedom in the world: Zambia. Available at https://freedomhouse.org/report/freedom-world/2011/zambia [accessed 9 November 2016].
6 Bertelmann Foundation (2014) BTI Country Report 2014: Zambia. Available at https://www.bti-project.org/fileadmin/files/BTI/Downloads/Reports/2014/pdf/BTI_2014_Zambia.pdf [accessed 9 November 2016].
7 Chêne M (2014, 16 April) Transparency International Helpdesk: Overview of corruption and anti-corruption. p. 4.
8 Bertelmann Foundation (2014) BTI Country Report 2014: Zambia. Available at https://www.bti-project.org/fileadmin/files/BTI/Downloads/Reports/2014/pdf/BTI_2014_Zambia.pdf [accessed 9 November 2016].
9 Ryder KE (2011) *Making hay while the Sun shines: Experiences with the Zambian Task Force on corruption.* Bergen: Chr. Michelson Institute.
10 Freedom House (2013) Freedom in the world: Zambia. Available at https://freedomhouse.org/report/freedom-world/2013/zambia [accessed 9 November 2016].
11 Chêne M (2014, 16 April) Transparency International Helpdesk: Overview of corruption and anti-corruption. p. 2.
12 Bertelmann Foundation (2014) BTI Country Report 2014: Zambia. Available at https://www.bti-project.org/fileadmin/files/BTI/Downloads/Reports/2014/pdf/BTI_2014_Zambia.pdf [accessed 9 November 2016].

USD 300 million of funding by the Global Fund to Fight AIDS, Malaria and Tuberculosis as a result of concern about corruption in the ministry of health,[13] but USD 100 million was restored in 2012 after several officials were fired.[14] Sweden also withheld USD 33 million from the ministry of health when USD 5 million went unaccounted for, while the European Union also halted a road-building project.[15] Prosecutions of high-ranking officials are rare and suspected by some critics to be politically motivated.[16]

Banda's anti-corruption commitment is referred to as ambivalent and achieving mixed results. The former president was arrested and prosecuted for abuse of authority of office involving a USD 2.5 million government-to-government oil deal between Zambia and Nigeria. However, in June 2015, the Lusaka magistrate's court largely acquitted Banda of this charge. Banda was, however, charged with one count of abuse of authority of office contrary to section 99(1) of the Penal Code; he responded by saying that the prosecution's evidence was grossly inconsistent, inconclusive and contradictory. He said the prosecution produced documents from the Zambian side but failed to produce any document from the Nigerian side to prove that this was a government-to-government deal. Mr Banda also said that there was no evidence that the he instructed his son, Henry Banda (who has since lived in exile for fear of prosecution), to determine where the proceeds of the oil deal were to be channelled. He said there was no evidence to prove that Henry opened an account under the name Izola where an initial payment of USD 500 000 was paid by SARB energy director, Akpan Ekpene.[17]

The National Anti-Corruption Policy (NACP) was launched in 2009, comprehensive audits of all major ministries and public agencies were ordered by Banda's administration in response to the 2009 health scandal, and whistleblowing legislation was passed by parliament in 2010. At the same time, the government removed the abuse of authority clause in the Anti-Corruption Commission Act No. 42 of 1996, which was an important tool for prosecuting high-level corruption in Zambia; former president Chiluba was acquitted, and the task force on corruption was dismantled in 2010. Upon coming into power, President Sata committed to intensifying the fight against corruption and launched investigations against several former ministers and senior officials. However, in 2012, the ACC opened corruption investigations into former justice minister Wynter Kabimba and defence minister Geoffrey Mwamba, both leading figures of Sata's party. The government reinstated the abuse of office clause in the Anti-Corruption Act No. 3 of 2012.

---

13 BBC (2010, 16 June) Global Fund freezes Zambia aid over corruption concerns. Available at http://www.bbc.com/news/10331717 [accessed 10 November 2016].
14 Freedom House (2013) Freedom in the world: Zambia. Available at https://freedomhouse.org/report/freedom-world/2013/zambia [accessed 9 November 2016].
15 Freedom House (2011) Freedom in the world: Zambia. Available at https://freedomhouse.org/report/freedom-world/2011/zambia [accessed 9 November 2016].
16 Chêne M (2014, 16 April) Transparency International Helpdesk: Overview of corruption and anti-corruption. Bertelmann Foundation (2014) BTI Country Report 2014: Zambia. Available at https://www.bti-project.org/fileadmin/files/BTI/Downloads/Reports/2014/pdf/BTI_2014_Zambia.pdf [accessed 9 November 2016].
17 Mwale C (2015, 14 October) ACC hits back over 'lost' files – at no point has the Commission lost documents, says Moono. *Zambia Daily Mail.* p. 2.

When the new government came into power in 2011, it established a number of commissions of inquiry to investigate alleged misconduct and malpractices against the previous MMD regime. These gave an opportunity to a broad spectrum of society (including ordinary citizens) to present any relevant evidence. However, little progress has been made to date on the recommendations of the commissions' reports, and law enforcement agencies have not acted upon those. For example the Zambian Revenue Authority Commission of Inquiry and the Oil Procurement Commission of Inquiry reports have revealed abuse of office and corrupt practices but little or no action has been taken, leading CSOs such as TIZ to question their effectiveness and purpose.[18]

Currently, there is some debate as to whether Banda's immunity should be restored since one of his cases was disposed of in court. The lesson that Zambia has learnt is that despite strong accusations of corruption against former heads of states, they still survive without being sent to jail. In the case of the late Dr Chiluba, he was also acquitted of his criminal cases and the UK court judgment did not force the money's recovery.

Status of corruption in Zambia

The 2014 ZBPI – conducted and produced jointly by TIZ and the ACC based on citizens experiences – revealed that the overall aggregate bribery index, calculated from 22 public service institutions, is 8.5%. However, when compared to the 16 public institutions covered in the 2012 ZBPI, the overall aggregate bribery index in 2014 was 11.9% and in 2012 it was 9.8%. This means that in 2014 the likelihood of paying a bribe to a public institution worsened from 2012 to 2014.

Figure 1: Overall bribery aggregate index (likelihood to encounter corruption)

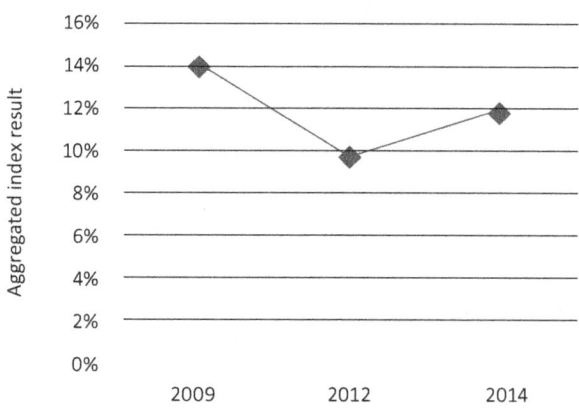

18 Chêne M (2014, 16 April) Transparency International Helpdesk: Overview of corruption and anti-corruption; (TI Zambia 2012) Transparency International Zambia 2012 to 2016 Strategic Plan.

In 2014 the prevalence of bribery considerably worsened. While in 2012, 44.6% respondents paid a bribe, this increased to 57.1% in 2014. This is due, in part, to the increasing trend of paying a bribe when demanded.

The ZBPI survey is a tool for measuring corruption. It seeks to provide empirical evidence of bribery incidences in public institutions, as well as an indication of progress thereof every two years. The sectors that have always been cited as being the most prone to corruption in the past five years have included the police, the road transport and safety agency (RTSA), local authorities, health services and the judiciary. The table below demonstrates all sectors affected by corruption comparatively between 2012 and 2014.

Table 2: Comparison of aggregate bribery indices 2012 and 2014

Name of institution	Aggregate index (%)		Change in %
	2012	2014	
Zambia police	48.30	78.28	-30.0
Local authorities (councils)	7.45	17.50	-10.1
Road traffic & safety agency	14.40	14.72	-0.3
Ministry of education	6.35	13.02	-6.7
Ministry of agriculture and livestock	2.25	10.13	-7.9
Passport office	8.00	8.24	-0.2
Zambia revenue authority	8.90	7.87	1.0
National registration office	12.30	9.11	3.2
Ministry of health	12.40	9.02	3.4
Judiciary (courts)	8.30	7.38	0.9
Immigration department	4.70	4.87	-0.2
Ministry of lands	11.60	6.05	5.5
Zambia Electricity Supply Corporation (ZESCO)	8.35	3.89	4.5
Patents and companies registration agency (PACRA)	0.45	0.55	-0.1
Ministry of works and supply	1.45	0.17	1.3
Zambia Telecommunication (ZAMTEL)	1.10	0.05	1.0
	9.8	**11.9**	**-2.1**

Source: Zambia Bribe Payers Index 2014.

The prevention and suppression of corruption features prominently in political speeches in Zambia. On 18 September 2015, President Edgar Lungu during his official opening of parliament speech reiterated that his government would continue the fight against corruption. In his speech on the official opening of the fifth session of the 110th national assembly, he reaffirmed that he was not going to protect any public officers involved and found wanting in corrupt practices. President Lungu further committed himself not to interfere with ACC operations.[19] Commenting on the president's national assembly speech, TIZ hoped that it would be translated into appropriate, visible and tangible action by civil servants and law enforcement agencies that seemed to have adopted a business-as-usual approach. TIZ indicated in a press statement that it hoped such major pronouncements would result in the closing of all the loopholes which had led to the loss of millions of unaccounted for public funds well documented in a number of reports, including the auditor general's.[20]

The Transparency International CPI from 2009 to 2014 showed slight improvements. In 2009 Zambia's CPI, Zambia had an improved score of 3.0 out of 10 points. In 2012, Transparency International changed the scoring range from the traditional 0 to 10 to a new range of 0 to 100. In 2013 and 2014, Zambia's score remained the same at 38.

Figure 2: Transparency International Corruption Perception Index and trends analysis

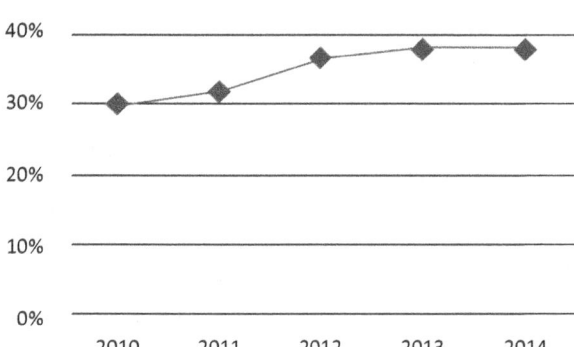

The World Bank corruption control indicators for Zambia show that there has been both a success and a minimal decline. In 2010, the country was rated at 32.85%, which increased to 46.88% in 2012. However, by 2014, it had declined again to 41.34%.[21] The table below illustrates these scores.

---

19 President Edgar Lungu, President of Zambia (2015, 18 September) Speech Delivered to the fifth session of the eleventh national assembly of Zambia.
20 Transparency International Zambia (2015, 21 September) TIZ Welcomes President Lungu's Commitment to Fighting Corruption. Press Statement.
21 World Bank (2015) Worldwide Governance Indicators. Available at http://data.worldbank.org/data-catalog/worldwide-governance-indicators [accessed 27 September 2016].

Figure 3: World Bank, control of corruption indicator, five-year trends analysis

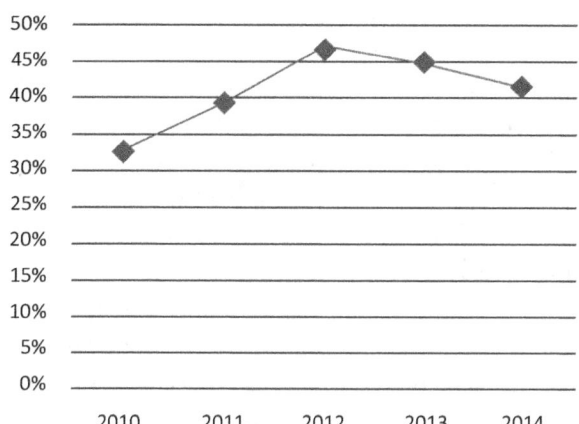

D. Civil society, donors and media engagement

Zambia has a number of key CSOs that have activities related to the prevention and suppression of corruption in the country, including: TIZ, Caritas Zambia (CZ), the Southern African Centre for Constructive Resolution of Disputes (SACCORD) and the Civil Society for Poverty Reduction (CSPR).

TIZ is implementing activities such as procurement monitoring, which is aimed at advocating for the implementation of anti-corruption principles and systems in selected public procurements. TIZ also engages in public contract performance monitoring, which involves empowering and facilitating third party (community) monitoring of contract performance that not only provides accountability but also creates a sense of ownership in the intended beneficiaries. It has developed easy-to-understand materials aimed at empowering citizens to monitor public contract performance. In this project, TIZ trains groups of citizens to monitor public procurement implementation. TIZ is also undertaking public finance monitoring by tracking all actions undertaken by the state in mitigating all reported cases of public finance misuse. It produces a book called *Show Me the Money*, which provides evidence of public financial misuse and ways to prevent it.[22] This book explores how government spends and accounts for public money. The exploration is based on the auditor general's report, which measures a government's accountability record on public expenditure. It is estimated that about USD 29.5 million in public money is misappropriated, stolen or grossly mismanaged every year in Zambia.[23]

---

22 Transparency International Zambia 2012 to 2016 Strategic Plan.
23 Transparency International Zambia (2007) *SHOW ME THE MONEY! How Government Spends and Accounts for Public Money in Zambia.* p. 11.

The media also covers corruption stories prominently. For instance, on 5 October 2015 *The Post* newspaper published a story in which auditor general Anna Chifungula called the ACC inept. In this story, the auditor general (AG) complained that the ACC loses files and closes corruption cases without investigating. She has stated that her office has received a number of letters from the ACC confirming its inability to prosecute cases her office has givien them, owing to documents that they lose or are missing. She adds that her office was getting demoralised as investigative wings were not keen on prosecuting suspicious activity.[24] However, the ACC spokesperson refuted the auditor general's remarks, saying that the 'ACC does not lose documents obtained from the auditor general's office or indeed from any other source'. He added that, after receiving photocopies and during the course of investigations, the ACC approaches the institutions in question to access original documents and that it is the original documents that are found missing. He confirms that it is at this stage that the ACC writes to the AG's office to inform them that the original documents were missing.[25] It is clear that these cases are not resolved.

Zambia launched the NACP in 2009 to harmonise the various anti-corruption efforts by various state and non-state actors. The NACP, which is the first ever comprehensive policy on corruption in Zambia, provides a framework for developing ways and means of preventing and combatting corruption in a comprehensive, coordinated, inclusive and sustainable manner. It acknowledges that corruption is a complex crosscutting problem that requires a multi-faceted approach. The policy provides for the participation and involvement of all sectors, institutions and individuals in tackling corruption. The policy identifies the institutionalisation of integrity programmes, in both public and private institutions, through the establishment of integrity committees as an effective implementable strategy to enhance good governance. It identifies and provides for the need to coordinate and harmonise the various good governance reforms and programmes, as well as providing for the re-orientation and strengthening of governance institutions. The NACP Implementation Plan actuates the legal, institutional and social measures as envisaged by the policy.

E. Legal framework

Commitment to international conventions

Zambia signed the African Union Convention on Preventing and Combatting Corruption on 3 August 2005, ratified it on 30 March 2007 and deposited the signature of ratification on 26 April 2007. With regard to the SADC Protocol Against Corruption, Zambia signed it on 14 August 2001 and ratified it on 8 July 2003. Zambia signed the United Nations

---

24 Mwanza T (2015, 6 October) ACC Inept ... they lose files, close corruption cases without investigating – Chifungula. *The Post* newspaper. pp. 1 & 3.
25 Mwale C (2015, 14 October) ACC hits back over 'lost' files – at no point has the Commission lost documents, says Moono. *Zambia Daily Mail*. p. 2.

Convention Against Corruption (UNCAC) on 11 December 2003 and ratified it about four years later on 7 December, 2007.

Domestication of international conventions

Zambia has domesticated and made most of these anti-corruption conventions part of its substantive laws. It has also enacted a number of additional pieces of legislation in compliance with these conventions. The key laws include the following;
- Public Interest Disclosure (protection of whistleblowers) Act No. 4 of 2010;
- The Anti-Corruption Act No. 3 of 2012;
- The Plea Negotiations and Agreements Act No. 20 of 2010;
- The National Prosecution Authority Act No. 34 of 2010;
- The Forfeiture of Proceeds of Criminal Act No. 19 of 2010; and
- The Financial Intelligence Act of 2010.

These laws are what form part of the strong legal framework in fighting corruption in Zambia.

The government communicates the ratification of international instruments when these are done. Other players such as CSOs also highlight such progress when making public speeches. The UN and AU anti-corruption conventions have mechanisms for reviewing how far the government has implemented them; the SADC protocol does not.

Under the AU, there is the Africa Peer Review Mechanism (APRM) to which Zambia belongs, which is similar to the UNCAC (though the APRM is voluntary). Zambia is currently in the process of implementing its national programme of action under the APRM. The governance department under the ministry of justice forms the secretariat of the APRM process in Zambia.

The Zambian UNCAC review process was undertaken in 2011. TIZ was part of the team that was invited by government to prepare the required compliance self-assessment in a workshop held from 20 to 25 March 2011. However, as at the time of publication, the self-assessment report had not yet been published by the government.

In Zambia, there is no clearly stated mechanism on how the implementation of international conventions is supposed to be reported to the public. This is only done when there are local and international events such as the annual United Nations Anti-Corruption Day, where government officials update the country on how some articles in the UNCAC have been domesticated into local legislation.

Despite Zambia signing, ratifying, and domesticating most international instruments on corruption, their actual implementation and record of compliance has not been very impressive. It is apparently only important to be seen to be up-to-date with international trends. One key indicator is that, in the past three years, there have been well documented cases of financial scandals reported in the 2012 auditor general's report, without any follow up action. The table below clearly demonstrates that there has been abuse of office and of public resources under the 2012 anti-corruption act; however, so far only one person has been convicted under this clause despite the numerous reported abuses in the auditor general's report of 2012.[26]

In Zambia, there is no clearly stated mechanism on how the implementation of international conventions is supposed to be reported to the public. This is only done when there are local and international events such as the annual United Nations Anti-Corruption Day, where government officials update the country on how some articles in the UNCAC have been domesticated into local legislation.

Table 3: Abuse of office and public funds

Finding	Constituency development funds K	Grants to local authorities K	Total K
Misapplication of funds	662 501 095	2 735 524 080	3 398 025 175
Misappropriation	69 607 070	-	69 607 070
Irregular payments	10 012 678 075	393 991 740	10 406 669 815
Unaccounted for stores	870 741 278	191 647 284	1 062 388 562
Unaccounted for funds	267 700 000	191 647 284	459 347 284
Failure to follow tender guidelines	8 242 102 460	-	8 242 102 460
Fraudulent payment	-	16 340 996	16 340 996
Overpayment to suppliers	767 885 450	-	767 885 450

1996 Constitution of Zambia

The preamble to the constitution guarantees and pledges the accountability of the state in terms of human rights, adherence to the law and use of resources. In particular, it mandates that the citizens 'resolve to uphold the values of democracy, transparency, accountability and good governance'.[27] The constitution also establishes state institutions such as the auditor general's office, which is charged with the responsibility of promoting accountability. However, the ACC itself is not a creation of the constitution but a parliamentary piece of legislation. The 2015 draft constitution provides for the establishment of the ACC to be enshrined within the constitution.

Pending access to information bill

Zambia has no access to information law to guarantee the public's access to administrative information; it is generally agreed that such a law is necessary for greater corruption control. In February 2015, information minister Chishimba Kambwili promised that the

---

26   2012 Auditor General's Report for Zambia.
27   Constitution of the Republic of Zambia, 1996.

draft access to information bill would be presented to parliament soon.[28] As at the end of August 2015, the bill had not yet been presented to parliament. Citizens bemoan the delay as they believe that it is an important tool that can help hold civil servants and leadership accountable with a view to greater corruption prevention.

Anti-Corruption Act No. 3 of 2012

Zambia has a specific anti-corruption law called the Anti-Corruption Act No. 3 of 2012 that replaced the ACC Act No. 38 of 2010. This act has undergone several previous amendments and repeals. It was first enacted in 1980 under an act of parliament, the Corrupt Practices Act No. 14. This act has, over the years, been reviewed in a bid to strengthen the anti-corruption legislation. The main purpose of the act is to enable the ACC to professionally execute its mandate through the investigation and prosecution of suspected offenders, establish corruption prevention mechanisms, mobilise support and to enlighten the citizenry of Zambia through community education programmes.

Under section 6(1), the mandate of the ACC in general is to combat corruption in Zambia and:

a) Prevent and take necessary and effective measures for the prevention of corruption in public and private bodies …;

b) Initiate, receive and investigate complaints of alleged or suspected corrupt practices, and, subject to the directions of the director of public prosecutions, prosecute …;

c) Investigate any conduct of any public officer which, the commission has reasonable grounds to believe may be connected with, or conducive to, corrupt practices;

d) Be the lead agency in matters of corruption;

e) Co-ordinate or co-operate, as applicable, with other institutions authorised to investigate, prosecute, prevent and combat corrupt practices so as to implement an integrated approach to the eradication of corruption;

f) Consult, co-operate and exchange information with appropriate bodies of other countries that are authorised to conduct inquiries or investigations in relation to corrupt practices; and

g) Adopt and strengthen mechanisms for educating the public to respect the public good and public interest …

On its visibility in public contracts, the law provides for taking preventive, investigative and prosecutorial measures against public officers involved in corrupt practices in public procurement. Section 29 prohibits:

---

28 Kambwili promises table access information bill (2015, 12 February) *Lusaka times*. Available at https://www.lusakatimes.com/2015/02/12/kambwili-promises-table-access-information-bill/ [accessed 27 September 2016].

1. A public officer who, directly or indirectly, by oneself, or by, or in conjunction with, any other person, corruptly solicits, accepts or obtains, or agrees to accept or attempts to receive or obtain, from any person for oneself or for any other person, any gratification as an inducement or reward for or otherwise on account of, that public officer giving assistance or using influence in, or having given assistance or used influence in—
   a) The promotion, execution or procurement of any contract with a public body or private body for the performance of any work, the provision of any service, the doing of anything or the supplying of any article, material or substance.

Section 28 defines conflict of interest thus:

1. Where a public body in which a public officer is a member, director, employee or is otherwise engaged proposes to deal with any person or company, partnership or other undertaking in which that public officer has a direct or indirect private or personal interest, that public officer shall forthwith disclose, in writing to that public body, the nature of such interest and shall not take part in any proceedings or process of that public body relating to such decision.
2. Where a public officer or a relative or associate of such public officer has a personal interest in a decision to be taken by a public body, that public officer shall forthwith disclose, in writing to that public body, the nature of such interest and shall not vote or take part in any proceedings or process of that public body relating to such decision.
3. A public officer who contravenes subsection (1) or (2) commits an offence.

The aforementioned international instruments have been domesticated and are part of the Anti-Corruption Act No. 3 of 2012. In its preamble, the act recognises all such conventions and protocols. It recognises that its aim is to:

Provide for the domestication of the United Nations Convention Against Corruption, the African Union Convention on Preventing and Combatting Corruption, the Southern African Development Community Protocol Against Corruption and other regional and international instruments on corruption to which Zambia is a party.

On matters relating to electoral corruption, the Anti-Corruption Act under section 35(1) provides that:

1. The commission has jurisdiction to investigate and prosecute any offence of bribery prescribed under section seventy nine of the Electoral Act, 2006.

2. A person who uses any funds acquired through illegal or corrupt practices to fund a political party or for any purpose related to an election commits an offence.

However, from the time Zambia started holding competitive elections in 1991, the commission has not successfully prosecuted or investigated any person under this section despite having been present in its acts of parliament.

A limitation of the act is that it does not state that the ACC has a direct, specific mandate to investigate, prevent or combat cases of corruption in the extractive industries in Zambia. However, the ACC has a broad mandate to prevent and take necessary and effective measures for the prevention of corruption in public and private bodies. Since most extractive industries in Zambia are privately owned, this section mandates the ACC to take the aforementioned measures. Additionally, under section 20, the ACC is mandated to investigate and prosecute corrupt transactions by or with private bodies. The act also mandates the commission to 'do all such things as are incidental or conducive to the attainment of its functions'.

With regards to cheating in examinations and competitions, the ACC in Zambia carries out both awareness and monitoring exercises during examinations, with a view to reducing malpractices.

Public Interest Disclosure Act No. 4 of 2010

This act provides for the disclosure of conduct adverse to the public interest in the public and private sectors. The act provides for a framework within which public interest disclosures can be independently and rigorously dealt with. It also provides for procedures for employees in both the private and the public sectors to disclose information regarding unlawful or irregular conduct. The act provides a framework within which persons who make public interest disclosures (whistleblowers) are be protected. One key weakness of this act is that it is mostly preoccupied with protecting those in formal employment and not ordinary citizens. It does not, for instance, explain how ordinary citizens who are informers and journalists can get protection under this law. The law has also not been fully tested in Zambia, as the guidelines on how this law can work have not been made public.

Prohibition and Prevention of Money Laundering (amendment) Act No. 44 of 2010

Besides providing for the prohibition and prevention of money laundering, this act also provides for the constitution of an anti-money laundering authority and an anti-money laundering investigations unit. The law provides for the disclosure of suspicions of money laundering activities by supervisory authorities and regulated institutions. It also provides for the seizure of property related to money laundering, as well as for international cooperation in investigations, prosecution and other legal processes for prohibiting and preventing money laundering. An anti-money laundering authority has not yet been created; but, the law has been implemented by the Drug Enforcement Commission's anti-money laundering unit.

Bank of Zambia Anti-Money Laundering Directives of 2004

The Bank of Zambia directives require, under section 6, that 'a regulated institution shall put in place such anti-money laundering measures and adopt such practices as are necessary for the detection and prevention of money laundering as set out in the directives'.[29] These directives involve scrutinising all commercial banks and financial institutions, clients and transactions with a view to detecting and reporting money laundering.

2009 National Anti-Corruption Policy (NACP) and Implementation Plan

The NACP and Implementation Plan embodies the key elements of corruption prevention internationally identified as including:
- Regulating official discretion;
- Reducing procedural complexity;
- Increasing transparency in the allocation of public resources;
- Motivating employees and creating positive incentives;
- Results- and facts-based management;
- Internal reporting procedures;
- Eliminating conflicts of interest; and
- Disclosing assets.

Accordingly, the plan chiefly involves:[30]

a) Legal review to strengthen anti-corruption legislation;
b) Increasing transparency and accountability in the public service;
c) Reducing opportunities for corruption at points of delivery of public goods and services to the general public through reducing complexities in public service delivery, and decongesting points of service delivery;
d) Capacity building in anti-corruption; and,
e) Social mobilisation against corruption.

Evaluation

A 2015 evaluation of the implementation of the NACP by TIZ shows some key successes: the establishment of integrity committees (ICs); and the procurement reforms culminating in the enactment of legislation and the implementation of the treasury single account (TSA). The TSA is aimed at enhancing cash management and has so far been rolled out at the ministry of finance. The results of the evaluation reveal that, among the institutions

---

29 The Bank of Zambia Anti-Money Laundering Directives of 2004
30 National Anti-Corruption Implementation Plan. Zambia, 2009.

interviewed, 55% stated that they engaged in public sensitisation, employing approaches such as workshops, seminars and media productions (both print and electronic). Out of all the efforts to involve the public, 46% were partially successful while 29% had no success. The study also reveals that there is not enough emphasis on citizen participation in fighting corruption, rather, emphasis has been placed on improving systems in institutions. In addition, the harmonisation of implementation by ministries, departments and agencies (MDAs) and non-governmental organisations (NGOs) was rated to have been unsatisfactory. The positive effects of the NACP cited by respondents were a slight improvement in institutional co-ordination, the harmonisation of the laws on corruption, the enactment of some new laws and the establishment of 46 ICs. ICs are created in institutions to act as corruption-prevention focal points. The purpose of their creation was to mainstream corruption prevention in the routine business of government agencies and the private sector. They were said to be at either average or below average levels of success. The existence of active ICs would ensure the implementation of NACP activities within institutions.

It was apparent from the general lack of knowledge about the NACP among respondents that citizen sensitisation and participation were still at very low levels and needed urgent attention.

Furthermore, the policy is facing an ownership crisis in that most implementing institutions do not feel that they own it. Ownership (and the burden of implementation) seems to fall heavily on the ACC. Unfortunately, positioning the ACC to oversee policy implementation does not give it adequate leverage to ensure compliance by other institutions. For example, the ACC has neither the mandate, access nor capacity to ensure that all planned NACP activities under the strategic plans of implementing institutions are guaranteed funding.[31]

F. Anti-corruption commission in Zambia

Historical development and stability of the agency

A previously stated, the ACC was established through the enactment of the Corrupt Practices Act No. 46 of 1980. Prior to 1980, cases of corruption were handled by the police. This act was later repealed by the Anti-Corruption Commission Act No. 42 of 1996, which, among other things, gave operational autonomy to the ACC in order to safeguard it from the influence of the executive.

Independence and political will

The Anti-Corruption Act No. 3 of 2012 provides that 'subject to the constitution, the commission shall not, in the performance of its functions, be subject to the direction or

---

31 Transparency International Zambia (2015) Evaluation of the National Anti-corruption Policy. pp. 5–7.

control of any person or authority'. The preceding Anti-Corruption Act No. 42 of 1996 had the same provision.

Despite this, the executive is on record going against such a provision. For instance, on 6 December 2012, the late Michael Sata castigated the ACC for not getting permission from him when investigating senior party officials. He explained that, by law, the commission was supposed to get permission from him to investigate any senior party official. Mr Sata wondered why the commission was not approaching him to get permission to investigate senior party officials when the law was clear.[32] This is in contrast with the act's aforementioned guarantee of independence.

The question of the commission's independence is highly contested. The ACC has continued to receive public criticism that it is not independent as its chief executive officer and commissioners are appointed by the president. Some citizens contend that, in its current state, the commission cannot be completely independent as the appointing authorities may exert some form of influence on its operations. It is strongly proposed that the ACC head and commissioners should be appointed by an independent body and only ratified by parliament so that its allegiance is not to the president. Most analysts also agree that the ACC's effectiveness would be bolstered by popularising public will and not political will in the fight against corruption.

The commission also relies on government funding for its operations like any other government MDA. Although this is a standard practice globally, it has the inherent risk of the commission's operations being deliberately or poorly funded, and its independence compromised.

Section 4 of the anti-corruption act guarantees its continued existence:

> The Anti-Corruption Commission continued under the repealed act shall continue to exist as if established under this act, and shall be a body corporate with perpetual succession and a common seal, capable of suing and of being sued in its corporate name and with power, subject to this act, to do all such acts and things as a body corporate may, by law, do or perform.

The legal basis on which the commission was established has evolved over time; it has after all been in existence for the past 34 years and is one of the oldest in Africa. There have been major enhancements in terms of expanding the mandate of the ACC since the original act. In 1996 for instance, the anti-corruption law enhanced the mandate of the commission to investigate and prosecute cases of public procurements. Under this law, procurement fraud was criminalised and the mandate was given to the ACC to both investigate and prosecute such offences. In addition, the 2010 and 2012 anti-corruption laws were enhanced further

---

32 President Sata castigates ACC for not seeking permission from him to investigate senior party officials (2012, 6 December) *Lusaka Times*. Available at https://www.lusakatimes.com/2012/12/06/president-sata-castigates-acc-seeking-permission-investigate-senior-party-officials/ [accessed 27 September 2016].

to criminalise acts of corruption in the electoral process under section 35, and acts of corruption in sporting events under section 27.

The 2012 act also expanded the mandate of the ACC to include under section 20 'corrupt transactions by, or with, private bodies' and in section 24, 'corruption of members of public or private bodies with regard to meetings'. These sections mandate the ACC to not only investigate and prosecute cases of corruption in the public sector but also in private bodies. The participation of citizens in the fight against corruption was also guaranteed under the 2010 and 2012 acts under section 81, which has never been the case previously. Section 81 confirms that 'the commission shall ensure that public participation in the prevention and eradication of corruption is undertaken'.

The ACC has continued implement and enforce its mandate since it was established in 1980. Table 4 shows its budget allocations over the years. Table 5 shows the expenditure patterns against the budgets. The overall impression of the budget allocation shows that it has been fluctuating, mainly due to the fact that the allocations are dependent on the overall amounts of funds available each year.

Table 4: ACC 2011 to 2015 annual budgets

Year	Amount
2011	USD 4 730 979
2012	USD 5 098 512
2013	USD 4 983 120
2014	USD 7 105 073
2015	USD 6 773 223

Table 5: ACC 2013 to June 2015 income and expenditure summary statement

Year	Budget amount	Supplementary	Other income/ donors	Amount released by 31 December	Expenditure by 31 December
2013	USD 4 547 772	USD 684 958	USD 1,245,020	USD 5 436 654	USD 5 604 917
2014	USD 7 527 245			USD 7 225 994	USD 6 592 465
				Amount released by 30th June 2015	Expenditure as at 30th June 2015
2015	USD 6 664 964		USD 438 861	USD 2 271 169	USD 3 462 333

Source: Finance ministry website.

Agency staff

The head of the ACC is the director general who is appointed under section 9 of the anti-corruption act. The entire commission staff contingent stood at 341 at the end of 2014.

However, only 322 officers were in post by end of the year and this implied that there were 19 vacancies and these were as a result of resignations, redundancies and retirements.

On appointment of the head of the ACC, section 9 stipulates that:

> (1) There shall be a director general of the commission who shall be the chief executive officer of the commission.
> (2) The director general shall be appointed by the president, subject to ratification by the national assembly, on such terms and conditions as the president may determine.

The ACC has a five-member governing council that is provided for under the anti-corruption act schedule. Section 2 of this schedule stipulates that:

> (1) There is hereby constituted a board of commissioners which shall be the governing body of the commission.
> (2) The board shall consist of the following commissioners:
> a) The chairperson, who shall be a person who has held, or is qualified to hold, high judicial office;
> b) The vice-chairperson; and
> c) Three other persons.
> (3) The commissioners shall be appointed by the president, subject to ratification by the national assembly.

The section 12(1) further confirms that 'the commission shall appoint a deputy director general on such terms and conditions as it may determine'. For other senior officials these are appointed under section 13 which provides that:

> The commission may appoint directors, the secretary, investigating officers, and such other staff of the commission, on such terms and conditions as it may determine, to assist the director general in the performance of the director general's functions under this act.

Recruitment

In terms of eligibility and qualifications of members of the commission, these are determined and prescribed by law through the anti-corruption act. The profiles and criteria, and duration of tenure are fixed and clearly set. On these matters, section 2 of the schedule states that:

> 1. The commissioners shall be appointed by the president, subject to ratification by the national assembly.
> 2. A person is eligible to be appointed as a commissioner if that person —

a) Is a citizen of Zambia;
b) Is permanently resident in Zambia;
c) Is of high integrity; and
d) Has served with distinction at a senior level in a government office or a registered profession or vocation.
3. A person shall not be appointed as a commissioner if that person —
a) Holds office in, or is an employee of, any political party; or
b) Has been convicted of an offence involving fraud or dishonesty, or any other offence under this act or any other written law and sentenced therefore to a term of imprisonment of six months or more without the option of a fine.

As well as in section 3:

1. A commissioner shall, subject to the other provisions of this schedule, hold office for a period of three years and may be appointed for a further period of three years: provided that a commissioner shall only hold office for two terms.
2. A commissioner may resign upon giving one month's notice, in writing, to the president.
3. The office of a commissioner shall become vacant —
a) If the commissioner is absent, without reasonable excuse, from three consecutive meetings of the commission of which the commissioner has had notice;
b) If the commissioner is adjudged bankrupt;
c) If the commissioner is convicted of an offence under this act or any other written law and sentenced therefore to imprisonment for a term of six months or more, without the option of a fine;
d) If the commissioner is declared to be of unsound mind; or
e) Upon the commissioner's death.

Security of tenure
The director general of the ACC enjoys security of tenure, and is protected from criminal and civil proceedings for acts committed in the exercise of her duties. Section 17 of the anti-corruption act guarantees this immunity as it states that:
1. No proceedings, civil or criminal, shall lie against the director general, deputy director general, directors, secretary, an officer or member of staff of the commission for anything done in good faith in the exercise of the officer's or member of staff's functions under this act.
2. Subject to the provisions of this act, the director general, deputy director general, an officer or member of staff of the commission shall not be called

to give evidence before any court or tribunal in respect of anything coming to such person's knowledge in the exercise of such person's functions under this act.

Section 10 of schedule of the anti-corruption act also extends the immunity protection to members of the commission. This section states:

An action or other proceeding shall not lie or be instituted against a commissioner or a member of a committee of the commission for, or in respect of, any act or thing done or omitted to be done in good faith in the exercise of or performance, or purported exercise or performance of any of the powers, functions or duties conferred under this act.

This section also stipulates the procedure for removing the director general and protects their security of tenure:

1. Subject to subsection (2), a person appointed director general shall vacate that office on attaining the age of sixty-five years: provided that the president may permit a person who has attained that age to continue in office for such period as may be necessary to enable that person to do anything in relation to proceedings that were commenced before the person attained that age.
2. A person appointed director general may be removed from office for inability to perform the functions of office, whether arising from infirmity of body or mind or from any other cause, or for misconduct, and shall not be removed except by, or in accordance with, a resolution passed by the national assembly pursuant to subsection (3).
3. If the national assembly, by resolution supported by a simple majority, resolves that the question of removing the director general ought to be investigated, the speaker of the national assembly shall send a copy of such resolution to the chief justice who shall appoint a tribunal consisting of a chairperson and two other persons to inquire into the matter.
4. The chairperson and one other member of the tribunal shall be persons who hold or have held high judicial office.
5. The tribunal shall inquire into the matter and send a report on the facts of that matter to the president and a copy to the national assembly.
6. Where a tribunal appointed under subsection (3) advises the president that the director general ought to be removed from office for inability as aforesaid or for misconduct, the president shall remove the director general from office.
7. If the question of removing the director general from office has been referred to a tribunal under subsection (2), the president may suspend

the director general from performing the functions of office, and any such suspension shall cease to have effect if the tribunal advises the president that the director general ought to be removed from office.
8. The director general may resign by giving three months' notice, in writing, to the president, of the director general's intention to resign.

In case of this procedure being followed to remove the director general, the law provides that the deputy director general ought to be appointed to act as director general. This is supported by section 12:

4. If the office of the director general is vacant or the director general is absent from duty or unable for any other reason to perform the functions of that office, the deputy director general shall, save where the commission otherwise directs, act as director general.
5. If both the director general and the deputy director general are absent from office or unable for any other reason to perform the functions of their offices, the president shall appoint another person to act as director general.

Most anti-corruption activists agree that such a lengthy procedure helps to protect the security of tenure of the director general and constitutional office holders in Zambia.

The ACC has the authority to recruit both its technical and support officers. Their authority is enshrined in section 13:

The commission may appoint directors, the secretary, investigating officers, and such other staff of the commission, on such terms and conditions as it may determine, to assist the director general in the performance of the director general's functions under this act.

This is a practice that the ACC has been implementing since its establishment in the 1980s. The ACC recruits its staff according to its needs, free of any interference from the executive or legislature. The commission normally runs public advertisements in print media for recruitment of its staff.

However, the ACC seeks approval from the ministry of finance before recruiting. This is argued to be a public service procedure to guarantee the required funding. The ACC also gets approval from cabinet for any expansion in its staff structure. These two aspects may be the only restricting factors on the ACC's recruiting procedures.

The termination procedures for ACC officers are quite clear and transparent. The anti-corruption act states that such reasons need to be communicated to any affected officer. Under section 13:

4. The director general may, if satisfied that it is in the best interest of the commission, terminate the appointment of any officer of the commission and shall assign the reasons therefore, subject to any directions by the commission.
5. A person aggrieved with the decision of the director general to terminate that person's employment pursuant to subsection (3) may appeal against that decision to the board. This is a very rare procedure in making the reasons for employment termination mandatory and known as other organisations withholds such information in Zambia.

Ethics, conduct, capacity and remuneration

Members of staff are required to adhere to the commission's code of ethics including adherence to the provisions of the 2012 act which provides regulations for conflicts of interest. The ACC code of ethics is enforced through the ACC disciplinary code, which provides a wide range of measures to deal with abrogation of the code of conduct by staff.

Imposition of these regulations, particularly the code of ethics, creates problems of acceptance and non-adherence among staff. Members of staff need to believe in the ethical core values on an individual level.

Commission staff do benefit from specialised training in the prevention and combatting of corruption. A training plan exists in the commission that gives guidance on staff training needs. Resources are often set aside to meet such training requirements. The commission is responsible for nominating staff to attend training and the selection criteria are transparent. In addition, training is often specific or tailored to meet specific skills deficiencies among staff.

Although the salaries of commission staff are comparatively better than in mainstream government ministries, they are not adequate to attract the most highly qualified workers. Highly qualified workers are retained and resist corruption ostensibly because of their belief in the anti-corruption ideals of the commission.

Investigative and prosecutorial powers and responsibilities

The ACC has a clearly defined mandate in terms of prevention, prosecution, sensitisation, and education of the public in the fight against corruption. This mandate is elaborated on in section 6 of the act. In this section, the mandate and functions of the ACC are as follows:

1. The mandate of the Anti-Corruption Commission in general is to combat corruption in Zambia and among its key functions are to —
    a) Prevent and take necessary and effective measures for the prevention of corruption in public and private bodies ...;
    b) Initiate, receive and investigate complaints of alleged or suspected corrupt practices ...;

c) Investigate any conduct of any public officer which, the commission has reasonable grounds to believe may be connected with, or conducive to, corrupt practices;
d) Be the lead agency in matters of corruption;
e) Co-ordinate or co-operate, as applicable, with other institutions authorised to investigate, prosecute, prevent and combat corrupt practices so as to implement an integrated approach to the eradication of corruption;
f) Consult, co-operate and exchange information with appropriate bodies of other countries that are authorised to conduct inquiries or investigations in relation to corrupt practices; and
g) Adopt and strengthen mechanisms for educating the public to respect the public good and public interest and, in particular.

The commission has a clear mandate in terms of reporting cases of corruption, as stated above. The ACC has toll-free lines and email addresses and encourages citizens to walk in to report cases of corruption at their various offices around Zambia. In 2014, the ACC received 2 080 cases, of which 703 contained elements of corruption, which was an improvement on the 1 987 in 2013. Out of these complaints received only 724 were assessed to be related to corruption. The 2013 annual report demonstrates that the ACC has a clear mandate in terms of reporting cases of corruption. In 2013, the ACC Annual Report further confirmed that 62% of the reports the ACC receives are submitted in person by complainants, 22% through letters while the rest are received by email or fax, and 5.7% are generated by the ACC itself after assessing information that comes to its attention.[33] The target of the ACC is to process the reports it receives within 48 hours.

Public feedback mechanisms and witness protection

The ACC has both a centralised and decentralised system of receiving complaints against corruption. As at end of August 2015, the commission had offices in nine out of ten provinces of Zambia, which were also mandated to receive complaints of corruption. The ACC has made public statements assuring informers of their protection.

However, there have been a few instances where informers have ended up being dismissed from their employment. On 10 September 2015, the *Daily Nation* newspaper reported that two dismissed workers of First Quantum Minerals (FQM) had given the ACC a five-day ultimatum to compensate them following their dismissal as a result of ACC officers leaking information to the FQM. The article alleged that an ACC investigation report had confirmed that the ACC officers deliberately exposed the two informers.[34]

---

33 Anti-Corruption Commission (2013) *Annual Report*. p. 6.
34 ACC boss faces court action (2015, 10 September2015) *Daily Nation*. Available at http://zambiadailynation.com/2015/09/10/acc-boss-faces-court-action/ [accessed 27 September 2016].

EFFECTIVENESS OF ANTI-CORRUPTION AGENCIES IN SOUTHERN AFRICA

The ACC has developed a feedback channel for its informers. In 2013, the ACC reported that, out of the total number of complaints received, it responded to 75.7%, giving feedback within five days, up from 42.8% in 2011.[35]

The commission has a clear mandate to investigate, prosecute and bring civil suits in its own right on cases of corruption, but it has no stipulated deadlines for case completion.

An assessment of ACC targets set under its 2012–2016 strategic is shown in Table 6.

Table 6: Analysis of performance targets against results

Performance indicator target	Results reported in 2013 annual report
80% of complainants informed of the action taken within seven days.	Out of the total number responded to, 75.7% were given feedback within five days.
50% of full scale investigations conducted and concluded within 12 months.	399 cases authorised, 56% completed.
70% of complaints received and processed within 48 hours.	The ACC processed 54.8% of the complaints they received within 48 hours.

The ACC has a positive working relationship with parliament. It has held joint meetings with the African Parliamentary Network Against Corruption. From time to time, the ACC is invited to make submissions to parliament on all presidential constitutional appointments to determine such candidates' suitability before parliamentary committees. The ACC also makes regular parliamentary submissions on all governance and anti-corruption legislation that has a bearing on the fight against corruption in Zambia.

The commission has a good working relationship with the Zambia Police Service despite the strong perception from police officers that the commission largely targets them in its investigations and prosecutions. This is evidenced by the large number of officers investigated by the ACC being arrested for corruption. In 2013, the ACC received 78.9% of the complaints against police officers under the ministry of home affairs category.[36]

The commission has a cordial working relationship with the director of public prosecutions. It is obliged under the act to get consent from the director to prosecute cases of corruption.

In terms of the ACC's working relationship with the auditor general, there is a strong public perception that the two institutions do not collaborate and achieve the same results. This emanates from public comments from the auditor general, who has made public statements to the effect that law enforcement agencies were not helping to curb the financial mismanagement that her office routinely reports in its annual audit reports. For instance, on 25 July 2015, auditor general Dr Anna Chifungula said 'the challenges we are facing in audits is that when audit queries are raised in the auditor general's report

---

35 Anti-Corruption Commission (2013) *Annual Report*. p. 7.
36 Anti-Corruption Commission (2013) *Annual Report*.

no action is taken to show that misuse of public resources should not be condoned'.[37] Similarly, on 13 December 2011, Chifungula called on government to start prosecuting officers who misappropriated government funds. She regretted that action was not taken on culprits cited in her reports.[38] In October 2015, she castigated the ACC for being inept and ineffective in taking action on the basis of her reports. Her statements clearly show there is a disconnection between her expectations of the ACC to take action on the misappropriation of public funds and their understanding of their mandate. Her views are shared by many civil society organisations in Zambia.

On 9 May 2014, TIZ observed that there was no political will in dealing with the auditor general's report. TIZ executive director Goodwell Lungu noted that no one appeared to prepared to take responsibility for taking action against those found wanting. He said most of the issues start with controlling officers who exhibit lack of control, hence the TIZ's expectation that the president dismiss them immediately to pave the way for investigations.[39]

TIZ has always expressed concern with the ACC's slow pace of investigations into allegations of misappropriation of public funds. For instance, during a media briefing on 8 January 2014, ACC spokesperson Timothy Moono disclosed that of the 62 cases cited in the 2011 auditor general's report, only 47 cases have been investigated, with just three cases concluded and closed in 2014. Lungu wonders how the ACC could have only concluded and closed three cases out of the many the auditor general draws to their attention in her reports; he stated that it borders on public-funds abuse, adding that it allows the culprits to continue misappropriating public funds because the ACC may not catch up with them in time.[40]

The commission's mandate also covers the private sector. Sections 20 and 24 of the anti-corruption act mandate the commission to investigate, prosecute and even go to the extent of seizing property suspected of being the proceeds of crime. Section 20 outlines that:

> A person who, by oneself, or by, or in conjunction with, any other person, corruptly solicits, accepts or obtains, or agrees to accept or attempts to receive or obtain, from any person for oneself or for any other person, any gratification as an inducement or reward for doing or forbearing to do, or for and having

---

37 Chifungula calls for stiffer action on her AG reports (2015, 25 July) *Lusaka Times*. Available https://www.lusakatimes.com/2015/07/25/chifungula-calls-for-stiffer-action-on-her-a-g-reports/ [accessed 27 September 2016].
38 Auditor General asks Government to prosecute people cited in the report (2011, 13 December). *Lusaka Times*. Available at https://www.lusakatimes.com/2011/12/13/auditor-general-asks-government-prosecute-people-cited-report/ [accessed 27 September 2016].
39 TIZ questions political will to punish people named in auditor general's report (2014, 9 May) *Lusaka Times*. Available at https://www.lusakatimes.com/2014/05/09/tiz-questions-political-will-punish-people-named-auditor-generals-report/ [accessed 27 September 2016].
40 ACC is too slow says Transparency International Zambia (2014, 9 January) *Mwebantu*. Available at http://www.mwebantu.com/2014/01/09/acc-is-too-slow-says-transparency-international-zambia/ [accessed 27 September 2016].

done or forborne to do, anything in relation to any matter or transaction actual or proposed, with which any private body is or may be concerned, commits an offence.

This clearly shows that the commission has jurisdiction in the private sector. This is reinforced in section 24(1), which says:

A person who being a member of any public or private body by oneself, or by, or in conjunction with, any other person, corruptly solicits, accepts or obtains, or agrees to accept or attempts to receive or obtain, from any person for oneself or for any other person, any gratification as an inducement or reward for ... committing an offence.

The ACC has a mandate to seize property or assets suspected of being the proceeds of crime. It has such a mandate under both the anti-corruption act and the Forfeiture of Proceeds of Crime Act No. 19 of 2010. Under section 58 of the anti-corruption act, the commission can seize property. Section 58(1) stipulates:

Where in the course of an investigation into an offence under this act, an officer has reasonable grounds to suspect that any movable or immovable property is derived or acquired from corrupt practices, is the subject matter of an offence or is evidence relating to an offence, the officer shall, with a warrant, seize the property.

On recovery of stolen assets, the ACC can also use its mandate to enforce the Forfeiture of Proceeds of Crime Act No. 19 of 2010, which provides for the confiscation of the proceeds of crime. This law also facilitates the tracing of any proceeds, benefits or property derived from the commission of any serious offence. In particular, section 4(1) of this act outlines that

Subject to subsection (2), where a person is convicted of a serious offence committed after the coming into force of this act, a public prosecutor may apply to the court for one or both of the following orders: (a) a forfeiture order against property that is tainted property in respect of the offence; (b) a confiscation order against the person in respect of benefits derived by the person from the commission of the offence.

The ACC can cooperate with any local law enforcement agency or foreign jurisdiction to enforce the recovery of stolen assets or seize property suspected of being the proceeds of crime. For offences committed abroad, the ACC relies on section 88, which states that 'the Mutual Legal Assistance in Criminal Matters Act applies to offences under this act, except where the provisions of that act are inconsistent with this act'. The Mutual Legal Assistance in Criminal Matters Act No. 19 of 1993 provides for the implementation of treaties for mutual legal assistance in criminal matters and to provide for matters connected with or incidental to the foregoing. Section 8 stipulates that 'assistance under this act may be provided to a foreign state subject to such conditions as the attorney general may determine'. In addition, section 9 provides that 'a request by Zambia for international assistance in a criminal matter may be made by the attorney general'.

Additionally, the ACC can recover stolen assets or property under the Penal Code, which establishes a code of criminal law. Section 318 states:

1. Any person who receives or retains any chattel, money, valuable security or other property whatsoever, knowing or having reason to believe the same to have been feloniously stolen, taken, extorted, obtained or disposed of, is guilty of a felony and is liable to imprisonment for seven years.
2. Any person who received or retains any chattel, money, valuable security or other property whatsoever, knowing or having reason to believe the same to have been unlawfully taken, obtained, converted or disposed of in a manner which constitutes a misdemeanour, is guilty of a misdemeanour and is liable to the same punishment as the offender by whom the property was unlawfully obtained, converted or disposed of. (As amended by No. 26 of 1940)

Section 319 states:

Any person who shall be brought before a court charged with – (a) having in his possession anything which may be reasonably suspected of having been stolen or unlawfully obtained; or (b) conveying in any manner anything which may be reasonably suspected of having been stolen or unlawfully obtained; and who shall not give an account to he came by the same, is guilty of a misdemeanour.

And section 320:

Every person who, without lawful excuse, knowing or having reason to believe the same to have been stolen or obtained in any way whatsoever under such circumstances that if the act had been committed in Zambia the person committing it would have been guilty of felony or misdemeanour, receives or has in his possession any property so stolen or obtained outside Zambia, is guilty of an offence of the like degree (whether felony or misdemeanour) and is liable to imprisonment for seven years. The law is therefore applicable to even foreign jurisdictions.

Financial resources

The commission management is responsible for budgetary planning of its financial resources. On an annual basis, the ACC convenes budgeting meetings where it determines its needs according to activity based budgeting (ABB). The budgets are then submitted to the ministry of finance. An ACC contingency then goes to meet a committee at the ministry of finance, chaired by the secretary to the treasury to justify their budgets. This committee gives feedback to the institution but does not confirm the final budget allocations. These are confirmed once the figures in the yellow book are debated and passed by the national assembly.

In its 2013 annual report, the ACC confirmed that it could not implement some of its planned training activities due to inadequate funding.[41] In 2014, during the end of year press briefing, the ACC indicated that there had been an increased demand for funds to cover the increase in activities being undertaken by the commission and it confirmed that inadequate funding was one of its three main challenges. It was also confirmed that the ACC lacked the presence at district level needed in order to enhance its accessibility to the public.[42]

The ACC receives funding mainly from the government and one donor agency namely the Department for International Development (DfID) of the UK. In 2013, for instance, the ACC received a budgetary allocation of K 58 million from the government and K5 million from the DfID. This allocation covered both personnel and non-personnel emoluments for operations. The DfID allocates these funds directly to the ACC, which is allowed to obtain financial support from donors/cooperating partners.

In its annual reports from 2010 to 2013, the ACC confirms that the resources allocated are not adequate for the efficient accomplishment of the various missions it has.

The commission, like other government ministries, often receives timely funding releases in accordance with the profiles of the activities and budgets submitted to the ministry of finance. However, these financial resources are often delayed, partially released or not given at all for some months in the financial year, due to other commitments by government.

The ACC enjoys managerial autonomy and it does have effective control of the financial resources necessary for its operations. The commission applies rules of transparency to deter any questionable management or abuse of funds. It is audited by both internal auditors and external auditors. Internal auditors audit all financial transactions that take place on a daily basis while external auditors are engaged at the end of each financial year to conduct the audit.

The commission confirmed in its 2013 annual report that internal audits were conducted, finding the ACC's internal financial controls to be satisfactory. It also put in place measures to address all concerns highlighted in its ten auditable units and operational

---

41 Anti-Corruption Commission (2013) *Annual Report*. p.30.
42 Anti-Corruption Commission (2015, 6 January) End of 2014 Media Briefing.

areas. The external audits carried out by the office of the auditor general also confirm that the ACC's financial controls were in accordance with the International Standards for Supreme Audit Institutions (ISSAIs).[43]

It is worth noting that the commission has never appeared before the parliamentary accounts committee to answer to any irregularities from the external audit report and the office of the auditor general has commended the commission for prudent management of financial resources.

The commission's resource administration is the responsibility of management, which reports to the board, who are in turn accountable to the public through parliament. Below is a table showing the commission's budget in the last three years and the actual financial releases received. Note that the amounts show the total budgets including funds that may have been received from cooperating partners.

Table 7: Approved budget and actual expenditure

Year	Approved budget	Total budget released	% of budget release
2014	USD 7 527 245	USD 7 225 994	96.0%
2013	USD 5 194 190	USD 5 173 240	99.6%
2012	USD 5 921 783	USD 5 691 356	96%

G. Agency performance

The ACC has performed relatively well over the years. For instance, in the strategic plans for 2009–2013 and 2013–2016, one of the commission's strategic objectives was to increase the number of convictions. Some arrests were made, but there needs to be an increase in its investigation and prosecution capacity for there to be more conviction.

The table below indicates reported improvements in the conviction rates over a four-year period, against concluded cases in the courts of law.

Table 8: Prosecutions and convictions

Year	Total prosecution cases concluded	No. of convictions achieved	Convictions as % of total
2010	27	16	59.25%
2011	24	14	58.33%
2012	22	13	59.09%
2013	32	26	81.25%
2014	17	11	64.70%

---

43 Anti-Corruption Commission (2013) *Annual Report*. pp.30 & 35.

An average of 16 convictions every year for the past five years may not be satisfactory, compared to an average of 2000 reports that the commission receives each year.

A second strategic objective has been 'to increase citizen participation in the fight against corruption'. To this end, the commission has, over the years, heightened its outreach programmes and recorded an increase in the number of people reached during these sensitisation activities. These people have been empowered by information on corruption and what they should do in the face of it. As a result, the commission has witnessed a rise in citizens' participation in the fight against corruption; as is evident from the number of reports the commission has received.

Table 9: People reached and complaints received

Year	No. of people reached	No. of complaints received
2010	102 752	1 407
2011	136 000	1 404
2012	842 705	2 388
2013	293 907	1 987
2014	5 693 906	2 080

Another strategic objectives was 'to effectively and efficiently prevent corrupt practices in order to reduce incidences of corruption in both public and private bodies'.

Among the strategies employed to achieve this were the following:
- Develop and implement interventions for mainstreaming anti-corruption in the routine business of public and private bodies; and
- Develop and implement programmes in collaboration with both public and private bodies to prevent corruption.

In implementing the above strategies, the commission has since established 46 integrity committees (ICs) in MDAs which have been instrumental in institutionalising the prevention of corruption; particularly by instating codes of ethics, service charters and customer service centres. Furthermore, the commission has been conducting corruption vulnerability assessments as a means of establishing corruption loopholes in the routine business of institutions and coming up with interventions to prevent corruption.

The successes recorded over the years are also revealed in the surveys conducted by international institutions such as the World Bank, Transparency International and the Mo Ibrahim Foundation. Below are the graphs showing the results of these surveys.

Figure 4: Control of corruption aggregate indicator

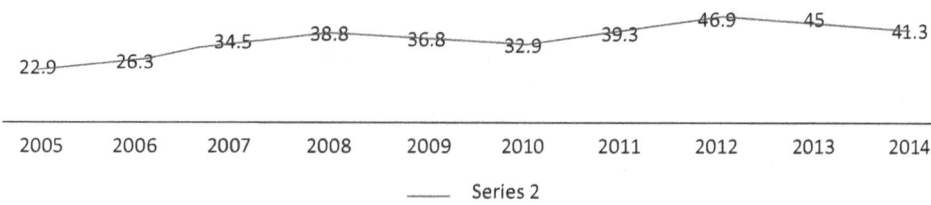

Table 10: Transparency International corruption perception index

Year	2010	2011	2012	2013	2014
Score	30	32	37	38	38

Figure 5: Mo Ibrahim index on African governance: Overall governance scores and ranking

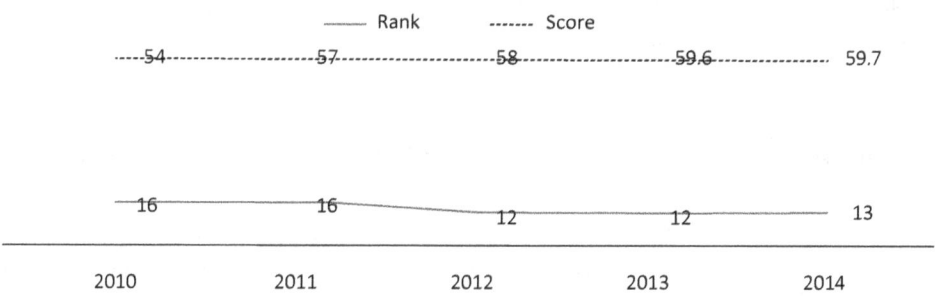

Figure 6: Accountability scores: Ibrahim Index on African Governance

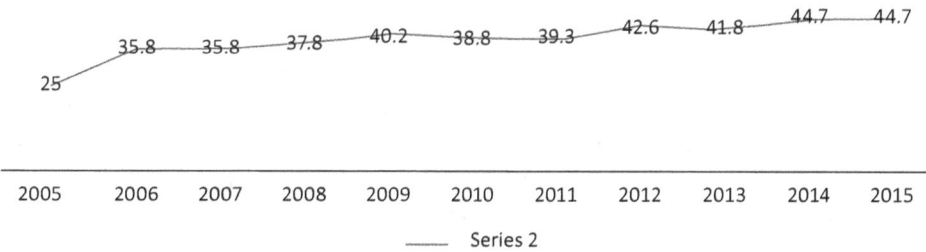

The financial absorption capacity of the ACC is quite high. In 2014 the total budget provision for funding amounted to USD 7 527 245 and the ACC received USD 7 225 994 being 96% of the budgeted for amount. In terms of its absorption capacity, it was able to utilise USD 6 592 465 (81.40%) as at the 2014 financial year end.[44]

---

44 Ministry of Finance and National Planning (2014) *Financial Reports Quarterly Budget Execution Report 2014 As At December 2014.* Available at http://www.mofnp.gov.zm/jdownloads/Financial%20Reports/Quartely%20Budget%20Execution%20Report%202014/As%20At%2031%20December%202014/expenditure_by_head_2014_as_at_31st_december_2014.pdf [accessed 27 September 2016].

In 2015 (as at June 2015), the ACC had only received funding amounting to USD 2 271 169 out of the total budget provision of USD 6 664 954 (34.08%). One would have expected that by midpoint of the financial year, the institution would have received close to 50% of the earmarked funding. This confirms that the ministry of finance does not release funds to the ACC in full, in a timeous fashion.

Strengths of the ACC

According to the ACC's 2013 to 2016 strategic plan, the following were documented as its key strengths.

Availability of enabling legislation

The major strength of the commission is the availability of anti-corruption and related legislations. These include the 2012 anti-corruption act, Public Interest Disclosure (Protection of Whistle Blowers) Act of 2010, Forfeiture of Proceeds of Crime Act of 2010 and Plea Negotiations and Agreements Act of 2010. Although these laws are new, they are expected to enhance the efficacy of preventing and combatting corruption.

Highly educated staff

The commission has a pool of well-educated staff, the majority of whom are university graduates. This enhances the commission's capacity to deliver on its mandate. The high level of education also enhances professionalism in the conduct of official business. Because constant training for up-grading skills and better handling of corruption cases, resources can be optimised elsewhere. Furthermore, exchange programmes in all core functions for purposes of benchmarking and sharing experiences should continue and be enhanced.

Presence in nine provincial centres

Having offices at regional level, the commission has managed to perform its various functions in nine provinces. Apart from providing interpersonal and timely responses to citizens, regional offices provide a useful base for further expansion of ACC interventions in the respective provinces. It is intended that the ACC will continue decentralising to district level as well as cover the newly created Muchinga Province as a step towards being more responsive to the demands of the public.

Availability of baseline information

The availability of baseline information in all the departments in the commission is an essential tool in the monitoring and evaluation of its performance. This has helped in identifying the weaknesses and strengths of the institution.

Availability of strategic plan

The availability of the 2009-2013 strategic plan provides background information to cover the next four years.

Weaknesses of the ACC

In spite of the strengths highlighted above, the commission has a number of weaknesses which affect the implementation of the strategic plan and, if not addressed, are likely to negatively affect its effective implementation.

Inadequate staffing

The commission's staffing levels have been extremely inadequate to meet the demands of the public to deliver on its mandate. With a total staff establishment of 362, which includes management, professional and support staff, the number is highly inadequate to effectively deal with the insidious scourge. In view of this, it is necessary that staffing levels be increased in all core functions in order to effectively deal with corruption.

Low career progression

There is low career progression due to structural rigidities which in turn lead to low staff morale and low productivity. Low career progression has had a negative impact on the commission in that well trained and skilled staff have often left for better career prospects. This situation, if not addressed, is likely to continue and result in failure to deliver on the commission's mandate and meet the expectations of the public. This therefore raises the need for restructuring.

Non-alignment of strategy and fragmented programmes

The 2009-2013 strategic plan was sanctioned prior to the approval of the NACP and Against Corruption Together (ACT) programmes, hence a lack of the harmonisation that came after the said documents were approved. The strategic plan has since incorporated provisions of these and all other relevant policy and programmes documents, however.

Lack of experts on the monitoring and evaluation

Currently, most of the officers working under the monitoring and evaluation unit were placed there on the basis of seniority and may not be fully qualified or have the expertise required. However, skills training in monitoring and evaluation are being provided to officers in this unit on an on-going basis.[45]

Two case studies of major investigations

Case study 1: Sports Deputy Minister Hon. Steven Masumba convicted for obtaining pecuniary advantage by using a fake certificate to obtain a job

On 20 November 2013, the Lusaka magistrate court sentenced Sports Deputy Minister Stephen Masumba to 12 months imprisonment with hard labour for obtaining pecuniary advantage by using a fake certificate to obtain a job. This follows a successful investigation

---

45 Anti-Corruption Commission (2012) 2012 to 2016 Strategic Plan.

by the ACC. After the conviction of Masumba, the late Michael Sata dismissed Hon Masumba as sports deputy minister in November 2013.

Masumba was convicted by the Lusaka magistrate court after being found guilty of obtaining employment at the Lusaka Business and Technical College as an accounting officer, using a forged accounting diploma that said had been awarded to him by the National Institute of Public Administration. Masumba's argument has been that the National Institute of Public Administration gave him the diploma by mistake.[46]

He was charged with one count of obtaining pecuniary advantage by false pretences contrary to the laws of Zambia and prosecuted by the ACC. On 29 September 2014, the Lusaka high court upheld the 12 months sentence. Lusaka High Court Judge Chalwe Mchenga said the lower court proved beyond reasonable doubt that Masumba obtained pecuniary advantage when he was employed as a lecturer at Lusaka Business and Technical College.[47] In 2014, acting President Guy Scott issued a presidential pardon on Masumba and he was released from jail where he was serving his jail sentence.

Table 11: Case of Hon. Steven Masumba timelines

Item	Date	Period between last event
Complaint received/investigation starts		
Investigation concluded		
Date of arrest by ACC and commencement of court trial	23 April 2012	
Magistrate judgment date	20 November 2013	19 months
High court judgment date	29 September 2014	10 months
Supreme court judgment date	Nil	Nil

Case study 2: Former Zambia Railways Limited (ZRL) managing director, Professor Clive Chirwa acquitted of abuse of office

On 17 August 2015, former Zambia Railways Limited (ZRL) Managing Director Clive Chirwa was acquitted by the Lusaka magistrate court for two counts of abuse of authority of office and one count of failing to declare interest. The commission arrested Chirwa for alleged corrupt practices involving over USD 23 728.

Prof Chirwa was arrested 8 October 2013 and charged with two counts. In the first count, he was charged with failure to disclose interest contrary to section 28(1) of the Anti-Corruption Act No.3 of 2012. Between 1 November and 31 December 2012, it was

---

46 Sports Deputy Minister Stephen Masumba sentenced to 12 months imprisonment with hard labour (2013, 20 November. *Lusaka Times*. Available at https://www.lusakatimes.com/2013/11/20/sports-deputy-minister-stephen-masumba-sentenced-12-months-imprisonment-hard-labour/ [accessed 27 September 2016].

47 High Court upholds 12 months jail time for Steven Masumba (2014, 29 September) *Lusaka Times*. Available at https://www.lusakatimes.com/2014/09/29/high-court-upholds-12-months-jail-time-steven-masumba/ [accessed 27 September 2016].

revealed that Clavel Incorporated Limited, a company in which he was a shareholder, was to be given a contract to train ZRL employees without disclosing interest.

In the second count, Chirwa was jointly charged alongside Ms Regina Mwale (finance director of ZRL) for abuse of authority of office in contravention of section 99 (1) of the Penal Code. Between 1 November 2012 and 30 April 2013, Chirwa and Mwale abused the authority of their offices by authorising a total payment of USD 24 502 to Fallsway Apartments of Lusaka for accommodation for the benefit of Prof Chirwa without following laid down procedures.[48]

Magistrate Obisster Musukwa convicted Mwale on two counts of abuse of authority of office, while Chirwa was acquitted. Musukwa said Mwale abused her authority when she authorised the payment, but the prosecution failed to provide documentary evidence before the court to prove that professor Chirwa directed Mwale to pay for his accommodation.[49]

Table 12: Case of Professor Clive Chirwa timelines

Item	Date	Period between last event
Complaint received/investigation starts	June 2013	NA
Investigation concluded	October 2013	4 Months
Date of arrest by ACC and commencement of court trial	8 October 2013	1 Month
Magistrate judgment date	17 August 2015	22 Months
High court judgment date	Nil	Nil
Supreme court judgment date	Nil	Nil

Analysis of cases received and concluded

During 2014, the commission received a total of 2 080 reports of suspected corruption, showing an increase of 93 reports from 2013. Even though this was said to be a sign of public confidence in the work of the commission, it could only investigate and prosecute cases falling under its mandate. Out of the reports received in 2014, a total of 1 377 were non-corruption-related (compared to 1 263 in 2013). This shows that there were more non-corruption-related complaints in 2014 than in 2013. Advice was subsequently given to all those who made these reports on how best to address the reported matters.

Of the 2 080 cases received in 2014, 703 reports contained elements of corruption; 426 were authorised for investigations; a total of 1 377 lacked sufficient detail to warrant investigation; and 277 reports with some elements of corruption were not authorised for investigation. Some cases were referred to the relevant institutions for administrative

---

48 Professor Clive Chirwa Arrested (2013, 10 September) Lusaka Times. Available at https://www.lusakatimes.com/2013/09/10/professor-clive-chirwa-arrested/ [accessed 27 September 2016].
49 Professor Clive Chirwa acquitted (2015, 17 August) Lusaka Times. Available at https://www.lusakatimes.com/2015/08/17/professor-clive-chirwa-acquitted [accessed 27 September 2016].

action while others were closed with no further action. The complainants in these matters were also advised accordingly.

In 2014, the commission also conducted investigations into 220 cases arising from the auditor-general's reports. By the close of the year, there were a total of 1 316 cases under investigation. That year, the commission recorded 35 arrests country-wide and 64 prosecutions cases went before the courts of law. The commission secured 27 convictions and recorded ten acquittals. Eight cases were withdrawn from court due to legal technicalities and 12 judgments were appealed.[50]

The timelines for matters being investigated from the time complaints are lodged to the time a conclusion is reached varies with each complaint. The amount of time these take depends on the availability and accessibility of the required evidence and key information. The ACC has its own prosecutors who prosecute all corruption cases. The commission must, however, obtain consent to prosecute from the director of public prosecutions in accordance with section 64(1) of the 2012 anti-corruption act which states: 'A prosecution for an offence under part III shall not be instituted except by, or with, the consent of the director of public prosecutions.'

Table 13: ACC Zambia complaints analysis 2012 to 2014

Item	2012	2013	2014
Total complaints received	2 388	1 987	2 080
Non corruption related	1 623	1 263	1 377
With elements of corruption	765	724	703
Authorised for investigations	466	439	426
Number of arrests nationwide	38	35	35
Number of convictions	13	26	27
Number of acquittals	9	7	10

Table 14: Complaints conclusion timelines within the same year being received

	2012	2013
Total number of investigations	856	1091
Number successfully concluded	164 (19.2%)	223 (20.4%)
Number of investigation cases carried forward	682 (80%)	868 (79%)
Referred to various institutions for administrative action	42	43

---

50 Anti-Corruption Commission (2014) End of Year Media Briefing. pp. 11 & 12.

Relationships with other stakeholders

The ACC has a cordial working relationship with state organs and local authorities in terms of complementarity. The ACC is positioned as the lead agency as well as being responsible for provision of advisory services for sector-specific (MDA-level) design and implementation of corruption-prevention measures. The NACP recommends that the MDAs that include local authorities actively participate in the design of internal/sector-specific corruption measures in order to 'own' them. In addition, individual local authorities assume full responsibility for their consistent implementation, including funding for NACP activities, although the ACC still provides backup. There is normally minimal conflict between state institutions and the ACC.

Civil society

The ACC works closely with CSOs. In 2014, for instance, they worked together in conducting sensitisation activities in rural areas across the country under the Corruption Awareness Fund. A total of 144 applications for funds from all provinces were received by the commission, out of which a total of 69 CSOs were selected for the final evaluation. As at the end of 2014, 30 CSOs had been shortlisted and 14 were selected for funding. The ACC (as at the end of 2014) had a total of USD 63 559 set aside to fund the CSOs' various anti-corruption activities.

Working with CSOs has helped the commission reach out to more rural areas where the ACC has no presence.

At national level, the ACC has a working agreement with TIZ to produce the ZBPI and conduct a number of other activities together to complement each other's efforts in the fight against corruption. The ACC and TIZ also have collaborative roles during the commemoration of International Anti-Corruption Day every year. The commission has also worked very well with TIZ in conducting public sensitisation activities on the dangers of corruption across the country.

The media

The ACC works with various media organisations in disseminating anti-corruption information. It also trains and sensitises journalists on corruption awareness. For instance, in 2014, a media workshop was conducted in the Northern Province of Zambia for journalists based there, aimed at sensitising them on anti-corruption issues. Through this workshop, the journalists assured the commission of their support in the fight against corruption; this resulted in more media coverage of corruption stories and media inquiries on commission activities.[51]

---

51 Anti-Corruption Commission (2015, 6 January) End of 2014 Media Briefing.

Private sector
The commission enjoys cordial relations with a number of private sector organisations, including CSOs such as TIZ, the Governance Foundation of Zambia, the Young African Leaders Initiative (YALI) and the Southern Africa Centre for the Construction Resolution of Disputes (SACCORD).

The commission has a collaborative memorandum of understanding signed with TIZ towards the production of the annual bribe payers index. Furthermore, TIZ, through its watchdog and advocacy roles, complements the commission in calling for accountability and integrity in all public sector business dealings.

In addition, some private institutions have been eager to form ICs in their institutions and, so far, two private firms have established such committees as a complementary measure to institutionalise the prevention of corruption.

Development partners
The commission has also enjoyed good relations and tremendous support from various development partners in the country. The commission, has over the years, received a lot of financial, technical and material support; particularly from the British government, through the DfID.

There has been no conflict arising from the different roles that the commission and its partner institutions perform as the mandates for each institution are different from the others.

Sub-regional, regional and international institutions
Zambia is party to the aforementioned international instruments. As such, the commission reports on the measures taken towards implementing these international protocols, through the ministry of foreign affairs and other channels.

The ACC is a member of the International Association of Anti-Corruption Authorities, the Eastern and Southern Africa Anti-Money Laundering Group, the Association of Commonwealth Anti-Corruption Agencies in Africa (ACACAA) as well as the Southern Africa Forum Against Corruption (SAFAC).

In addition, the director general of the commission Mrs Rosewin Wandi is also a member of the Corruption Hunters Network. The commission does not contribute any financial resources to this network but contributions have been made towards the running of SAFAC. The commission has also previously been chair of the ACACAA and SAFAC and has made valuable contributions to the operations of these organisations as it shared lessons learnt in the implementation of the international protocols. The influence has not been directly as a result of financial or technical contribution. Other collaborative platforms have been through:
- Joint programmes and investigations;
- Mutual legal assistance;
- Benchmarking and exchange visits;

- Joint training programmes, such as those held through the ACACAA Centre in Botswana; and
- Sharing of regional anti-corruption strategies.

The ACC has developed an obligation to communicate the results of its activities and investigations to the public. It holds quarterly media press briefings to communicate the results of its activities to the public.

The ACC collaborates with the public directly and indirectly. Section 81 of the Anti-Corruption Act No. 3 of 2012 mandates and compels the ACC to ensure they cooperate and work with the public, under section 81 which states that:

3. The commission shall inform the public of the various authorities involved in combatting corruption and the services available to the public and how the public may assist and otherwise participate in ensuring the effective functioning of the authorities.
4. The commission and the appropriate authorities shall establish mechanisms to collect and respond to public comments, concerns and questions relating to the fight against corruption including public debates and hearings.

In 2014 for instance, the ACC implemented various programmes where they collaborated with the public. This was done under its community education mandate. The commission conducted various awareness activities targeting members of the public and stakeholders so that they were made aware of the harmful effects of corruption to individuals and society at large. The following educational activities were conducted that year:[52]

- Two rural sensitisation exercises were conducted, one in Western Province and another in North Western Province. These exercises are meant to reach remote parts of the country where information isn't easily found, and to raise awareness on corruption. Members of the community were empowered with information; this has led to the traditional leadership and their subjects to be more vigilant and become change agents.
- Public rallies were also held in in Choma and Chipata districts at which over 3 000 people were reached with anti-corruption messages. It is anticipated that with the knowledge acquired, the public will be supportive in the fight against corruption.
- The commission also worked with CSOs in conducting sensitisation activities in other rural areas across the country under the Fund for Corruption Awareness. 14 CSOs are due to receive funding while the others will be funded in due course. Working with CSOs has helped

---

52 Anti-Corruption Commission (2014) End of Year Media Briefing. pp. 11 & 12.

the commission reach out to more rural areas where the commission has no presence.
- A media workshop was conducted in Northern Province for local journalists, aimed at sensitising them to anti-corruption issues. Through this workshop the journalists assured the commission of support in the fight against corruption; this has been witnessed through more coverage of corruption stories and media inquiries on commission activities.
- Several lectures were conducted at various institutions throughout the country, through which over 9 000 people were reached with anti-corruption messages. The institutions visited were equipped with information and it is hoped that they will become ambassadors in preventing and reporting corrupt practices.
- Study circle meetings/sessions were held with various groups from different institutions with the recent ones being the University Teaching Hospital and Vivid Media Agency. Members of staff in institutions where sessions were conducted were made aware of what constitutes corruption and their role in fighting it.
- On 9 December each year, Zambia joins the rest of the world in commemorating the International Anti-Corruption Day. The commission participates in a weeklong series of programmes that include public rallies and information displays across the country. Through this commemoration, the public are made aware of the national and international efforts being made in combatting corruption.
- The commission realises the importance of involving the youth in the anti-corruption campaign from an early age; because, as they develop into adults, they carry with them the values they learn as children. In this regard, the commission has continued engaging young people through activities such as the formation and support of school and community anti-corruption clubs.
- The commission also participated in a number of exhibitions throughout the country, including district and provincial agriculture shows and distribution of educational materials in form of leaflets, posters and booklets.

The commission believes that an informed public is vital to the fight against corruption and, through these outreach initiatives, the public will be armed against the temptation of corruption, as well as be equipped to recognise and report it.[53]

---

53 Anti-Corruption Commission (2014) End of Year Media Briefing. pp. 11 & 12.

Reporting mechanism and public perception

The ACC reports its activities on a quarterly basis to its board of commissioners. It also submits an annual report to the president of the republic before it is made public.

The ACC works in conjunction with TIZ to objectively assess its perception on its performance. It does this by jointly advertising and calling for open bids for independent consultants to carry out such perception surveys. Some of the public perceptions about the ACC's performance are collected during such surveys and submitted directly to the ACC. These are done every two years, alongside the ZBPI. The commission (in conjunction with stakeholders like the governance department under the ministry of justice) also periodically conducts corruption diagnostic studies.

The public perception of the ACC as reported in the 2014 ZBPI is that respondents recognise the ACC as the leading anti-corruption stakeholder organisation (37.2%), with the Zambia Police Service (19.2%) and the Drug Enforcement Commission (12.4%) coming in second and third. Furthermore, of survey findings on the assessment of the government's efforts in dealing with the issue of corruption in 2014, 17.3% noted that the efforts have been effective, 39.7% somewhat effective and 13.5% very ineffective.[54]

The ACC in Zambia has sub-offices in nine out of the ten provinces of Zambia. These offices can be accessed by people in the districts where they are. However, Zambia has over 100 districts and these offices are only in 11 of these districts. The rural districts in certain cases are far from where these offices are, as Zambia is a big country with a land surface of 752 000m^2 and is estimated to be the 37th biggest country in the world.

H. Conclusion and recommendations

Overall legal framework for combatting corruption

Zambia has a strong legal framework in the fight against corruption, although the levels of compliance and enforcement are low. It is recommended that the ACC upscale and enhance the levels of compliance and enforcement of all anti-corruption laws and regulations in the country. There is also a need to improve coordination between the ACC and the office of auditor general to improve investigations and prosecutions of public sector financial mismanagement.

Agency status

There is need to showcase that the ACC is both legally and operationally independent and enshrined in its autonomy proclaimed in the law. However, just as other law enforcement agencies have a tendency of investigating and prosecuting public officials only when their political party loses elections, so too does the commission. This tendency should be avoided through ensuring that public officials are investigated whilst their political party is still

---

54 Zambia Bribe Payers Index 2014.p. 41.

in power. The anti-corruption act should be revised to empower the ACC to sanction all public and private bodies that do not implement their recommendations.

National anti-corruption policy

The monitoring and evaluation approaches to anti-corruption in Zambia are flawed in that they disregard any inputs from non-state actors in order to provide an independent perspective on progress made. Looking at the potential impact that independent civil society monitoring can generate, this missing element should be considered. In addition, the impact of other government policies or laws that are expected to have an indirect bearing on reducing corruption should be assessed.

It is self-evident that cross-cutting anti-corruption reforms are particularly dependent on good communication between all implementing agencies and the public at large. Nevertheless, communication on anti-corruption strategies is weak in Zambia. The anti-corruption documents are not easily available to those interested (public officials and citizens) and most public agencies and politicians have little awareness of their existence. Also, the fact that the goals and progress of the anti-corruption strategies are not proactively communicated to the public does not allow for the creation of a sustained political debate and resultant pressure to move anti-corruption policies forward.[55] It is therefore recommended that there be pro-active communication to the public on progress being made on the implementation of anti-corruption policies.

Funding for the implementation of NACP activities should also be guaranteed, to ensure that all government agencies that mainstream anti-corruption activities are implementing it.

Mandate and strengthened collaboration

The ACC should be empowered through the ZACC Act to have the legal authority to collaborate with state and non-state actors as well as regional bodies. At the moment, state institutions treat the coordination role of the ACC as something that cannot compel them to implement recommendations.

In 2012 and 2013, the commission's success rate only stood at an average of 20% of cases concluded in each year. Its capacity to conclude these cases needs to be enhanced.

It is also recommended that the ACC carry out an internal case review to determine what factors lead to such a low success rate. Such an internal review should include clear recommendations on what needs to be done to improve the recommended completion timelines.

---

55 Hussmann K (2007) Anti-corruption policy making in practice: What can be learned for implementing Article 5 of UNCAC? Report of six country case studies: Georgia, Indonesia, Nicaragua, Pakistan, Tanzania and Zambia. 2007. pp. 34–38.

Funding

The government should provide adequate funding to the ACC in order for it to fulfil its mandate without major resource hindrances. Donors should also consider providing funding to the ACC to uplift its operations.

Whenever the salaries of commission staff are too low for a living wage, the commission engages the government for consideration of an increase in the salaries, or indeed for the entire conditions of service to be reviewed. This review happens as and when necessary. It is recommended that salaries for ACC staff should always be reviewed upwards every year to both motivate and retain its well-trained staff.

There should also be financial resources set aside for the ACC to consider funding all forums and some of the programmes being implemented by non-state actors.

Administration

There should be more specialised training for ACC officers. The ACC structure should be expanded to allow for recruitment of more officers, especially at district level.

Independence

Many analysts argue that the inherit weakness of the executive appointing the head of the ACC and its commissioners makes it difficult for the ACC to operate independently, despite public pronouncement of political will by President Edgar Lungu. It is strongly proposed that the ACC head and commissioners should be appointed by an independent body and only ratified by parliament so that its allegiance is not to the president.

Overall performance

The overall performance of the ACC needs to be improved – especially the minimal recorded convictions. It is also recommended that case management be improved so that more cases are concluded on time.

12
ZIMBABWE

Ms Teresa Mugadza

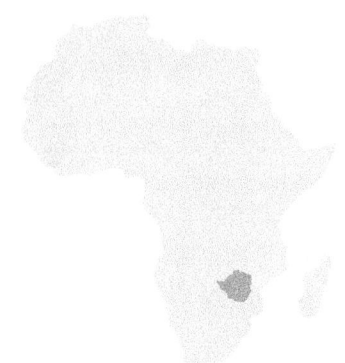

A. Executive summary

Corruption in Zimbabwe is so rife it has reached endemic proportions. The rot cuts across both the public and private sectors and has, in recent years, been exacerbated by a protracted and severe economic meltdown. The police and the political elite, otherwise vanguards against graft, have themselves been identified among the major culprits. A recent survey by Transparency International Zimbabwe (TIZ), for instance, revealed that the police are now regarded as the most corrupt agency in the country. As a result, there is a lack of public confidence in the government's commitment or ability to combat corruption, with many alleging lack of political will by those in authority.

Oddly, Zimbabwe has a fairly substantial legal framework to combat corruption. Corruption itself is defined and criminalised through the Criminal Law (Codification and Reform) Act (the Code). The Code creates distinct crimes relating to corruption. These are bribery; giving or receiving a bribe as an inducement or reward; corruptly using a false document; the intentional non-disclosure of, or the concealment of, a transaction from one's principal in order to deceive; and the deceitful non-disclosure or concealment from one's principal of a personal interest in a transaction. These crimes apply equally to the public and private sectors. Moreover, these crimes penalise the conduct of both agents and employees who corruptly try to obtain undue benefits by abusing their positions of employment or authority and members of the public who either try to corrupt the agents or participate in the corrupt transactions by the agents in equal measure. The Code also creates the 'conspiracy to commit' offences, which criminalise any corrupt agreement or arrangement between any agent and any other person even if the agreement or arrangement does not actually result in a corrupt transaction, thus casting the net even wider. With respect to public officials, under the offence of criminal abuse of power by a public officer, public officials would also be criminally liable for acting in a manner that is inconsistent with their public duties.

To make prosecution of some of the crimes easier, criminal intent – the legal requirement that the accused person must be shown to have intended the alleged crimes – will be presumed once one commits any of the specified acts constituting corruption. It will be for the person concerned to show that his conduct was not intended to be corrupt. Corruption is thus defined well and in broad terms, and there is a deliberate attempt to make it easier to prosecute.

With respect to the enforcement mechanisms, the constitution creates an independent anti-corruption agency, with a fair measure of authority. Appointed through an open process involving public interviews and consultations between the president and a committee of parliament, the Zimbabwe Anti-Corruption Commission (ZACC) is cushioned against external influence or pressure through a number of measures. Its independence is constitutionally guaranteed and interference with its work is expressly prohibited. Members of the commission are also protected from arbitrary dismissal and the commission's staff is not part of the public service. Political interference is further curtailed by the requirement that members of the commission must not engage in active politics. Members may also not act in a partisan manner or show bias or prejudice towards any political party or cause. With respect to its powers, the ZACC has fairly substantial authority. The commission is constitutionally charged to lead the fight against corruption and in so doing may summon the assistance of other law enforcement agencies. It has the power to direct the commissioner general of the police to investigate any matter to do with corruption and report back to it.

Besides the constitutional provisions, there are also other statutory measures to complement those in the constitution. The Prevention of Corruption Act, for instance, provides a procedure where, if it is in the national interest, the minister of home affairs may specify any individual for alleged acts of corruption specified in the Act and place such individual under investigations. The powers of the investigator in this process are quite immense. The investigator enjoys investigative and quasi-judicial functions, including powers of search and seizure, the power to compel the production of documents and other evidence, and the power to summon and question a suspect or anyone else associated with the suspect, or closely related to the suspected acts of corruption. Spousal privilege and other legal protections like banker/client confidentiality do not apply to the investigative proceedings. Statutory measures to help combat corruption include the provision for the protection by law of those who make reports of corruption in terms of both the Prevention of Corruption Act and Anti-Corruption Commission Act. Equally noteworthy, is the right to information in the constitution, which is regulated through the Access to Information and Protection of Privacy Act.

While the ZACC lacks independent arresting or prosecuting powers and must rely on the police and the national prosecuting authority (NPA), it still has enough authority to be effective. Moreover, the commission's lack of these powers only becomes a weakness impacting its effectiveness when it fails to get the support of the other agencies. In a thriving democracy, there is no reason why either the police or the prosecuting authority should not cooperate with another constitutional body. Yet, in practice, despite the clear letter of the law, the ZACC suffers several debilitating institutional challenges, including the lack of and/or inadequate support from other government bodies, including the police. The ZACC, for instance, has so far been deprived of an independent budget and must rely on its line ministry, previously the ministry of home affairs and now the office of the president, which has in turn assumed de facto oversight powers over the commission. Within that context, this paper thus posits that the major setbacks to the ZACC's effectiveness are more institutional than legal and may consequently best be addressed through concerted programmes to entrench constitutionalism in Zimbabwe. The law, it is contended, is only as good as those who implement it.

B. Introduction

State of corruption

The corruption index in Zimbabwe, like the economy – from which it feeds – is grim. Ranked 156th of 176 most corrupt countries,[1] corruption now pervades all aspects of life. In a recent local survey by Transparency International Zimbabwe (TIZ),[2] 65% of the respondents positively asserted that they understood the meaning of corruption, with one resident retorting: 'who in Zimbabwe doesn't know what corruption is; everyone is corrupt and everyone knows corruption'. Amongst the respondents, 74.3% were of the view that corruption had increased in the last two years; and 68% felt that the government was ineffective in addressing the issue, with one of the participants categorically pointing to a lack of political will. Nearly 80% (77.4) of the respondents professed that they had been asked for a bribe, with the following institutions being implicated the most: schools, the police, the passport office, courts (the magistrates and prosecutors), city council officials and the vehicle inspection department. The police topped the corruption list. 34% of the respondents said they had been asked for a bribe to speed things up; another 30%, to avoid arrest; 15% to get a cheaper service; and 14% to guarantee obtaining a service. 50% of the respondents indicated that they had refused to pay a bribe, while 40% admitted to paying one.

A number of people indicated a willingness to fight corruption through various initiatives such as joining an anti-corruption organisation as a member (25%); petitioning the government for more positive action (19%); anti-corruption social media campaigns (14%); paying more for a corrupt free company (13%); and peaceful protest (14%). Only 11% would report incidents of corruption. 43% of the respondents felt that reporting would make no difference, while 37% said they were afraid and 20% were not sure where to report. Asked which institutions they would trust to fight corruption, 35% vested their trust in an independent non-profit organisation, compared to 20% who said they would trust the government's anti-corruption body and the police.

---

1 See, 2014 Transparency International Corruption Perceptions Index, available at http://www.transparency.org/cpi2014/results [accessed 11 October 2016].
2 Transparency International Zimbabwe (2014) Daily Lives and Corruption in Zimbabwe: Public Opinion Survey on Corruption, Perception and Experiences.

The figures are grim and depressing. More telling though is the public's distrust of government institutions, which have either been implicated directly in corrupt activities or are seen to be ineffective in fighting corruption. While Zimbabwe has a fairly substantial legal framework to combat corruption, as the elaborate discussion below will show, corruption itself has become so entrenched it is now almost institutionalised. That the police are perceived as one of the main culprits makes the situation all the more tragic and renders any attempt to fight the social ill nearly futile. The problem is also exacerbated by a perceived lack of political will by those in positions of authority, who, allegedly, also feed off the trough. As the oft-repeated National Indigenisation and Economic Empowerment Board (NIEEB) scandal, involving senior government ministers (discussed below[3]), clearly showed, it is true that the commission is still liable to political influence. In the words of one irate respondent in the TIZ survey:

> If the government is really committed in fighting corruption, it can stop it, just like how they forcibly removed everyone from Chiadzwa in 2008. The government is not serious in fighting corruption; politicians have only denounced corruption while their colleagues who are corrupt walk scot free [sic] in the street.

Politics of corruption
Corruption, money and politics

To understand corruption in Zimbabwe one must consider the context. Corruption does not operate in a vacuum. Rather, it operates in a social, economic and political environment from which it is, in many respects, directly linked. It can be said that there is a direct relationship between corruption and a weak economy, just as there is a direct link between corruption and a poor political system. Zimbabwe suffers the dual tragedy of both, and direct links can be traced between the country's political and economic decline and the rise of corruption. In his seminal presentation, The State of Corruption in Zimbabwe,[4] Dr G Shana – himself a former commissioner of the ACC – traced the rise of corruption in Zimbabwe from 1980, when the country gained majority rule and observed that: 'The first seven years of independence were basically characterised by the paradox of a country run by a Socialist-Marxist revolutionary party whose internal ideology appeared at odds with the way the economy was speedily [growing]'. Inherited from an isolated white supremacist regime that had survived an onslaught on international sanctions through fiscal discipline, the performing economy attracted very isolated incidents of corruption. In part owing to the socialist outlook of the nascent democracy, which eschewed the private accumulation of wealth:

---

3   See summary of the facts of the scandal in this report.
4   The state of corruption in Zimbabwe, a paper presented by Dr G Shana at the Mass Public Opinion Institute Seminar, Crowne Plaza Hotel, 9 May 2006. Excerpts available at https://www.newsday.co.zw/2014/02/08/birth-corruption-zimbabwe/ [accessed 20 November 2016].

The most unanimous opinion condensed from audit reports, donor reports, household surveys, business environment and enterprise surveys, legislative reports and diagnostic studies available between 1980-1987 was that the incidences of corruption though present were minimal no matter how they were defined. During this period the state enjoyed a relatively high level of integrity save the few incidences of grand corruption that emerged in the form of two cases (*State vs. Paweni, State vs. Charles Ndhlovu*) received wide spread societal condemnation.

Shana further observes that 'from 1980 to 1987 corruption was largely opportunistic corruption or greed corruption; from 1987 to 2001 we witnessed the emergence of political elite corruption or network corruption'. It is important to state that the emergence of 'political elite corruption' in Zimbabwe cannot be entirely associated with economic decline. (Corruption, in the form of graft which is linked to economic decline has been more a phenomenon of the post 2000 era.) Rather, corruption in Zimbabwe can be traced back to the nascent years when, due to political and social developments at the time, the ruling party (and by extension, the state) started to consolidate power and limit space for scrutiny by citizens. It is important to state that in the aftermath of Gukurahundi,[5] the state clamped down on dissent and scrutiny of many of its actions for national security reasons. Thus began the consolidation of power by the state during the period 1980–1995 and Zimbabwe became a de facto one party state. Internationally, Zimbabwe was considered a model country, proving that it is possible for a post liberation nationalist government to transition into a democracy, even with some internal destabilisation. However, on the ground, the situation created was one where those in authority (or connected to authority) both in government and the ruling party, became accustomed to acting without accountability, using offices and positions to access resources for personal gain, and generally acting to self-enrich without remorse. This was because, at the time, it was easy to label those dissenting as seeking to destabilise peace/being anti the party and therefore the state. In turn, this led to those seeking to curry favour with the ruling elite engaging in or facilitating corrupt activities (hence the scandals such as Willowgate scandal).[6] Related to this, those in political leadership also used their political clout to manipulate state systems and institutions for their personal benefit (such as the War Victims Compensation Scandal). It is also during this period that the culture of patronage was cultivated as the political system rewarded those considered instrumental in the consolidation of the ruling party's power. Shana notes: 'This (emergence of corruption) was fast followed by patronage corruption as the networks needed protection and ensured political loyalty and leverage by the patrons.' Exacerbating the emergence of the corrupt political elite, were citizens

---

5   See https://en.wikipedia.org/wiki/Gukurahundi.
6   Willowgate happened because politicians abused their right to access vehicle, however by implication, those at Willowvale Motor Industries also facilitated the politicians' abuse of the motor vehicle facility as the analysis of the case will show.

who had been cowered by the events of the first ten years of independence when dissent was clamped. Thus, even though citizens were aware of the corruption, their voices were muted by their experiences and even though they were disgruntled by it, very few took any significant action or stance against the excesses by the political elite.

As Shana observed:

> From 1987, Zimbabwe saw an exponential rise in cases of corruption, from two in seven years to an average of three to four cases a year (until 2002 when the lid fell off). The vast majority of the cases, if not all involved high ranking politicians some of whom are still active in politics and or government having been surreptitiously recycled back into positions of authority even when they had been convicted and sentenced. Involvement in corruption appears to have enhanced their political careers not damaged them [sic].

It is apposite to note the direct connection between corruption and politics here. Patronage as a result of conflation between state and party has become an integral part of politics and the economy in Zimbabwe. It was commonly understood that you do not conduct business in Zimbabwe unless you are known by those in the ruling party. Coupled with the economic decline that had started in 1997,[7] corruption has become the way through which one conducts successful business or rises through political rank. This is what Shana describes as 'political corruption, chaotic corruption'.

Shana suggests a number of reasons why 2002 marked the watershed in the rise of corruption. He argues that the 2002 elections ushered in a new level of political polarisation, combativeness and aggression that 'would define Zimbabwe's political and economic landscape'. The emergence of a viable opposition party in the form of the MDC radically changed the way politics and national discourse would be conducted. Political survival, political expedience and political party affiliation now overrode and dictated all aspects of national, social and economic discourse. As a result,

> partisan politics and especially ruling party politics captured national and state operations ... demanding party loyalty as a pre-requisite to the exercise of right or privilege. The distinction between party and government, party and national interest, party and national patriotism became increasingly blurred in the nationalisation of party politics.

Thus for example, this period saw the implementation of a national youth service programme that purportedly recruited young people to teach them ideals of the revolution, who were in fact the ruling party's youth wing being integrated into the state system, on state resources to help the ruling party recover political ground lost to the opposition. These 'graduates'

---

7 Commonly referred to as Black Friday, when the Zimbabwean Dollar lost over 70% of its value against the United States Dollar in one day in November 1997.

became embedded into the civil service and received stipends/state assistance for tertiary institution learners, and yet they were in fact a creation of the ruling party to consolidate its power, including by the use of violence as evidenced by their role in elections between the 2002–2008 elections.[8] Thus the youth in the ruling party benefitted from state resources to advance the party agenda, while those youths perceived to be linked to the opposition were generally excluded.

This nationalisation of party politics in turn resulted in the national integrity systems, such as parliament, the judiciary, the law enforcement and watch dog institutions, and the civil service in general, losing their relative autonomy, professionalism and accountability.

With accountability and professionalism now subordinated to party politics, it was inevitable that immoral, criminal and corrupt activities that serve political advantage would be given immunity and impunity only judged and chastened if they did not. The result was that corruption could now be justified as political strategy and patronaged for political protection from the various camps that were emerging.

The politicisation of national institutions and the system of political patronage not only encouraged corruption, it also nurtured a culture of impunity where those politically connected would be shielded from prosecution.[9] As will be shown, those in authority or connected thereto have been able to avoid sanction for corruption for a variety of reasons but largely because of political protection, while those without political clout have been sacrificed.[10] As such, the prosecution of corruption in Zimbabwe has largely been low level.

C. Civil society, donors and media engagement

The media

One of the earliest watchdogs to raise alarm against corruption in Zimbabwe was probably the media. The country's most famous case involving grand corruption, the 'Willowgate Scandal', was broken by the state-owned daily, *The Chronicle* in 1989,[11] and became widely

---

8   See generally http://www.solidaritypeacetrust.org/205/national-youth-service-training/ [accessed 20 November 2016].
9   There are many examples of those connected to the ruling party being shielded from sanction for corruption or impropriety; for example, the 2012 Constituency Development Fund scandal (that saw several MPs across the political divide being implicated in abuse of the funds that had been advanced to MPs for development initiatives in the constituencies), when the net began to close in on those in the ruling party, even the opposition MPs managed got away with a slap on the wrist as arrests and criminal sanction were abandoned because of the impact the criminal actions would have had on the ruling party. See http://www.herald.co.zw/govt-to-descend-on-cdf-looters/ and http://www.herald.co.zw/blitz-cdf-thieves-corrupt-councils/ [accessed 20 November 2016].
10 The case of the deposed former vice president is a case in point. She was only accused of corruption when she had fallen out of favour with the party, although she still has not been held criminally liable for the alleged corruption. See http://www.herald.co.zw/top-detectives-probe-mujuru/ [accessed 20 November 2016].
11 *The Chronicle* received a letter that had erroneously been sent to a Bulawayo businessman, Obert Mpofu, now a senior government minister. It was this letter that prompted the investigation by Geoff Nyarota and Davison Maruziva that led to the 'car racket' story that ultimately become the Willowgate Scandal. See generally https://en.wikipedia.org/wiki/Willowgate.

reported by the local and international media. Notably, in the first decade or so after independence, although the state – which was virtually a one party state – had a monopoly over the media, the state media was at the fore front in exposing corruption and other improprieties by key government officials. With the emergence of the opposition politics in the late 90s, which coincided with the 'politicisation of national institutions phase',[12] there also emerged a vibrant private press, which would henceforth lead the fight against corruption. In this period, as the public media had become politically compromised and subject to political patronage, it fell upon the private media to expose corruption and other excesses by the political establishment; at times facing reprisals.[13] To date, the private and independent media remains as vociferous against corruption and other abuses by those in positions of political authority as it is about corruption in the private sector. The state media, on other hand, has increasingly become a political instrument and primarily reports allegations of corruption against the opposition movement, perceived government critics, and those who fall out with the ruling party, such as the sacked former vice president, Joice Mujuru and her close allies. Allegations of corruption against them were only made after they had been fired from the party for supposedly plotting to overthrow the president. Thus, allegations of corruption in the state media have become just another front in the on-going succession war – the infighting within ZANU PF on who will succeed the president.[14]

Civil society

In the first decade after independence, while civil society existed in various forms, it was not so vocal against corruption. One of the reasons is simply that in the first decade or so after independence, corruption was generally frowned upon and minimal, and consequently of no immediate concern. The few incidents of corruption that occurred were roundly condemned and decisive actions taken against the culprits. The role of civil society in that regard was therefore minimal. Besides, civil society itself was also still in its budding stage and was not yet as vibrant as it is today. However, as the economy began to decline and corruption proliferated – a period, which as noted earlier, coincided with a general political and economic decline in the country – civil society became as vocal against corruption as it was in relation to other abuses. By the mid-90s, civil society had become a formidable voice against corruption and political repression. A number of CSOs focusing on specialised areas arose in this time, including TIZ, which became and remains a formidable voice against corruption in Zimbabwe. Its programmes include: advocacy and legal advice; policy, legislative and institutional monitoring; and research

---

12 As observed by Shana - The state of corruption in Zimbabwe, a paper presented by Dr G Shana at the Mass Public Opinion Institute Seminar, Crowne Plaza Hotel, 9 May 2006. p. 4. Excerpts available at https://www.newsday.co.zw/2014/02/08/birth-corruption-zimbabwe/ [accessed 20 November 2016].
13 For example, the Harare International Airport scandal was exposed by the *Daily News* in 2000, see generally http://www.canadafreepress.com/2005/cover020805.htm [accessed 20 November 2016].
14 http://harare24.com/index-id-news-zk-24038.html quoting *The Herald*, the largest daily circulated by the state media on 24 October 2014 [accessed 20 November 2016].

and information on corruption. Today civil society is one of the leading voices against corruption and other state abuses. While organisations such as TIZ and the local chapter of the Anti-Corruption Trust lead the fight against corruption, there is also widespread condemnation by civil society in general, as part of the protracted campaign to check the excesses of the ruling regime. This arises from the fact that there is a direct link between corruption and political abuse of power, as observed above.

Donor community

In the early days, the donor and development community, like everyone else, was not particularly concerned with corruption because, as already indicated, it was minimal. Besides, during that time, the country enjoyed a fair measure of international good will and small incidents of corruption could have been overlooked. The primary concern, it would appear, was to help the young democracy's social, economic and political transition to majority rule. While the donor community primarily channelled resources to help the country cater for an enlarged constituency, especially the marginalised rural communities where social services were underdeveloped; development partners, including the international financial institutions – besides helping develop social amenities – were preoccupied with ensuring economic stability and growth. Suspicious of the country's socialist outlook, development partners and international agencies were concerned with ensuring that Zimbabwe's economy – hitherto designed primarily to cater for a very small white minority – would not buckle under the pressure of an enlarged black majority constituency, and continued to grow, and that the country continued to meet its debt obligations. As a result, between 1991 and 1996, the Zimbabwean government was forced to embark on the International Monetary Fund and the World Bank-sponsored Economic Structural Adjustment Programmes (ESAP), designed towards a free market economy and, ostensibly, economic growth. The measures, it is generally agreed, left the economy worse off and, it could be argued, indirectly resulted in the rise in corruption. It was at this stage, when the economy visibly began to flounder and instances of corruption in the public sector began to manifest, that the donor community and development partners became more vocal on the need for fiscal discipline, transparency and accountability. Today, they are as vocal about corruption as they are about the general political decadence in Zimbabwe.

Most donors and development partners are now attaching stringent conditions, including the need for transparency and accountability, as pre-requisites for aid or financial support to the government. Others are also engaged in the fight against corruption through provision of direct aid to organisations such as TIZ. More recently, some donors have also become proactive and are availing resources and capacity building support towards the fight against corruption to state institutions through intergovernmental organisation initiatives such as Zimbabwe United Nations Development Assistance Framework (ZUNDAF).[15]

---

15 2012–2015 Zimbabwe United Nations Development Assistance Framework (ZUNDAF) for example provides

One of ZUNDAF's priorities is good governance, including 'enhanced accountability in the management of public resources and service delivery'. This includes direct support to institutions such as the ZACC and others.

D. Commitment to international conventions

One of the paradoxes with Zimbabwe is that, much as corruption continues to thrive almost unabated – as the discussion to follow on the legislative framework will show – the country has an elaborate legal framework to combat the vice, including commitments to a number of key anti-corruption conventions. Notably, Zimbabwe has signed and ratified the United Nations Convention Against Corruption (UNCAC) (2007); the AU Convention on Preventing and Combating Corruption, (AUCPCC) (2006); and the SADC Protocol Against Corruption (SPAC) (2004). None of these has however been domesticated directly, which has raised questions as to why the country ratifies international conventions, other than – as some critics might argue – for public posturing on the international scene.

However, to be fair, while the government has been slow to domesticate anti-corruption conventions, it has significantly incorporated some of the principles in the conventions in the anti-corruption legal framework discussed herein. Moreover, through the relevant line ministries and institutions, like the ministries of justice and ministry of home affairs or the office of the prosecutor general and the Zimbabwe Police Service, the country actively participates in UNCAC structures and submits periodic reports as required of states parties under the treaty. Zimbabwe has also complied with the UNCAC by creating an anti-corruption agency and enacting legislation to deal with corruption and other ancillary matters. Besides, Zimbabwe also participates in UNCAC processes, such as peer reviewing other states' implementation of the UNCAC.[16] According to the 2013 review of the country's compliance with the UNCAC,[17] while Zimbabwe has significantly complied with the provisions of chapter III of the convention, the country could benefit from consolidating the legal framework on corruption.

As a member of the African Union and SADC, Zimbabwe has also ratified the African Union Convention on Preventing and Combating Corruption and the SADC Protocol against Corruption. The country is an active member of various platforms involved in combating corruption, including the Southern African Forum Against Corruption (SAFAC), and has participated in all SAFAC meetings and activities. Zimbabwe has also previously chaired SAFAC and hosted its secretariat. The country's participation in SAFAC activities in the last few years has however been erratic, possibly owing to

---

for support to good governance initiatives which include support to transparency and accountability initiatives including support to ZACC at http://www.zw.one.un.org/togetherwedeliver/2012-2015-zimbabwe-united-nations-development-assistance-framework .

16 Zimbabwe participated in the country reviews of Benin and Zambia in 2012; while Zimbabwe was reviewed by Malawi and Madagascar under the auspices of the UNODC.

17 See report at https://www.unodc.org/documents/treaties/UNCAC/COSP/session5/V1387724e.pdf [accessed 20 November 2016].

financial challenges, but also because of institutional handicaps. Zimbabwe, for instance, missed the last two SAFAC meetings because there has been no substantive commission in place. Additionally, Zimbabwe is also a member of both the African Association of Anti-Corruption Authorities (AACA) and the International Association of Anti-Corruption Authorities (IAACA). The country is also a member of the Asset Recovery Inter Agency Network of Southern Africa (ARINSA); the Eastern and Southern Africa Anti-Money Laundering Group (ESAAMLG); Interpol; and the Southern African Regional Police Chiefs Cooperation Organisation (SARPCCO).

Zimbabwe's commitment to international conventions is thus marred by lack of resources. At the same time, as this paper will show, there also appears to be no firm political commitment to the principles of the conventions.

E. Legislative framework

The legal battle against corruption in Zimbabwe has been a long and winding trail that in some ways reflects the country's chequered political history. The fight found legal expression for the first time in 1985, when the nascent democracy[18]– possibly inspired by its socialist values – passed the Prevention of Corruption Act.[19] Hitherto, corruption was just an incident of the common law crimes involving dishonesty, such as theft, bribery and fraud. It was not its own crime. The Prevention of Corruption Act was thus significant in two respects. First, this was the first time corruption was legally defined and recognised as a distinct punishable offence. Secondly, the definition debunked the myth that corruption was a cancer only common to the public sector. The statutory definition extended to the private sector as well. This inclusive definition basically encompassed all individuals (agents), who, while acting for another (the principal), obtained or tried to obtain undue material advantage, by abusing their office or official position.

Prevention of Corruption Act (chapter 9:16)

The Prevention of Corruption Act provided two legal regimes: one which generally applied to agents – persons working for another; and another specifically for public officials, although the agency provisions also applied to public officials. With respect to agents, the act enumerated a number of corrupt practices, which were proscribed. These involved:
- Any agent soliciting, accepting or obtaining, agreeing to or attempting to obtain a gift or consideration for himself from another person;
- Any other person giving or agreeing to give an agent a gift or consideration as inducement or reward, in order to influence the

---

18 Zimbabwe, under the leadership of ZANU PF, then a Socialist party, gained majority rule in 1980.
19 The Prevent of Corruption Act [chapter 9.16] was promulgated on in 1985 but came into effect in on 7 February 1986.

agent's decision on any issue relating to his principal's affairs or business;
- The use of false documents where any agent, with intent to deceive his principal, uses, or any other person, with intent to deceive the agent's principal, gives to an agent, any receipt, account or other record in respect of which the principal is interested, which contains a statement that is false or erroneous or defective in a material particular;
- Any agent who, by arrangement with any seller of goods or supplier of services, secretly obtains any gift or consideration for himself or for any other person in connection with his principal's affairs or business;
- Any seller of goods or provider of services, who secretly offers a gift or consideration to an agent for himself or for any other person in regard to the sale of the goods or to the employment of his services in connection with the affairs or business of the agent's principal; or
- Any agent who, with intent to deceive his principal, or to obtain any gift or consideration for himself or any other person, fails to disclose to his principal the full nature of any transaction carried out in connection with his principal's affairs or business.

At the heart of these criminal offences was the unjust enrichment of any agent or any other person in the course of the agent's official business at the expense of the principal. Notably, corruption was criminalised from both the perspective of an agent and that of a third party, generally members of the public. With respect to public officials, the act also went on to criminalise any conduct either inconsistent with the official discharge of public duties or showing bias or prejudice, even where it could not be shown that the public officer had gained any undue material advantage. Any public officer who, in the course of his employment, does anything that is contrary to or inconsistent with his duty, or omits to do anything, which it is his duty as a public officer to do, for the purpose of showing favour or disfavour to any person, would be guilty of an offence. The act also went on to empower the minister to make regulations for 'the disclosure by persons of the origin, extent and nature of their past and present assets and liabilities' and for 'the disclosure by public officers and other agents of interests in contracts or proposed contracts or other matters connected with the business or affairs of their principals'.[20]

In order to make it easier to prosecute corruption, by its nature insidious and elusive, criminal intent – the legal requirement that the accused must have intended the alleged crime – would be presumed whenever one committed any of the corrupt practices above. It would be for that person to prove that his/her conduct was not meant to be criminal.[21] With respect to corporate entities, also to make it easier to prosecute corruption, the corrupt

---

20 Section 18(2)(a) and (b).
21 Section 15(2)(a)–(e).

practices of one company which is a subsidiary or part of a group of companies, unless the contrary were proved, would also be imputed on all the other related companies.[22] To ensure that the general public – both victim and theatre for corruption – also participates in the fight against the corruption, the act also provided for 'whistleblower' protection. Any person who, without lawful excuse, either prevents any other person from giving any information, threatens or does any other thing calculated or likely to deter any other person from giving any information, or does anything calculated or likely to prejudice any other person because that other person had given any information concerning any corrupt practice, whether in terms of the act or otherwise, would be guilty of an offence.[23] Additionally, the act also authorised the minister to make regulations for, 'the better protection from victimisation or other prejudice of persons who give information, whether in terms of this act or otherwise, concerning any corrupt practice or other dishonest or unlawful conduct'.[24]

Notably absent, however, the act did not create any standing body to combat the newly defined crime. Rather, save for the limited specification procedure considered below, this onerous task was largely left to the regular law enforcement and prosecutorial agencies. The specification procedure, on the other hand, authorised the minister[25] – acting on reasonable grounds – to, by publication in the Government Gazette, specify any person suspected to have been involved in or to have benefited from corruption or related crimes. Specification would effectively place the person specified under the curatorship of an investigator appointed by the minister to investigate that person, and the specified person may not conduct any official business without the authorisation of the investigator.[26] On his part, the investigator would be responsible for investigating the affairs and business of the specified person to establish whether or not he/she was involved in any corrupt practice as defined in the act. If so, whether any third party had any claim against the person specified as a result; and to determine the extent and nature of any such claim and the most expeditious or advantageous method of enforcing or preserving such claim. The investigator must then report the result of the investigation to the minister.[27] It is important to highlight here that the act contemplates restitution or compensation to victims of corruption.

---

22 Section 15(4).
23 Section 14(2). Note: In terms of section 19, the minister may also regulate the protection of whistleblowers further through subsidiary legislation. See also section 15(3).
24 Section 19(2)(c).
25 The minister of justice, legal and parliamentary affairs; since the act was reassigned to the ministry of homes affairs; it is now the minister of home affairs who specifies persons.
26 Section 10(7). Whether directly or through another person he/she may not, without the approval of the investigator, expend, agree to, or dispose of any property; operate any back account; increase his indebtedness or adversely affect his estate; act as a director of a company or as a partner in a partnership and so forth. Any transaction relating to the foregoing shall be void and, where property has been transferred, the investigator shall have the right to recover such property through court.
27 Section 8(1).

For the investigator to discharge his/her extensive brief effectively, he/she is conferred with tremendous statutory powers. He/she has the power to call for the production of and to take control of any documentary evidence belonging to or in the custody of the specified person, his employee/s or other associates;[28] to examine the property of the specified person;[29] or to enter any property belonging to or controlled by the specified person, or any property where there might be evidence of suspected acts of corruption by or on behalf of that person.[30] The investigator also has the power to summon the specified person or any other person, including his/her spouse, who may be able to give material information concerning the affairs or property of the specified person, or concerning any transaction carried out by him/her or on his/her behalf, or any person who has possession or custody of any relevant documentary evidence, to appear before him for 'examination'.[31]

During the examination, the investigator may interrogate any person so summoned concerning all matters relating to the affairs, business or property of the specified person, or concerning any transaction carried out by or on his behalf, and require that person to produce any book, document or record.[32] Persons under investigation are not protected from self-incrimination and the marital/spousal privilege does not apply. Banker or client privilege in relation to accounts held by the specified person, his spouse or by any person who is or was in any way associated with or was party to any transaction with the specified person or his spouse does not apply too. Wilful failure or refusal to cooperate with the investigator or contempt of the investigator is an offence.[33]

The potential for the specification procedure to combat corruption is quite immense. Its biggest drawback, however, is that this process is legally, institutionally and practically limited. To start with, the proviso that specification may only be invoked in cases of corruption where it is in the national interest to do so makes it clear that this is an exceptional procedure that was not meant to apply to the day to day incidents of corruption. This is also confirmed by the fact there is no standing investigative unit and investigators are appointed on an ad hoc basis. Secondly, the entire process is subject to the minister's discretion, which, in a questionable democracy, is susceptible to abuse. The specification procedure, although useful and profound, does not address one of the most glaring omissions in the act – the absence of a statutory watchdog against corruption.

---

28 Section 8(2)(a).
29 Section 8(2)(b.).
30 Section 8 (2)(d).
31 Section 9.
32 Section 9(3).
33 Section 13(1)(a)–(f). Any person who threatens, resists, hinders or obstructs or uses foul, abusive or insulting language towards or at an investigator; or having been summoned or required to appear at any proceedings by the investigator, fails without lawful excuse to appear, or having appeared at the proceedings, refuses to be sworn; or without lawful excuse, fails or refuses to answer fully, to the best of his/her ability, any question put to him by an investigator or fails or refuses to produce any book or record when required to do so by an investigator, shall be guilty of an offence.

Zimbabwe Constitution Amendment Act (No. 16)

As corruption continued to thrive, with two major scandals – the GMB (Paweni) scandal,[34] and the Willowgate scandal[35] – rocking the young socialist democracy, it would appear the legislature eventually came to appreciate the need for a standing watchdog. In 2000, the Zimbabwean constitution was amended to provide for an ACC.[36] Section 108A, of Amendment No. 16, provided for the ACC, whose members would be appointed by the president.[37] The members would be chosen for their integrity, knowledge and experience in administration, prosecutions, criminal investigations, or other qualifications, and would comprise at least one lawyer, one auditor or public accountant, and a veteran of more than ten years' experience in criminal investigations.[38]

The constitutional amendment charged the ACC with, 'combating corruption, theft, misappropriation, abuse of power and other improprieties in the conduct of affairs in both the public and private sectors'.[39] To accomplish this enormous and difficult task, the commission was given the power to, among other things: conduct investigations and inquiries, either of its own initiative or on receipt of complaints; to require assistance from members of the police force and other investigative agencies of the state; and, through the attorney general, to secure the prosecution of persons for corruption and other related crimes.[40] Besides, the commission would also be responsible for recommending to the government and the private sector, 'measures to enhance integrity and accountability and to prevent improprieties'.[41] The functions of the ACC were brief and its powers terse, presumably on the understanding that an act of parliament would elaborate on them further.

Anti-Corruption Commission Act (chapter 9:22)

Five years after Amendment No. 16, the ACC Act, which would pave the way for the appointment of a commission, was eventually enacted in January of 2005. The act, among other things, provided for the qualifications, appointment, and terms of conditions of members of the ACC provided for in the constitution.[42] The act also expounded on the powers of the commission. The commission would be responsible for:

- Monitoring and examining the practices, systems and procurement procedures of public and private institutions;

---

34 See http://www.theindependent.co.zw/2013/09/27/corruption-now-time-walk-talk/ [accessed 21 November 2016].
35 See https://en.wikipedia.org/wiki/Willowgate.
36 Constitutional Amendment (No. 16) Act, Act 5 of 2000, also referred to herein as Constitutional Amendment No. 16.
37 Section 108A(1).
38 Section 108A(2).
39 Section 108A(3).
40 Section 108A(4)(a)-(c).
41 Section 108(A)(3).
42 Section 4–7.

- Enlisting and fostering public support in combating corruption in society;
- Educating the public on the dangers of corruption in society;
- Instructing, advising and assisting any officer, agency or institution in the elimination or minimisation of corruption;
- Receiving and investigating complaints alleging corruption;
- Investigating the conduct of persons suspected to be involved in corruption; and
- Assisting in the formulation of practices, systems and procurement procedures of public and private institutions with a view to the eliminating corrupt practices; advising on ways of strengthening anti-corruption legislation; and recommending to the government the ratification and domestication of relevant international legal instruments aimed at combating corruption.[43]

In terms of its powers, the commission was empowered to:
- Make recommendations to the police to arrest and detain any person reasonably suspected of corruption, or of committing any of the statutory offences that were enumerated in the schedule to the act, and to communicate any such recommendation to the attorney general;
- Obtain search warrants from a magistrate or justice of the peace;
- Seize any travel documents or anything which is reasonably believed to contain evidence of the commission of an offence related to corruption;
- Seek, through the attorney general's office, court orders for the freezing of any assets or accounts of persons suspected to be involved in any offence related to corruption;
- Protect and safeguard any persons assisting in investigations involving any offence related to corruption;
- Enter any public or private premises and require any public officer or agent of a public officer to answer any questions related to the investigation of any offence related to corruption;
- Cause to be prosecuted through the attorney general's office, any person reasonably believed to have committed any offence related to corruption;
- Seek court orders through the attorney general's office for confiscation of proceeds of corruption;
- Recommend that any public officer, agency or institution follow a recommended system to improve administrative efficiency; and

---

43 Section 12. See also the commission's objectives set out in section 11.

- Make standing orders related to the control and administration of the commission, the discipline, training, classification of and promotion of officers, the duties of officers and the financial regulation of the commission, and any other matters expedient or necessary for preventing the abuse or neglect of duty and for upholding the integrity of the commission.[44]

As the act effectively conferred the commission policing powers, in terms of section 13(2), the commission would exercise its powers concurrently with those of the Zimbabwe Republic Police (ZRP). In some instances, the commission would however have to act only with the assistance of the police. In relation to searches, entry or seizures, unless in urgent or exigent circumstances, the commission would have to notify the officer commanding the police district concerned and be accompanied by an assigned police officer.[45] The potential for conflict between the police and the commission as a result of the overlap was quite obvious. The lawmaker thus provided for the resolution of any conflict between the commission and the ZRP through the office of attorney general. The attorney general was given the power to intervene and direct the parties as necessary to resolve any conflict.[46]

The first commission was appointed in terms of the act in September 2005.

Criminal Law (Codification and Reform) Act (chapter 9:23)

In 2006, as part of a comprehensive legislative review process, corruption was re-defined when the Criminal Law (Codification and Reform) Act, came into force. The Code, essentially codified (in some instances also re-defining the law) all the criminal offences operative in Zimbabwe which, previously, were largely unwritten (common law) or scattered in various statutes. Corruption, which was criminalised alongside bribery – a nearly indistinguishable cousin – was re-defined and the prohibited corrupt practices, under the Prevention of Corruption Act, were provided as distinct criminal offenses. The act of soliciting, obtaining or agreeing to obtain or accepting a gift or consideration as an inducement or reward by any agent, or the act of offering, giving or agreeing to give any agent a gift or consideration as an inducement or reward by any third party, knowing or realising that there is a real risk or possibility that such gift or consideration is not due to the agent, were criminalised as bribery.[47] The use of a false document by any agent in order to deceive or prejudice his/her principal, or the use of a false document by any third party to deceive any agent, was criminalised under the crime of 'corruptly using a false document'.[48]

---

44 Section 13(1) as read with the schedule thereof.
45 Section 13(4).
46 Section 13(5).
47 Section 170(1).
48 Section 171.

The crime involving the failure by any agent to fully disclose an interest in a transaction relating to his/her principal's business under the Prevention of Corruption Act was amplified into four separate criminal offences. The first is the crime of, 'corruptly concealing a transaction from a principal', where any agent, carrying out any transaction in connection with his/her principal's affairs or business, fails to disclose to the principal the full nature of the transaction in order to either deceive the principal or realising that there is a real risk or possibility that the principal may be deceived, or intending to obtain a consideration, knowing or realising that there is a real risk or possibility that such consideration is not due to him/her. This crime also extends to any person (third party) who carries out with any agent or assists any agent to carry out any transaction in connection with the affairs or business of the agent's principal, knowing that the agent does not intend to disclose to the principal the full nature of the transaction.[49] By extension, any agreement between any agent and any other person not to disclose to the agent's principal the full nature of any transaction by the agent in connection with the principal's affairs or business in order to deceive the principal, or where there is a real risk or possibility that the principal may be deceived, or intending that the agent should obtain a consideration knowing or realising that there is a real risk or possibility that such consideration is not due to him/her,[50] was also criminalised as a separate crime of, 'conspiracy to commit the crime of corruptly concealing a transaction from a principal'.[51]

A further category relating to, 'corruptly concealing from a principal a personal interest in a transaction', was also created where, any agent carries out any transaction in connection with his/her principal's affairs or business without disclosing to the principal that he/she holds a personal interest in the subject-matter of the transaction in order to either deceive the principal, or realising that there is a real risk or possibility that the principal may be deceived, or in order to obtain a consideration knowing or realising that there is a real risk or possibility that such consideration is not due to him/her. The crime also extends to any person (third party) who carries out any transaction with any agent or assists any agent carry out any transaction in connection with the affairs or business of the agent's principal, knowing that the agent does not intend to disclose to the principal a personal interest which the agent or the other person holds in the subject-matter of the transaction.[52] This provision also provided for the crime of 'conspiracy to commit the crime of corruptly concealing from a principal a personal interest in a transaction', where any agent and any other person agree or arrange not to disclose to the agent's principal any personal interest held by the agent in the subject-matter of any transaction in connection with the principal's affairs or business in order to deceive the principal or where there is a real risk or possibility that the principal may be deceived, or intending that the agent

---

49 Section 172(1).
50 Section 173(2).
51 Section 172(2).
52 Section 173(1).

should obtain a consideration knowing or realising that there is a real risk or possibility that such consideration is not due to them.[53]

With respect to public officials, the original crime in the Prevention of Corruption Act remained the same,[54] subject to the affirmative action qualification.[55] Also, as in the previous act, to make it easier to prove the crimes, criminal intent will also be presumed once it is shown that acts of corruption were committed in the manner and circumstances above. It would be for the person concerned to prove that in acting as he/she did, he/she did not intend to act in a criminal/corrupt way.[56] The Code, however gives a wider and more systematic enunciation of corruption. Notably, where the Prevention of Corruption Act placed emphasis on the corrupt practices of/by an agent, the Code criminalises corruption from both the perspective of any agent and that of any participating third party squarely. Also noteworthy, the Code not only penalises wilful acts of corruption, where any agent or any third party knowingly acts in a particular corrupt way or knowingly desires a particular corrupt result, but the Code equally criminalises reckless conduct, where any agent or any third party acts in the realisation that there is a real risk or possibility that his/her conduct or the result therefore may amount to corruption. Reckless failure to verify readily verifiable facts or wilful blindness designed to mask corruption is thus criminalised. Also noteworthy, the act not only criminalises completed acts of corruption; that is, where a corrupt transaction actually takes place. Known as inchoate crimes in legal terms, under the 'conspiracy to commit' offenses,[57] the mere act by any agent and any other person of agreeing or arranging to withhold any information from the agent's principal – failure to disclose a transaction or an interest in a transaction – in order to mislead the principal or to secure a benefit for the agent, is also criminalised. The transaction itself need not have been completed. Nor is it necessary that the principal actually be deceived or prejudiced. What is prohibited is simply the agreement or arrangement.

The scope of the new definition is quite immense. Yet again, the law was well-defined and what was left was for the enforcement mechanisms to match its letter. Sadly, as the country's economy continued on a downward spiral, amid political instability, corruption continued to thrive, with the law enforcement agencies appearing to be out of their depth, or complicit.

Constitution of Zimbabwe Amendment Act (No. 19)

In 2009, the Zimbabwean constitution was amended yet again, after a coalition government between the ruling ZANU PF party and the opposition movement, MDC (in

---

53 Section 173(2).
54 Section 174(1).
55 Section 174(3): any public officer who does or omits to do anything in the exercise of his/her functions for the purposes of favouring any person on the ground of race or gender pursuant a government policy for the advancement of historically disadvantaged groups shall not be guilty of abuse of duty.
56 See sections 170(2); 171(2); 172(3) 173(3); and 174(2).
57 Section 172(2) and 173(2).

its two formations, MDC-T and MDC[58]), came to power, following a disputed presidential election victory for ZANU PF. (In the same election, the opposition had obtained a majority in parliament.) A compromise political settlement, Constitutional Amendment No. 19,[59] introduced a number of institutional changes that were designed to accommodate the opposition in government and to assuage some of their standing concerns.

Possibly a function of the opposition's involvement in government, as well as its numerical strength in parliament, Section 100K of Constitutional Amendment No. 19, reconstituted the ACC as the Zimbabwe Anti-corruption Commission (ZACC). Comprising the same old number of members,[60] chosen on the same basic criteria,[61] the only notable change was that members would be appointed by the president, 'in consultation with the committee on standing rules and orders'.[62] This is a committee of parliament appointed in terms of what is now Section 151 of the constitution. This added qualification was clearly meant to curb the previously unfettered executive discretion of the president in the appointments to ensure the independence and integrity of the commission. The functions of the commission otherwise remained the same.[63]

Zimbabwe Constitution Amendment Act (No. 20)

As Constitutional Amendment No. 19 was for all intents and purposes an interim arrangement,[64] as soon as the unlikely coalition government came to power, one of its immediate concerns was to undertake a comprehensive review of the Zimbabwean constitution – itself a compromise document which, at inception, tried to balance the interests of the defeated White supremacist regime and the victorious African majority, and had subsequently survived an onslaught of nineteen subsequent piecemeal amendments and was generally considered outdated. Following a widespread public consultation process under the stewardship of the coalition government, a new constitution, the Constitution of Zimbabwe Amendment (No. 20) Act, 2013, was enacted. The amendment, which

---

58 Originally conceived as the Movement for Democratic change (MDC), the party split into two in October 2005. After the split, as both splinter groups laid claim to the popular name and brand, the two formations became known as, MDC-T, after the leader, Morgan Tsvangirai, and MDC after the erstwhile leader, Arthur Mutambara.
59 The Constitution of Zimbabwe Amendment (No. 19) Act, 2009.
60 At least four but not more than nine members – section 100K(1).
61 That the members be persons of integrity chosen for knowledge and experience in administration or the prosecution and investigation of crime or for their general suitability for appointment, and that at least one of them should be lawyer, one auditor or public accountant, and one someone with not less than ten years' investigative experience – section 100K(2).
62 Section 100K(1)
63 Section 108A of the amended constitution was replicated word for word in section 100L of the Amendment.
64 Under the Global Political Agreement between ZANU PF and the MDC, one of the terms was that the coalition government would guide the nation through a constitutional reform process that would result in a free and fair election under a new constitution. See article VI of the, 'Global Political Agreement (Government of National Unity), 15 September 2008'.

introduced a new constitution all-together,[65] came into force on 22 May 2013, but some of the provisions were staggered over time.[66]

Perhaps, because of the involvement of a corruption-weary public directly in its formulation, the new constitution attempted to take the fight against corruption to the next level. The constitution not only provided for a reinvigorated independent anti-corruption commission, the need for transparency and accountability underlined the new constitutional dispensation. The need to combat corruption, especially in the public sector, was recognised as one of the national objectives underpinning the new constitution. As such, the constitution is replete with provisions designed to promote good governance, accountability and probity in the public sector, as well as specific mechanisms against corruption.

Substantive provisions designed to combat corruption in the constitution

The commitment to stamp out corruption in the public sector was affirmed from the onset in the constitutional, national objectives under the heading, 'Good governance', where the state was enjoined to, 'adopt and implement policies and legislation to develop efficiency, competence, accountability, transparency, personal integrity and financial probity in all institutions and agencies of government at every level and in every public institution', and in particular, to ensure that appointments to public offices are made primarily on the basis of merit, and to put in place measures to expose, combat and eradicate all forms of corruption and abuse of power by those holding political and public office.[67] For these purposes, 'the state must ensure that all institutions and agencies of government at every level, in particular commissions and other bodies established by or under (the) constitution, are provided with adequate resources and facilities to enable them to carry out their functions conscientiously, fairly, honestly and efficiently'.[68]

Under the heading, 'Basic values and principles governing public administration', the constitution went on to provide for a public administrative system, 'governed by the democratic values and principles enshrined in (the) constitution, including the principles that, 'a high standard of professional ethics must be promoted and maintained';[69] 'public administration must be accountable to parliament and to the people';[70] and that, 'transparency must be fostered by providing the public with timely, accessible and accurate information'.[71] With respect to state owned companies, the constitution enjoined companies and other commercial entities owned or wholly controlled by the state to conduct their operations so as to maintain commercial viability and abide by generally accepted

---

65 Section 3(1).
66 Section 3(1), sixth schedule.
67 Section 9(1).
68 Section 9(2).
69 Section 194(1)(a).
70 Section 194(1)(b).
71 Section 194(1)(c).

standards of good corporate governance.[72] Also, that they must establish transparent, open and competitive procurement systems – a requirement no doubt inspired by the everyday allegations of rampant corruption with respect to public tenders.

Possibly a direct response to the perceived partisan conduct of some senior officials in strategic government institutions like the security agencies or the electoral bodies – some of whom have publicly declared their political allegiance – the constitution also underscored the need for a professional and apolitical civil service. Under the heading, 'Responsibilities of public officers and principles of leadership', the supreme law reiterated that the, 'authority assigned to public officers is a public trust which must be exercised in a manner which,' among other things, 'promotes public confidence in the office held by the public officer'.[73] Section 196 further provided that:

> (2) Public officers must conduct themselves, in public and private life, so as to avoid any conflict between their personal interest and their public or official duties, and to abstain from any conduct that demeans their office, and
> (3) Public officers in leadership positions must abide by the following principles of leadership:
> (a) objectivity and impartiality in decision making;
> (b) honesty in the execution of public duties;
> (c) accountability to the public for decisions and actions; and
> (d) discipline and commitment in the service of the people.

In the fight against corruption, it is indeed true that information is power. Section 62 of the constitution thus provided for access to information. The provision provides that:

> Every Zimbabwean citizen or permanent resident, including juristic persons and the Zimbabwean media, has the right of access to any information held by the state or by any institution or agency of government at every level, in so far as the information is required in the interest of public accountability.

This right of access to information held by the state, it is important to observe, is guaranteed as fundamental freedom protected under the bill of rights and is justiciable under the generous and accessible terms of section 85.[74] When looking at this right, it is also important to consider the provisions of the Access to Information and Protection of Privacy Act,[75] which amplifies on the right and regulates access.[76]

---

72 Section 195(1).
73 Section 196(1)(c)
74 Section 85 provides a locus for the enforcement of fundamental human rights and freedoms and provides very liberal grounds for standing.
75 Access to Information and Protection of Privacy Act [chapter 10:27].
76 Although the act predates the constitution, it remains applicable to the extent that it does not conflict with the supreme law.

Institutions against corruption

In order to ensure the level of transparency and accountability envisaged under the new dispensation – possibly a learning from history, when the substance of the law was not always matched by the enforcement mechanisms – chapter 12 of the constitution, creates a number of 'Independent Commissions Supporting Democracy', namely: the Zimbabwe Electoral Commission, the Zimbabwe Human Rights Commission, the Zimbabwe Gender Commission, the Zimbabwe Media Commission; and the National Peace and Reconciliation Commission. In addition to their respective specific mandates, one of the general objectives of these commissions is 'to promote transparency and accountability in public institutions'.[77] Especially noteworthy, for present purposes, however, are the functions of the Zimbabwe Media Commission, in particular its mandate to, 'uphold, promote and develop freedom of the media',[78] and to, 'ensure that the people of Zimbabwe have a fair and wide access to information'.[79] The importance of access to information in the fight against corruption, as stated earlier, cannot be overemphasised. One of the biggest corruption scandals in Zimbabwe, the Willowgate scandal,[80] was broken by the press. Offshore, there was the Watergate scandal.[81]

The principal agents against corruption under the new constitution are however the 'Institutions to Combat Corruption and Crime', provided for in chapter 13, namely the ZACC and the NPA. The ZACC is considered in detail below.

F. Prevention and combatting of corruption bureau: The ZACC

Historical development of institutional framework to combat corruption

As indicated above in the elaborate discussion on the legislative framework, the ZACC was introduced in 2009 under Constitutional Amendment No.19. The ZACC replaced the Anti-Corruption Commission, which was provided for in Constitutional Amendment No. 16 of 2000 and established in 2005. The ZACC was then incorporated into the new constitution – Amendment Act No. 20 – subject to changes to its powers and terms of appointment. Constitutional Amendment No. 20, it will be recalled, was a people driven constitution that, as already mentioned, was promulgated following a widespread public consultation process and subsequent referendum. It could therefore be said that the commission, at least in its present form, was a direct creation of the people.

---

77 Section 233(d).
78 Section 149(1)(a).
79 Section 149(1)(f).
80 Willowgate scandal, which involved the illegal buying and selling of motor vehicles at super profits by senior government officials. See: https://en.wikipedia.org/wiki/Willowgate.
81 See: https://en.wikipedia.org/wiki/Watergate_scandal.

Stability of the agency

Like its predecessor, the Anti-Corruption Commission, the ZACC is a constitutional body. It derives its existence from the constitution and draws its powers therefrom. In that context, at least as far as the law is concerned, it enjoys the highest level of legal protection. However, in practice, the agency's stability is often affected by political interference as will be shown later herein.

Agency staff

ZACC staff may be said to fall into two categories: the commissioners – who constitute the 'commission' and are collectively clothed with the statutory powers provided in the constitution – and the employees, who are in turn employed by the commission and act as its administrative delegates and secretariat. It is the conditions of service of the commissioners that are most germane to this discussion although consideration is also given to those of the employees of the commission.

Section 254 of the constitution constitutes the ZACC, which shall comprise a chairperson and eight other members.[82] All are appointed by the president in consultation with the committee on standing rules and orders.[83] With respect to the eight members (less the chair), the committee on standing rules and orders must however submit to the president a list of not fewer than twelve members from which the eight shall be appointed.[84] in order to identify eligible members, for transparency's sake, the committee on standing rules and orders must follow the steps set out in section 237(1). The committee must: advertise the positions, invite the public to make nominations, conduct public interviews of prospective candidates, prepare a list of the appropriate number of nominees, and submit the list to the president. Interviews for the incoming commission were held for the first time in June 2015. This elaborate appointment procedure serves two immediately visible purposes. The process curtails the exerting influence of the executive (the president) and gives the commission an aura of independence. At the same time, by involving the public, directly as well as through elected representatives, the process also lends the commission public confidence and legitimacy. That said, the fact that the president has the final say somewhat dilutes the public's input in the appointment process and also raises questions on the commission's absolute independence from the executive.

In terms of their tenure, under section 320(1) of the constitution, members of the ZACC shall hold office for a five-year term, which is renewable only once. During their tenure, members are however protected from arbitrary dismissal. They may only be removed on the grounds clearly set out in the constitution – mental incapacity, gross incompetence, gross misconduct or disqualification in terms of the constitution – under the same independent disciplinary process as the judiciary. The procedure is set out in section 187

---

82 The basic requirement for eligibility for the commissioners remains the same under the old constitution from section 100K (2), 254(2) which borrows verbatim the eligibility requirements.
83 Section 254(1).
84 Section 254(2)(b).

of the constitution. The disciplinary proceedings are presided over by an independent tribunal of not less than three members, one of whom must be a retired judge in Zimbabwe, or a judge from a comparable English speaking jurisdiction; and the other, a seasoned lawyer chosen from a list of three nominees by the Law Society of Zimbabwe. The tribunal shall decide whether a commissioner must be removed or not and make recommendations to the president. The tribunal's recommendations shall be binding on the president.

It must however be observed that section 320(1) does not offer absolute security of tenure, firstly in that – unlike the judiciary, which enjoys unlimited tenure until mandatory retirement – the commissioners' terms are limited to a maximum of two five-year terms, subject to reappointment after the first term. Security of tenure is generally considered integral to independence. In the present case the limited nature of the tenure and especially the reappointment provision raises concerns of the ZACC's absolute independence. It leaves the commissioners vulnerable to the vagaries of politics in a bid to secure reappointment or to be considered for other appointments after the ZACC.

Also incidental to the commission's independence, which also goes to the question of ethics and conduct in terms of section 254; the ZACC, like the other independent commissions: shall be independent and not subject to the direction and control of anyone; must act in accordance with the constitution; must exercise its functions without fear, favour or prejudice; and shall only be accountable to parliament. Members of the ZACC must not exercise their functions in a partisan manner or further or prejudice the interests of any political party or cause. Persons who are members of a political party must relinquish their position forthwith or within 30 days of their appointment to the commission. Likewise, commissioners who take political office or fail to relinquish political positions held shall cease to be members of the ZACC immediately. In terms of section 320(7), commissioners shall be paid from the consolidated revenue fund.

Regarding employees of the ZACC, also an incident of the ZACC's independence, the employees do not form part of the civil service. They shall be employed by the ZACC as provided for in section 234 of the constitution. Effectively, their terms and conditions are determined by the commission subject to the country's protective labour laws.

Responsibilities of the agency

With respect to the commission's functions, section 255 expands on the functions conferred under the repealed constitution.

(1) The ZACC has the following functions:
   (a) To investigate and expose cases of corruption in the public and private sectors;
   (b) To combat corruption, theft, misappropriation, abuse of power and other improper conduct in the public and private sectors;

(c) To promote honesty, financial discipline and transparency in the public and private sectors;
(d) To receive and consider complaints from the public and to take such action in regard to the complaints as it considers appropriate;
(e) To direct the commissioner general of police to investigate cases of suspected corruption and to report to the commission on the results of any such investigation;
(f) To refer matters to the national prosecuting authority for prosecution;
(g) To require assistance from members of the police service and other investigative agencies of the state; and
(h) To make recommendations to the government and other persons on measures to enhance integrity and accountability and prevent improper conduct in the public and private sectors.

While some of these functions reflect those in Amendment No. 19, or in the ZACC Act,[85] the scope of commission's powers under section 255 makes it apparent that the legislature clearly envisaged the ZACC as the primary gatekeeper against corruption. The commission was specifically charged to combat corruption both in the public and private sectors, through various mechanisms, including investigations, either on its own or through the law enforcement agencies; prosecutions, through the NPA, as well as stamping out corruption through other non-legal measures as 'naming and shaming', either through its reports to parliament,[86] or pursuant to its general powers to, 'expose cases of corruption in the public and private sectors'. With respect to policing powers, notably, the ZACC was conferred the power, not only to, 'require assistance from members of the police service and other investigative agencies of the state', but also, where necessary, to 'direct the commissioner general of police to investigate cases of suspected corruption and to report to the commission on the results of any such investigation'. The commissioner general must comply with such directions.[87] This, it is observed, gives the commission more investigative powers than previously held under the ZACC Act, when it could only exercise its policing powers concurrently with those of the police.

Besides the policing and enforcement functions, the ZACC was also designated the official policy advisor on corruption and related matters.[88] The ZACC was empowered to make 'recommendations to the government and other persons on measures to enhance integrity and accountability and prevent improper conduct in the public and private sectors'.[89] While there is no specific requirement that government must implement the commission's recommendations, it is possible that the commission may still pressure the

---

85 Unless repealed or amended, the act will remain in force to the extent that it is not inconsistent with the new constitution.
86 Section 257.
87 Section 255(2).
88 Section 255(1)(c).
89 Section 255(1)(h).

executive by reporting any government inaction or lack of cooperation to parliament. In terms of the constitution, the ZACC may make special reports to parliament on any 'improper conduct' by government or the private sector, over and above the mandatory annual reports.[90] This reporting procedure – naming and shaming – could be used to pressure both government and errant companies. Ultimately, the commission could also use this parliamentary report procedure to recommend legislative reform where either or both the government and the private sector fail to comply with significant recommendations of a policy nature.

Some critics have however argued that the commission's lack of independent powers of arrest affects its effectiveness. The commission must still rely on the police to effect arrests. In terms of section 257(3), the government must ensure, through legislation and other means that the ZACC has the power, 'to recommend the arrest and secure the prosecution of persons reasonably suspected of corruption, abuse of power and other improper conduct which falls within the commission's jurisdiction' (emphasis added). This restriction of the commission's powers to merely recommending arrests reflects the wording in the ZACC Act, whose provisions on the issue,[91] unless repealed or amended, remain relevant as they do not conflict with the constitution. An officer of the commission who intends to make any search, entry or seizure, it appears, must therefore still notify the officer commanding the police district concerned and be accompanied by an assigned officer, except in urgent or exigent circumstances. Others have also questioned the need for the ZACC to submit its reports to parliament through the line ministry – home affairs[92] – although at least on paper, that should merely be a formality.

Feedback mechanism and witness protection

While both the Prevention of Corruption Act and ACC Act provide for protection of those who give information on corruption, not much detail is provided and the provisions have not operationalised. Indeed, this is one area that Zimbabwe has been found to be consistently weak under the UNCAC review mechanism. The government has however stated that it is working on whistleblower protection.[93] The delay in addressing this gap however raises concerns as to the government's commitment to combat corruption, as whistleblower protection has a direct bearing on the reporting of corruption, especially high level corruption.

There is nothing in the existing legislative framework for a feedback mechanism, although there appears to be nothing that should stop such measures being implemented at a policy level.

---

90 Section 257.
91 Section 13(4), Zimbabwe Anti-Corruption Commission Act.
92 Section 257 of the constitution.
93 See https://www.newsday.co.zw/2014/07/10/govt-still-crafting-whistleblowers-act/ [accessed 20 November 2016].

Seizure, forfeiture, recovery of assets and mutual legal assistance

The Criminal Procedure and Evidence Act provides for seizure, forfeiture and recovery of assets in relations to criminal prosecutions. These provisions would apply to cases of corruption, which as stated above, are adequately defined and criminalised in the Code.

Mutual legal assistance with other countries is provided for under the Criminal Matters (Mutual Assistance) Act of 1990. This act is designed to facilitate search, seizure, forfeiture and recovery of assets to and from other countries that have reciprocal mutual legal assistance arrangements with Zimbabwe in terms of section 3. The act also specifies that its provisions do not preclude the operation of other arrangements for search, seizure, forfeiture and recovery of assets. Thus it is possible for such further additional arrangements to be made through Interpol as well as through inter-governmental cooperation in terms of extradition arrangements.

Financial resources

In terms of section 322, parliament must ensure that funds are appropriated to the commission to enable it to exercise its functions effectively. Moreover, in terms of section 305, the minister of finance must, in the national annual budget, provide a separate budget for the commission. In practice this has however not been implemented. Rather, as a matter of practice, the ZACC receives its budget allocation through the ministry of home affairs, which, until November 2015, was the line ministry. The ZACC now falls under the office of the president and cabinet (OPC). This has been the position operationally since the ZACC was established and results from the fact that there are no accounting mechanisms through which the ZACC can receive funds directly from the consolidated revenue fund. It does not appear that any measures are being taken to operationalise section 305, which means that the ZACC will continue to be subject to financial management by the OPC.

The ZACC's lack of an independent budget poses challenges and has often incapacitated the commission's execution of its mandate. It denies the commission the capacity to plan, organise and prioritise its work. On a number of instances, the ZACC has failed to receive adequate resources for operations from the line ministry, other than salaries and benefits for its commissioners and staff, thus effectively rendering it a white elephant. This has been interpreted in some quarters as further indication of the lack of political will by the state to support the commission's core mandate – the fight against corruption.

Detailed operational budget and auditing

Since the ZACC is funded through the line ministry, it is also audited as part of the ministry, previously, the ministry of home affairs. It is noteworthy even though the ZACC has submitted full operational budgets to the ministry of finance since its establishment; it has never received the full budget requirements.[94]

---

94 As discussed earlier herein.

Relationship with the public and other stakeholders

The ZACC's interaction with the public in general has somewhat been limited. The commission is only located in the capital city and nowhere else in the country. This means that for the more remote parts of the country, the ZACC is inaccessible at best and non-existent at worst. Besides, even in the cities, the ZACC has failed to maintain a visible and accessible profile. The commission does not have comprehensive and consistent engagement strategies with the public, such as outreach awareness campaigns. As shown in the TIZ study referred to earlier, a number of people did not know where to report corruption or where to find the ZACC. Because of its inaccessibility, some members of the public have a low regard for the commission and are of the impression that the entity can be done away with. Indeed, even at parliamentary level, there appears to be a lack of confidence in the ZACC. In 2014, the legislature went so far as to vote for the setting of up a special parliamentary committee to combat corruption despite the existence of the ZACC. The proposal was only rescinded after the speaker, at the intervention of some members, ruled that the establishment of such a committee would be inconsistent with the existence of the ZACC and violate the constitution.[95]

With respect to the other stakeholders, the ZACC has endeavoured to maintain its independence. As such, the ZACC does not have any relationship with any of the political parties, although there are misgivings that some of the commissioners might be politically aligned. In the same way, the ZACC has also maintained a safe distance from non-governmental development partners. It is primarily state funded and has not actively or directly sought material assistance from any development partner. Its interface with some development partners has been limited and indirect. The interface has been largely through established government and development partner platforms such as the ZUNDAF, which brings together the UN agencies represented in Zimbabwe and the government of Zimbabwe on an agreed to development agenda for a fixed period. Likewise, the ZACC's interface with civil society organisations has also been limited. In recent years, the ZACC has however partnered with various CSOs on anti-corruption public awareness campaigns. To this end, the ZACC collaborated with such entities as Transparency International Zimbabwe and the Southern Africa Human Rights Trust. These relationships are however not formalised and remain ad hoc despite overtures for formal arrangements by civil society.

The ZACC's relationship with the media is typical of any relationships between the media and any public body that holds information of a public interest or executes an important and contentious public mandate. The ZACC will not readily offer interviews, press releases or other engagement with the media and the press continues to hound the commission for information or commentaries on matters of interest. This position is quite regrettable as the media should ordinarily be a strategic partner in the fight against

---

95 See http://www.zimbabweonlinenews.com/zimbabwe-parliament-speaker-rules-against-establishing-ad-hoc-committee-on-corruption/ [accessed 20 November 2016].

corruption. This is in spite of the fact that a number of investigations by the ZACC resulted from stories that were broken by the media. Moreover, the media, particularly the private media, has also provided the ZACC the platforms to clarify matters when it has been under attack. The media has also been instrumental in highlighting the challenges that the ZACC has faced such as lack of resources. The ZACC's aloofness from other stakeholders is regrettable as it has resulted in it losing out on opportunities to partner with institutions that have access to greater audiences and resources such as the media and civil society organisations.

Agency relationships with the private sector

In terms of the constitution, the ZACC is also supposed to preside over corruption in the private sector, its relationship with the corporate world is almost non-existent. This is partly because corruption in Zimbabwe has largely been perceived as a public sector issue. There is thus currently no direct collaboration between the ZACC and the private sector. Any interaction between the two parties has been ad hoc and upon request. In most instances, this has mainly been through invitations for the ZACC to attend specific functions and speak to corruption and how it is dealing with the issue. On the other hand, it is important to note that the private sector has also initiated a number of anti-corruption interventions on its own without seeking the assistance of or partnering with the ZACC. For instance, a number of accounting firms are part of a consortium with a toll free anti-graft telephone line. This telephone line is however not linked to the ZACC and the reports received are not forwarded to ZACC. It would appear that the private sector perceives corporate corruption as different from that in the public sector and does not see the benefit of collaborating with the ZACC, which focuses mostly on public sector. This lack of cooperation could also be an indictment against the ZACC, which is still perceived as 'toothless'.

Agency reporting mechanisms and public perception

In terms of its reporting systems – that is, how the ZACC receives reports of corruption from informants – the commission largely relies on three mediums: in person reports, written reports, and telephone reports. As the ZACC has offices only in Harare, only those who live in or can travel to the capital report cases in person. The rest are otherwise forced to make telephonic or written reports, which is not very reassuring when one is divulging very sensitive information. Those who report are not compensated in any way, even by way of reimbursement for direct costs. Moreover, although legislation provides for whistleblower protection, as considered above, the ZACC and the police do not have the resources or capacity to offer effective protection for those persons reporting corruption or other impropriety. These institutional deficiencies thus affect the effective reporting of cases of corruption. With respect to the actual filing of a report by an individual, the system is also not automatically designed to guarantee anonymity, which can be discouraging.

The standard practice is for informants to disclose their identifying particulars. While anonymous reports may also be taken, this appears to be the exception and not the norm.

Performance

In spite of the available comprehensive constitutional and legal framework, Zimbabwe has still struggled to effectively combat or contain corruption. A lack of resources (both financial and human), is clearly one of the reasons, although that could be overstated. A closer analysis of the way the ZACC is constituted and how it operates, however, also points to other factors, which affect its effectiveness. These can be classified under two broad categories. First, the structural/institutional challenges, which relate to the manner in which the ZACC is set up; its mandate and its relationship with collaborating partners like the police, the judiciary, and the prosecuting authority. These then give rise to the second aspect: the operational challenges, which affect the daily execution of the commission's mandate. Ultimately, critics suggest, these weaknesses can be traced back to a lack of political will by those in power, who – it has been argued – are themselves the major culprits in corruption.

G. Structural and institutional challenges

Interaction with parliament, reporting procedure

As discussed, while the constitution provides for the ZACC to report directly to parliament, the same provision also requires that the reports be submitted through the 'responsible minister'. While it appears this was intended as a mere formality, in practice, the line ministry has somehow arrogated itself editorial or veto power with respect to these reports. Between 2010 and 2012, for instance, the ZACC produced its annual reports and forwarded them to the responsible ministry. The minister however never tabled the reports before parliament, thus denying the commission access to the legislature at the same time denying the lawmakers their oversight powers as the constitution envisages. On its part, parliament has never taken the ZACC or the 'responsible minister' to task for not submitting annual or other reports to parliament. This obvious lapse in oversight raises questions about parliament's commitment to preventing and combating corruption.

Financial arrangements: lack of an independent budget

Another critical issue is the ZACC's dependence on the responsible ministry for budget allocation, disbursements, and financial accounting. Although in terms of the constitution, constitutional commissions are supposed to be provided independent and separate budgets, in practice the ZACC has only received its funding through the ministry of home affairs, and with effect from November 2015 it will be through the OPC, ostensibly for 'accounting purposes'. As a result, the commission lacks financial independence and must rely on the responsible ministry, which determines its budget allocation, and by extension, the scope of its activities and the priority areas. In practice, the ministry has released funds to the commission piecemeal and for specific purposes like salaries. This has effectively reduced the ZACC to an organ of the ministry and seriously curtailed its effectiveness.

Recruitment of staff
The ACC Act allows the ZACC to recruit its own staff, in consultation with the minister responsible, which in practice resulted in the responsible ministry assuming control over the ZACC recruitment. Although the new constitution now provides for full autonomy on staff issues, in view of the current structure where the ZACC accesses resources through the responsible ministry, this provision is not likely to be followed through and the responsible ministry will likely continue to influence the recruitment process.

Operational challenges
Control by the responsible ministry
As the discussion immediately above clearly shows, despite its guaranteed constitutional independence until November 2015, when it was transferred to the OPC, the ZACC has effectively operated within and through the ministry of home affairs, as the responsible ministry. Among others, the ministry has controlled the ZACC's budget as well as its access to parliament, thus effectively rendering the commission a subordinate entity, which, as stated earlier, affects its effectiveness.

Inadequate budget allocations
Because, in practice, the ZACC has no independent budget and must bid for a budget allocation through the responsible ministry, since inception, it has never received its full budget request from treasury. Between 2011 and 2014, the ZACC received only between 7-12% of its total request. Subsequently this incapacitates the operations of the commission, which, in the past, would sometimes only receive salaries for the commissioners and staff and little else for investigations and other core activities.

Lack of cooperation and institutional relationship issues
As already discussed, the ZACC's lack of independent powers of arrest and prosecution, and its reliance on the police and the prosecuting authority, affect its effectiveness where it fails to secure the support of these agencies. At a second level, there was always potential for conflict between the ZACC and other 'sister' state organs, also administered by the ministry of home affairs, such as the police, the department of immigration and the registrar general's office. The fact that some of these departments have also been identified among the most corrupt put them and the ZACC on a collision course. As indicated above, the ZACC was however recently reassigned under the OPC and it is hoped that this should ease this potential conflict. It is also hoped that this should help strengthen the ZACC's capacity.

In short, the ZACC's performance has traditionally been severely curtailed by limited resources, dependence on the responsible ministry, and (at times) lack of support from other state agencies. The latter aspect – the ZACC's reliance on other agencies like the police and the prosecutor general's office for the successful execution of its mandate – coupled with the existence of other anti-corruption agencies like the department of anti-corruption and anti-monopolies in the ministry of home affairs, thus raises the question of whether it would not be better to adopt a unitary system and an all-powerful anti-corruption agency. This would clearly take care of the cooperation problems and possibly the funding issues. While arguments have been made for increased autonomy and more power to the ZACC, including full policing and prosecuting authority, there is also a compelling case for various actors to remain involved in the anti-corruption crusade. In countries that do not have anti-corruption agencies, like South Africa for instance, corruption is handled successfully by various agencies, such the police, specialised crime units, and public protectors. This multidimensional approach spreads the task and promotes specialisation, thus presenting greater opportunities for success from different angles. Clearly, both approaches are viable. All to say that the question is not so much as to form, and in the Zimbabwean context, more to do with political will.

Political support

Most critics (as one of the respondents to the TIZ survey earlier suggested) however argue that the biggest drawback to the fight against corruption in Zimbabwe is a lack of political will by the political elite for political and economic reasons. In the fight against corruption, scholars postulate four indicators of political will: adequate legal support to anti-corruption agencies; independence of the anti-corruption agencies; level of anti-corruption budget; and zero tolerance policy on corruption. It is in the latter that the government in Zimbabwe is solely lacking. While senior government officials, including the president, are on record for denouncing corruption – the president even going to the extent of naming and reprimanding some members of his own party for alleged corrupt activities[96] – these public denunciations have yielded marginal deterrence, with some closest to the president continually implicated in corruption. Critics have thus argued that these public denunciations are lukewarm, convenient, and cosmetic at best. Others have even gone on to allege that the president has shielded or continues to shield known corrupt allies for political expediency. Indeed, that the president should only denounce the former vice president, Joyce Mujuru, for corruption after the two fell out, critics argue, only serves to confirm this contention.

Besides the president, most politicians are wont to adopt anti-corruption rhetoric for electioneering purposes even as they themselves are allegedly corrupt. Indeed, as empirical surveys have shown, members of the public believe that politicians, alongside the police, are among the most corrupt in Zimbabwe. Besides, there also appears to be no direct interest in the work of ZACC within the executive and in parliament. From the discussion

---

96 Former ZMDC Chairman Mr Masimirembwa was publicly reprimanded for corruption by the president See http://www.herald.co.zw/ex-zmdc-boss-in-6m-scandal/ [accessed 20November 2016].

on the legislative framework above, it will be recalled that it took five years from the time the constitution first provided for an anti-corruption agency to the appointment of the first commission. Moreover, since inception, despite the financial independence envisaged in the constitution, the ZACC is yet to be allocated an independent budget and it continues to be funded through the line ministry, hitherto, the ministry of home affairs. Moreover, since August 2013, when the former commission relinquished office at the end of its term, there was no substantive commission in place until the end of November 2015 when new commissioners were appointed. On its part, although mandated to submit annual reports to parliament, the ZACC has never done so, and parliament has never called it to account. During the tenure of the erstwhile commissioners, only the parliamentary committee on home affairs twice summoned the commission to give evidence on its operational challenges. As critics argue, these facts cast serious doubt on the commitment of those in office to fight corruption. As one of the respondents in the TIZ survey alleged, it appears there is lethargy because those who are supposed to superintend corruption are some of the most corrupt.

Successes

Yet, despite all the setbacks highlighted above, the ZACC (including its predecessor the ACC) has done considerable work. The commission has achieved the following key successes:

- Notable cases by the commission include the mission led by the ACC to ascertain activities in the Chiadzwa diamond fields, although the report was never made public. The ZACC was also instrumental in unearthing the FIFA match fixing scandals of 2010/11,[97] in which the local football authority, the Zimbabwe Football Association (ZIFA) was implicated. The local investigation led to the arrest and prosecution of the former CEO of ZIFA.[98] the ZACC also involved in the NIEEB investigations, already mentioned;
- Besides investigations, the commission has also played an important advisory role in line with the constitution. In 2009 the ACC undertook a study on the nature and prevalence of corruption in the country. The report is however yet to be made public.
- In collaboration with the ministry of state enterprises, the ACC was involved in the creation and launching of the National Corporate Governance Framework for State Enterprises and Parastatals;

---

97 See generally the Ebrahim Commission *Asiagate Report* October 2012.
98 *State vs. Henrietta Rushwaya*, the accused was eventually acquitted but several players, coaches and journalists were implicated in the criminal trial, and a FIFA mandated tribunal found several of the accused persons guilty of impropriety.

- The ZACC was also a key participant in developing the National Corporate Governance Code,[99] recently launched; and
- The ZACC has also been invited by several government ministries and departments to undertake forensic audits of their operations, with a view to reducing opportunities for corruption.

H. Conclusion

From the discussion above, it can reasonably be said that Zimbabwe has fairly advanced legal mechanisms to fight corruption. The major drawbacks however appear to be political and institutional. There appears to be a lack of political will to tackle corruption, as if to confirm the allegation that the politicians are the ones who are the most corrupt. This lack of political interest also manifests in the institutional problems highlighted above, where, as we have seen, the ZACC has at times failed to discharge its functions effectively because of inadequate support from other complementing state organs like the ministry of home affairs, the police, and the national prosecuting authority. This political lethargy has in turn reared a sense of hopelessness, despondency and apathy among the general public, rendering the situation more desperate. Where the public could individually and collectively take a stand against corruption, it would appear it has lost all hope and energy. As the survey by TIZ shows, many people are resigned to the fact that they just have to oil the system to make things happen, while others have given up on reporting corruption altogether.

When corruption reaches such levels where it has become institutionalised, eradicating it becomes very difficult and requires a systematic and multi-faceted approach involving different players. The challenge is largely how to change attitudes. How to tame the corrupt and how to make the victim the hunter. How to ensure that members of the public refuse to be complicit and begin to demand transparency and accountability. In other words, how restore to the rule of law.

I. Recommendations

The following measures are proposed, although they are by no means conclusive.

Public participation
- Where the law provides enough protection and the problem is institutional, any positive change must necessarily come from the people themselves. In the fight against corruption, it is therefore imperative to ask how members of the public could be motivated

---

99 There are indications that the NCGC will soon be made into a law to augment the anti-corruption regulatory framework.

to take a stand and begin to bring about positive change? This is a difficult question with no single answer. Perhaps, to start with, what is required is just an honest and open public debate on corruption. General discourse on the origins of corruption, its causes, effects and how it can be stamped out, etc. In the same way Zimbabweans were once reticent to talk about HIV/AIDS, but now discuss the issue openly, there is need for the same open dialogue on corruption. For these purposes, given the political dimension to corruption, members of the public must shed off the culture of fear, which often stifles open and honest debate where politics is involved. CSOs could lead this process.

- At the same time, there must also be some form of incentive to motivate public engagement. The people's efforts must be seen to count for something. The ZACC, as the principal agent against corruption, must take the lead on this aspect. To start with, it must itself be visible and must inspire public confidence. As the TIZ report shows, already, most people have no confidence in the commission, while others do not even know of its existence.
- Measures to increase visibility might include decentralising to other centres outside the capital, presently, the commission's sole seat. To instil confidence, the ZACC must also try to implement such measures as whistleblower protection programmes, already provided for at law level, as well as other measures to ensure anonymity or to guarantee the personal security of informants. Other measures to encourage reporting may also include reimbursements for direct expenses incurred as a result of reporting.
- The ZACC must also make its reports public to give the people a sense of what it is doing, what it has achieved and what its challenges are. It does not help build confidence that the commission has never publicised any of its reports or researches. Nor that it has an outdated and incomplete website. Ultimately, the ZACC must prove its worth through the successful prosecution of cases of corruption, in particular high level corruption. The commission's record in relation to high level corruption is still thin, possibly because of the political influence mentioned herein.

Policy and institutional reform

- Along with the other initiatives proposed herein, there is also an urgent need to ensure that all public institutions, as well as the private sector, introduce user-friendly, efficient and transparent systems. Most instances of corruption, especially low level corruption in the public sector, result from opaque or inefficient systems, which give rise to illicit backdoor practices. As highlighted in the discussion on the legal framework already the constitution provides for an efficient and transparent public service. All that is required, therefore, is intensive lobbying to ensure implementation of these constitutional imperatives. CSOs, including corruption watchdog, Transparency International (Zimbabwe), could play a significant role in this process. The CSOs would need to come up with programmes of action that would include comprehensive audits of public service systems to identify the ones that do not work and thus breed corruption, and then come up with proposed recommendations, before engaging or lobbying the appropriate authorities.

Capacity building

- This relates to the need to strengthen the institutions, which impact on corruption, including the ZACC itself, the NPA, parliament, the judiciary and others. As the main watchdog against corruption in Zimbabwe, the ZACC's teeth must be sharp and its eyes open. There is need to ensure, through lobbying and other means, that the ZACC is adequately resourced both in terms of human capital and finance. The legal foundation is already there. The constitution provides for an independent and separate budget for the commission. The present practice where the commission survives on hand outs from the line ministry is simply untenable. Moreover, it violates the constitution. In the circumstances, should lobbying fail, there is also the possibility of taking the matter to court for breach of the constitution.
- Other measures to capacitate the ZACC would include training and professional development courses on such matters as investigative techniques, preservation of evidence and presentation of evidence. In this regard, collaboration with other agencies in Zimbabwe and abroad, or corporates and non-governmental organisations with technical skills and expertise in these areas, would be helpful. The ZACC's aloofness, as noted earlier, does not help.
- The same applies to the NPA and the courts, which could also benefit from the experiences and expertise of other courts or agencies in other countries as well as other specialised entities. This is especially critical because prosecuting or presiding over corruption cases sometimes can be very difficult as some of the cases raise very complex factual and technical issues beyond the scope of a regular police officer or judge. Indeed, in the same way the police and the courts created specialised units to deal with the victims of sexual offences, it might also be

desirable to create special units in the police and the judiciary to deal with cases of corruption. The scope of work of the serious frauds unit in the police or the economic crimes unit in the judiciary, for instance, could be extended to deal with cases of corruption.

- There is also a need to capacitate parliament, through conscientisation, training and lobbying, so that it becomes more engaged and assertive on the issue of corruption. That parliament has never received any report from the ZACC in five years and has never called the commission to account betrays a lack of engagement. Parliament, as already mentioned, is after all the sole body with oversight functions over the ZACC. There appears to be a need to teach parliament its role in combating corruption and ensuring that the legislature is in fact effective. CSOs and anti-graft organisations like TIZ could take a lead in this process.

Economic reform

- As corruption in Zimbabwe cannot be divorced from the country's economic meltdown, one of the lasting solutions is therefore to rejuvenate the economy. This process, most business analysts have argued, involves the government adopting consistent policies that promote investment and guarantee security of property. There is therefore a need for continuous lobbying of the government by business and other players to ensure that the country adopts consistent and business-friendly laws and policies. Business could lead the engagement and lobbying process.

Political reform

- Ultimately, especially in relation to high level corruption, the people must, through the ballot and other lawful means, reject a leadership that is either corrupt or shields corruption. This power solely lies in the hands of the people. Civic education by CSOs therefore continues to be relevant.

As indicated, there are number of measures that could be adopted to try and stamp out corruption in Zimbabwe. There is, however, no magic bullet. All efforts are incremental and complementary, and there are no small measures. The fight, as they say, starts with one small step.

Appendix A

Case study of failed investigation
National Indigenisation and Economic Empowerment Board (NIEEB) and three others

The facts of this case are in the public domain and are common cause. In early 2013, the ZACC began an investigation into the operations of the National Indigenisation and Economic Empowerment Board (NIEEB), which was charged to supervise the government's indigenisation policy compelling all companies to cede 51% of their shareholding to local Zimbabweans. The investigation had been prompted by media and other reports suggesting impropriety in the way NIEEB was awarding tenders to service providers. The ZACC approached NIEEB to conduct preliminary investigations and to obtain documentary evidence relating to indigenisation transactions involving the ministry of mines, the ministry of indigenisation and economic empowerment and the ministry of transport, communications and infrastructure development. NIEEB refused to cooperate, forcing the ZACC to approach the courts for search and seizure warrants in relation to NIEEB itself, the relevant ministers, the Zimbabwe Mining Development Corporation (ZMDC) (responsible for marketing the country's minerals) and the Zimbabwe National Roads Authority (ZINARA). After the magistrates' court refused to grant the application, the ZACC proceeded to the high court, which granted the warrants.

When the ZACC attempted to affect the searches at the respective offices of NIEEB and ZMDC, armed riot policemen refused its officials entry. On an earlier attempt, they had also been denied entry. Thereafter, NIEEB also approached the high court seeking cancelation of the warrant. A different judge of the high court granted the application and the ZACC's efforts were thwarted. This case raises a number of issues, which illustrate the difficulties of investigating high-level corruption, which must be noted here. First, the allegedly partisan and politically compromised state media led an onslaught against the ZACC, alleging corruption by the commission itself. The allegations raised, however, related to actions by members of the previous commission. Secondly, a senior member of the government and a leading politician in the ruling party who was himself implicated in the scandal initiated a campaign to tarnish the commission's image and to rubbish its NIEEB investigations. The essence of the campaign was to paint the ZACC as a partisan institution that was targeting ZANU PF while overlooking corruption by the MDC. Third, the use of the riot police to thwart investigations by a constitutional body armed with a search warrant issued by the courts was quite curious and telling. It illustrated the point laboured herein that the major problems in fighting corruption in Zimbabwe are institutional and manifest the absence of the rule of law. Fourth, the case also illustrated another point also laboured herein that, despite all the right words in the constitution, until there is a political will to fight corruption, the ZACC will only be effective in fighting low level corruption against those who are not politically sheltered.

Case study of successful prosecution
State vs. Godfrey Tanyanyiwa

Godfrey Tanyanyiwa (GT) was the town clerk, the principal accounting officer, of Chitungwiza Municipality, a satellite city of the capital, and the third largest in Zimbabwe by population. The ZACC received a report sometime in 2012, that GT had, in the course of his duties, defrauded his employer of over USD 80 000, abused his office, and had failed to declare interest in a house he was leasing to council. In the end, the investigation by the ZACC focused on the charge of fraud in relation to the house GT had acquired using council funds and had proceeded to lease out to council without declaring his interest in it.

Investigations revealed that GT had authorised the transfer of USD 85 000 from the Chitungwiza Municipality's bank account to a real estate agent on the pretext that the estate agent had been hired to service residential stands in the city. However, the money was in fact transferred to the estate agent as part payment for the purchase of a residential property for GT himself in one of Harare's premier suburbs. In the second instance, GT had then proceeded to offer the house he had purchased for himself using municipality funds to the municipality for rental. Investigations also revealed that, using the same estate agent, GT had offered the said house to the municipality for use by the director of urban planning. GT did not disclose that he in fact was the owner of the house that the municipality was now renting. Instead he proceeded to charge rentals in the sum of USD 1 300 for five months. GT was subsequently convicted of three counts of fraud and one count of concealing a transaction from the principal in terms of the Criminal Code. He was jailed for an effective two-and-a-half years by the high court.

www.ingramcontent.com/pod-product-compliance
Lightning Source LLC
Chambersburg PA
CBHW080354030426
42334CB00024B/2871